WESTERN TRADITION

World Religions

CANADIAN PERSPECTIVES

Edited by

Doris R. Jakobsh
University of Waterloo

M. Darrol Bryant
Renison University College

Ken S. Coates
University of Saskatchewan

Douglas E. Cowan
Renison University College

William Rory Dickson
Wilfrid Laurier University

Shari Golberg
University of Toronto

Scott T. Kline
St. Jerome's University

Meena Sharify-Funk
Wilfrid Laurier University

NELSON EDUCATION

NELSON EDUCATION

World Religions: Canadian Perspectives—Western Traditions
Edited by Doris R. Jakobsh

Vice President, Editorial Higher Education:
Anne Williams

Acquisitions Editor:
Maya Castle

Senior Marketing Manager:
Amanda Henry

Developmental Editor:
Jacquelyn Busby

Editorial Intern:
Jeremy Lucyk

Permissions and Photo Researcher:
Lynn McLeod

Senior Content Production Manager:
Natalia Denesiuk Harris

Production Service:
MPS Limited, a Macmillan Company

Copy Editor:
Gillian Watts

Proofreader:
Jennifer A. McIntyre

Indexer:
Edwin Durbin

Senior Production Coordinator:
Ferial Suleman

Design Director:
Ken Phipps

Managing Designer:
Franca Amore

Interior Design:
Sharon Lucas

Parchment Image:
© Neosiam/Dreamstime.com

Cover Design:
Sharon Lucas

Cover Image:
Courtney Milne

Compositor:
MPS Limited, a Macmillan Company

Printer:
Edwards Brothers

Printed and bound in the United States of America
1 2 3 4 14 13 12 11

For more information contact Nelson Education Ltd., 1120 Birchmount Road, Toronto, Ontario, M1K 5G4. Or you can visit our Internet site at http://www.nelson.com

Library and Archives Canada Cataloguing in Publication Data

World religions : Canadian perspectives : western traditions / edited by Doris R. Jakobsh ; [contributing authors] M. Darrol Bryant ... [et al.].

At head of title: Western traditions.
Includes bibliographical references and index.
ISBN 978-0-17-650118-1

1. Religions. 2. Canada—Religion. I. Jakobsh, Doris R. (Doris Ruth), 1963– II. Bryant, M. Darrol

BL80.3.W647 2011 200
C2011-907320-X

ISBN-13: 978-0-17-650118-1
ISBN-10: 0-17-650118-5

The front cover image is a photograph by Courtney Milne. Courtney Milne is a photographer, an artist, author, educator, keynote speaker, and philanthropist. His career has taken him on a global journey that has spanned all seven continents. He has published 12 books of photography, including *The Sacred Earth*, with a foreword by His Holiness, The Dalai Lama. Milne's multi-media shows have attracted audiences worldwide, and his photographs have been shown in more than 200 exhibitions. His limited edition collections are held by more than 25 galleries, museums, and universities. Courtney Milne lives on the Canadian prairie near Saskatoon, Saskatchewan.

CONTENTS

EDITOR'S INTRODUCTION

DORIS JAKOBSH

Welcome to the study of world religions. Contrary to scholarly and media claims in the late twentieth century that "religion is dead" or "religion is no longer relevant," religion is indeed alive and well in the twenty-first century. In an increasingly globalized, multicultural Canada, where every possible form of religious affiliation can be found, it is very likely that you personally will come into direct contact with many peers whose belief systems are different from your own. Your own religious affiliation may not be very important to you; you may not even call yourself religious. However, it is quite possible that despite not "feeling" very religious or perhaps not knowing much about your own religious background, you still have some sort of religious affiliation. I'm reminded of a time when I was in a market in Chiang Mai, Thailand. I stopped to chat with the owner of a little stall and noticed that she had a small shrine set up to Buddha. I asked her about her religion, and she instantly remarked that she wasn't religious! When I asked her about the shrine, the sticks of incense, and the candle that she had lit, she said that was just "tradition." I found her statements remarkable. If a storeowner in Canada were to tend to a religious shrine in the shop while setting up for the day, customers would identify that storeowner as being highly religious.

Often people take part in religious traditions because of parental expectations, or because they might wish to introduce their own children to the traditions of their grandparents. You might not think twice about celebrating Diwali if you are of Hindu, Sikh, or Jain heritage—it is simply what is "done" in your family. Or you might find yourself wanting to have a traditional Christian wedding, and so start discussing being married in a local church or in one to which your family once had connections. If you take some time to look at your development as a child or young adult, it is very likely that religious values have played a role in shaping your life in some way. It is difficult to get away from religion, even if you have grown up in an entirely secular home.

Whether or not you as an individual consider yourself to be religious, the study of religion is important, given that so much of history and culture is steeped in religious traditions. Religious beliefs have had a fundamental role in shaping society, both within families and more broadly at the institutional and political levels. In an increasingly globalized world, most of us are becoming aware of the role played by religion, whether it is in working toward peace or in the stirring up of conflict. A solid understanding of religion is beneficial in negotiating the complexity of worldviews that surround us all, both locally and globally.

Students from the University of Waterloo's 'The Living Traditions of India' visited the city of Hampi in Karnataka, South India. Hampi was the medieval capital of the Vijayanagara empire that was founded in the fourteenth century. Remains of the capital city include an amazing array of religious sites, palaces, and public architecture that is spread over a beautiful, hilly landscape along the Tungabhadra River. Today, the ruins are a UNESCO World Heritage Site.

Source: Ketussa Sotheeswaran

In the fall of 2010 I had the privilege of taking a group of twelve students from the University of Waterloo, where I teach in the Department of Religious Studies, for a three-month course in India titled "The Living Traditions of India." The purpose of this full term of study was to allow students an opportunity to experience, in a truly in-depth manner, the religious traditions of India. This included staying at a yoga ashram in the Himalayas, where, upon being awakened at four thirty a.m., we took part in meditation and yoga classes for hours at a time. We were also invited to listen to Sufi musicians, called *qawwali* singers, perform at the Nizammudin Shrine in Old Delhi. Their beautiful, masterful voices soared and fell as they sang about the separation of the lover and the Beloved, Allah.

We had an opportunity to sit at the feet of enlightened women and men across India, individuals who had devoted themselves to the spiritual quest and lives of intense discipline. One of these remarkable individuals was a British-born Tibetan Buddhist nun, Jetsumna Tenzin Palmo, who had spent twelve years of her life in a cave high in the Himalayas, learning the discipline of intense meditation practices. We met Dr. Sadhvi Sadhna, a Jain nun who is the current acharya (leader) of a Jain ashram in northern India. She received us with incredible graciousness and then proceeded to teach us about important principles of Jainism that are applicable to the entire human race, and of the importance of interfaith dialogue in the quest for world peace. Father George, the head of the "Old Seminary," a Syrian Orthodox centre in Kerala, taught us about the long history of Christianity in India, beginning with the travels of Saint Thomas in the early years of the developing Christian movement—making all of us rethink our notions of Christianity as an exclusively Western tradition. We were invited to Dr. Vandana Shiva's biodiversity farm near Dehradun and there were privileged to learn about her vision, her understanding of justice, the ecological movement that she has led for the past twenty years, and how that intersects with her understanding of religion and a deep reverence for Mother Earth. All of these encounters allowed the students to gain a solid experiential knowledge base in the living religions and cultures of India, and, perhaps even more important, to open themselves up to the possibilities and responsibilities of being citizens in an increasingly globalized world.

Our group, which came from diverse religious, ethnic, and cultural backgrounds, was able to discover the variety and depth of religious practices and worldviews other than our own. At times we came face to face with deeply embedded, largely subconscious cultural preconceptions that only our own traditions were normative. Through our interactions with religious leaders and devotees of the varied traditions we were studying, as well as looking at the philosophical, cultural, educational, and political systems that undergird Indian society, all of us were able to come to an understanding that there are alternative worldviews, based on different fundamental premises. It then became our mission to discover how the many religions that we had discovered in India came to be transplanted in Canada, and how those traditions had changed or were still similar to the forms we had encountered in India.

AN INVITATION TO STUDENTS

This textbook is an invitation to study the many and varied religions of humankind, and some of the alternative worldviews that stem from regions far from Canada yet have taken root within Canadian soil. Having taught numerous introductory religion courses, I am excited by the potential for such courses to be engaging and relevant—particularly for Canadian students, and particularly at this time in history. Designed to address both the historical and current impacts and influences of religion, this volume covers areas traditionally considered foundational to the study of religion, but it also adds materials to address contemporary concerns. As the editor of this particular textbook, I had a number of goals and expectations for each chapter as well as for the volume as a whole.

1. It is important that you get a thorough understanding of each particular religion presented in the text, including its history, its central beliefs, and its practices. All of the contributors to this volume are recognized scholars in their fields, and all of them have written extensively on their topics. Perhaps even more important, they have taught introductory courses on their particular areas of expertise.

Their rich experience with the subject matter, as well as with teaching, has enabled them to communicate complex concepts in a manner that, without losing depth, is accessible and comprehensible.

2. Each chapter, by and large, includes stories and insights drawn from the writers' experience. Many of the contributors have spent significant amounts of time not only learning about a specific religion from texts or manuscripts but also engaging with it while doing field research and collecting data. Some have immersed themselves within religious communities, both in Canada and internationally. You will find accounts of some of these experiences and insights in the chapters you are about to read, and it is my hope that this more personal approach will contribute to your own interest in the subject matter.
3. The study of religion has traditionally focused on examining and learning about sacred texts. In fact, historically, most scholars of religion were trained almost exclusively in textual studies. While this is changing, often when we teach about religion, we tend to focus on texts. What I have found, however, in speaking and interacting with students, is that many of you seem more interested in the "doing," or performative, aspects of religion than in discussion of sacred texts. As I began to think about how to organize and focus this particular volume, I observed how the history, beliefs, celebrations, and rituals of various religious communities are presented in most introductory textbooks. I found that very often texts do not give sufficient attention to *practical* and *lived* aspects of religious expression. This has often led to students being unable to relate what they are reading to their personal experiences in a particular religion or with people of other faiths.

   This textbook has not downplayed the importance of sources within religions, especially the sacred writings and other texts of each specific tradition; contributors were asked to carefully choose material for you to read in each chapter. However, close attention is also paid to "lived" religion. Some authors have addressed this by providing guides to what to expect when visiting a particular worship centre or shrine or participating in various celebrations or rituals. Others have described their own experiences—the sights, smells, and sounds—when they visited a particular religious site. Also, some scholars have explored how religion has implications far beyond specific rituals or notions of "the sacred," including wider social and cultural norms such as family and kinship roles, caste, class, and race. These, which at first glance appear not to have any connection to religion per se, upon further exploration can often be seen to be rooted in particular religious and ethical worldviews. This approach will allow you to come to a deeper and richer understanding of the many and varied strands of what constitutes religion.
4. A significant and unique feature of each chapter has been a concerted effort to bring a Canadian perspective to each religious tradition covered in this textbook. This includes a substantial history of the religion in the Canadian context, changes that may have taken place within religions as a result of their transplantation to Canada, and also those beliefs, rituals, ethical worldviews, and practices that connect adherents of a particular tradition globally. The volume is primarily directed toward a Canadian student population, and as such it seeks to speak to the religious realities and experiences of you or your peers as you study at a university here in Canada. It is my hope that you will see your own experiences reflected in some way in the discussions to follow. I also trust that some of the issues that are raised will lead to discussion and debate, both within and outside the classroom setting.

   This substantial Canadian focus is also significant in terms of specific content. For instance, the history and development of Sikhism in Canada is significantly different from the American experience. In the United States, many of the earliest Sikh settlers married Mexican women and quickly formed family ties that bound them to America. In contrast, the first Sikhs in Canada did not have similar options; therefore, by and large, the early Canadian Sikhs on the West Coast who were largely male were focused on either returning to their native Punjab in India to join their families or eventually sponsoring them to immigrate to Canada. The significance of this point would be missed in a textbook written for a wider North American audience.
5. The study of women in religion is also an important dimension of this volume. Many of us who teach introductory world religion classes are often

dismayed at how little attention is given in textbooks to women's religious realities. This volume has made great strides in moving beyond the general apathy toward and underrepresentation of women in the study of world religions. While it does not claim an overarching feminist approach, contributors were asked to consider women's roles in the religious traditions of their chapter. This meant going beyond the occasional mention of a remarkable woman in a religion's history. Attempts have been made to address women's roles, rituals, and status, both historically and within the contemporary world. This allows for a richer, more complex and encompassing exploration of "world religions."

6. Scholar Eileen Barker has warned that academics who do not engage in the phenomenon of cyber-religion do so at their own peril (Barker 2005, 81). This warning has been taken to heart in this textbook. Each contributor was asked to move beyond a simple listing of important URLs to address, if only at a rudimentary level, the significance of religion online as it pertains to each religion. Virtually every religion has a presence on the Internet, but scholars have found that the Internet has had a greater impact on some religions than others. For example, the adherents of new religious movements (NRMs) find that the Internet provides an unprecedented presence among the historically established religions. Modern Paganism, for instance, which does not have an established institutional hierarchy and is relatively small numerically, has a significant presence online. This opens up issues of authority: who speaks for modern Pagans, or for any other religious tradition online? This volume will thus be an invaluable resource both for you as students and also for your instructors, to begin examining the ramifications of the Internet for the study of religion generally. The hope is that the issues raised by scholars will be useful to those who may turn to the Web as an initial point of information-gathering about religion.
7. It is also beneficial to learn *how* to study religion. Getting a grasp of the methodologies of the discipline is vital. Sometimes when I am asked what I do for a living, I say that I teach religion. Some people wonder what one could possibly teach, since religion is obviously "about God," and God is something that cannot be proved or disproved. Many comment that religion is a personal, mystical experience, something that is not quantifiable, something that should stay in the realm of faith, not in academia. Some of this perception can be traced to the great scholars of religion, such as Mircea Eliade (1907–86), who wrote that religion is about non-rational experience—something he defined as "the sacred." How can one study the sacred? Rudolf Otto (1869–1937), who is known best for his influential volume *The Idea of the Holy* (1917), believed that "the holy" "is beyond our apprehension and comprehension . . . before which we recoil in a wonder that strikes us chill and numb" (1958: 28).

   However, while there are elusive elements in religious experience, there are also many aspects within religions that can be studied empirically. The study of religion in this volume moves beyond a theological and historical approach into the realm of other academic disciplines. Scholars here will look to wider social changes, perhaps economic or political, that may have had an effect on the development of a religion over time. For example, when examining religion in India or in Canada, the impact of colonialism must be taken into consideration.

   There are systematic approaches that may be taken in studying a religious tradition, including varied theories of religion and religious knowledge, specific terminologies that are used, methodological considerations, and analytical approaches. These methodologies originate from a wide variety of disciplines, both in the humanities—including the study of history, literature, women's studies, and philosophy—and within the social sciences—for example, in sociology, anthropology, or psychology. You will come to know how the study of religion developed over time, particularly in the first chapter of this volume, which is entirely dedicated to the 'study' of religion.
8. Each author in this volume was asked to carefully choose images that would contribute to your understanding of the tradition being examined. Take the time to look at the images and read their captions. These too will add to your comprehension of the course material.

This is the general format for each chapter:

- Central beliefs
- Sources of the tradition

- History and development
- Spiritual/religious practices
- Authority (or authorities)
- Religious identity
- Religious diversity
- The Canadian context
- Religion and the Internet
- Key terms
- Critical thinking questions
- Recommended reading and viewing
- Useful websites

Adopting this format meant creating a consistency that allows for easy comparisons and a comprehensive understanding of each religion. However, in several chapters the format has been adjusted slightly to allow for a more accurate presentation of the religion in question. Rather than organizing their chapter artificially according to an editorial structure, authors were given the freedom to modify the format when doing so would more genuinely represent the religion.

You will also encounter four types of boxes throughout the textbook that draw attention to texts, rituals, people, places, and other items of particular significance.

- **Perspectives:** In the Perspectives boxes, concepts, symbols, and theories are highlighted to show how their meanings can be understood in different ways and how the significance of objects and principles can depend on the perspective of the observer.
- **Practices:** Each tradition has unique customs or practices that are performed at certain times. Some are still actively carried out while others are no longer practised; some are performed by a select few, others by the masses. The Practices boxes focus on the behaviour associated with each religious tradition.
- **People and Places:** These boxes feature important people and places in each tradition's history: prominent scholars and theorists, temples and churches, innovators, heroes, deities, and much more.
- **Words:** Words, both written and spoken, hold a significant place in the history and culture of the traditions. Hymns, prayers, poems, and stories are featured, as well as excerpts from both sacred and academic texts.

A NOTE TO INSTRUCTORS

You will find Chapter 1, on the study of religion, an excellent resource for students who may be taking a religion course for the first time. The chapter allows students to get a broader understanding of how religion is studied within the different disciplines of academia. The approaches outlined in this chapter, however, were not included in the guidelines for the contributors. Instead, each author was given the freedom to retain his or her own voice and to approach the religion from the perspective of his or her own discipline and research, whether explicitly stated or not. This textbook exemplifies a diverse approach in teaching world religions.

CONCLUSION

As you begin your journey into the study of religions, it is my hope that you will discover the complexities and nuances of the many and varied world religions explored in this textbook. I invite you to move to a greater understanding of the beliefs and practices of your friends and colleagues with whom you share a workplace or a classroom yet whose worldview and belief system may be quite different from your own. Finally, Hindu temples, Jewish synagogues, Christian churches, Muslim mosques, and Sikh gurdwaras, to name just a few, will welcome you warmly should you ask about visiting and even taking part in a religious service. As well, there are rich and varied Native traditions in Canada that are open to inquiry and dialogue. This approach allows for a potentially rich experiential dimension and a deepening of understanding, beyond what you may learn in the classroom. You may even be able to convince your professor to organize a class trip!

Doris R. Jakobsh, Editor
Waterloo, Ontario, Canada

REFERENCES

Barker, Eileen. 2005. "Crossing the Boundary: New Challenges to Religious Authority and Control as a Consequence of Access to the Internet." In *Religion and Cyberspace,* ed. Morten T. Højsgaard and Margit Warburg, 67–85. London: Routledge.

Otto, Rudolf. 1958. *The Idea of the Holy.* Oxford: Oxford University Press.

A NOTE FROM THE PUBLISHER

INSTRUCTOR ANCILLARIES

The **Nelson Education Teaching Advantage (NETA)** program delivers research-based instructor resources that promote student engagement and higher-order thinking to enable the success of Canadian students and educators.

In consultation with the editorial advisory board, made up of dedicated instructors, Nelson Education has completely rethought the structure, approaches, and formats of our key textbook ancillaries. The result is the Nelson Education Teaching Advantage and its key components: *NETA Engagement, NETA Assessment,* and *NETA Presentation.* Each component includes one or more ancillaries prepared according to our best practices, and a document explaining the theory behind the practices.

NETA Engagement presents materials that help instructors deliver engaging content and activities to their classes. Instead of instructor's manuals that regurgitate chapter outlines and key terms from the text, NETA Enriched Instructor's Manuals (EIMs) provide genuine assistance to teachers. The EIMs answer questions such as "What should students learn?"; "Why should students care?"; and "What are some common student misconceptions and stumbling blocks?" EIMs not only identify the topics that cause students the most difficulty but also describe techniques and resources to help students master these concepts. Dr. Roger Fisher's *Instructor's Guide to Classroom Engagement (IGCE)* accompanies every Enriched Instructor's Manual.

Under *NETA Assessment,* Nelson's authors create multiple-choice questions that reflect research-based best practices for constructing effective questions and testing not just recall but also higher-order thinking. Our guidelines were developed by David DiBattista, a 3M National Teaching Fellow whose recent research as a professor of psychology at Brock University has focused on multiple-choice testing. All Test Bank authors receive training at workshops conducted by Prof. DiBattista, as do the copyeditors assigned to each Test Bank. A copy of *Multiple Choice Tests: Getting Beyond Remembering,* Prof. DiBattista's guide to writing effective tests, is included with every Nelson Test Bank/Computerized Test Bank package.

NETA Presentation has been developed to help instructors make the best use of PowerPoint® in their classrooms. With a clean and uncluttered design developed by Maureen Stone of StoneSoup Consulting, NETA Presentation features slides with improved readability, more multimedia and graphic materials, activities to use in class, and tips for instructors on the Notes page. A copy of *NETA Guidelines for Classroom Presentations* by Maureen Stone is included with each set of PowerPoint slides.

IRCD

Key instructor ancillaries are provided on the *Instructor's Resource CD* (ISBN 978-0-17-664865-7), giving instructors the ultimate tool for customizing lectures and presentations. (Downloadable Web versions are also available at www.WorldReligions.nelson.com.) The IRCD includes

- **NETA Engagement:** Written by Scott Wall of Wilfrid Laurier University, the Enriched Instructor's Manual is organized according to the textbook chapters and addresses eight key educational concerns, such as typical stumbling blocks students face and how to address them.
- **NETA Assessment:** The Test Bank was written by A. W. Barber of the University of Calgary. It includes multiple-choice questions written according to NETA guidelines for effective construction and development of higher-order questions. Also included are short-answer and essay questions. Test Bank files are provided in Word format for easy editing and in PDF for convenient printing, whatever your system.

  The Computerized Test Bank by ExamView® includes all the questions from the Test Bank. The easy-to-use ExamView software is compatible with Microsoft Windows and Mac OSX. Create tests by selecting questions from the question bank, modifying these questions as desired, and adding new questions you write yourself. You can administer quizzes online and export tests to WebCT, Blackboard, and other formats.

- **NETA Presentation:** Microsoft® PowerPoint® lecture slides for every chapter, created by Scott Wall of Wilfrid Laurier University, feature key figures and photographs from *World Religions: Canadian Perspectives.* NETA principles of clear design and engaging content have been incorporated throughout.
- **Image Library:** This resource consists of digital copies of figures, short tables, and photographs used in the book. Instructors may use these jpegs to create their own PowerPoint presentations.

STUDENT ANCILLARIES

World Religions: Canadian Perspectives also offers an interactive student companion site. This site includes flashcards, crossword puzzles, quizzes, weblinks, and other useful online resources. Go to www.WorldReligions.nelson.com to access these engaging materials.

ACKNOWLEDGEMENTS

When I was approached to produce a new world religions textbook that was to have a significant impact on the way Canadian courses in religion are taught, and as the extent of this endeavour took hold, I became increasingly aware that it could not be a one-person job. This two-volume textbook would never have come to fruition without the support, advice, critique, and cajoling efforts of numerous individuals throughout its long process. I am grateful to Bram Sepers, acquisitions editor at Nelson at the time of this text's inception, with whom I had many "visioning" conversations about the necessity and possibility of a new world- and Canadian-focused textbook on religions. Since then I have had the distinct pleasure of working with Heather Parker, Anne-Marie Taylor, Jacquelyn Busby, Maya Castle, and Natalia Denesiuk Harris, among others at Nelson Education, as well as copyeditor Gillian Watts. Their insistence that this work maintain a high degree of integrity and academic excellence was heartening. I will be forever grateful for their encouragement, humour, patience, and overall kindness.

For their thoughtful commentary, I would like to thank the following reviewers:

Martin T. Adam, University of Victoria
A. W. Barber, University of Calgary
Herbert W. Basser, Queen's University
Amila Buturovic, York University
Robert Campbell, University of Toronto
Philippa Carter, McMaster University
Minoo Derayeh, York University
Ellen Goldberg, Queen's University
Aaron W. Hughes, University of Calgary
James Linville, University of Lethbridge
Fadel H. Zabian, Fanshawe College

To each contributor, my thanks for signing on to the mandate and vision of this textbook. You have my sincere admiration for the academically solid, creative, and, perhaps most important, student-focused chapters written. Thank you for every attempt made to accommodate the writing, editing, and production timeline, never an easy task for those of us ensconced in the intensive research, teaching, and service milieu of academia. To the many scholars and teachers I have had along the way, whose love for the study of religion continues to inspire—Harold Coward, Mary Malone, Darrol Bryant, Diana Eck, among others—my deepest gratitude. I am also indebted to my chair and friend, David Seljak, for making time—always a rare commodity—to offer insight, critique, and editing prowess. To Maureen Fraser, thank you for your generous and kind support. To the many students at the University of Waterloo who have also been my teachers, I offer my appreciation.

To my inner circle of friends, who have given far more than they have received for far too long, my enduring gratitude. To my parents, Josef and Sonja Jakobsh, I am truly at a loss to know where one begins to say thank you. To Kaira and Jesse, who seem so easily to embody all that I strive to be, and to Paul Roorda—partner, best friend, beacon, and foundation—all my love.

Doris R. Jakobsh

ABOUT THE CONTRIBUTORS

Scott T. Kline is Associate Professor of Religious Studies at St. Jerome's University at the University of Waterloo. His area of research is religious ethics and politics. He has published in a variety of journals, including *Peace and Change: A Journal of Peace Research, International Relations,* and the *Journal of Religion and Popular Culture,* on topics such as interreligious ethics, the role of religion in South Africa's Truth and Reconciliation Commission, Christianity and U.S. politics, and consumer religion. He is the regionally elected coordinator of the Eastern International Region of the American Academy of Religion (AAR) and a former director on the AAR national board. He is currently writing a book titled *Ethical Being.*

Shari Golberg is a Ph.D. candidate in religion, women's studies, and Jewish studies at the University of Toronto. Her work explores feminist approaches to classical religious texts in Judaism and Islam and contemporary text-based collaborations between Jewish and Muslim women. She was awarded a SSHRC CGS grant for this research in 2006. In the past few years she has written extensively on issues of gender and law in Judaism and Islam and has taught classes on scriptural interpretation, gender, and anthropology of religion. She also coordinates and facilitates When Beruriah Met Aisha, a grassroots community-based text-study project for Jewish and Muslim women living in Toronto.

M. Darrol Bryant is a Distinguished Professor Emeritus at the University of Waterloo and Director of the Centre for Dialogue and Spirituality in the World's Religions at Renison University College. He was educated at Concordia College (B.A., philosophy and political science), Harvard Divinity School (S.T.B. in theology), and the Institute of Christian Thought, University of St. Michael's College (M.A. and Ph.D., special religious studies). He is the author and/or editor of more than twenty volumes in the study of religion, including *Religion in a New Key; God: The Contemporary Discussion; Muslim-Christian Dialogue; Woven on the Loom of Time: Many Faiths and One Divine Purpose;* and, most recently, *On Spirituality and Mahayana Buddhism: History and Culture.* He has travelled extensively, has been a visiting professor in India and Kenya, and has lectured worldwide.

Meena Sharify-Funk, Ph.D., is an Associate Professor in the Religion and Culture Department of Wilfrid Laurier University; she specializes in Islamic studies with a focus on contemporary Muslim thought and identity. Her current research focuses on the construction of contemporary Canadian Muslim identity in a post-9/11 world. It is a continuation of her first manuscript, *Encountering the Transnational: Women, Islam, and the Politics of Interpretation* (2008), which examined the impact of transnational networking on Muslim women's identity, thought, and activism. She has also co-edited two books, *Cultural Diversity and Islam* (2003) and *Contemporary Islam: Dynamic, Not Static* (2006).

William Rory Dickson is a doctoral candidate in the Laurier and Waterloo universities joint Ph.D. in religious studies and is a recipient of a doctoral fellowship from the Social Sciences and Humanities Research Council of Canada. He specializes in Islamic studies, and his current research focuses on Sufism in North America. Dickson has published articles in the *Journal of Contemporary Islam* and *Studies in Religion.*

Ken S. Coates is a faculty member in the Johnson-Shoyama Graduate School of Public Policy at the University of Saskatchewan. He has written extensively on Aboriginal history and rights, including such works as *Best Left as Indians: Native–White Relations in the Yukon; The Marshall Decision;* and *Aboriginal Rights in the Maritimes.* His writing includes several articles and chapters on Aboriginal–missionary relations. Raised in the Yukon, he has taught at universities from British Columbia to New Brunswick, as well as at the University of Waikato in New Zealand. Ken has worked with many Aboriginal organizations, including Northern Native Broadcasting Yukon, and has been a consultant on Aboriginal affairs with various governments and non-governmental organizations.

Douglas E. Cowan is Professor of Religious Studies at Renison University College at the University of Waterloo in Ontario, Canada. He is the author of a number of books, including *Sacred Space: The Quest for Transcendence in Science Fiction Film and Television* (Baylor, 2010), *Sacred Terror: Religion and Horror on the Silver Screen* (Baylor, 2008), and *Cults and New Religions: A Brief History* (with David G. Bromley; Blackwell, 2008).

ABOUT THE EDITOR

Doris R. Jakobsh is Associate Professor and the current Director of Women's Studies at the University of Waterloo, where she was nominated for the Distinguished Teacher Award in 2010. She has degrees from the University of Waterloo, Harvard University, and the University of British Columbia. She is the author of *Relocating Gender in Sikh History: Transformation, Meaning and Identity* (Delhi: Oxford University Press, 2003/2005) and *Sikhism*, in the Dimensions of Asian Spirituality series (Hawaii: University of Hawaii Press, 2011), and has edited *Sikhism and Women: History, Texts and Experience* (Delhi: Oxford University Press, 2010) as well as having numerous other publications. Professor Jakobsh is a member of the Steering Committee of the Sikh Consultation of the American Academy of Religion. She also serves on a number of local and international editorial boards and advisory committees associated with the study of religion and Sikh studies.

CHAPTER 1

The Study of Religion

Scott T. Kline

INTRODUCTION

It is an early Sunday morning in mid-February and some 40,000 people have been camped out for weeks awaiting the commencement of this year's three-hour-long procession. For many this is an annual pilgrimage, marked by family reunions, feelings of patriotism, and a sense of community. By noon there will be roughly 200,000 people surrounding the event's site. Many of them will be dressed in brightly coloured jackets and shirts. A few will be wearing hats and clothes to commemorate the tragic death of one of their heroes at a previous gathering. Another forty million people will watch the event unfold on global television. The infield grass is a lush green, which provides contrast to the brightly coloured murals painted around it. Following tradition, the forty-three men who have qualified for this year's event are introduced and ceremonially paraded before the crowd. After the introduction and parade, the master of ceremonies asks everyone in attendance to stand and pray. A prayer leader then asks God to protect the forty-three men in the procession, everyone in attendance, and the country. Immediately following the prayer, a choir sings the national anthem. As the anthem comes to an end, three fighter jets fly low in formation over the grounds, generating a thunderous roar that reverberates off the grandstands and viewing boxes. The mass of people raise their arms in joy and let out a collective scream. As they begin to settle, the master of ceremonies introduces the grand marshal, who takes the microphone and declares, "Gentlemen, start your engines!"

A few months earlier, a larger pilgrimage took place on the other side of the globe. Since at least the seventh century of the **Common Era (C.E.)**, pilgrims have converged on a small tract of land near the Red Sea for a weeklong act of worship. With more than two million people expected to attend, the government has had the city's major sites cleaned and repainted. Security forces have been training for months to deal with the onslaught of visitors. A newly installed air conditioner, one of the world's largest, is set to provide relief to weary travellers as they gather in one of the city's most revered sites. The pilgrims, all dressed in white, follow the same basic itinerary: On the first day they walk counterclockwise seven times around a cube-shaped building. Each time they pass a black stone at the corner of the building, the pilgrims blow kisses and point toward the stone. When they have finished, they make their way to a nearby town, where they will stop to pray and to gather stones. Many will be transported in air-conditioned coaches, while others will choose to make the 15-kilometre walk.

Common Era (C.E.): the term used by scholars instead of A.D. (Anno Domini).

Circumambulation: the act of moving around a sacred object or space.

Hajj: the annual pilgrimage to Mecca, Saudi Arabia, and the fifth pillar, or duty, of Islam. Pilgrims on the hajj are called hajji.

The courtyard of al-Haram Mosque, full of hajji, or hajj pilgrims.

Source: Photos.com

On the second day, the pilgrims arrive at another town not far away to pray and to gather more stones. Later that evening they camp in the open air and pray for much of the night. On day three they journey to another town, where they will spend the next few days praying and waiting for the appointed time to throw their stones at three 26-metre-long walls, an act that represents stoning the devil. After they have hurled their stones, and before leaving town, many make sure to obtain a certificate confirming that an animal has been sacrificed for them; others perform the sacrifice themselves. The final day returns the pilgrims to the city with the cube-shaped building, where they repeat the **circumambulation** ritual from day one. The pilgrimage comes to an end with the pilgrims drinking from a well and offering final prayers.

The two events described here have no obvious connections. The first one is the Daytona 500, the most important car race associated with the National Association for Stock Car Auto Racing (NASCAR) series. Held every year since 1959 at Daytona International Speedway in Daytona Beach, Florida, the 500-mile (805-kilometre) race is commonly referred to by NASCAR fans as "The Great American Race." It is traditionally the first event in the NASCAR season, which runs from mid-February until early November. The second description is of activities associated with the **hajj**, the pilgrimage to Mecca, which is the fifth pillar, or duty, of Islam. Every able-bodied Muslim has an obligation to make the pilgrimage at least once in his or her lifetime, finances permitting. Many save money for years to attend. Some who cannot personally afford the hajj are supported by their villages, which are often quite poor and may have to save for years to send a single person.

The Daytona 500. With 200,000 spectators on-site and forty million TV viewers, it is the most important NASCAR race of the season.

Source: Chris Graythen/Getty Images

In spite of some obvious differences, the Daytona 500 and the hajj do share certain formal similarities. For instance, they both maintain sets of rituals that are well established and known to those in attendance. Both have defined spaces and structures where the events take place. And both have stories of heroes, saints, and villains that provide complementary narratives for both the NASCAR race and the hajj.

We begin with general descriptions of these events to raise two foundational questions. The first is "What is religion?" This is an important question because it helps us define and limit our field of study. It helps us understand why many religious studies scholars do not treat NASCAR races, any other form of popular culture, or mythical figures such as Santa Claus, the Tooth

Fairy, or the Easter Bunny as objects of study—that is, as religion. It also helps us understand why a number of scholars actually *do* think popular culture, myths, professional sports, and gaming, for example, ought to be studied as religion. And it helps us appreciate the complexities associated with defining *religion*.

The second question is "How do we study religion?" Or, to put it another way, what theoretical and methodological approaches have religious studies scholars employed to analyze and explain the phenomena they consider "religious"? To answer this question, we will need a greater understanding of both the general history of the field, including the scholars who helped shape it, and the scholarly approaches that make up the field of religious studies. We will discover that our approaches often yield different conclusions, even though we are apparently examining the same phenomena. And we will begin to learn and to use the language of religious studies, especially the key terms and concepts that enable us to study religion as an academic pursuit.

In short, our task in this chapter is to introduce you to the study of religion, an expansive field of academic inquiry that draws generously from the humanities (e.g., philosophy, theology, history, literature) and the social sciences (e.g., anthropology, sociology, psychology, linguistics). In this respect, the study of religion is neither a subject nor a discipline with its own distinct methodologies. Rather, as Walter Capps once put it, religious studies is "a *subject field* within which a variety of disciplines are employed and an enormous range of subjects are treated" (1974, 727). If we perform our task well, this chapter should help you understand the field of religious studies, the language we use in the field, and the academic approaches used by religious studies scholars.

WHAT IS RELIGION?

The term *religion* has a long, multi-layered, and obscure history. One of the most plausible etymologies has the term deriving from an early Indo-European root **leig*, which means "to bind." From this root stems the Latin verb *ligare*, which means "to tie" or "to bind"—the English word *ligament* is derived from this verb as well. From *ligare* comes the Latin verb *religare*, which means "to retie" or "to bind fast"; it is a verb that connotes a sense of interconnectedness and permanency.

Catholic: from Latin and Greek words meaning "universal," referring to people and organizations associated with the Catholic Church, the largest Christian communion and, prior to the Protestant Reformation in the sixteenth century, the Christian church of western Europe.

Religious orders: communities and organizations of men or women who seek to lead a life of piety and often to perform some type of service. Members normally commit themselves to poverty, chastity, and obedience to lead a dedicated life.

Historical usage clouds the next etymological stage. The current consensus is that the verb *religare* provided a basis for the Latin noun *religio*, which conveys a sense of reverential awe and respect that one might experience in the presence of a spirit, god, honoured leader, or anyone else held in high esteem. However, *religion* has not always been understood in these terms. In fact, between the fourth and sixteenth centuries C.E., *religion* was thought to derive from the Latin verb *relego*, which means "to reread" or "to be careful." *Relego* was used to denote an action that required conscientious repetition or ritualistic discipline. Vestiges of this understanding of *religion* survive today in the adverb *religiously*, as in "She studies her notes religiously before every class." It is this transformation of the meaning of *religion*—from ritualistic devotion to something that binds—that is crucial to our understanding of religion and the field of religious studies.

Inventing "Religion"

As the historian of religion Jonathan Z. Smith has demonstrated, prior to the sixteenth century, the Latin noun forms *religio, religionis* (religion), the adjective *religiosus* (religious), and the adverb *religiose* (religiously) were terms "referring primarily to the careful performance of ritual obligations" (1998, 270). Western European explorers and **Catholic** missionaries who travelled eastward to China and India and westward to the Indies and Latin America in the fifteenth and sixteenth centuries commonly used *religion* to describe the indigenous peoples' rituals and ceremonial practices. Their frame of reference for *religion* and *religious* was, of course, European Catholicism and those who belonged to Catholic **religious orders**. Members of religious orders,

Ritual: a set of repetitive actions, often coordinated and regulated, that relates to a religion's myths and concept of ultimate meaning.

Idolatry: from a Greek term meaning "image worshipper." Nineteenth-century scholars of religion used the term to designate practices that violated Christian religious practices. Contemporary scholars avoid using the term as an academic category because it is a normative category that assumes a Christian standard.

Virtue: moral excellence or rightness.

Piety: devoutness, usually expressed through spiritual and worldly practices.

Faith: trust in the truth or authenticity of a person, idea, or concept. In the nineteenth century, the term became a designation for religion.

referred to as monks and nuns, were characterized by their devotion to the Church, their monastic life, their commitment to prayer, and their disavowal of worldly possessions. As these explorers and Catholic missionaries began to report on the cultures of China, India, the Indies, and Latin America, they used *religion* and *religious* to describe social arrangements, ceremonies, and political structures that resembled those in Spain, Portugal, and much of Western Europe.

Distinctions between *religion*, *custom*, and *superstition* began to define comparative qualities in belief and practice. These comparative qualities were, however, rarely explicitly defined, in part because the Western European Christian frame of reference was taken for granted. In assuming this Western European Christian frame of reference, any perceived differences between Europe and these "foreign" practices were typically filtered through a normative European Christian lens. *Superstition*, for example, generally implied practices that Europeans would associate with irrational belief, magic, and actions that would violate their cultural sensibilities, while *religion* implied **ritual** practices that, at the very least, formally resembled those taking place in churches across Western Europe. This close association between religion and ritual was not, however, without controversy. Back in Europe, theologians and some Church leaders were raising concerns that priests abroad were being too accommodating, if not deceitful, in their attempts to find similarities between Christian practices and "native rituals." Even when the term *ritual* was used to describe practices that would indicate differences from Christianity—such as cannibalism or "**idolatry**"—the close connection between ritual and religion within Catholicism meant that medieval theologians had to provide arguments for why and how "ritual" could lead to practices that violated Christian doctrine and practice.

By the end of the seventeenth century, the Catholic conception of religion as ritual performance and obligation had begun to give way to an understanding of religion as "**virtue**" and "**piety**." Influenced by Protestant Reformation leaders such as Ulrich Zwingli (1448–1531), John Calvin (1509–64), and to a lesser extent Martin Luther (1483–1546), post-Reformation scholars recast *religion* in more individualistic terms, that is, as a frame of mind oriented toward God that would lead to individual acts of virtue and piety, rather than participation in ritual performances. During this same time, terms such as *service* and *worship* lost much of their ritualistic connotations. Moreover, in line with key tenets of Protestant Christianity, ***faith*** became increasingly preferable to *religion* because *faith* emphasized the human subject's relationship with God and the subject's capacity to comprehend divine truth apart from the mediating authority of a Catholic priest, bishop, or pope. This Protestant emphasis on the human subject's ability to encounter God and to discover truth apart from the Catholic Church represented a fundamental challenge to medieval church, political, and social power structures. Indeed, the Protestant Reformation forever changed European Christianity. Not only did the Reformation split Western European Christianity into separate Protestant and Catholic traditions, but it also set the stage for various forms of Protestantism to take shape. By the beginning of the eighteenth century, then, Western Europe was no longer simply a geographical region under the authority of a single church—the Catholic Church. Rather, it operated with an ever-increasing variety of Christian traditions, each with different doctrines, rituals, and relationships with political authorities.

Along with the different types of Christianity, there was growing recognition of other "religions," which in the seventeenth and eighteenth centuries were often sorted into four primary species, namely, Christianity, "Mohametanism" (which later became

Islam), Judaism, and what was typically labelled "idolatry" or "**paganism**," which functioned as a miscellaneous category cataloguing cultural practices and social arrangements that fell outside the first three. While recognizing the differences between religions, scholars in the seventeenth and eighteenth centuries remained more interested in their similarities. This preoccupation with finding similarities among the different religions led to a long debate over "**natural religion**"—a debate that would dominate the study of religion for nearly two centuries.

Paganism: a broad category used by nineteenth-century scholars to identify groups that were polytheistic.

Natural religion: characterized by the belief that divine truth was manifest in natural phenomena and accessible through human reasons. Natural religion was popular in the seventeenth and eighteenth centuries.

Analects of Confucius: a text written between the fifth and third centuries B.C.E. traditionally believed to contain the sayings and teachings of the Chinese philosopher Confucius (c. 551–c. 479 B.C.E.) and his followers.

Bhagavad-Gita: a Hindu scripture focusing on the story of Lord Krishna; part of the ancient Hindu epic the Mahabharata.

Rig-Veda: a collection of old Indian Sanskrit (Vedic) hymns and one of the four sets of Vedas that comprise Hinduism's authoritative texts.

Pali canon: the collection of scriptures used in Theravada Buddhism.

The basic thesis of natural religion was that any human being willing and able to commit to rational questioning and study could discover religious beliefs and practices based on rational understanding. Initially this thesis was the foundation for disputes among Christians, especially between Protestant groups. The idea was that Christians of good faith and will could settle matters through reason. Eventually the thesis was expanded to include non-Christian religions as well. The strong inclination toward harmony in the natural-religion thesis meant that scholars tended to privilege similarities between the religions. The Christian roots of the thesis also meant that scholars often concentrated on a religion's universal claims, its central texts (especially stories of creation), its conception of life after death, its innate impulses to seek truth and the divine, and other topics central to Protestant Christianity. For many eighteenth- and nineteenth-century scholars of natural religion, the issue at stake was not whether another religion was true or not (although it was presumed that Christianity was the truest of them all) but rather the manner in which religion revealed unified truth to different people. There was, in other words, a common universal truth that surfaced in each religion, and it was the scholar's task to observe, classify, and explain "religious phenomena" in their various forms. This process signalled a significant transformation in the understanding of *religion*: it introduced the idea that religion was no longer a theological category but an anthropological category that relied on scholarly observation, classification, and interpretation of data.

By the turn of the nineteenth century there was no shortage of data. Scholars had become fluent in non-European languages. Moreover, colonial officials, travellers, and merchants had begun to learn Hindi, Arabic, Chinese dialects, certain African tribal languages, and other languages that made good political and economic sense. It was an age of expanding empires, increased international mobility, economic globalization, and post-Enlightenment curiosity, and there was growing demand for literature that could explain the social and cultural practices of peoples in faraway places. As a result, translations of "religious" texts began to appear. For example, an English translation of Confucius's **Analects** appeared in the late sixteenth century. Excerpts from the **Bhagavad-Gita** appeared in English in the late eighteenth century. The East India Company financed scholars to write a four-volume translation of the **Rig-Veda** in the middle of the nineteenth century, just before establishment of the British Raj in South Asia. Excerpts from the **Pali canon**, Theravada Buddhism's central texts, began to appear in the late nineteenth century with the assistance of the Pali Society, which was created by three British civil servants posted in Ceylon (now Sri Lanka).

Sweeping studies of foreign cultures and religions were also published and widely read in Europe. For instance, early in the nineteenth century, the twenty-four-volume *Descriptions of Egypt* appeared in France; the scholars had been part of Napoleon's expeditionary forces that invaded Egypt in 1798. This work, which anchored the new field of Egyptology, guided European

Naturalistic religion: a concept developed by anthropologists and scholars of religion in the nineteenth century to categorize the practices of non-supernatural religions, especially those linked with "primitive" peoples (e.g., animism, totemism, fetishism, magic).

Supernatural religion: a concept developed by anthropologists and other scholars of religion in the nineteenth century to categorize beliefs and practices that assumed the presence of a being beyond nature.

Fetishism: a category used by nineteenth- and early-twentieth-century scholars of naturalistic religion to refer to the practice of using objects believed to have supernatural powers. A fetish is the object that is believed to have such powers.

Totemism: a category used by nineteenth- and early-twentieth-century scholars of naturalistic religion to refer to the practice of using an animal or another natural figure to represent a community of people. A totem is the animal (e.g., an eagle or a wolverine) or natural figure.

Shamanism: a category used by nineteenth- and early-twentieth-century scholars of naturalistic religion to refer to groups of people who believe that an intermediary or a messenger (a shaman) can communicate with the spiritual world.

Animism: a category used, especially by nineteenth- and early-twentieth-century scholars of naturalistic religion, to refer to the belief that spirits exist not only in humans but also in other animals, plants, rocks, mountains, rivers, clouds, thunder, and other naturally occurring phenomena.

Magic: a category used, especially by nineteenth- and early-twentieth-century scholars of naturalistic religion, to refer to the belief that human beings can manipulate the natural world through supernatural power or through esoteric knowledge of natural laws.

In this famous painting titled *Napoleon before the Sphinx*, two powerful figures meet face to face: one the face of the first French empire, the other the face of an Egyptian tradition dating back to at least 2500 B.C.E. Nineteenth-century studies of religion were often the result of European empires invading foreign lands.

Source: Apic/Getty Images

thinking on Islam and Coptic Christianity in Egypt for almost a century. Other studies, such as John Bellamy's *The History of All Religions* (1812) and Henri-Benjamin Constant's *Considerations on the Source of Religion: Its Forms and Developments* (in French, *De la religion,* 1824–31), were published to receptive audiences. By the end of the nineteenth century scholars had invented the terms *Hindooism* (1829), *Taouism* (1839), and *Confucianism* (1862). Above all, these scholars created systems of classification (in technical terms, *taxonomies*) that resembled those used by natural scientists to classify and define organisms. The result of this process was that, by the mid-nineteenth century, the study of religion was no longer a theological pursuit or a natural history but a social science.

As Smith has noted, "the most common form of classifying religions, found both in native categories and in scholarly literature, is dualistic and can be reduced, regardless of what differentium is employed, to 'theirs' and 'ours' " (1998, 276). One of the most important distinctions in nineteenth-century research on religion was between **naturalistic** and **supernatural** religions. Naturalistic religions, which were sometimes called "primitive" religions, were often traced to "primitive peoples," or in German *Naturvölker*, which literally translates as "nature peoples." Naturalistic religion was broken down into smaller segments: **fetishism**, **totemism**, **shamanism**, **animism**, and **magic**, as well as tribal, imperial, and ancestor worship, to name just a few. By contrast, supernatural religion placed belief in a divine otherworldly power, being, or beings that would affect worldly affairs from time to time. Influenced by the English naturalist Charles Darwin (1809–82) and Herbert Spencer (1820–1903), who popularized Darwin's theories in the field of sociology, a number of influential scholars, including anthropologists Edward B.

Tylor (1832–1917) and James G. Frazer (1854–1941), thought that these "primitive" religions were in the early stages of evolutionary development, and that with each stage they would begin to look more and more like supernatural religions.

These scholars of naturalistic religion maintained classification categories that privileged religions resembling Protestant and, to an ever-decreasing extent, Catholic Christianity in Europe. The supernatural or spiritual religions, which tended to be synonymous with "high religion," were limited to Christianity, Buddhism, and Mohammedanism (later Islam). In some classifications, Judaism was called a "reformed natural" religion and a "fleshly" religion because it was a "spontaneous" religion and limited to a single "race," as compared to Christianity, for instance, which grew out of Judaism "rationally" and was open to all races. This marked a major shift in the study of religion. The old system of classification, which had the three Abrahamic religions—Judaism, Christianity, and Islam—set against "idolatry" or "paganism," had been replaced by a new model, which classified Buddhism, Mohammedanism, and Christianity as the *supernatural religions* while assigning all other religions, including Judaism, to various classes of *naturalistic religion*.

The invention of "world" or "universal" religions occurred during this wave of interest in non-European religion. The Dutch scholar Cornelius Petrus Tiele (1830–1902) introduced the concept of "the world's religions" in his *Outline of the History of Religion to the Spread of Universal Religion* (1876). He divided the world's religions into two broad classifications: natural (or "naturalistic") religion and ethical religion. Consistent with the nineteenth-century trend to interpret data in evolutionary terms, Tiele thought that naturalistic religion was the lower stage in human development, with animism being the lowest form of religion, totemism being a transitional phase, and **polytheism** being characteristic of the highest form of naturalistic religion.

Tiele divided ethical religion, the higher stage, into two categories. The first was called "national nomistic religious communities." With this category, Tiele attempted to capture religions that were founded on a law or scripture and drew their adherents from a particular nation or ethnic group. These religions included Daoism, Confucianism, "Brahmanism" (later Hinduism), Jainism, primitive Buddhism, and Judaism. The second category of ethical religions was called "universalistic religious communities." These religions practised universal **proselytization**, which meant that they accepted followers from all ethnic groups. Tiele included only three "universalistic" or "world" religions: Islam, Buddhism, and Christianity.

Polytheism: belief in more than one god.

Proselytization: the practice of converting someone or some group of people to a religion.

The category "world religions" was, from the outset, a controversial designation. In particular, scholars sought to expand the number of world religions by combining Tiele's two categories of ethical religion. Jonathan Smith has captured the profound lack of scientific rigor involved in this process. It was, he wrote, "an odd venture of pluralistic etiquette: if Christianity and Islam count as world religions, then it would be rude to exclude Judaism. . . . Likewise, if Buddhism is included, then Hinduism cannot be ignored. And again, if Buddhism, then Chinese religions and Japanese religions" (Smith 1998, 280).

In many respects, then, "world religions" is a political category, signifying that these religions matter to the academy because they affect global politics. The political foundations of world religions are made even more evident by the scholarly practice of dividing these religions along an East–West geographical line. This East–West orientation is radically political because it assumes a centre of the world: traditionally Europe, the continent that both dominated geopolitics throughout the nineteenth century and the early part of the twentieth century and invented the study of religion. Consequently, the category "Eastern religions" typically meant the religions that originated in the Arabian Peninsula, China, Japan, South Asia, and Southeast Asia. These "Eastern" religions included Islam, Buddhism, Confucianism, Daoism, Hinduism, and Sikhism. It was only in the first half of the twentieth century that Islam became a "Western" religion. Currently the designation "Western religions" means the religions that originated in the Middle East and North Africa but became politically significant in Europe and later in the Americas—Judaism, Christianity, and Islam. Often lost in this "world religions" paradigm are the so-called minor religions, which are commonly designated as spirituality and

Substantive definitions of religion: sometimes known as essentialist definitions, they maintain that religion has an essence that is universal (e.g., the holy, the sacred, or a belief in spiritual beings).

Sacred: something or someone that is set apart or holy. It is often used in contrast with *profane*.

Sui generis: a Latin phrase meaning "of its own kind." It is used by scholars of religion, especially those from the *Religionswissenschaft* school, who believe that religion is "of its own kind" and must therefore be studied with an appreciation for the irreducible truth that is in religion.

tribal groupings because they demand so little political attention. Based almost solely on political criteria, then, many studies of "the world's religions" exclude the beliefs of indigenous peoples in the Americas and Oceania as well the religions of sub-Saharan Africa.

Defining Religion

So we return to our question "What is religion?" By now it should be clear that defining religion is not an easy task. As we discovered in our brief history of the term *religion*, it has been wrought with theological biases, philosophical and anthropological assumptions about absolute truth, and political agendas. There is, in short, no "pure" or "true" definition of religion. As sociologist Peter Berger wrote in *The Sacred Canopy*, "Definitions cannot, by their very nature, be either 'true' or 'false,' only more useful or less so" ([1967] 1969, 175). So why, then, should we attempt to define religion? The short answer is this: in order to set limits on our field of study, we must establish some boundaries on the phenomena that we wish to study; otherwise, to say that we are "studying religion" means that we are studying everything—which is to say nothing in particular.

Substantive and Functional Definitions

Historically, definitions of religion have fallen into two broad categories: the substantive and the functional. **Substantive definitions** typically provide definitive answers to the question "What is religion?" In general, substantive definitions, which are sometimes called *essentialist* definitions, tend to emphasize three features of religion. First, they focus on the "things" of religion, such as gods, belief in higher powers, sacred scripture, the divine, and the holy. A classical substantive definition of religion comes from the anthropologist E. B. Tylor, who defined religion as a "belief in Spiritual Beings" ([1871] 1974, 383).

Second, substantive definitions make claims about the essence of religion. For instance, the German theologian Friedrich Schleiermacher (1768–1834) believed that the essence of religion is to be found in the "feeling of an absolute dependence" ([1830] 1999, 12–18, 26–29). For Schleiermacher, religion is essentially an affective, or emotional, response. Rudolf Otto (1869–1937), also a German theologian and the author of the widely read *The Idea of the Holy* (1917), offered a definition that emphasized a subjective response to an object outside oneself. For Otto, the holy is a non-rational mystery that generates experiences of both fear and fascination. "The truly 'mysterious' object," Otto wrote, "is beyond our apprehension and comprehension, not only because our knowledge has certain irremovable limits, but because in it we come upon something inherently 'wholly other,' whose kind and character are incommensurable with our own, and before which we recoil in a wonder that strikes us chill and numb" (1958, 28).

Similarly to Otto, Mircea Eliade (1907–86), the legendary figure who turned the University of Chicago into a hub for North American religious studies, believed that religion was rooted in a non-rational experience of what he called "the **sacred**." For Eliade, religious phenomena have an essence, "the sacred," that is the cause of religious behaviour and not the effect. Eliade wrote, "A religious phenomenon will only be recognized as such if it is grasped at its own level, that is to say, if it is studied *as* something religious. To try to grasp the essence of such a phenomenon by means of physiology, psychology, sociology, economics, linguistics, art, or any other study is false; it misses the one unique and irreducible element in it—the element of the sacred (1963, xiii). Students who adopt Eliade's definition of religion believe—and we use *believe* deliberately, since there is no way to demonstrate it academically—that religion is essentially ***sui generis*** (Latin for "of its own kind" or "self-caused"), extraordinary, inscrutable, and common to all humans. (The term Eliade used for people who have this natural inclination to seek the sacred was ***Homo religiosus.***)

And third, substantive definitions of religion tend to posit a normative standard that provides moral, spiritual, and psychological guidance for human beings. An excellent example of this normative type of definition comes from William James (1842–1910), the philosopher and psychologist, who stated in his popular book *The Varieties of Religious Experience* (1902) that religion "consists of the belief that there is an unseen order, and that our supreme good lies in harmoniously adjusting ourselves thereto" (1958, 58). Another good example comes from Paul Tillich (1886–1965), one of the most celebrated theologians of the twentieth century, who wrote, "Religion is the state of being grasped by an ultimate concern, a concern which qualifies all other concerns as preliminary and which itself contains the answer to the question of the meaning of our life" (1963, 8).

Substantive definitions create tremendous concern for scholars of religion who work in the social sciences and are accustomed to engaging with phenomena by using empirical frameworks. While these scholars raise a number of objections, there are two that stand out. First, substantive definitions assume realities called the "spiritual" and the "supernatural." The problem with this assumption is that both the spiritual and the supernatural exist outside the realm of academic inquiry. To understand the spiritual and the supernatural as realms of being and existence requires a subjective encounter with "the sacred," "the holy," or any other spiritual being or state. Critics therefore argue that the study of religion in substantive terms eventually becomes an "insiders'" study that may exclude "outsiders" who reject notions of a spiritual or supernatural reality. In the eyes of these critics, substantive claims cannot be proven empirically through scientific means.

Second, critics often argue that substantive definitions are merely parochial theological assertions operating under the guise of universal pretensions. The result, they contend, has been that substantive definitions of religion have yielded studies that have more in common with theological studies than with the social sciences. In more precise terms, the process emanating from substantive definitions of religion assumes certain attributes of liberal Protestant theology: they assert (a) that there is an essence to religion, (b) that this essence is "true," (c) that all human beings either do or may experience this "true" essence in some manner or another, and (d) that this experience leads to a better state of being, whether it is called "salvation," "enlightenment," "**moksha**," "higher consciousness," "**nirvana**," or "oneness with reality."

Functional definitions generally answer the question "What does religion do?" In functionalist terms, religion meets certain human needs, such as providing social cohesion, emotional or psychological support, and intellectual meaning. Functional definitions tend to facilitate studies into the behaviour of religious people rather than their beliefs. Consequently, scholars who use functional definitions are often interested in the sociology, anthropology, and psychology of religion. A classic functional definition of religion is found in the work of the sociologist Émile Durkheim (1858–1917), who wrote, "A religion is a unified system of beliefs and practices relative to sacred things, that is to say, things set apart and forbidden—beliefs and practices which unite into one single moral community called a church, all those who adhere to them" ([1912] 1915, 419). For Durkheim, religion provides social stability, a means to express group identity, and a forum for community gatherings.

Like Durkheim, Karl Marx (1818–83) defined religion in terms of its social function: "Religion is the sigh of the oppressed creature, the heart of a heartless world, just as it is the spirit of a spiritless situation. It is the *opium* of people" (1964, 42). Marx thought that religion only placated the feelings of alienation that the masses were experiencing as they toiled away in their dehumanizing

Homo religiosus: a phrase coined by Mircea Eliade to refer to the human quality of being religious.

Moksha: a Sanskrit term meaning "release," it means the escape from the cycle of birth and rebirth. Nirvana is its equivalent in Buddhism and mukti in Sikhism, although the manner in which humans are liberated from the cycle differs in each religion.

Nirvana: the state of being free from suffering, a central concept in the religions of India.

Functional definitions of religion: favoured by sociologists and others scholars interested in studying what religions "do," they focus on the behaviours of people and how those behaviours are connected to other aspects of the community.

jobs. Religion was an "illusory happiness," a numbing drug that had to be jettisoned in order to discover "real happiness" (1964, 42). Moreover, religion was a bourgeois tool of oppression employed by those who owned the means of production (the bourgeoisie) to control the working class (the proletariat). To achieve authentic happiness, the working class had to rid itself not only of religion but also of capitalism, which in Marx's view meant nothing less than a socio-economic revolution.

Sigmund Freud (1856–1939), one of the founders of psychoanalytic psychology, also believed that religion was an illusion. "Religion," he wrote, "is an attempt to get control over the sensory world, in which we are placed, by means of the wish-world which we have developed inside us as a result of biological and psychological necessities. . . . If one attempts to assign religion its place in [human] evolution, it seems . . . a parallel to the neurosis which the civilized individual must pass through on his way from childhood to maturity" (1918). Daniel Pals, a scholar who specializes in theories of religion, has accurately described the profound reductionism in Freud's thinking. He writes that Freud "does not just say that, *among other things*, religion seems to have certain psychological functions. He asserts that religion arises *only* in response to deep emotional conflicts and weaknesses" (2006, 77).

PERSPECTIVES

The Insider/Outsider Problem

The Canadian scholar of religion Wilfred Cantwell Smith (1916–2000) is widely known for privileging the perspective of the insider in the study of religion. He writes, "no statement about a religion is valid unless it can be acknowledged by that religion's believers" (1959, 42). In effect, Smith is proposing a rule that insiders are the final authority in determining whether or not a scholar's statement about their religion is correct. This rule, however, creates problems for researchers who are interested in studying why insiders act and believe differently. Which insider should be the final arbiter? Or what happens if (or more likely, when) the researcher finds that an insider's claims contradict his or her behaviour? Does the researcher then make a judgment based on criteria outside those of the insiders?

In the 1950s Kenneth Pike, a linguist, coined the terms *emic* and *etic* to help analyze human language. According to Pike, the emic viewpoint studies phenomena from inside a system and relies on insiders to judge the accuracy of a description or, for example, the proper way to say the word *about* in Canada. An etic viewpoint studies phenomena from outside a system and uses criteria derived from extrinsic concepts and categories that are meaningful to the researcher. For Pike, etics are a way of accessing emics; but etic perspectives can claim no priority over emic perspectives. In the 1960s, Marvin Harris, an anthropologist, borrowed Pike's emic/etic concept to study cultural anthropology. Harris disagreed with Pike. For Harris, etics are useful for making relatively objective determinations of fact, which is an essential component of disciplines that purport to be sciences.

Today, insider/outsider debates occur most often when scholars attempt to extrapolate a universal human characteristic from the study of religion while other scholars attempt to refute such universalistic claims as going beyond the scope of academic study. For example, Wendy Doniger and Diana Eck have conducted a number of comparative studies of religion and found that certain shared experiences underlie many myths and rituals, even though they may appear in different forms in various religions. In response, scholars such as Russell McCutcheon, a Canadian academic, maintain that these attempts to locate universal experience are remnants of a liberal humanism that privileges an essentialist understanding of religion over a functionalist one.

Of course, not all functional definitions are as reductionist as those offered by Marx and Freud. For instance, Clifford Geertz (1926–2006), the leading figure in twentieth-century North American anthropology, constructed a definition that is both functional and "realistic" (a term we will discuss below), to the extent that it has enabled scholars to examine the objects of religious experience without reducing them to their fundamental status or nature:

> Religion is (1) a system of symbols which acts to (2) establish powerful, pervasive, and long-lasting moods and motivations in [people] by (3) formulating conceptions of a general order of existence and (4) clothing these conceptions with such an aura of factuality that the moods and motivations seem uniquely realistic. (1979, 79–80)

Geertz's definition of religion maintains wide appeal among scholars in large part because of its flexibility and scope. Other definitions provide even more flexibility and scope. For example, Wilfred Cantwell Smith, the Canadian scholar and former director of the Harvard Center for the Study of the World Religions, recommended using the language of "traditions" to include both religion and secular humanism. Ninian Smart (1927–2001), who helped pioneer secular approaches to the study of religion, suggested using "worldviews" as the common term for nationalism, socialism, and religion.

One common criticism of functional definitions is that they can be too sweeping. While they allow scholars to examine a variety of phenomena that many might associate with religion, such as prayer, ritual performance, and structures of religious authority, functional definitions generally have trouble limiting phenomena. Because functional definitions orient the student to examine structures, forms, and patterns of human activity, it is often difficult to exclude phenomena that appear to bear attributes similar to "religious" phenomena. Examples of this blurring between religion and other, similar forms of human behaviour might include a NASCAR race, the Olympics, the fan culture around a sports team (e.g., "Leafs Nation" or "Habs Nation"), a nationalist political party such as the National Socialist Party in Germany or the Khmer Rouge in Cambodia, a political ideology such as communism, an intentional community committed to living in an ecologically sustainable way, or a virtual online community that gathers regularly to play World of Warcraft. The danger with functional definitions is that the terms *religion* and *religious* grow to be so all-encompassing that they become academically useless categories.

PERSPECTIVES

Functional definitions of religion have allowed scholars to examine contemporary sports as religion. In the United States, football fans cheer for professional teams that have animal mascots—such as the Bears, Colts, Seahawks, Broncos, Dolphins, Cardinals, and Eagles—which are strikingly similar to the clan totems identified in early studies of religion. These totems/mascots provide identifying markers for communities/fans as they gather to support their respective clans/teams. In Canada, Olivier Bauer (2009) has published a book that analyzes the correlations between Montreal Canadiens fans who refer to the Habs jersey as *la sainte flanelle* ("holy

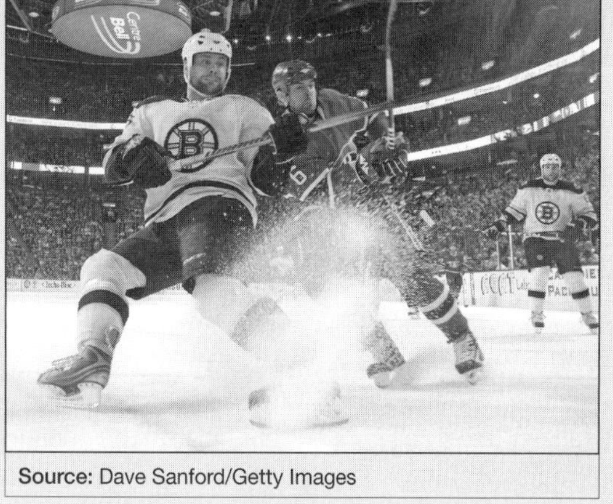

Source: Dave Sanford/Getty Images

Deity: an entity that exists beyond the natural world and is believed to affect the lives of the natural world, often in the form of a god.

Toward a Stipulative Definition of Religion

Students in my introductory courses in religious studies will often ask me this question in some form or another: "If you're searching for a definition of religion, why not just go to the dictionary?" While the question is typically posed with the best of intentions, such as to help alleviate their fellow students' frustration and confusion over why defining religion is so complicated, the problem is that dictionary, or lexical, definitions are limited to ordinary usage. Definitions found in dictionaries such as the *Oxford Dictionary of the English Language* or *Merriam-Webster's* dictionary state only "the actual way in which some actual word has been used by some actual person" (Baird 1973, 10). A lexical definition of *religion*, then, is simply a cataloguing of the most common ways in which the term has been used. For example, the *Canadian Oxford Dictionary* (2004) contains five separate definitions for *religion*. The first one reads: "the belief in a superhuman controlling power, esp. in a personal God or gods entitled to obedience and worship." For students pursuing an academic study of religion, this definition is unsatisfactory, since not all religions have an absolute **deity** or gods who wield power or demand obedience. For instance, in Theravada Buddhism, which is found in many parts of Southeast Asia as well as India and Sri Lanka, the Buddha (the "Enlightened One") is revered as a sage but not as a god. Because lexical definitions convey popular usage, students of religious studies should avoid them as much as possible.

Another way to define religion is by making empirical statements about religion. This type of definition is called a *real* definition. Such definitions rely on data and some form of proof in their formation. Because these definitions are deductive, which means they arise only at the end of study, scholars who use real definitions tend to rely on their definitions as an integral element in their overall argument. These real definitions are central propositions about the way things are. One good example of a real definition is the following: "Religion consists of very general explanations of existence, including terms of exchange with a god or gods" (Stark and Finke 2000, 91). While real definitions may be phrased in ways that appear to be the same as *substantialist* definitions, they are different. Substantialist definitions assert from the beginning that religion has an essence, while real definitions, which tend to be more functional in orientation, attempt to demonstrate through social scientific methods that religion corresponds to certain objects and phenomena.

Given the nature and objectives of this text, we will adopt a *stipulative* definition of religion. Stipulative definitions are somewhat arbitrary statements designed to limit the range of study for a particular purpose and audience. These are useful working definitions that are subject to revision. Moreover, stipulative definitions can be either substantive or functional. For example, a Christian theologian could, following Paul Tillich, stipulate that religion is "ultimate concern" and then proceed to enquire into the essential nature of higher beings in different

PERSPECTIVES

A Note Regarding Dictionaries

Not all dictionaries should be avoided by the student of religion. Technical dictionaries edited, written, and reviewed by scholars in the field can provide students with reliable information. These dictionaries include the *Penguin Dictionary of Religions* (2005), edited by John Hinnells, and the thorough *Harper Collins Dictionary of Religion* (1996), edited by Jonathan Z. Smith. There are also dictionaries that focus on specific religions, including new religious movements, and theoretical approaches to the study of religion. Unlike the general language lexicons, these technical dictionaries often provide historical context and commentaries outlining the usage of the terms. Readers should consult the bibliography at the end of each chapter for help in finding resources.

religions. Alternatively, a sociologist of religion could, following Durkheim, stipulate that religion consists of "unified systems of beliefs and practices" and then proceed to examine the ways in which religious institutions function to provide social stability.

Since the authors in this text tend to emphasize the social, cultural, historical, and political aspects of religion, let us stipulate the following definition, which we construct with the help of Bruce Lincoln (2003) and Thomas Tweed (2006): *Religions are systems of discourses, practices, communities, and institutions that draw on human and suprahuman powers to provide adherents access to ultimate meaning.*

Suprahuman: an adjective relating to abilities and modes of existence that are greater than human.

Theism: a broad term signifying belief in at least one god.

Myth: in the field of religious studies, a story that communicates a community's norms and values. For scholars of religious studies, a myth is neither true nor false, but important data that enables scholars to understand the various roles that the myth plays in a religion.

Doctrine: the formal teachings of a religion, typically in written form and promoted by authority figures or experts trained in interpreting the teachings.

Before the Common Era (B.C.E.): before the C.E. Used by scholars instead of B.C. (before Christ).

The Usefulness of Our Definition

Notice that this definition invites us to study the religions in this text as coherent systems that maintain ways of communicating, acting, gathering, and regulating behaviour. It stipulates that religions present humans with special pathways to authentic knowledge and truths. This knowledge and truth could be intellectual (i.e., rational) or experiential (i.e., nonrational). Following Tweed (2006), our definition uses the term **suprahuman** instead of terms such as *God*, *gods*, or *spiritual beings*. With this definition we are suspending our judgment as to whether such suprahuman beings exist, but we are acknowledging that religions do typically include such beings. This choice allows for religions that do not affirm **theism**, such as Theravada Buddhism and certain new religious movements, to be captured by our definition. Furthermore, our definition recognizes that some religions, including Christianity and some forms of Buddhism, believe that suprahuman powers can operate through human beings. We should also note that, because our definition includes references to suprahuman beings and ultimate meaning, we have effectively excluded the study of NASCAR races, fairy tales, most political and social movements, and popular culture as religions.

Our definition is useful because it enables us to study the various expressions of religious phenomena. For instance, through a study of a religion's *discourses*—that is, the formal ways in which people communicate—we can examine two of the primary ways in which religious communities disseminate knowledge about reality, morality, the meaning of life and death, and other core beliefs: **myth** and **doctrine**. The term *myth* comes from the Greek word *mythos*, meaning "word" or "story." Prior to the sixth century B.C.E., the word *mythos* was synonymous with the Greek word *logos*. But as Greek intellectuals such as Plato (429–347 B.C.E.) and Herodotus (c. 484–c. 425 B.C.E.) began to question the stories of the Greek gods, *mythos* came to mean "implausible story" or "irrational story," while *logos* took on the meaning of "reasonable story" or "reason." This Greek legacy remains with us today. Many of us associate myth with fictitious stories such as the classical Greek myth *The Odyssey*, the medieval stories of King Arthur, or the contemporary myth *The Lord of the Rings*. We may also associate myth with a false story or cultural narrative, much as Naomi Wolf did in her book *The Beauty Myth* (1992).

In the academic study of religion, a myth is a narrative that conveys a community's central values and understanding of the world. As scholars of religion, we do not make judgments about whether a myth is literally true or not. Instead, our primary purpose in studying a myth is to help us understand the various roles it plays in a community's network of communication. In this regard, we treat myth as something ordinary. Common myths include stories about creation, heroes, tricksters, salvation/enlightenment, redemption, and the afterlife. We can find them in scripture, oral histories, and collections of teachings by revered leaders, as well as in a religion's art and architecture.

In comparison to myth, which takes the form of stories, doctrine often appears as creeds, confessions of faith, or legal declarations. Doctrine may also appear as theology or a philosophy. In general, doctrine tends to explain the core tenets of a religion by clarifying its myths. Take, for example, the biblical myth about the expulsion of the two original human beings from the Garden of Eden because they disobeyed God (Genesis 3). Christianity interprets this story through its doctrine of original sin, which was developed in the writings of third- and fourth-century C.E. theologians. In effect this doctrine teaches that all human beings are born with the inherited sin of the first man and woman in the Garden of Eden. It explains why people do bad things, why there is human suffering in this world, and why there is a severed relationship between human beings and God. It also points to the Christian doctrine of salvation, which holds that Jesus died as a sacrifice for the sins of not only the first humans but all humankind.

Through a study of a group's *practices*, we can understand the performative aspects of a religion. Religious practices can take many forms, such as singing, dancing, praying, meditating, drawing, painting, writing, dreaming, bathing, walking, running, eating, fasting, having sex, not having sex, dressing in a particular way, working, begging, and so on. Religious practices are rooted in tradition and conducted according to custom. Religious practices can be performed in public or in private. *Ritual* is the name scholars give to a set of practices that is repeated over time, often for the purpose of symbolically retelling or reliving meaningful events in a religion's tradition. In many cases, rituals are carefully choreographed to coincide with a religion's myth, such as in the case of the hajj and the pilgrims who reenact aspects of the prophet Abraham's life.

Two integral aspects of religious practice are time and space. Scholars have long observed that many religious rituals are cyclical. For example, Jewish Passover, Christian Easter celebrations, Islam's month of fasting (Ramadan), and the Hindu Festival of Lights (Diwali) occur according to their respective calendars. Other rituals, such as the obligation to pray five times a day in Islam (*salah*), are daily practices that are linked to the position of the sun or the time of day. A number of religions, including Judaism, Christianity, Islam, and Theravada Buddhism, maintain weekly rest days, which are traditionally set aside for purification and contemplation. Based on observations of religious festivals and rituals, scholars such as Mircea Eliade have developed the concept of "sacred time" in order to distinguish it from ordinary, or profane, time. In sacred time, these scholars argue, religious people move from the routine of profane time into a time that enables them to perform their rituals.

Whether in temples, churches, mosques, prayer rooms, rice fields, tents, or cubicles in an office, religious practices take place in space. In some cases, mythic spaces become focal points for contemporary religious practices, including pilgrimages. For instance, Judaism regards the Temple Mount in the heart of Jerusalem as the holiest site on earth, because it was there, Jews believe, that God's presence dwelled at times in a series of temples that were eventually destroyed. Muslims, too, regard the Temple Mount/Noble Sanctuary as a holy site—it is home to the oldest Islamic building still standing, the Dome of the Rock, which was built in the late seventh century C.E. However, the holiest site in Islam is Mecca, the city where the Prophet Muhammad proclaimed Islam in the seventh century. It is home to the Ka'aba, the cube-shaped building that is the focal point for Muslims at prayer all around the world and the centre of the hajj circumambulation. Although perhaps not directly linked to a religion's myth, a local temple, church, or mosque provides formal spaces where religious practices can take place. Like mythic sites, these places typically have rules that govern the conduct of those who enter. On a smaller scale, there are also informal sites of religious practice that for a period of time become meaningful to religious people. These may be public spaces where someone, for example, stops to pray or meditate (a park, an office building, a shopping mall) or private spaces where someone has created a special place to perform individual rituals (e.g., a shrine or chapel in one's home).

The twofold task of the scholar studying religious practices is (1) to observe the performance, where it takes place, and when, and (2) to raise questions about the meaning it has for the individual and the community. Take, for instance, a young Jewish man living in a suburb of Montreal who decides to grow a beard. Is he letting his beard grow because he is following a Jewish tradition, which is based on a reading of scripture that forbids the shaving of the "corners of the head" (Leviticus 19:27), or is he growing a beard because of aesthetic preference? Unless we understand the context and the traditions, we are prone to misinterpret the practice and its significance.

Through the study of a *community* organized around religious discourses and practices, we can understand the social structures and boundaries for those inside the community. A study of a religious community might involve an examination of its gender roles, its understanding of the family, and its class structure. A study of a religion's social structure could focus on how and why some religions have divided into various **sects** or **denominations**. If we are interested in the politics of the community, we might examine the nature of religious authority within the community and how the community challenges that authority. Or we might ask questions about the role of religion in a country's political and governing structure.

Through a study of a group's *institutions*, we can encounter the ways in which religious discourse and practices take place and cohere around authoritative figures, offices, and leaders who are charged with nurturing and defending the community, its practices, and its modes of communication. Scholars sometimes make a distinction between formal institutions (e.g., a temple, a church, a mosque, a **gurdwara**, or a religious school) and informal institutions, which are socially constructed norms and customs that provide social order, even when they appear to contravene a religious doctrine. Studies of informal institutions typically concentrate on gender, family, civil society, informal governance, and emerging challenges to authority.

Sect: the term has multiple meanings in religious studies and for this reason is often avoided by contemporary scholars. Traditionally it means a group that is opposed to and set apart from a recognized political or religious body. Some sociologists remain interested in the term because it enables them to examine groups that separate from other groups because they claim to be more authentic.

Denomination: a subgroup of a religion.

Gurdwara: a place of worship for Sikhs.

The Erawan Shrine in Bangkok, Thailand, situated in front of the Erawan Grand Hyatt Hotel in one of the city's busiest shopping districts. Amidst the commotion of a busy city, worshippers, both Thai and foreign, stop to pray at the shrine. The figure in shrine, Phra Phrom, is a Thai representation of the Hindu god Brahma. Despite Thailand's being a predominantly Buddhist country, the shrine remains an important site for many Thai citizens.

Source: © Piti Vedeer/Alamy

PERSPECTIVES

An Important Caveat Regarding Data

Now that we have stipulated a definition, we need to add one important caveat: *religion*, as an essence or a unique ethos, does not exist. Jonathan Smith explains:

> While there is a staggering amount of data, of phenomena, of human experiences and expressions that might be characterized in one culture or another, by one criterion or another, as religious, *there is no data for religion.* Religion is solely the creation of the scholar's study. It is created for the scholar's analytic purposes by his [or her] imaginative acts of comparison and generalization. Religion has no independent existence apart from the academy. For this reason, the student of religion . . . must be relentlessly self-conscious. Indeed, this self-consciousness constitutes [the student's] primary expertise, his [or her] foremost object of study (1982, xi).

The issue is not whether the data we study are authentic—people do indeed go to temple, church, and mosque, and some ground their actions in moral codes found in scripture and authoritative teachers. Rather, it is the category we use to classify and define these data that is in question. To put matters simply, *religion* is a category imposed by the religious studies scholar, from the outside, on aspects of a particular culture. The "outsider"—in this case, European explorers and Christian missionaries, colonial bureaucrats and merchants, as well as modern scholars from Europe and North America—is responsible for the term (Smith 1998, 269). *Religion* is therefore not a native category but a category created by the outsider to identify and classify characteristics of phenomena. As students of religion, then, we must recognize that our definitions of religion are always in flux and imperfect.

HOW DO WE STUDY RELIGION?

Religious studies scholars in North America share a common story about studying religion as graduate students. It goes something like this: We are somewhere (usually on an airplane or a bus or at a party) making small talk with someone we have never met, when suddenly our new acquaintance asks, "So, what is it you do?" For those of us who tell the truth and say, "I'm a grad student in religious studies," the conversation typically leads to the question "So, you're studying to be a minister or a priest, are you?" While this story is purely anecdotal, it nevertheless represents a prevalent misconception in North American society that associates religious studies with theological and pastoral training. For many North Americans, *religion* is something personal, it is something we do, so to study religion must inevitably mean that we are "religious" and likely working toward a religious vocation such as pastor, priest, rabbi, or imam. But the academic study of religion does not mean that we must or even should identify with a particular religion. Nor does it imply that we aspire to be religious leaders. Rather, to engage in the academic study of religion means that we use scholarly methods to examine, classify, analyze, and explain phenomena that we call "religion."

Because religious studies is a subject field and not an academic discipline, there is no science or prescribed methodology directly associated with the study of religion. Instead the academic study of religion relies on methods used in disciplines such as sociology, anthropology, psychology, philosophy, history, and many more sub-disciplines, including archaeology, ethics, linguistics, gender studies, the sociology of knowledge, and ethnomusicology. Consequently, in many North American colleges and universities it is common for a religious studies program to be housed in either the anthropology or philosophy department, and perhaps called the department of anthropology (or philosophy) and religious studies.

In the United States, religious studies departments began to emerge as independent units within the university only in the late 1960s and 1970s. To create stand-alone departments of religious studies in publicly funded universities, scholars from the humanities and social sciences were often granted joint appointments in both their core discipline and the new department. These new departments of religious studies were secular (that is, non-theological) in orientation and consciously organized to teach the major world religions. To emphasize the cross-cultural nature of this new religious studies curriculum, some departments chose to describe their activities as studies in "comparative religion." Amidst the changing social norms of the late 1960s and 1970s, undergraduates flocked to courses on Buddhism, Hinduism, and new religious movements such as the International Society for Krishna Consciousness (ISKCON, or the "Hare Krishnas"), the Jesus movement, and various "hippy" intentional communities.

Unlike the situation in the United States, where the doctrine of **separation of church and state** means that theology was never welcomed in publicly funded universities, in Canada a number of Canadian universities maintain either links to or their own theology faculties and departments. Much like privately funded universities in the United States, such as Harvard, Yale, and Princeton, many Canadian universities owe their existence to previously existing church schools. Moreover, a number of large research universities have agreements with smaller theological colleges to provide training to students seeking a vocation in the church. While courses in theology continue to exist in many of Canada's universities, since the early 1970s the vast majority of the courses offered in religious studies departments are not theologically oriented and do not assume any type of faith commitment on the part of the student.

Whether in the United States or in Canada, students taking religious studies courses will most likely encounter not just one approach to the study but several. Let's highlight a few of the most widely used approaches.

Separation of church and state: a phrase first used by Thomas Jefferson (1743–1826) in 1802 to describe the "freedom of religion" and "non-establishment" clauses in the First Amendment of the U.S. Constitution. The Supreme Court of the United States affirmed this separation in 1878 and in a series of rulings beginning in 1947, leading to it becoming "settled law."

Ontology: the branch of philosophy that studies being, existence, and reality.

Epistemology: a branch of philosophy that is concerned with knowledge and ways of knowing.

Philosophical Approaches

Philosophical approaches to the study of religion use reason to engage with central areas of belief, claims about truth, and the human capacity to construct systems of logic and meaning. Philosophers of religion are typically not interested in social and cultural conceptions of religion. Rather, they attempt to think about questions of meaning and value without resorting to a faith perspective or relying on a faith community. Following the Greek philosopher Plato, many philosophers of religion have, over the years, asked metaphysical questions—that is, questions about non-physical, non-scientific things: Does God exist? How does one speak about God? What is the nature of ultimate meaning? Philosophers of religion often focus on one branch of philosophy called **ontology**, which is the investigation of the nature of being, existence, and reality. Philosophers of religion have also been interested in questions of **epistemology**, which focus on knowledge, how we acquire knowledge, and how we know.

In the Western tradition, philosophy and theology have long worked in conjunction with each other. From the second to the sixteenth century C.E., philosophy and theology were complementary methods of thinking about truth. Jewish, Christian, and Muslim thinkers mounted sophisticated philosophical arguments to uphold the basic tenets of their respective religious beliefs. Toward the end of the Middle Ages, for example, Jewish, Christian, and Muslim thinkers used the Greek philosopher Aristotle's (384–322 B.C.E.) philosophical system to revitalize their respective religious traditions.

Agnosticism: the belief that human beings cannot know whether or not God exists.

Middle Ages: the period in European history between the fifth and fifteenth centuries C.E.

The famous Jewish scholar Maimonides (1138–1204) refashioned Aristotle's philosophical framework to develop arguments on a wide array of topics, from the nature of God's relationship with humanity to the problem of evil. Thomas Aquinas (1225–74) adapted Aristotle's philosophy to develop a comprehensive guide for Christian thought called the *Summa Theologica*. And perhaps the most important Aristotelian thinker of the Middle Ages was the Islamic philosopher Averroes (1126–98; his Arabic name was Ibn Rushd), who is often credited with reintroducing Aristotle into Western philosophy and setting in motion the European Renaissance in the fifteenth century.

By the seventeenth century and the Age of Reason, philosophers had started to distance themselves from theological claims. During this time, two general schools of thought began to emerge: the rationalists and the empiricists. The rationalists argued that, in principle, all knowledge could be gained by the power of human reason alone. In contrast, the empiricists argued that all knowledge had to come through the senses, from experience, which meant a reliance on the physical sciences. The German philosopher Immanuel Kant (1724–1804) attempted to strike a compromise between the rationalists and the empiricists. Kant concluded that using reason without applying it to experience would lead only to illusion, while resorting to experience without first subsuming it to reason would lead only to pure subjectivism. This conclusion could be applied to God's existence as well. In Kant's view, even though we might believe that there is a God, it is impossible to maintain a rational argument for the existence of God. The only viable philosophical position, then, is **agnosticism**; that is to say, we simply do not and cannot know if God actually exists. At the core of Kant's philosophy is the human subject who has thrown off the shackles of "self-incurred tutelage" and begun to think as an autonomous (self-legislating), modern human being. Kant's famous dictum sums up not only his philosophy but also much of philosophy after the Enlightenment: "*Sapere aude!* Have the courage to make use of your own intellect!" (1991, 54).

Modern analytic philosophy, with its agnostic premises, has tended to focus on the logic and meaning of religious language, including the ways in which religious language generates claims about knowledge and truth. For instance, when someone says, "God loves us," what kind of language is that—a statement of fact or an assertion? For some philosophers, this type of statement cannot be a statement of fact because it is not falsifiable; in other words, it is equally possible to claim that God hates us. While many might believe the statement "God loves us" to be true, from a philosophical perspective the statement is an assertion, rooted perhaps in emotion or illusion. Other philosophers, however, make the argument that such methods of language analysis fail to account for the variety of ways in which knowledge and truth are generated through various discourses. Influenced by European social philosophers such as Michel Foucault (1926–84) and Jürgen Habermas (b. 1929), these philosophers attempt to show that truth is determined by the structures of knowledge and meaning in a particular discourse, whether it is scientific, political, artistic, religious, medical, economic, or moral discourse. This project often takes the form of a genealogy that accounts for the historical forces—many of which were contradictory—that helped generate knowledge and the authoritative discourses that legitimate "truth." While this genealogical approach to the study of religion is philosophical in orientation, many anthropologists, sociologists, historians, and other scholars also engage in this type of historical deconstruction.

Theological Approaches

The term *theology* comes from two Greek words: *theos*, which means "god" or "gods," and *logos*, which means "speech" or "inquiry." Plato used the term *theologia* to describe the rational study of the divine, and contrasted theology with poetic stories about the gods. The early Christian church, under Plato's influence, adapted the term to refer to the biblical account of God's relationship with humanity. Prior to the creation of universities in the eleventh century, theology was closely associated with the activities of Christian monasteries and cathedral schools, which trained young men for the clergy. By the **Middle Ages**, however, *theology* had taken on a narrower meaning. Theology had become a discipline of study in Europe's newly created universities and it competed with the disciplines of law and philosophy for the best students. Between the eleventh and sixteenth centuries, the term *scholasticism* (from a Latin word meaning "that which belongs to the school") was often used to describe the type of theology that was taught in European universities. One classic definition of theology took shape during this period through the work of the Benedictine monk and early "scholastic" Anselm of Canterbury (1033–1109): theology, he argued, is "faith seeking understanding" (in Latin, *fides quaerens intellectum*). Theology continued to be a mainstay of European universities until the late 1960s, when students began to become interested in comparative religion and the social sciences.

The inclusion of theology as a legitimate academic approach to the study of religion has been a topic of intense debate within the field of religious studies since its inception in the 1960s. One objection is that theology presumes that the study of religion is the study of God or gods, which, as we discovered earlier in this chapter, would effectively exclude religions that either have no gods or do not place much importance in deities. Another objection is that many religions, including Judaism and many religions of India, do not conceive of their intellectual heritage in theological terms. Many Jewish scholars, in fact, are quite reluctant to use the term *theology*: it seems to presuppose that human beings can know about the inner life of **G-d**, which according to some Jewish thinkers verges on idolatry. And perhaps the most common objection is that theology is merely a Christian interpretive framework that is ultimately accessible only by "insiders"—that is, by Christians—who must adhere to the tenets of their theological tradition.

In response to the first two objections, many theologians freely admit that the study of theology is not intended to be a framework universally applicable to understanding all religions. But in some instances theological engagement with another religion can provide important insight into both Christianity and the other religion. Gregory Baum, for example, in his book *The Theology of Tariq Ramadan: A Catholic Perspective* (2009), provides an accessible introduction to a contemporary Islamic reform movement led by Tariq Ramadan, which he then compares with modern reform movements within the Catholic Church. This type of scholarship, which seeks to understand a particular faith in theological dialogue with another religious tradition, is called *comparative theology* and is often associated with *inter-religious dialogue*.

G-d: the term often used by Jewish writers who believe it is wrong to write the name of their deity.

In response to the third objection, defenders of theological approaches point out that there are many different types of theology. Generally these types fall into two broad categories: a sectarian theology that is accessible only to insiders and an academic theology that is open to critical examination by all. *Sectarian theology* is aimed at promoting and transmitting doctrine to like-minded believers. This type presumes that everyone undertaking a study of theology is either already associated with the particular religious group (sometimes termed a *denomination*) or is seeking to become a member. For this reason, sectarian theology is found exclusively in seminaries and church-related colleges in the United States and Canada. By contrast, *academic theology* adheres to the scholarly conventions of the modern university by ensuring that theological examination is open to everyone, that no conclusion can be based on privileged beliefs, and that all conclusions are subject to critical examination.

Sociological Approaches

The sociology of religion considers religion to be a social institution that exists alongside the economy, government, health care, education, and other social institutions. Taken as a whole, these institutions give structure to society and transmit meaning that becomes deeply interwoven with a group's collective identity and self-understanding. The earliest sociologists—Émile Durkheim and Max Weber (1864–1920)—were particularly interested in studying religion because they saw how foundational religion was to the social, political, and economic changes taking place in nineteenth-century Europe.

Durkheim's understanding of history and humanity is based on a theory of social order that brings human beings together through political, moral, and religious activities. According to Durkheim, social behaviour involves people acting as both physical and social beings. Physically, humans act on egoistic (self-interested) needs and desires. Socially, humans construct a social order to govern those egoistic needs and desires. The primary task of the social order, then, is to socialize individuals to conform to the group's norms. A social order provides cohesion when people share the same moral beliefs and worldviews and when these moral beliefs and worldviews are reinforced by collective rituals and symbols. According to Durkheim, religion is the prototypical institution that generates and cultivates the rituals and symbols that continually reaffirm a society's moral beliefs and categories of knowledge. Religion does all of this by separating phenomena into two categories: the sacred and the profane.

In his book *The Elementary Forms of Religious Life* (1912), Durkheim famously argues that the origins of religion are located in totemic religion. Using the Aboriginal people of Australia as his case study, Durkheim observed that the totemic animal functioned as an emblem for the clan, and as the representation of all that was good about the clan, the totemic animal had to be treated as sacred. To harm or to mistreat the totem was therefore often perceived by the clan's leaders as a rejection of social norms, which meant wrongdoers had to undergo some form of rehabilitation or punishment. In more complex societies, Durkheim concludes, religion will likely not be the institution that conveys and nurtures social norms; that role will fall instead to politics, economics, and especially science. In Durkheim's social theory, the waning of religion in modern societies is cause for neither celebration nor lament, for all societies develop and adapt institutions over time to provide social stability. Any differences between religion and other social institutions are, Durkheim believes, only a matter of degree and not a matter of type. For Durkheim, every institution that provides social cohesion functions in the same basic way, but religion remains an important element in society because it is, foundationally, the institution that unites people, links them to their common history, and strengthens their collective identity.

Max Weber, unlike Durkheim, was not particularly interested in the role of religion in social alienation or in religion's capacity to provide social order and integration. Instead Weber sought to understand and explain the foundations of Western society's regulatory structures by focusing on the situations and decisions facing social actors in specific contexts. For Weber, modern societies had become overregulated, not underregulated, as Durkheim contended. There were, Weber observed, fewer and fewer spaces in society for people to act outside the dominant principles of efficiency, institutional control, and management—that is, the very same principles that fostered industrial and political bureaucracy. In the modern age of bureaucracy, people found it increasingly difficult to act with integrity and

Jacob Zuma, president of South Africa, and his fifth wife, Thobeka Madiba, celebrate their marriage in a traditional Zulu ceremony. According to Émile Durkheim, religious gatherings provide social cohesion and group identity.

Source: AFP/Getty Images

to take responsibility for decisions that directly affected their lives. Modern bureaucracy had, in effect, become a system of external control. On the specific issue of religion in the modern society, Weber argued that if religion were going to survive in modern society, it would have to become bureaucratic and eventually follow the logic of efficiency, performance, and usefulness.

While Weber's work on bureaucracy is an important topic, students of religion are usually better acquainted with his classic study of the relationship between Christianity and capitalism, titled *The Protestant Ethic and the Spirit of Capitalism* (1905). Weber observes that capitalism in northern Europe in the eighteenth century emerged as Protestant Christianity taught people about the virtues of hard work and financial planning. Whereas the Catholic Church taught that only the clergy and those who belonged to religious orders were fulfilling a vocational calling, the Protestant churches told the faithful that work in the secular world was in fact a vocation ordained by God. The values of hard work, coupled with secular jobs that were divinely sanctioned, provided capitalism with a labour force and a cultural spirit that enabled capitalism to flourish. Weber surmised that the religious aspects of capitalism were eventually discarded, but not before Western society had undergone a rationalization process that, with the unwitting help of the Protestant churches, had turned individuals into self-interested maximizers of their utilities and justified the economic structure of modern society.

The work of Durkheim and Weber continues to guide sociologists as they consider contemporary issues such as secularization, civil religion, multiculturalism, religion and nationalism, religious violence, and implicit (or invisible) religion.

Anthropological Approaches

Anthropology is the systematic study of the origins, development, customs, and beliefs associated with human culture. As a social science, anthropology has much in common with sociology. Like Durkheim and Weber, the earliest anthropologists studied religions as human creations and not as divinely inspired or essentially truthful phenomena. One early anthropologist was E. B. Tylor, who hypothesized that humanity had developed the concepts of the soul and the spirit, as well as spiritual beings, to explain non-rational experiences such as dreams, trances, and hallucinations. Influenced by the evolutionary thought of the late nineteenth century, Tylor theorized that the most basic form of religion was animism, an original form of religion that ascribed spiritual characteristics to natural phenomena such as trees, oceans, and mountains. Tylor further postulated that the basic spiritualism of animism was eventually replaced by polytheism and **monotheism** in higher-order peoples. For Tylor there was a "psychic unity of humankind" that linked primitive peoples to their more highly developed relatives. This perceived unity and his preoccupation with discovering the origins of religion led Tylor to develop a cross-cultural approach to anthropology that was closely shared by another British anthropologist, James Frazer, author of the widely read *The Golden Bough* (1890).

Monotheism: belief in one god.

Etic: analysis of cultural phenomena from the perspective of one who does not participate in the culture being studied.

Emic: analysis of cultural phenomena from the perspective of one who participates in the culture being studied.

Among contemporary scholars of religion, the most widely read anthropologist is Clifford Geertz, whose essay "Religion as a Cultural System," published in 1966, remains requisite reading in many comparative religion courses in North American and European universities. For Geertz, religion is a complex cultural system that maintains symbols for the purpose of establishing moods and motivations in people, leading to what he called a "worldview." According to Geertz, this cultural system constitutes an inner world of emotions and sentiments that, when bound together through commonly shared symbols and ritual practices, creates the phenomenon "religion." Following Max Weber's method of "understanding" (*Verstehen*), Geertz thinks that the anthropologist's primary task is to understand completely the symbol system of a particular culture in order to gain access to the group's cultural actors. For Geertz this means that anthropologists should provide a "thick description"—that is, an interpretation of the indigenous actors' own perceptions and interpretations of events, based on the scholar's empirical knowledge. Geertz's method marks a change in anthropology from **etic** approaches, which examine culture from the outside and use broader principles, to **emic** approaches,

Collective unconscious: a part of the unconscious mind, it is manifested in similar forms (archetypes) in all humanity because the human psyche organizes experiences in similar ways.

Archetype: an innate form of expression generated by the collective unconscious, it is a base or prototypical idea (e.g., the hero, the trickster, spatial representations such as wheels).

which examine culture from the inside using categories generated from scholarly engagement with the culture.

Geertz's legacy in the subfield of anthropology of religion is open to much debate. Anthropologists such as Talal Asad (b. 1932) have criticized Geertz for presuming that religion maintains an autonomous essence that remains unaffected by political and economic discourses. Others have targeted Geertz for blurring traditional methodological lines in anthropology between ethnography, which entails empirical qualitative research on a particular culture and people through fieldwork and participant observation, and ethnology, which tends to focus on theoretical and historical interpretations.

Psychological Approaches

Psychology is the study of mental functions and their relationship to both individual and social behaviours. As an academic discipline, psychology is relatively new. Many of the pioneers of psychology were philosophers, including William James (1842–1910), the first person to teach a course in psychology in the United States, at Harvard University in 1875. James was particularly interested in religion, and by the time his book *Varieties of Religious Experience* appeared in 1902, he was already a widely respected philosopher of religion. In this first extensive study of religion from a psychological approach, James identified two broad types of religion: institutional and personal. *Institutional religion* refers to a religious group or organization that plays an important role in a society's culture. *Personal religion*, which is characterized by an individual's having a mystical experience, can be experienced regardless of the culture. James was most interested in personal religion because he believed the mystical experience provided the purest access to the structure of the mind. For James, then, the proper object of study was not the social, the cultural, or even the institutional aspects of religion but rather the "religious genius" (or religious experience) that provided the foundations for social and cultural movements. James subdivided the religious experience into two types: the "healthy-minded" and the "sick-souled." The healthy-minded maintained a generally optimistic outlook on life and excluded the category of evil, while the sick-souled retained evil as a central category. James believed that, while the healthy-minded worked in limited circumstances, the sick-souled was ultimately the experience that would most adequately account for life in the real world, where bad things do happen.

The psychoanalytic theories of Sigmund Freud and Carl Jung (1875–1961) were quite popular in religious studies throughout much of the twentieth century. Freud famously argued that religion is simply a projection of unconscious wants and desires. Moreover, religion sublimates or redirects psychic energy and anxiety into socially acceptable behaviours. It thus acts as a regulatory device that enables individuals to function in a society that is, Freud asserted, itself repressed and largely dysfunctional. At the root of this dysfunction, on both an individual and a social level, was the unwillingness of people to confront their parental relationships. Freud believed that lingering anxieties and guilt stemming from these unexamined relationships were manifested in primitive humans through the creation of gods, which functioned as supernatural parents. Religion continues, Freud theorized, because people need to feel secure and wanted, and religion provides the necessary illusion to alleviate unconscious anxiety and guilt. But, of course, Freud did not believe that religion provided the antidote to fear, anxiety, and guilt. On the contrary, he thought religion was a primary contributor to human pathology. For true liberation, people had to outgrow their infantile reliance on religion and face reality squarely.

Carl Jung, one of Freud's students, criticized Freud for focusing too much on repressed childhood experiences with parents and negative sexual experiences. Instead, Jung postulated that the unconscious mind is a repository of human creativity that was generated from a shared **collective unconscious**. Jung believed that the unconscious contains, among other things, **archetypes** (or recurring patterns) that enable the human ego to find itself in relation to the collective unconscious. There is, Jung thought, a process of discovery that each individual must undergo in order to achieve a sense of self—the *self* being one of the most important archetypes in Jung's theory. Through a three-stage process that corresponds with infancy, adolescence, and adulthood, individuals are eventually able to integrate their psychic weaknesses with their strengths. In Jung's theory, religious symbols play an integral role in achieving a healthy balance because they deflect any totalizing—and thus potentially destructive—tendencies in the unconscious. These symbols, which often take the form of spirits or gods, provide direction and meaning as we work through the anxieties of life and death.

Since the late 1940s, psychoanalytic studies of religion have given way to methods that are more in keeping with the empirical approaches found in contemporary psychology labs and departments. For instance, Gordon Allport (1897–1967) developed the Religious Orientation Scale to determine the various psychological dimensions of religious practice. Allport suggested that there are two types of religion: (1) intrinsic religion, which displays characteristics of deeply held faith and devotion, and (2) extrinsic religion, which displays characteristics of utilitarian manipulation such as attending church or a temple to gain social status. Daniel Batson challenged Allport's binary distinction of intrinsic and extrinsic religion by adding a third orientation, the quest, which allows for acceptance of doubt and critical questioning on the part of the subject. According to Batson, the Quest Scale permits scholars to understand the complexity of religious motivation of subjects because it provides an open-ended, active approach to existential questions and rejects pat answers that may be categorized easily as either intrinsic or extrinsic religion.

Four mandalas of the Vajravali series, c. 1429–56, central Tibet. According to Jungian scholars of religion, a mandala (from the Sanskrit, meaning "circle" or "sacred circle") is an archetypical symbol of wholeness.

Source: Kimbell Art Museum, Fort Worth, Texas/Art Resource, NY

Current research in the psychology of religion continues to be predominantly empirical. Major topics include social control, the relationship between emotions and spirituality, and personality traits associated with traditional theological concepts such as virtue, humility, and forgiveness (Emmons and Paloutzian 2003).

Phenomenological Approaches

Phenomenological approaches to the study of religion have their foundations in a nineteenth-century philosophical movement that focused on data (phenomena) that could be presented to and experienced by human consciousness. These phenomenologists were not interested in explaining experiences or phenomena by using sociological, anthropological, or psychological frameworks. Instead they advocated for robust descriptions of data. They thought that scholars had to suspend their personal judgments about matters under consideration and, furthermore, that any attempts to explain the "truth" of data philosophically or theologically had to be bracketed out of the inquiry. This approach to philosophy was aptly named after the Greek word *phainomenon*, which means "that which appears."

While the phenomenology of religion is related to these nineteenth-century philosophers (Flood 1999), contemporary phenomenological approaches to the study of religion are more closely associated with the work of two scholars, Mircea Eliade (1907–86) and Ninian Smart (1927–2001). For Eliade and many other phenomenologists of religion, religion is irreducible: it exists *sui generis*. Because it is *sui generis*, religion is unlike any other social institution or experience. Assessments about the truth or reality of religious claims—such as the existence of God, the emancipation of human suffering in nirvana, or the healing power of a shaman—must be avoided, Eliade argued, since the truth of the truth and reality of these claims is essentially embedded in the

Religionswissenschaft: from the German meaning "study of religion" or "science of religion." Most often translated into English as "history of religions," it is commonly associated with the work of Mircea Eliade.

phenomenon. As a result, Eliade wanted to study only the public forms or manifestations of religion's essence. This pursuit of studying the essence of religion led to volumes on comparative religion. Eliade focused on stories of birth and rebirth, belief systems that geographically divided space into sacred and profane spheres, and instances where the "holy" broke into the historical world and linked together all of reality.

Eliade's insistence that religion was *sui generis* helped create a school of thought within the field of religious studies called ***Religionswissenschaft***, a German term meaning "study of religion," but most often translated as "history of religions." The main methodological characteristic of the "history of religions" school is that scholars must both bracket any preconceived notions about the phenomena being studied and at the same time empathize with their subjects.

Ninian Smart's approach to religious studies is, in comparison to Eliade's, considerably more modest. Although a phenomenologist, Smart was not particularly concerned with establishing a school of thought or even developing a grand theory to situate all religious phenomena. Rather, he often employed basic historical methods, which also relied on rigorous descriptions, to chronicle the characteristics of phenomena commonly called "religion." To help categorize these phenomena, he devised the "dimension theory" of religion, which identified aspects (or family resemblances) among the world's religions. Smart's seven dimensions of religion are

- **Doctrinal and philosophical:** the systematic formulation of religious teachings in a systematic form.
- **Mythical and narrative:** the stories, which are often in the forms of revelation, that communicate meaning and concepts that are integral to the religious community.
- **Ethical and legal:** the moral customs and legal rules that regulate human behaviour in a group and in many cases are regarded as revealed.
- **Ritual:** the forms and orders of religious ceremonies, which may be public or private and in many cases are regarded as revealed.
- **Experiential:** the private emotions of group members, including feelings of awe, guilt, ecstasy, bliss, mystery, love, and liberation.
- **Institutional:** the social frameworks and belief systems practised by a group and often the bases for determining community identity and membership.
- **Material:** ordinary objects or places that have become sacred or supernatural, either symbolically or manifestly.

These seven dimensions connect to each other, Smart argued, to form a multidimensional organism. For Smart the study of religion was a fine balance between objective scientific method and subjective participation. This perspective led him to the conclusion that the study of religion is a "human science" because it involves a careful, rational, and verifiable method that recognizes data derived from both impartial observation of sensory experience (objective phenomena) and impartial observation of psychological experience (subjective phenomena). In other words, Smart believed that the study of religion is not simply a science corresponding to its objects but a science that takes into account the inner feelings and attitudes of religious peoples, for without these subjective experiences, understanding human life and activities is simply impossible.

Phenomenological approaches to religion are among the most widely used in the field of religious studies. This is due in part to the enormous influence that Eliade and Smart had on students for nearly thirty years. In spite of phenomenology's success, however, these approaches have faced serious challenges. For instance, critics who tend to favour empirical methods often charge phenomenology of religion with lacking scholarly rigour. They argue that phenomenology is unscientific because scholars (a) enter into their study with predetermined assumptions about the data they are looking for, and (b) interpret the phenomena based on subjective participation, including intuition. Moreover, many critics, especially those who are concerned with the roles of gender, race, class, and nationality in scholarship, contend that phenomenological approaches do not pay adequate attention to the biases of the scholar and the assumptions built into phenomenological approaches. It is these biases, they charge, that lead many North American phenomenologists to claim that there are universal structures, ways of being, and essences common to all religions.

PEOPLE & PLACES

Some Important Scholars of Religious Studies

Friedrich Schleiermacher (1768–1834)—a German theologian who defined religion essentially as "a feeling of absolute dependence."

Karl Marx (1818–83)—a German social theorist who thought the bourgeoisie used religion to serve their own interests by politically immobilizing the proletariat with the "opium of the masses."

Sigmund Freud (1856–1939)—the founder of psychoanalysis, who believed religion is an illusion we humans create to help us cope with feelings of weakness, anxiety, and unworthiness.

Émile Durkheim (1858–1917)—a founder of modern sociology who thought religion provides cohesion, group identity, and a moral framework for societies.

Max Weber (1864–1920)—a German sociologist who sought to understand the causes of human behaviour by examining how people's beliefs and ideas affect actions.

Rudolf Otto (1869–1937)—a German theologian who defined religion as "the holy," a non-rational mystery that is both terrifying and fascinating.

Paul Tillich (1888–1965)—a theologian who defined religion as "ultimate concern."

Sarvepalli Radhakrishnan (1888–1975)—president of India from 1962 to 1967 and a scholar of religion who attempted to make "Hinduism" intelligible to Western audiences.

Mircea Eliade (1907–86)—founder of the "history of religions" school at the University of Chicago and the most significant scholar of the late twentieth century to argue that religion is *sui generis*, that is, unique.

Wilfred Cantwell Smith (1916–2000)—a Canadian scholar who helped develop the idea of world religious traditions and who understood religion as essentially an inner experience.

Clifford Geertz (1926–2006)—a American anthropologist whose best-known work, "Religion as a Cultural System" (1966), provided the field of religious studies with a definition of religion for more than a generation.

Ninian Smart (1927–2001)—a scholar who popularized a phenomenological approach to the study of religion and who, beginning in the 1960s, helped establish departments of religious studies in the United Kingdom and the United States.

Talal Asad (b. 1932)—a postcolonial anthropologist who is critical of European assumptions built into established approaches to the study of religion.

Jonathan Z. Smith (b. 1938)—an American scholar who has published on a wide range of subjects, including approaches to the study of religion.

Wendy Doniger (b. 1940)—Mircea Eliade Distinguished Service Professor of the History of Religions at the University of Chicago and a scholar specializing in the religions of India, religious myth, and ritual.

Diana Eck (b. 1945)—director of the Pluralism Project at Harvard University and a scholar known for her humanistic approach to religion and interreligious dialogue.

Amina Wadud (b. 1952)—an American-born Islamic scholar and imam who takes a feminist approach to readings of the Qur'an.

Tariq Ramadan (b. 1962)—a Swiss-born public intellectual who advocates for a politically responsible form of Islam that engages in dialogue with the cultures where Muslims reside.

"Other" Approaches

As with most academic fields, historically the field of religious studies has been dominated by white North American and European men of economic means. While there certainly remains a great deal of male white privilege, since the late 1960s important movements in the academy, and particularly in the field of religious studies, have sought not only to include marginalized voices in course curricula but also to

Feminism: a political, cultural, and economic movement as well as a critical framework aimed at the liberation of women from structures and situations of injustice.

Postcolonial: a broad approach to academic study that examines and critiques the lasting effects of colonialism on people who were colonized.

Orientalist: an increasingly outdated term for one who studies the cultures and peoples of "the East." *Orientalism* is the term used by Edward Said to describe an inherent bias in Western scholarship that assumes an imperial view of the world.

maintain faculty who have been historically marginalized because of gender, race, class, or nationality. These were the people and perspectives often objectified in scholarship as "the other"—that is, they were either objects of study or simply overlooked. Today, however, these "other" voices are revitalizing religious studies scholarship and playing integral roles in reshaping religious studies programs. For the most part these "other" approaches are not rooted in discrete methodologies such as sociology, anthropology, or psychology. Rather, they are integrated into virtually all aspects of religious studies, and particularly into the areas of philosophy, theology, sociology, anthropology, and psychology.

For example, **feminism**-based approaches to the study of religion attempt to overcome androcentric (male-centred) scholarship by advocating for gender-balanced and gender-inclusive scholarship. Feminist scholars reject the notion that scientific studies of religion emanating from the social sciences were truly objective or neutral, for the simple reason that they normally overlooked the role of women in society and women's experiences. One way to correct the androcentrism is to reexamine both the methodologies and the data in order to recover once-lost women's perspectives. Feminist scholars typically argue that it is possible to have a normative perspective—such as the equality of women—and yet remain relatively objective within a certain methodology. Claims of absolute neutrality and objectivity simply do not hold up to scrutiny, since a scholar always maintains a perspective. For this reason, feminist scholars of religion attempt to adhere to the scholarly protocols of a particular approach while at the same balancing the view that women should not be underrepresented in research or in the academy. Another way to correct the androcentrism is to mount courses focusing on women in religion. As Rita Gross notes in her book *Feminism and Religion* (1996), one ironic, if not ill-informed, response to courses on women in religion is that they are biased because they include more information about women than men. "But," Gross contends, "these kinds of claims only mask a desire to hear familiar perspectives and emphases, a wish that assumptions that have been taken for granted should not be challenged" (15).

Postcolonial approaches to the study of religion are also raising penetrating questions about who and what has been historically included or excluded in the study of religion. More specifically, postcolonial scholars seek to identify and analyze the social, political, economic, and cultural practices that arise in response to and resistance to colonialism. They argue that, in spite of the widespread political decolonization of Africa, Latin America, the Caribbean, and parts of Southeast Asia in the twentieth century, vestiges of colonialism remain firmly embedded in the logic systems of modern institutions, including the academy and the study of religion. Postcolonial scholars often cite the work of Frantz Fanon (1925–61), who in his book *The Wretched of the Earth* (1961) explored the psychological and social effects of colonization on the people of Algeria. Another important figure in the development of postcolonial theory was Edward Said (1935–2003), who in his book *Orientalism* (1978) highlighted the ways social scientists, specifically **Orientalists** (Western scholars who study Eastern cultures), have disregarded the views of those they actually study. Said wrote:

> To the extent that Western scholars were aware of contemporary Orientals or Oriental movements of thought and culture, these were perceived either as silent shadows to be animated by the Orientalist, brought into reality by them, or as a kind of cultural and international proletariat useful for the Orientalist's grander interpretive activity. (208)

In the broad field of religious studies, Talal Asad is one of the leading figures bringing postcolonial critiques to bear on approaches to the study of religion. As we discovered earlier in this chapter, Asad has raised serious questions about the structural biases and unexamined privileges embedded in the field of religious studies,

Mohandas K. Gandhi (1869–1948) on the Salt March, 1930. Gandhi's leadership in India's overthrowing of British colonial rule inspired anti-colonial struggles in Africa and Southeast Asia, as well as black civil rights struggles in the United States.

Source: Time & Life Pictures/Getty Images

especially in the subfield of anthropology of religion. A new generation of postcolonial scholars has begun to investigate specific cases of secular modernity in postcolonial societies such as Egypt, Turkey, South Africa, India, and Pakistan. Scholars who study the Aboriginal peoples of the Americas, Australia, and other regions may also identify themselves as postcolonial theorists. On the whole, the postcolonial scholars often focus their attention on issues of gender, class, and the formation of the human subject within a colonial and postcolonial context.

"Other" approaches that have begun to take hold in the field of religious studies also include studies that concentrate on the plight of the poor in a society: lesbian, gay, bisexual, transsexual, and queer (LGBTQ) people, and persons with disabilities. While feminist and postcolonial approaches and those that focus on the economically oppressed, LGBTQ people, and persons with disabilities are not identical, they do share certain critical perspectives in response to the imposition of categories and methods of study that are not only inappropriate but also complicit in the further marginalization of women, the colonized, the poor, lesbians, gays, bisexuals, transsexuals, queers, and persons with disabilities. At a minimum, these scholars share a basic belief that all students of religion, whether senior professors or students in a class on introductory religious studies, should be critically aware of the "other" and their relationship to the "other" as they engage in cultures, societies, and religions that are not their own.

CONCLUSION

At the outset you may have wondered why a text on world religions would begin with a chapter on the study of religion. Would it not be more interesting to jump right into an examination of a specific religion? Indeed, we recognize that you are reading this text because you want to learn something about the world's religions. However, now that you are at the conclusion of this chapter, we hope you understand that learning about the world's religions first requires a basic grasp of the definitions, concepts, and scholarly approaches used in the field.

As a student of religious studies, you are entering into a network of conversations that includes prior scholars, contemporary scholars, and your fellow students. To help you enter that network, this chapter has attempted to identify a number of the primary conversations taking place within the field, the terms used in those conversations, the general approaches or ways of speaking used by scholars, and certain critical challenges to the dominant ways of studying religion.

As you begin to examine specific religions in this text, the tendency will no doubt be to forget about some of the issues raised in this chapter. To help you avoid this, we encourage you to draw on our definition of religion to ask questions about a religion's ways of communicating, its ritual practices, its communal bonds, and its institutional structures. Use the key terms we highlighted in this chapter. Consider how various scholarly approaches to the study of religion might affect our understanding of the religion we are examining. Raise questions about how issues such as gender, race, class, ethnicity, and other marginalizing factors play out in a religion and in our understanding of that religion. In short, build on the material in this chapter to develop your critical thinking skills.

KEY TERMS

Agnosticism, p. 18
Analects of Confucius, p. 5
Animism, p. 6
Archetype, p. 22
Before the Common Era (B.C.E.), p. 13
Bhagavad-Gita, p. 5
Catholic, p. 3
Common Era (C.E.), p. 1
Circumambulation, p. 2
Collective unconscious, p. 22
Deity, p. 12
Denomination, p. 15
Doctrine, p. 13
Emic, p. 21
Epistemology, p. 17
Etic, p. 21
Faith, p. 4
Feminism, p. 26
Fetishism, p. 6
Functional definitions of religion, p. 9
G-d, p. 19
Gurdwara, p. 15
Hajj, p. 2
Homo religiosus, p. 9
Idolatry, p. 4
Magic, p. 6
Middle Ages, p. 18
Moksha, p. 9
Monotheism, p. 21
Myth, p. 13
Natural religion, p. 5
Naturalistic religion, p. 6
Nirvana, p. 9
Ontology, p. 17
Orientalist, p. 26
Paganism, p. 5
Pali canon, p. 5
Piety, p. 4
Polytheism, p. 7
Postcolonial, p. 26
Proselytization, p. 7
Religionswissenschaft, p. 24
Religious orders, p. 3
Rig-Veda, p. 5
Ritual, p. 4
Sacred, p. 8
Sect, p. 15
Separation of church and state, p. 17
Shamanism, p. 6
Substantive definitions of religion, p. 8
Sui generis, p. 8
Supernatural religion, p. 6
Suprahuman, p. 13
Theism, p. 13
Totemism, p. 6
Virtue, p. 4

CRITICAL THINKING QUESTIONS

1. Do you think it is possible for a scholar to engage in an objective study of religion? Is an objective study even desirable?
2. If you were to stipulate a definition of religion, what would it be? What would be the strengths and weaknesses of this definition?
3. What does it mean when we say that the field of religious studies is interdisciplinary?
4. If you were to invent a religion, what would it include? On what sources would you draw to invent your religion?
5. How have issues such as gender, race, class, and ethnicity affected the study of religion?

RECOMMENDED READING

Braun, Willi, and Russell T. McCutcheon, eds. *Introducing Religion: Essays in Honor of Jonathan Z. Smith*. London: Equinox Press, 2009.

McCutcheon, Russell T., ed. *The Insider/Outsider Problem in the Study of Religion: A Reader*. London: Cassell, 1999.

———. *Studying Religion: An Introduction*. London: Equinox Press, 2007.

Peach, Lucinda. *Women and World Religions*. Upper Saddle River, NJ: Prentice Hall, 2001.

Segal, Robert A. *Blackwell Companion to the Study of Religion*, new ed. London: Wiley-Blackwell, 2008.

Stausberg, Michael, ed. *Theories of Religion: A Critical Companion*. New York: Routledge, 2009.

USEFUL WEBSITES

American Academy of Religion:
An association of more than 10,000 teachers and scholars of religion.

Canadian Society for the Study of Religion:
Dedicated to interdisciplinary and critical research into religion.

The Pluralism Project at Harvard University: Conducts research into the diverse religions present in the United States and their impact on American society.

REFERENCES

Baird, Robert D. 1973. *Category Formation and the History of Religions.* Berlin: Mouton de Gruyter.

Bauer, Olivier. 2009. *La religion du canadien de Montréal.* Montreal: Fides.

Berger, Peter. (1967) 1969. *The Sacred Canopy: Elements of a Sociological Theory of Religion.* Garden City, NY: Doubleday.

Capps, Walter. 1974. "On Religious Studies, in Lieu of an Overview." *Journal of the American Academy of Religion* 42, no. 4: 727–33.

Durkheim, Émile. (1912) 1915. *Elementary Forms of the Religious Life*, trans. Joseph Ward Swain. New York: Macmillan.

Eliade, Mircea. 1963. *Patterns in Comparative Religion*, trans. Rosemary Sheed. New York: Meridian Books.

Emmons, Robert A., and Raymond F. Paloutzian. 2003. "The Psychology of Religion." *Annual Review of Psychology* 54: 377–402.

Flood, Gavin. 1999. *Beyond Phenomenology: Rethinking the Study of Religion.* London: Cassell.

Freud, Sigmund. 1918. "Civilization and *die Weltanschauung.*" http://www.fordham.edu/halsall/mod/1918freud-civwelt.html (accessed 24 August 2010).

Geertz, Clifford. 1979. "Religion as a Cultural System." In *Reader in Comparative Religion: An Anthropological Approach*, ed. William A. Lessa and Evon Z. Vogt, 1–46. New York: Harper & Row.

Gross, Rita. 1996. *Feminism and Religion.* Boston: Beacon Press.

James, William. 1958. *The Varieties of Religious Experience.* New York: Mentor Books.

Kant, Immanuel. 1991. "What Is Enlightenment?" In *Kant: Political Writings*, ed. Hans S. Reis, 54–60. Cambridge: Cambridge University Press.

Lincoln, Bruce. 2003. *Holy Terrors: Thinking about Religion after September 11.* Chicago: University of Chicago Press.

Marx, Karl. 1964. "Contribution to the Critique of Hegel's Philosophy of Right." In *Karl Marx and Friedrich Engels on Religion.* New York: Schocken Books.

Otto, Rudolf. 1958. *The Idea of the Holy.* Oxford: Oxford University Press.

Pals, Daniel. 2006. *Eight Theories of Religion*, 2nd ed. New York: Oxford University Press.

Said, Edward. 1978. *Orientalism.* New York: Random House.

Schleiermacher, Fredrich. (1830) 1999. *The Christian Faith.* New York: T & T Clark.

Smith, Jonathan Z. 1982. *Imagining Religion: From Babylon to Jonestown.* Chicago: University of Chicago Press.

———. 1998. "Religion, Religions, and Religious." In *Critical Terms for Religious Studies*, ed. Mark C. Taylor, 269–84. Chicago: University of Chicago Press.

Smith, Wilfred Cantwell. 1959. "Comparative Religion: Whither and Why." In *The History of Religions: Essays in Methodology*, 31–58. Chicago: University of Chicago Press.

Stark, Rodney, and Roger Finke. 2000. *Acts of Faith: Explaining the Human Side of Religion.* Berkeley: University of California Press.

Tillich, Paul. 1963. *Christianity and the Encounter of the World Religions.* New York: Columbia University Press.

Tweed, Thomas A. 2006. *Crossing and Dwelling: A Theory of Religion.* Cambridge: Harvard University Press.

Tylor, Edward B. (1871) 1974. *Primitive Culture*, vol. 1. New York: Gordon Press.

Timeline

- **c. 920 B.C.E.** Division of land of Israel into northern and southern kingdoms (Judah and Israel).
- **721 B.C.E.** Northern kingdom conquered by Assyrians and people led off into slavery.
- **586 B.C.E.** Destruction of First Temple in Jerusalem.
- **538 B.C.E.** Edict of Cyrus allows exiles to return to Israel and rebuild Temple.
- **70 C.E.** Destruction of Second Temple.
- **c. 500** Editing of Babylonian Talmud.
- **c. 1000 C.E.** Rabbi Gershom enacts ban on polygamy.
- **1096** First Crusade results in deaths of thousands of Jews in Europe.
- **late 1100s** Maimonides writes *Guide for the Perplexed,* the most significant text of Jewish philosophy until the modern period.
- **late 1200s** The Zohar, the foundational text of Jewish mysticism, published in Spain by Moses de Leon.
- **1492** Jews expelled from Spain.
- **c. 1500** Shulchan Aruch, the most authoritative code of Jewish law, composed by Rabbi Yosef Caro.
- **1666** Shabbetai Zvi, believed to be Messiah by many across Jewish world, dashes expectations by converting to Islam.
- **1700–60** Ba'al Shem Tov founds Hasidism.
- **1729–86** Moses Mendelssohn inspires beginning of Jewish Enlightenment in Germany and paves way for emancipation of Jews in Europe.
- **mid-1800s** Reform Judaism develops, followed by Orthodox Judaism and Conservative Judaism.
- **1880s** Waves of violent anti-Jewish riots in Russia lead many Jews to emigrate to United States and Canada.
- **1896** Theodor Herzl spearheads Zionist movement to establish Jewish homeland in Israel.
- **1933–45** Nazi party rises to power in Germany; its anti-Semitic policies result in systematic murder of six million Jews.
- **1948** State of Israel established and Israeli War of Independence breaks out.
- **1972** First woman ordained as Reform rabbi.
- **1993** First peace agreement signed between Israel and Palestinians.

CHAPTER 2

Judaism

Shari Golberg

INTRODUCTION

In Thornhill, Ontario, a suburb north of Toronto with a sizeable Jewish population, a local supermarket is bustling with customers readying themselves for Passover, a holiday that marks the Israelites' passage from slavery in ancient Egypt to freedom. It is the day before the beginning of the holiday and the doors and tills of the popular grocery store will remain open until midnight to accommodate Jewish shoppers trying to meet all their food requirements for the eight-day holiday. Aisles upon aisles of foods with special "Kosher for Passover" labels will be practically bare by the time the event is over.

According to the biblical book of Exodus, in the Israelites' haste to leave Egypt they were unable to wait for their dough to rise, so they were forced to eat **matzah**, a flatbread, on the run. To commemorate this event, according to Jewish law, bread and other grain products are forbidden during Passover. Hence, ritually observant Jews across Canada and throughout the world prepare for this festival by buying special foods and scrubbing down every inch of the house in order to rid their homes of any trace of prohibited ingredients. Indeed, for many the obsessive cleaning has become just as, if not more, significant than the **seder**, the festive meal associated with the holiday at which the story of the Exodus is retold through symbolic foods, children's games, songs, and traditional liturgy.

But Jews are a diverse group, and what is regarded as important for one Jew may not hold any meaning for another. As an old joke goes, "Two Jews, three opinions," and in many ways the holiday of Passover best captures this spirit of heterogeneity, disagreement, and debate within the Jewish tradition. A Jew of Polish descent might find the seder of a Moroccan Jew wholly unrecognizable: not only would the customs be strange but many of the traditional foods on the table would be completely prohibited for her. While some Jews fastidiously observe the festival's dietary restrictions and cleaning rituals, others may emphasize Passover's focus on family or its connection with spring. Indeed, Passover's central themes of freedom from slavery and rebirth have made it malleable enough to map onto many different struggles for liberation throughout time. As a result, it has continued to resonate with Jews of all social, cultural, religious, and political stripes.

In this chapter you will learn more about the historical development of Judaism, from its biblical roots to its transformation by the **rabbis** in late antiquity and its later evolution into distinct denominations in response to the Enlightenment and modernity. In the process you will also learn about the troubled history of the Jewish people and the multiple and often conflicting approaches to Jewish law, Jewish practice, and Jewish identity that exist in today's world. Judaism is complicated by the fact that, from its earliest days, it has been both a religious tradition and an ethnic and cultural identity. As such, today, many who choose not to participate in the religious practices may still consider themselves to be Jews. So, as you can see, Judaism is quite difficult to summarize.

Matzah: a flat, cracker-like bread eaten during the holiday of Passover.

Seder: the festive meal held during the holiday of Passover, which commemorates the Israelites' liberation from slavery in Egypt.

Rabbi: a Jewish spiritual leader and teacher, often regarded as an expert in Jewish law.

Torah: from a word meaning "instruction," this is the primary sacred scripture of the Jews, also known as the Hebrew Bible or the five books of Moses. The term can also refer to the entire corpus of Jewish teachings.

Talmud: a vast collection of rabbinic writings dealing with matters of law, ethics, philosophy, history, and folk practices. One version of the Talmud was compiled by the rabbinic community in the land of Israel while the other was compiled by the rabbis in Babylonia. The Babylonian Talmud would ultimately become the text to dictate Jewish practice.

As a non-proselytizing religion, Judaism is the smallest of the three great Western monotheisms. It is estimated that there are between twelve and eighteen million Jews worldwide, a mere 0.2 percent of the world population (Jewish People Policy Planning Institute). While the greatest numbers of Jews live in Israel, the United States, France, Canada, and Britain, Jews have lived all over the globe, and their texts and practices have been shaped throughout history by the places in which they have lived. Indeed, given the philosophical, legal, social, cultural, and historical diversity within Judaism, it might be better to discuss *a* Judaism rather than simply Judaism in general. As the scholar Jacob Neusner has put it, "there is not now, nor has there ever been a single Judaism. . . . Taken all together, Jews have believed everything and its opposite about the critical components of a religion: God, community and the holy way of life" (1991, 385).

This raises the matter of "defining" Judaism. In the introductory chapter of this textbook, you were asked to consider a stipulative definition of religion in order to delimit our field of study (see Chapter 1, page 13). Well, the same questions are just as pertinent to the sub-field of Judaism. Historically, definitions of Judaism tended to be substantive; they were essentialist in nature, usually attempting to exclude one group or another from what the author(s) understood as "normative" Judaism. While more contemporary scholarship has tried to avoid essentialist statements about Judaism by acknowledging that there are indeed "multiple Judaisms," as scholar Michael Satlow has pointed out, this has been equally ineffective in moving toward a definition, as it denies that there is any unity among Judaisms through time and space. Consequently, rather than devising another essentialist definition of Judaism, Satlow has suggested that any expression of Judaism, historical or contemporary, can be plotted along three different "maps": Jewish self-identity, textual tradition, and religious practice (2006, 8). Keeping these maps mentally on hand may be useful as we navigate our way through the history of different communities of Jews.

Nonetheless, one component that may cut across all three of Satlow's conceptual maps is the notion of a *covenant*, or agreement, between God and the Jewish people. Recurrent in Jewish texts, manifest in religious practice. and either embraced or rejected as part of a Jewish self-concept, this special relationship is characterized by a set of obligations or laws recorded in the **Torah**, also known as the Hebrew Bible. The primary sacred text of the Jewish people, the Torah is traditionally believed to have been revealed by God to the Israelites at Mount Sinai. In this chapter you will learn more about the Torah and other authoritative texts such as the **Talmud**, through which the Torah has been traditionally understood and interpreted.

Perhaps more than other religions, Judaism is at its core a text-based tradition. Although the term "people of the book" originally derived from Islam and was meant to refer to both Jews and Christians, it is a moniker that has been proudly adopted by Jews over the centuries as a label of self-identification. Since the Jews were continually being exiled from one land after another, the only constant bridging them throughout time and space was their "book," a set of texts that inevitably spawned many more texts of commentary and interpretation. Although the primary sources became fixed over time, their meaning and significance continued to adapt to fit each new context with which Jews were confronted. This adaptability is likely what enabled a landless people to develop and thrive in both hostile and friendly circumstances. Canada in particular is notable for being one of the friendlier environments to have accepted the Jews. In this chapter you will learn more about the history of the Jews in Canada and how they have exemplified the Canadian mosaic at work.

CENTRAL BELIEFS

The Uniqueness and Oneness of God

Biblical thought and rabbinic Judaism both regard Abraham as having been the first person to reject idolatry and recognize the existence of one true God. A traditional rabbinic story, or **midrash**, tells of Abraham's zeal to persuade others of the folly of idol worship. According to the tale, Abraham's father, Terah, owned a shop where idols were sold. One day while Terah was out, Abraham took a stick, smashed all the idols, and put the stick in the hand of the biggest idol. When Terah returned and asked what had happened, Abraham explained that the largest statue had fought with the smaller ones. When Terah retorted that such a thing was impossible, that the idols were inanimate and had no independent powers or thoughts, Abraham responded, "Listen to yourself! Do you not see that the very thing you worship is empty?"

Midrash: a rabbinic interpretation of scripture.

Other, similar legends tell of Abraham's turning to the sun, the moon, and the stars as sources of worship in his quest to discover the creator of the universe. Watching the movements of the heavens, Abraham recognizes that each of these celestial bodies is fleeting, and thus determines that there must be something greater ruling over each of them. In this way he awakens to the existence of one true God. This belief in one supreme deity is what unites Judaism, Christianity, and Islam, and it is precisely why Abraham remains a key figure in all three traditions.

Although Abraham's descendants, the Israelites, may not historically have been the first monotheists (it seems that the ancient Egyptians likely came to the practice first), to settle on monotheism and have their cosmology revolve around one divine being rather than a pantheon of gods and goddesses was quite a radical project, given the polytheistic Near Eastern context in which Judaism emerged. So it is not surprising to find that the Israelites often lapsed into worship of the surrounding gods, especially Canaanite fertility goddesses. Initially it seems that they saw their own god, known primarily as Yahweh (see box), as their national god; their god was supreme over others, but that did not preclude the existence of other gods. However, with the emergence of the biblical prophets—a class of inspired social critics and commentators whose writings are preserved in the Hebrew Bible—the message to the Israelites becomes unequivocal: Yahweh is the god of all creation, the only god, expecting exclusive loyalty and obedience.

Words

Names of God

The name Yahweh {hw<hy"} is represented by four Hebrew letters in the Bible—yud, hay, vav, hay—and its exact pronunciation is still debated to this day. By 70 C.E. this name was deemed by the rabbis to be too sacred to be pronounced, so instead it was replaced by *Adonai* ("my lord") or *Hashem* ("the name") when it was read aloud or used in everyday speech. In the nineteenth century *Yahweh* became the most widely recognized scholarly rendering of the word, although it is sometimes also vocalized as *Jehovah*. Since the name consists of four Hebrew consonants, it is also referred to as the *tetragrammaton*, meaning "four-letter word" in Greek. It is believed that the name may derive from a word meaning "being."

Another divine name that is thought to come from the same verbal root as the tetragrammaton is *Ehyeh Asher Ehyeh*. In the book of Exodus, when God first appears to Moses in the form of a burning bush and tells him he has been chosen to lead the Israelites out of Egypt, Moses asks, "If I come to the Israelites and say to them, 'The God of your ancestors has sent me to you,' and they ask me, 'What is his name?' what shall I say to them?" God responds, "Ehyeh Asher Ehyeh" (*JPS Tanakh* 1985, Ex 3:13–14), often translated as "I am that I am" or "I will be what I will be." This name only appears once in the entire Hebrew Bible, yet God's response to Moses is one of the most well-known verses in the Torah, for it depicts God as eternal, dependent on nothing and no one.

The Shema Prayer

This notion of God as singular, unique, and most-powerful became the central tenet of Israelite religion and later Judaism. It is best expressed in the form of the *Shema*, a line of text from the book of Deuteronomy (the fifth book of the Torah) that is recited twice daily as part of the morning and evening prayer services: "Hear, O Israel, the Lord is your God, the Lord is One" (Deut. 6:4).

The text goes on to command the people to love God with all their hearts and souls, to teach these precepts to their children, and to speak of them when they sit in their houses, when they go out, when they arise, and when they go to sleep. As a further reminder, the text implores that these words should be written on their hands and foreheads, their gates and doorposts—in short, the essence of the Shema prayer is that one's devotion to God and the affirmation of God's oneness should pervade every aspect of one's life. Indeed, later tradition would understand these directives as being more than mere figures of speech: the Shema prayer would literally be inscribed and affixed to the doorposts of Jewish homes in the form of a *mezuzah* (a piece of parchment, often in a decorative case) and worn on the arms and forehead in the form of *tefillin* (see synagogue attire, below).

Practices

Mezuzah

A word meaning "doorpost," the mezuzah is a piece of parchment bearing the Shema prayer, usually encased in a decorative container. In this photo of the Zion Gate in Jerusalem, the mezuzah case is made of bullet casings gathered after the 1948 Israeli War of Independence, when Israeli forces attempted to recapture the Old City of Jerusalem via this entrance. As is customary, the mezuzah here is placed on the top third of the right side of the doorway and is tilted inward as a compromise between the positions of two medieval sages, Rashi and Rabbeinu Tam, who differed on whether the mezuzah should be affixed vertically or horizontally.

While the mezuzah is meant to be a reminder of God's commandments, many Jews also popularly understand it as a protective amulet that keeps their homes safe from harm. This folk belief is deeply rooted in Jewish mystical traditions and actually hearkens back to the biblical account of the Exodus, when God warns of a plague that will kill the first-born sons of the Egyptians. To serve as a sign differentiating the homes of the Israelite slaves from those of their Egyptian oppressors, God commands the Israelites to sacrifice a lamb and spread its blood on their lintels and doorposts; wherever the blood is present, God will pass over the home (hence the name of the holiday Passover) and spare the children. Later writings tie this salvific blood to the commandment of the mezuzah. While the more rationalist among the rabbis repudiated these ideas, the frequent inscription of the divine name "Shaddai" on the mezuzah speaks to their persistence. *Shaddai* is thought to be an acronym for *Shomer Delatot Yisrael*, meaning "the Guardian of the Doors of Israel."

Source: © Israel images/Alamy

The Nature of God

Although monotheism is clearly a central value of Judaism, throughout Jewish history and thought there has never been one agreed-upon doctrine as to the nature of God. Furthermore, one's Judaism is not dependent on one's faith or on any particular dogma attesting to the role of the Divine in the world. Nevertheless, Maimonides, a twelfth-century rabbi, philosopher, and doctor, was the first to attempt to posit a theological creed for Judaism. In his *Thirteen Principles of the Faith*, Maimonides asserts that God is one, is the Creator of the universe, is unlike any other being, and is all-knowing, eternal, and without form.

The idea that God cannot be seen is articulated throughout early Jewish sources. Nevertheless, as God is also understood in the Jewish tradition to have intervened in history, there are moments when God must "reveal" Godself. When God gives the Torah to the people of Israel, God appears as thunder and lightning, smoke and cloud (Exod. 19). While God appears to most prophets and important biblical figures in the form of dreams, only Moses is described as speaking with God "face to face" (*JPS Tanakh* 1985, Ex 33:11). Yet even in the case of Moses, when he asks to see God's glory, he is told, "You cannot see my face; for no one shall see me and live" (Exod. 33:20). God's presence on earth, known in later Judaism as the *Shekhinah*, was understood as dwelling first in the Tabernacle, the sanctuary that accompanied the Israelites throughout their journey in the desert, and then later in the Temple in Jerusalem. But in the case of the Temple, the divine presence was not a physical manifestation. Rather, one's connection to God was thought to be most perceivable there, especially in the inner sanctum of the Temple, known as the Holy of Holies.

Despite the fact that the Jewish God is thought to be without form and, ultimately, beyond sexuality, traditional descriptions of God in both the Hebrew Bible and rabbinic literature tend to envision God as male, specifically as a husband, king, or father in relation to the people of Israel. These metaphors are meant to help the worshipper establish a more personal relationship with an unknowable deity. But in the modern period, many have noted the negative implications of conceiving of God as male and its impact on gender relations. As Jewish feminist theologian Judith Plaskow has argued, exclusive use of male imagery for the divine "justifies a human community which reserves power and authority for men" (1995, 228). Since the 1970s,

PEOPLE & PLACES

Maimonides and the Thirteen Principles of Faith

Maimonides was a Jewish philosopher of the twelfth century and arguable the greatest Jewish thinker of all time. Although quite controversial in its day and still not entirely accepted by all Jews, Maimonides' thirteen principles are the closest that Judaism comes to having a statement of belief. In addition to describing the attributes of God, Maimonides made several other beliefs integral to Judaism, including the uniqueness of Moses as a prophet, the authenticity of the Torah, the coming of the Messiah, and resurrection of the dead. This abridged version of the thirteen principles was adapted by Louis Jacobs:

1. God is the Creator of the Universe.
2. God is One.
3. God has no body, form, or likeness.
4. God is eternal. There was never a time when God did not exist, and there will never be a time when God will cease to exist.
5. One must pray only to God.
6. God revealed himself to the prophets.
7. Moses is the greatest of the prophets.
8. The Torah was given by God to Moses.
9. The Torah is eternal; God will not change the Torah, nor will God allow the Torah to be superseded.
10. God knows all the thoughts and all the deeds of people.
11. God rewards those who keep God's laws and punishes those who disobey them.
12. God will send the Messiah to usher in a new and better world.
13. God will revive the dead. (Jacobs 1984, 5)

feminists have attempted to correct this imbalance by focusing on the Bible's use of more feminine imagery in its description of God. For instance, Numbers 11:12 depicts God as "nursing" the Israelites, while Isaiah 42 alludes to God as having birth pangs. As a result, in several progressive communities attempts have been made to amend the liturgy in the traditional prayer book and alternate between female and male descriptions of God. However, to traditionalists this smacks of paganism: such language is too reminiscent of the goddess and fertility cults against which the biblical prophets railed. Although the debate rages on, feminist theologian Rachel Adler reminds us that Judaism's theological boundaries are immensely broad. From Maimonides to the more mystically inclined, it seems that there has always been room for numerous contradictory understandings of the Divine within the tradition (Adler 1993, 102).

Humanity

As has already been noted, stories play an important part in foundational Jewish beliefs. The Torah contains many different genres of writing, from poetry to law to history to liturgy, but its narratives are the key to understanding the relationship between God and human beings. According to the book of Genesis, humanity is the crowning act of creation, created by God on the sixth day, after the creation of the heavens and the earth, all plant life, and all the animals. There are actually two different accounts of the creation of humans in the opening chapters of Genesis, each having its own theological implications as well as implications for gender relations. In the first version, men and women are created simultaneously:

> Then God said, "Let us make humankind in our image, according to our likeness; and let them have dominion over the fish of the sea, and over the birds of the air, and over the cattle, and over all the wild animals of the earth, and over every creeping thing that creeps upon the earth." So God created humankind in his image, in the image of God he created them; male and female he created them. (NRSV 1993, Gen. 1: 26–27)

According to this account, both men and women were created "in the image of God." But what does it mean to be made in the image of God if, as we have already observed, God has no body, is beyond sexuality, and has no likeness to any other being? Medieval interpreters offered varying explanations of the phrase, suggesting that our discerning intellect or the immortality of our souls might be what most likens us to God and distinguishes us from all other forms of creation. Nevertheless, this version of creation was understood by many commentators as promoting the inherent value of all human beings, both male and female. Since every one of us shares something in common with God, we each, in essence, bear the stamp of the Divine, regardless of gender (Ross 2004, 38–39).

However, in the second rendition, man is created first out of the earth and animated with God's breath, while woman is created afterwards as man's "helper," out of one of the man's ribs:

> . . . the Lord God formed man from the dust of the ground, and breathed into his nostrils the breath of life; and the man became a living being. . . . Then the Lord God said, "It is not good that the man should be alone; I will make him a helper as his partner." . . . So the Lord God caused a deep sleep to fall upon the man, and he slept; then he took one of his ribs and closed up its place with flesh. And the rib that the Lord God had taken from the man he made into a woman and brought her to the man. Then the man said, "This at last is bone of my bones and flesh of my flesh; this one shall be called Woman, for out of Man this one was taken. Therefore shall a man leave his father and his mother, and shall cleave unto his wife, and they shall be one flesh." (NRSV 1993, Gen. 2:7, 18, 21–24)

It is this second account that has predominated in Western culture and has so often been used to justify the subjugation of women. Although most Jewish interpreters understood woman as being just as much God's creation, based on this account, some suggested that she was created as a lesser creature, as an afterthought, from substandard material (a bone, rather than the earth), with the primary function of serving man rather than God. One can see how the two different versions of the creation story could easily yield polarizing conceptions of the roles of men and women vis-à-vis the Divine.

Adam and Eve

Regardless of how one explains the differences between these two texts, the order and circumstances surrounding the moment of creation are, literally and figuratively, just the beginning in terms of understanding the Hebrew Bible's conception of humanity. In the narrative that follows, God places the first couple, known as Adam and Eve, in a garden and gives strict instructions to Adam that all the trees and plants within it are suitable for eating, save one: the Tree of Knowledge of Good and Evil. Should they eat from its fruit, they shall die. A little while later, a serpent entices Eve into eating from the forbidden tree, suggesting that the only reason it is off limits is that if she partakes of it, she will be like God, knowing good and evil. Eve evaluates what the serpent has suggested and her curiosity gets the better of her—she not only eats from the tree's fruit but gives it to a rather passive Adam to try as well. At this moment the couple suddenly become aware of their nakedness and, feeling ashamed, they fashion some clothes.

God then reappears in the garden, demanding an explanation for their transgression. Adam blames Eve and Eve, in turn, blames the serpent. No one wants to take responsibility for their actions. God then doles out punishments to all three of the offenders for their part in the violation of God's one simple decree. For instigating all the drama, the serpent is dealt with first—he is cursed to crawl on his belly for eternity and endure abuse from Adam and Eve's descendants. Eve is punished with pain in childbirth and is told that her husband will rule over her. Finally, Adam is told that the ground is now cursed because of his actions—no longer will food be easily available to him; instead he will have to endure hard, backbreaking work to make things grow. And, just as God had warned, the couple will die. Not immediately (Genesis tells us that Adam lives to be more than nine hundred years old), but Adam and Eve, and all of their descendants, now must accept mortality as a consequence for having partaken of the forbidden fruit.

In Jewish thought, the creation story has never been regarded as prescriptive—indicating how we should live our day-to-day lives—but rather as descriptive, or explaining how things are. The narrative is an attempt to explain the origin of things, how our present circumstances came into being. Hence we learn about the source of sexual attraction and sexual difference, why we are mortal, why we wear clothing, why women experience pain in childbirth, and why we must work to obtain our food. The text is not suggesting that God wants women to be ruled by their husbands, or that childbirth and agriculture must be painful processes. In fact, a close reading of the passage seems to indicate that those things actually fly in the face of the original divine plan. Accordingly, the creation story and its aftermath should be seen as a reflection of the human condition.

The Evil versus the Good: A Tale of Two Inclinations

Perhaps no other myth has been overlaid with so many divergent ideologies as the story of Adam and Eve. Many ideas not present in the original narrative have been read into it by both Jewish and Christian commentators (the Hebrew Bible is also considered scripture by Christians) through the centuries. It is worth noting that in the original story, the forbidden fruit is not described as an apple, the serpent is not associated with Satan, and Eve does not sexually manipulate Adam into eating the fruit. Both Jewish and Christian scholars were responsible for disseminating and popularizing these motifs, but Jewish sages did understand them slightly differently than their Christian counterparts. Unlike Christianity, which regards all human beings as having been born into original sin—a state of inherited guilt as a result of Adam and Eve's disobedience for which one has to atone—the rabbinic tradition does not understand all humanity as being implicated in the misdeeds of the first couple.

According to the rabbis, humans are given free will and are seen as struggling between two inclinations, one to do good and the other to do evil. The evil inclination is thought to be with us when we are born, while the good inclination develops in humans only around the age of thirteen, which is the age when we become responsible for our moral choices, according to the rabbis (Midrash Rabbah, Eccl. 1983, 4:13, 1). Still, the evil inclination is not regarded as a demonic force; rather, it is a drive to act according to our desires. In many ways it is what makes us human, for as the rabbis suggest, if it were not for the evil inclination, no one would get married, have children, build a house, or start a business (Midrash Rabbah, Gen. 1961, 9:7). So, according to this conception, it is the role of the good inclination to keep the evil inclination in check, to ensure that a desire for food does not become gluttony, a desire for sex does not become lewd and lascivious behaviour, and so forth.

Covenant

As alluded to above, a covenant—or *brit*, as it is known in Hebrew—is an agreement between two parties. In the ancient Near East it was not uncommon for two kings to enter into a treaty agreement in which the more powerful ruler (known as a suzerain) dictated to the leader of the smaller state (known as a vassal) how their affairs would be governed. The suzerain king would offer protection to the vassal king and his people as long as the latter agreed to submit to the greater king and abide by a series of conditions. In many cases the treaty would then be ratified by both parties' making a vow involving the ceremonial cutting of animals in half and laying down the pieces in two rows. To affirm their recognition of the terms of the treaty, the parties would then walk between the split carcasses, as if to say, *Should I not uphold my end of our deal, may the same fate that befell these animals also befall me.*

The covenant between God and Israel is not unlike these ancient treaties. In the book of Genesis, God, who could be compared to a suzerain king, enters into an agreement with the patriarch Abraham to multiply his progeny, make them into a great nation, and grant them the land of Canaan as their homeland. This is in return for Abraham's obedience in having left the only home he has ever known, in Ur of the Chaldees, to set out for Canaan upon God's urging. To seal the deal, God commands Abraham to cut in half a series of animals. God then appears to Abraham in a vision and passes between the animal pieces. In this way God assures Abraham that what has been promised to him will come to pass.

In return for the good fortune and privileges that God has offered him, Abraham and all his male descendants thereafter must also agree to be circumcised—to have their foreskins removed—on the eighth day after birth. Thus circumcision becomes an everlasting sign of this covenant, which will be passed on to Abraham's son Isaac, Isaac's son Jacob, and through Jacob on to his children, the twelve tribes of Israel.

At Mount Sinai, after the Israelites have been freed from slavery in Egypt and are on their way to the land that was promised to them by God, the covenant is renewed and spelled out in greater detail through the giving of the Torah. The Torah is Israel's special inheritance and explains the terms and conditions of the covenantal relationship with the Divine. So, with Moses as mediator, God explains to the Israelites what obedience to Yahweh entails and describes the catastrophes that will ensue should the people fail to follow God's commandments:

> ... be careful not to forget the covenant that the Lord your God made with you.... When you have had children and children's children, and become complacent in the land, if you act corruptly by making an idol in the form of anything, thus doing what is evil in the sight of the Lord your God, and provoking him to anger, I call heaven and earth to witness against you today that you will soon utterly perish from the land that you are crossing the Jordan to occupy; you will not live long on it, but will be utterly destroyed. (NRSV 1993, Deut. 4:23–26)

Words

The Ten Commandments

I am the Lord your God, who brought you out of the land of Egypt.
You shall have no other gods before me.
You shall not take the Lord's name in vain.
Keep the Sabbath day as holy.
Honour your parents.
Do not murder.
Do not commit adultery.
Do not steal.
Do not bear false witness.
Do not covet your neighbour's property.
(Exod. 20:2–17)

The land of Israel is not simply theirs for the taking; in order to conquer it, possess it, and keep it eternally, they must abide by God's laws. At the centre of these laws are the Ten Commandments (see "Words" box), which outline Israel's obligations to God as well as their obligations to one another.

But the Torah contains many other laws as well, which are revealed throughout the Israelites' sojourn in the desert and thereafter. From what to eat, how to dress, and when and with whom to have sex to how to go to war, care for the poor, compensate your workers, and worship God appropriately, Israelite laws essentially governed all aspects of human life, civil and criminal as well as public and private.

The rabbis of the Talmud, who would become the quintessential interpreters of the Torah, believed that all these injunctions in the Torah amounted to 613 laws, which could be further broken down into 248 positive laws, or prescriptions (e.g., "Keep the Sabbath day as holy"), and 365 negative laws, or prohibitions (e.g., "Do not steal").

Halacha: Jewish law as it developed from the time of the Mishnah (see page 35) until today. It is a combination of both the oral law and the written law as understood by the rabbis of the Talmud.

Oral Law

The early rabbis also believed that along with the written Torah that was provided to Moses, God also revealed an oral Torah, that is to say, a set of unwritten traditions that were passed down orally in an unbroken chain from one generation to the next, to both supplement what was in the written Torah and to help clarify its meaning. These oral traditions were eventually recorded in the Talmud. Although their interpretations often seem far from the plain sense of the text, the rabbis saw themselves as simply bringing to light what was already embedded in the scriptures; it was just a matter of having the right tools—the collected wisdom of the oral tradition—to glean the "hidden" meaning. And since the oral law was also thought to have a divine origin, in this way the rabbis imbued their own readings with authority. So Jewish law, known as **halacha**, meaning "the way of walking," became a synthesis of both the laws contained in the Torah and the legal traditions derived from the rabbis' reasoning.

Women and the Commandments

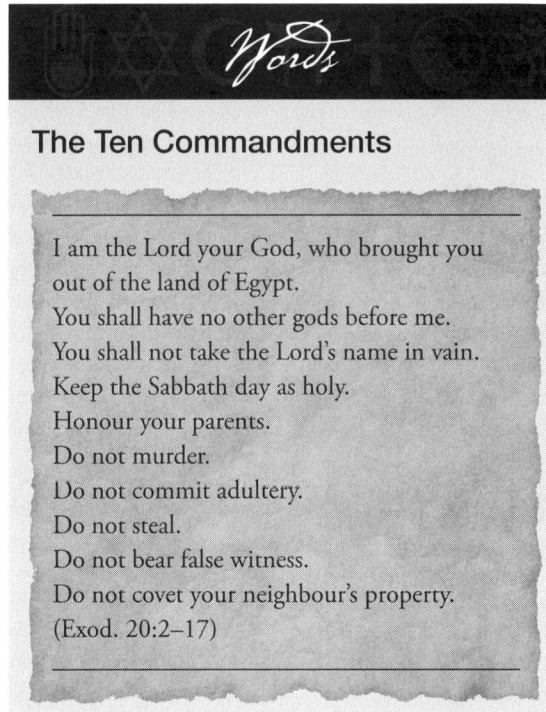

Although Jews understood themselves as having a special duty to fulfil God's commandments, not all Jews were considered to be equally obligated. The great majority of the commandments do apply uniformly to all Jews, but some are clearly divided along gender lines. In the case of laws pertaining to removal of the foreskin or the requirements of ritual purification after menstruation and childbirth, it is quite obvious that there is a biological basis for their not being equally relevant to both men and women. However, in other instances—when women inherit only when there are no male heirs, when only men can initiate divorce proceedings, or when a women's testimony is not considered valid—the reasoning for the differential treatment cannot be biological. Rather, the biases in the law seem to derive from some unwritten assumptions about women's place in the social order. Patriarchy, defined as "the institutionalization of male dominance over women and children in the family and the extension of male dominance over women in society in general" (Lerner 1986, 238), was certainly not unique to either biblical culture or rabbinic Judaism, but both systems arguably did little to overturn established class and gender hierarchies in the cultures in which they emerged.

Indeed, the rabbis of the Talmud took for granted that women, along with slaves and minors, were exempted from certain laws. In an attempt to systematize these rules and distinguish them from the ones that women were still required to perform, the early sages suggested that women were exempt from all positive, time-bound commandments. In other words, if a law was phrased as a prescription ("Thou shalt" as opposed to "Thou shalt not") and its performance was necessary at a certain time of day or on a certain day of the calendar, women were not obligated to fulfil such a law. For instance, the early sages exempted women from recitation of the Shema prayer, since it must be recited in the morning and the evening.

No specific rationale was provided by the Talmudic sages as to why women would be excused from this particular category of commandments to begin with. Often it was suggested that women had been freed from the burden of time-bound prescriptions for very practical reasons, so that those obligations would not interfere with their responsibilities as wives and mothers. In more modern times, rabbis and scholars recast the exemption as being a result not of women's domestic duties but rather her spiritual superiority; in other words, women, whose reproductive systems make them more in tune with the cycles of nature, do not require additional reminders of the sanctity of time the way men do. Still, despite this shift in rationale, women would continue to have an uneasy relationship with Jewish law and their place within the age-old covenant. Because the commandments are so essential to Jewish practice, being exempt from a significant chunk of them inevitably had an impact on women's self-perception as Jews. This is particularly true in the case of Torah study, which the rabbis elevated to the single most important ritual activity. By exempting women from the study of the Torah, the rabbis would limit women's opportunities for knowledge and authority within the tradition for thousands of years.

Today, from rights in marriage and divorce laws to leadership and ritual participation, women in all denominations have challenged the status quo regarding women and the commandments. Although the reasons for doing so vary among the different movements (see "New Denominations" below), in the past forty years, Conservative, Reform, and Reconstructionist authorities have all allowed women to be ordained as rabbis and have recognized the right of Jewish women to take on all the obligations and roles once reserved strictly for men. Even in Orthodox Judaism, women now study the Torah and Talmud at extremely high levels, and although they have encountered some resistance, women have responded to their exclusion from certain components of prayer by starting their own, women-only prayer groups. In a similar vein, some Orthodox women have sought and received private ordination from their teachers, although these ordinations are not generally recognized by mainstream Orthodoxy.

Chosenness

In the Jewish tradition, the commandments themselves are not seen as a punishment but rather as a great privilege. The Torah explains that Israel was chosen by God specifically for this role and that the people enthusiastically accepted the awesome responsibility:

> . . . the Lord called to [Moses] from the mountain, saying, " . . . If you obey my voice and keep my covenant, you shall be my treasured possession out of all the peoples. Indeed, the whole earth is mine, but *you shall be for me a priestly kingdom and a holy nation.* These are the words that you shall speak to the Israelites." So Moses came, summoned the elders of the people, and set before them all these words that the Lord had commanded him. The people all answered as one: "Everything that the Lord has spoken we will do." (Exod. 19:5–7)

Generally speaking, the notion of chosenness is understood by Jews not as their having a special status in the universe as much as it is connected to the receiving of the Torah and the obligation to live out God's covenant.

Early rabbis even suggested that it was not so much that God chose the Jews to receive the Torah as it was the Jews choosing God. A well-known midrash describes the Torah being offered by God to different nations, with each one wanting to know its contents before they agree to sign on. However, upon hearing the restrictions involved, including "Do not murder" and "Do not steal," they turn down God's offer. Only Israel accepts the divine gift unconditionally, agreeing to abide by God's laws even before they have heard and understood them.

Reconstructionist Judaism, the youngest of the four mainstream denominations, rejects the principle of chosenness on the grounds that it seems antithetical to other basic Jewish concepts, such as all humanity's being created in God's image. However, for the remaining streams of modern Judaism, which retain the chosen-people concept as part of their theology, being "chosen" does not make Jews innately superior, nor does it entirely exclude non-Jews from the divine plan. On the contrary, the fact that non-Jews can convert to Judaism and be considered full-fledged members of the community suggests that there is nothing innate about Jewishness at all. So although early scholars of religion classified Judaism as being a naturalistic religion limited in scope to one nation or ethnic group (see Chapter 1, page 7), this is a misunderstanding of some of Judaism's key teachings. Indeed, in traditional Jewish writings, God's laws have always been conceived of as pertaining to all humanity. The Torah itself includes the story of Job, a righteous non-Jew who believed in God, as well as the story of Jonah, who is sent to tell the non-Jewish nation of Nineveh to forsake their wicked ways. In fact, according to the Talmud, non-Jews are particularly obligated in the observance of a number of distinct biblical laws known as the *seven Noahide laws*. The term comes from the Flood narrative in Genesis, which tells of God, incensed by human corruption and violence, sending a great deluge to destroy all of creation. Wishing for a fresh start, God spares the righteous Noah, his family, and one pair from each animal species in order to repopulate the earth once the flooding stops. After forty days and nights the waters subside and God makes a covenant with Noah, promising that there will never be another flood that destroys the whole earth. As part of this covenant (which precedes the covenant that God makes with Abraham), the children of Noah must agree to abide by some basic rules: honouring life by not committing murder, theft, adultery, incest, blasphemy, or cruelty to animals, and by setting up courts to ensure that people are treated with fairness. Any non-Jew who lives justly by following these precepts is considered righteous and, according to the early rabbis, has a place in the world to come.

Afterlife

The existence of an afterlife is not clearly articulated in biblical texts. While some books such as Ezekiel and Daniel hint at the notion of resurrection of the dead, and other texts such as Numbers, Psalms, Job, and Lamentations make reference to a dark, mysterious place called *Sheol*, where the dead can briefly arise with God's assistance, elsewhere death is described as rather final. Nevertheless, with the advent of rabbinic Judaism and Jews' encounter with Hellenistic culture, the concept of an afterlife, known as *olam ha-bah* ("the world to come"), does emerge. One popular rabbinic dictum describes this world as being but a mere hallway to the next world. Accordingly, one must "prepare himself in the corridor in order to enter the banquet hall" (mAvot 4:21, Soncino Press). There are no elaborate descriptions of what the heavenly realm might look like, and in some instances it seems that references to the next world are merely descriptions of an idyllic age upon earth.

Messiah

The word messiah, or *mashiach* in Hebrew, simply means "anointed one," deriving from the practice of anointing a person with sacred oil when he is installed as king. In traditional Jewish thought the Messiah was not considered to be divine, nor was he considered to be Jesus of Nazareth, as in Christianity. Rather, the Messiah was expected to be an ideal king, descended from the line of King David, who would rule on earth in a time of righteousness. This time was also associated with resurrection of the dead, although whether this pertained only to the righteous in Israel or to all of humanity was a matter of debate among the sages. Throughout Jewish history, several people have claimed to be the Messiah, especially in times of peril and persecution (see "Shabbetai Zvi," below), but all have been rejected as false. Consequently, Jesus is understood by Jews as just one among many of these false messianic claimants. Today, more liberal Jewish denominations tend to reject the notion of the Messiah as embodied in an individual person, and instead understand the messianic references in the Bible as metaphors describing a utopian vision for the future.

For traditional Jews, on the other hand, it is believed that this future king will gather worldwide Jewry back in the land of Israel and usher in an era of peace.

Despite the existence of these precepts, whether in ancient, classical, or contemporary Jewish thought, the emphasis of religious devotion and spiritual activity tends to be more on the present world. One's obligation to follow God's commandments is seen as primarily having benefits in this world. Failure to follow the law is often described biblically as resulting in one's "being cut off from the people" or "being spit out of the land," while adherence to God's divine laws will "lengthen one's days" or allow one to "find favour in the eyes of the Lord," which for the patriarchs and other righteous biblical figures usually took the form of honour and wealth among men.

Tikkun Olam: Repairing the World

Originally *tikkun olam* was a post-biblical concept that referred to modifying Jewish law in the name of social order or the public good. However, with the popularization of Kabbalah, or Jewish mysticism, as developed by Isaac Luria in the sixteenth century, tikkun olam underwent a change and came to be associated with the "repairing of the world" (see "Kabbalah," below). Today more liberal branches of Judaism have further transformed the concept of tikkun olam; it is now synonymous with social justice and can refer to anything from giving to charity, volunteering with the elderly or the homeless, or initiating a political campaign. Consequently, many contemporary Jews act morally and ethically not because of a fear of what awaits them in the afterlife, but more out of a sense of duty to the world.

SOURCES

Torah

As already mentioned, the Torah is the primary sacred text of the Jews. The word *Torah* derives from a Hebrew word meaning "teaching" or "instruction." Most narrowly, the term refers to what is known as the five books of Moses, which includes Genesis, Exodus, Leviticus, Numbers, and Deuteronomy. But *Torah* can also refer to a larger collection of texts that encompasses the five books of Moses as well as the writings of the prophets (Nevi'im) and a section called "Writings" (Ketuvim), which includes wisdom literature, historical retellings of events, and post-exilic history. Collectively these texts are also called the Tanakh (an acronym for Torah, Nevi'im and Ketuvim); they include twenty-four books in all. In the broadest sense of the word, *Torah* can be used to refer to the entire corpus of Jewish teachings.

Words

The Twenty-Four Books of the Hebrew Bible

Torah

- Genesis
- Exodus
- Leviticus
- Numbers
- Deuteronomy

Prophets (Nevi'im)

- Joshua
- Judges
- Samuel I & II
- Kings I & II
- Isaiah
- Jeremiah
- Ezekiel
- The twelve minor prophets: Hosea, Joel, Amos, Obadiah, Jonah, Micah, Nahum, Habakkuk, Zephaniah, Haggai, Zechariah, and Malachi

Writings (Ketuvim)

- Psalms
- Proverbs
- Job
- Song of Songs
- Ruth
- Lamentations
- Ecclesiastes
- Esther
- Daniel
- Ezra and Nehemiah
- Chronicles I & II

The Five Books of Moses

By the late biblical period, the five books of Moses were already being written together on one continuous scroll and were considered a unit. Although *Torah* is often synonymous with *law* in post-biblical writings, to reduce the five books of Moses to a legal text would be a misnomer. First of all, there are several different genres of writing in these texts, from lists of laws and ethical teachings to genealogies, poems, and prayers, as well as narrative texts, many of which we have already alluded to. But while the Torah is not simply a book of law, it is not a straightforward narrative either. Each story comprises a hybrid of styles, with laws and moral exhortations often being introduced as an episode unfolds. Many of the stories do seem to be united by a particular theological vision, but no one single theme or philosophy encompasses all five books. Still, the plot does seem to follow a distinct chronology describing the coming into being of the people of Israel, starting with the creation of the world and continuing with the lives of the patriarchs Abraham, Isaac, and Jacob, the sojourn of the Israelites in Egypt, their enslavement by Pharaoh and liberation by Moses, their wanderings in the desert, and their eventual arrival in the Promised Land.

The Prophets

The next section of the Tanakh begins where Deuteronomy leaves off, with the conquering and settlement of the land of Canaan. It then goes on to chronicle the rule of the people by judges, the establishment of a monarchy in Israel, the division of that monarchy into northern and southern kingdoms (also known as Israel and Judah), the eventual exiles of both these communities, and the return of the Judeans (which is where the term *Jew* originates) after being granted permission by the Persian ruler, Cyrus. This section includes the more history-oriented books of Joshua, Judges, Samuel, and Kings, which are then followed by the books of Isaiah, Jeremiah, Ezekiel, and the twelve minor prophets, so named because the texts are relatively short.

The books of Joshua, Judges, Samuel, and Kings are infused with references to important prophets such as Samuel and Elijah, who are seen as inspired figures behind the key events being chronicled. However, the books of Isaiah, Jeremiah, Ezekiel, and the twelve minor prophets are prophetic writings in the more conventional sense, in that they record pronouncements associated with particular individuals. Prophets in ancient Israel should not be understood chiefly as people who predicted the future. Although they did sometimes purport to be foretelling events, these projections were always couched in generalities. Most often, the destruction and tragedies they described were intended to provoke people into correcting their behaviour, while at other times their visions were seen as simply reporting the inevitable consequences of the people's having forsaken their God. So the primary role of the prophet, as reflected in this section of the Tanakh, was that of social critic, commenting on both domestic and international affairs and trying to convince people to follow the will of God as they understood it.

The Writings

The name of the "Writings" section of the Tanakh is deliberately vague, as it contains material that seems on the whole to defy categorization. Despite their diversity, the texts known as *Ketuvim* were likely grouped together because they were deemed to be authoritative long after the five books of Moses and the prophetic writings were considered closed canons. The Talmud provides a glimpse into the late canonization of many of these texts, illustrating that accepting them as scripture was not necessarily a straightforward process. Texts such as the Song of Songs and the book of Esther were considered controversial, as neither contains any references to God. The Song of Songs, with its erotic descriptions of two lovers trying to find one another, was thought to be particularly problematic. While it would ultimately be interpreted as an allegory of the relationship between God and Israel, it took the great sage Rabbi Akiva to make a case for the Song's inclusion in the biblical canon: "All the writings are holy," he states, "but the Song of Songs is the Holy of Holies" (mYad 3:5, Soncino Press).

Authorship

Traditional Jews believe that all three sections of the Tanakh were divinely inspired, although the five books of Moses are regarded as the most sacred, since it is believed that the contents of this section were communicated directly to Moses by God. Nevertheless, even some of the earliest rabbis noted the difficulty of crediting Moses with writing the Torah, especially since Moses's death is recorded in the final verses of the book of Deuteronomy. To resolve this problem, one Talmudic tradition suggests that these last chapters were written by Moses's successor, Joshua, while another tradition holds that Moses's death was recorded by a tearful Moses himself, in anticipation of his own demise (bBB 15a, Soncino Press). With regard to the rest of the Tanakh, the titles of the prophetic writings were thought to be indicative of authorship. Hence the book of Joshua was written by Joshua, the book of Samuel by Samuel, and so on, and several of these key figures were thought to be responsible for composing other biblical texts as well. This would remain the traditional Jewish view until the modern era.

The Documentary Hypothesis

In the nineteenth century a scholarly movement known as *higher criticism* developed that stripped the Hebrew Bible of its divine origins. Its adherents dared to read the Bible as though it were any other text and concluded that the Torah was likely a composite text comprising numerous different sources or documents dating to different time periods. In 1883 German Bible scholar Julius Wellhausen synthesized the insights of his colleagues and penned what would become known as the *documentary hypothesis*, a theory that continues to dominate contemporary biblical studies. Although it has been modified over time by various biblical scholars, this view advocates that approximately four different authors or schools of authors can be identified in the five books of Moses. Despite having been woven together by a final editor to appear as a unified whole, the four sources can be teased out of the text, so the theory goes, based on the distinctive language they use, the literary style they employ, and the theological perspective that runs through their respective sources. While the dates and specific material deriving from each of the four sources continue to be debated by scholars, recognition that the Torah has multiple strands at work within it has been highly influential, much to the ire of traditional Jews who feel that it undermines the notion of the text's being the word of God.

What's in a Name: Differences between the Torah and the Old Testament

In addition to being called the Tanakh, the Torah is also sometimes referred to as the Old Testament. Many actually use the terms *Torah* and *Old Testament* interchangeably, but if we look a bit further into the meaning of the latter designation, we see that it carries some theological baggage. *Testament* is generally understood as being another word for covenant, and describing the Torah as "the old covenant" seems like a suitable epithet for an ancient text that chronicles the special relationship between God and the people of Israel. However, *old* here does not mean simply ancient but rather antiquated or outdated. It is described as old in relation to the New Testament, a text that contains the teachings of Jesus and is considered the foundation of Christian theology. Although Jesus's message of salvation is seen by Christians as continuing in the vein of the Israelite prophets before him, it is also regarded as overriding or superseding the earlier promise of an everlasting covenant between God and Israel. In Christian theology, with the arrival of Jesus, most of the laws given to Moses are no longer necessary; the people of Israel are disinherited and God's covenant is reinterpreted and renewed to pertain to Christians alone. Hence, more and more the term *Old Testament* is being replaced by the more neutral term *Hebrew Bible* to differentiate it from the New Testament, which was originally written in Greek.

Ritual Uses

The book of Deuteronomy includes a directive that the community assemble once every seven years to have the book of the law read aloud so that every man, woman, and child will be aware of their obligations to God and to one another. Current practice involves regular Torah readings during morning prayer services on Mondays, Thursdays, and Saturdays. The five books of Moses are thus divided into weekly portions so that the entire scroll can be read within a single year.

The Torah Scroll

Although printed versions of Torahs in book form are available for study and individual use, Torahs for more ceremonial purposes are to this day carefully copied by hand, by people specifically trained as scribes, onto scrolls made from animal skins. As the positioning and shape of each letter and space must follow strict requirements, it can take up to a year and a half to complete one Torah. When not in use, the Torah is kept in an ornamental cabinet reminiscent of the Ark of the Covenant, where the Ten Commandments were originally housed. As seen here, the Torah is traditionally belted with silk or satin, protected by a piece of fabric or a wooden case, and ornamented with a silver or gilded breastplate, scroll handles, and two crowns with bells that fit over the upper ends of the handles. All these adornments are meant to set the Torah apart as a sacred object. A silver pointer on a chain, called a *yad*, is generally hung over one of the handles, as it is not permissible to touch the Torah with one's bare hands: moisture from the fingers could blur the letters and render the entire scroll unfit for ritual purposes.

Source: Photos.com

Mishnah: an interpretation of the legal material in the Torah compiled by Rabbi Judah the Patriarch around 200 C.E.

The Mishnah

The **Mishnah** is an elaboration of the legal material in the Torah. It is arranged by topic and divided into six orders, focusing on agricultural laws, laws to do with festivals, and laws governing male and female relationships (especially marriage), damages, temple procedures, and ritual purification. This text is written tersely and seeks mostly to clarify ambiguities in the legal precepts outlined in the Torah. Originally an oral tradition, the Mishnah was compiled around 230 C.E. by a man named Rabbi Judah the Patriarch, who lived in the northern part of the land of Israel. It is a reflection of the law and practices that had been handed down by the sages who lived before him. The material in it does not purport to be new but rather is a collection of debates regarding the oral law from the years 70 to 230 C.E.

The need for a text such as the Mishnah came about as a direct result of the destruction of the Second Temple in Jerusalem in 70 C.E. When the Jews had a centre of religious worship in the Temple, religious rites were carried out by priests—descendants of Aaron, also known as Sadducees—who followed the laws as they understood them in the Torah. Because the monarchy was not restored after the Jews returned from exile but the Temple was rebuilt, both religious and political leadership of the community eventually fell to those responsible for the Temple as an institution: the priests. However, after the destruction of this sacred space, the Jews once again found themselves in a state of crisis. Without a religious centre, how would they worship?

Enter the Pharisees, a group of sages who were opponents of the ruling Sadducees. Believing that the Sadducees had come to power illegitimately, the Pharisees differed with the former on a variety of theological issues, especially on the existence of an oral law that had been handed to Moses at Sinai to help explicate the written law. The Sadducees rejected the notion of the oral law, and the Pharisees saw themselves as the only legitimate interpreters of that tradition. With the Temple gone, they saw an opportunity, and they started to devise a new system of religious worship that would not be dependent on a temple. For instance, instead of offering sacrifices to the deity, they instituted prayer as the primary form of divine worship.

However, the Pharisees still continued to talk about temple worship and how things such as sacrifice should be conducted in the event that another temple was built. They went back to the biblical text and found that the laws were often terse and enigmatic, so they proceeded to try to tease out

Practices

The Brevity of the Mishnah: Tractate Berachot 1:1

As the Shema prayer is one of the most important pieces of liturgy in Judaism, it is perhaps not surprising that a discussion about the correct time to recite it in the evening opens the very first chapter in the first tractate, or section, of the Mishnah. As there were no clocks back then, the text uses other indicators familiar to its target audience to pinpoint the correct time frame. The passage below conveys both the Mishnah's conciseness as well as how much expert or insider knowledge is needed to decipher its meaning. The words in square brackets are not in the original text but have been added to help clarify its meaning; italicized phrases are explained below.

From when may one recite the Shema in the evening?
From the time when the priests go in to eat their *sacred tithes*,
until the end of the *first watch*—so says Rabbi Eliezer.
And the Sages say: Until midnight.
Rabban Gamliel says: Until the break of dawn.
It once happened that [Rabban Gamliel's] sons came from a wedding banquet [after midnight].
They said to [their father]: "We have not recited the Shema."
He said to them: "If dawn has not broken, you are [still] obligated to recite it."
"[This is true] not only in this case [of reciting the Shema]; rather, in all cases where the Sages said that [some precept can be performed only] until midnight—the precept is [still in force] until the break of dawn . . . .
[But] if that is so, why did the Sages say, "until midnight"?
To distance a person from transgression.

Sacred tithes: The priests who served in the Temple were given tithes, or gifts of food, by the Israelites, but this food could be eaten only in a state of ritual purity. Consequently, if a priest became ritually impure through contact with a contaminating object (such as a dead reptile), he needed to immerse himself in water and then wait for nightfall before he could become pure again and eat the donated food. The Mishnah is indicating that the first opportunity to recite the evening Shema prayer would be when the recently purified priests went in to eat their tithes.
First watch: Either a third or a quarter of the way through the night. This is a source of debate in later rabbinic discussions of this text.
To distance a person from transgression: There are three opinions here as to the latest time that one might recite the evening prayer: until the first watch (Rabbi Eliezer), until midnight (the sages), or until the break of dawn (Rabban Gamliel). But Rabban Gamliel seems to suggest that he and the sages ultimately mean the same thing: they may have said until midnight, but until the break of dawn is still acceptable. So if that is the case, the text asks, why did the sages say only until midnight? This was to ensure that people would recite the Shema earlier and not accidentally sin by falling asleep before they had a chance to fulfil their obligation.

Source: Adapted from *The Book of Jewish Belief,* Louis Jacobs and others

the meanings of the text. They created laws where there was no clear-cut explanation, all the while claiming that their interpretations could be traced back to Moses. For instance, in the Torah there is no prescribed picture of how to go about getting married. These early rabbis found various models in the conduct of the patriarchs (Abraham, Isaac, and Jacob) and their wives (Sarah, Rebecca, Rachel, and Leah) and began to codify them into laws. There were often disagreements in interpretation, and these disagreements would be included in the text. Although the laws tended to follow the majority opinion, all these disagreements, including minority positions, are codified in the Mishnah.

The Talmud

A generation after the Mishnah was compiled, even it seemed insufficient for determining how to live on a day-to-day basis. So the rabbis began expanding on the Mishnaic text in both the land of Israel (by then known as Palestine) and Babylonia, where some Jews had remained after being exiled by the Assyrians. As a result there are two different versions of the Talmud, one Palestinian, compiled by the beginning of the fifth century, and the other Babylonian, compiled in the fifth to sixth centuries. These two texts overlap in many ways yet also reflect the particular concerns of each community. The Babylonian Talmud is much longer than its Palestinian counterpart (a printed version today fills more than thirty volumes), and today it is the one that dictates current practice for traditional Jews.

While the Mishnah generally records concluded legal opinions, the Talmud includes the debates and step-by-step reasoning processes used by the rabbis of this later period. The Talmudic rabbis are portrayed as having a dialogue about the meaning of the Mishnah; using back-and-forth questioning, they challenge one another's arguments, which address the language, logic, and legal conclusions of the earlier generations of rabbis. Biblical and mishnaic proof texts are employed in creative ways to support their positions and attempt to explain the derivation of a particular law. In the process, the rabbis explore numerous different scenarios to see how a given law might apply and they devise new laws as needed (although, strictly speaking, these are never understood as new but rather as a part of the revealed oral tradition). Debates between Talmudic sages are often left open-ended, with no formal conclusion.

A Page of the Talmud

Decoding a page of the Talmud can be quite daunting. As seen here, the name of the tractate and the chapter and page numbers appear in bold type across the top of the page; the wide column of text in the centre often has a few relevant lines of the Mishnah in Hebrew, followed by the Talmudic sages' discussion of that same topic in Aramaic, the most widely spoken language of the period. Along the sides of the page you will find the commentaries of various medieval scholars from the eleventh and twelfth centuries, cross-references to other parts of the Talmud, other legal codes, textual corrections from the sixteenth century, and sometimes more modern interpretations as well. So a single page of the Talmud is really a dialogue among several centuries of Jewish scholars. The Talmud and its long, often convoluted arguments are to this day studied in depth by traditional Jews.

Source: © Israel images/Alamy

Responsa: compilations of questions and answers addressed to community rabbis on everyday matters of Jewish law.

Zohar: the main text of Jewish mysticism, which understands God's manifestation in the universe as ten emanations of divine energy.

Midrash

The complex and creative principles behind the dissecting and interpreting of the Tanakh or the Mishnah that appear in the Talmud are known as *midrash*, which comes from a word meaning "to search" or "to inquire." Two types of midrash are found in the Talmud: *midrash halacha* and *midrash aggada.* The former pertains to questions of law and Jewish practice and follows a series of strict guidelines, while the latter is of a more fluid nature and encompasses the non-legal material in the Talmud, which consists of ethical teachings, rabbinic folktales, historical anecdotes, politics, geography, and even medical advice. Commenting on the difference between these two types of midrash, the German Jewish poet Heinrich Heine* (1797–1856) described the halacha as "that illustrious fighting school, where the expertest dialectic athletes . . . carry on their mental combats," while the aggada was more like "a garden . . . where the charming olden stories, tales of angels, famous legends, silent histories of martyrs, festal songs and words of wisdom . . . all glitter'd, bloom'd and sprung in such abundance" (1866, 472–73).

Other Sources

The question of which texts are considered traditional or authoritative in Judaism is fraught with controversy. The sheer number of texts and commentaries that stem from the Torah and the Talmud is awe-inspiring. Yet not all Jews would agree on the status of these texts. Jewish law certainly continued to develop after the Talmudic period, with the **responsa** literature—compilations of questions and answers addressed to community rabbis on everyday matters of Jewish law—and eventually the Shulhan Aruch, which is considered the ultimate code of Jewish law in Orthodox Judaism. However, other contemporary Jewish denominations do not necessarily deem these later sources as binding in the same way. In fact, for Reform and Reconstructionist Jews, the Talmud itself may not be considered binding. Nonetheless, while the Talmud may not dictate how one lives one's life among more liberal Jewish movements, it is still often regarded as a significant source of literature describing Jewish history, theology, and culture and serving as the basis of a communal Jewish practice.

Other important Jewish texts include the **Zohar**, the major text of Jewish mysticism (see "Kabbalah," below), as well as the *siddur*, or prayer book, and the Haggadah, which is the text used at the Passover seder to aid in retelling the story of the exodus from Egypt. Both the siddur and the Haggadah have a standard set text established during the Middle Ages, but they also have many different variations depending upon one's ethnic origin, local custom, and denominational affiliation.

HISTORY

The Biblical Period (2000–538 B.C.E.)

The Hebrew Bible is not so much a history book per se as it is a document with a particular theological agenda. The purpose of its narratives is not to provide an objective account of events as they happened; rather, people, places, and key moments are embellished in order to instruct the Israelites and instil in them pious behaviours. Furthermore, the events it describes were recorded exclusively by men, long after they were purported to have taken place, and there is little archaeological or material evidence to corroborate the mythic events and key figures described within its pages. Nonetheless, the Bible does give us a glimpse into the central episodes that became significant in the collective memory of the Jewish people, and it also provides us with some limited insight into Israelite social relations. Therefore, we will begin our discussion of "biblical history" with the Bible itself.

Exodus from Egypt

The book of Genesis, which describes the family intrigues of Abraham, Isaac, and Jacob, ends with Jacob's children having settled in Egypt because of

* Heinrich, Heine. *The Poems of Heine.* Translated by Edgar Alfred Bowring (London: Bell and Daldy, 1866).

a famine in the land of Canaan. When the book of Exodus begins, a regime change results in the family of Jacob no longer being welcome in the land; they are forced into hard labour and edicts are issued that their male offspring be killed to ensure that the populous clan does not overtake the native Egyptians. Moses, spared from death when fished out of the Nile by the pharaoh's daughter, emerges as the leader of the Israelites, and after several pleas—and ten plagues—Moses convinces Pharaoh to let the people go. However, Pharaoh soon regrets his decision and sends his troops after the escaped slaves. The Israelites' dramatic escape reaches its climax at the Red Sea as the Egyptians are closing in on them. According to the Torah, a corridor of land through the sea allows the Israelites to pass unharmed while the Egyptians are drowned, and the victorious Israelites then begin their journey to Canaan.

Although the historicity of this narrative is doubted by scholars, the outline of the story is plausible: Semitic peoples had moved into Egypt for centuries during times of famine, and mass escapes of slaves did occur in the ancient world, as did natural disasters much like those described in the plagues, although not usually in such rapid succession. If the exodus from Egypt did occur, the best guess of scholars dates the event to around 1200 B.C.E., when Egypt was ruled by Merneptah, son of Ramses II, since one of his inscriptions alludes to a victory over "Israel" (Tigay 2004, 104).

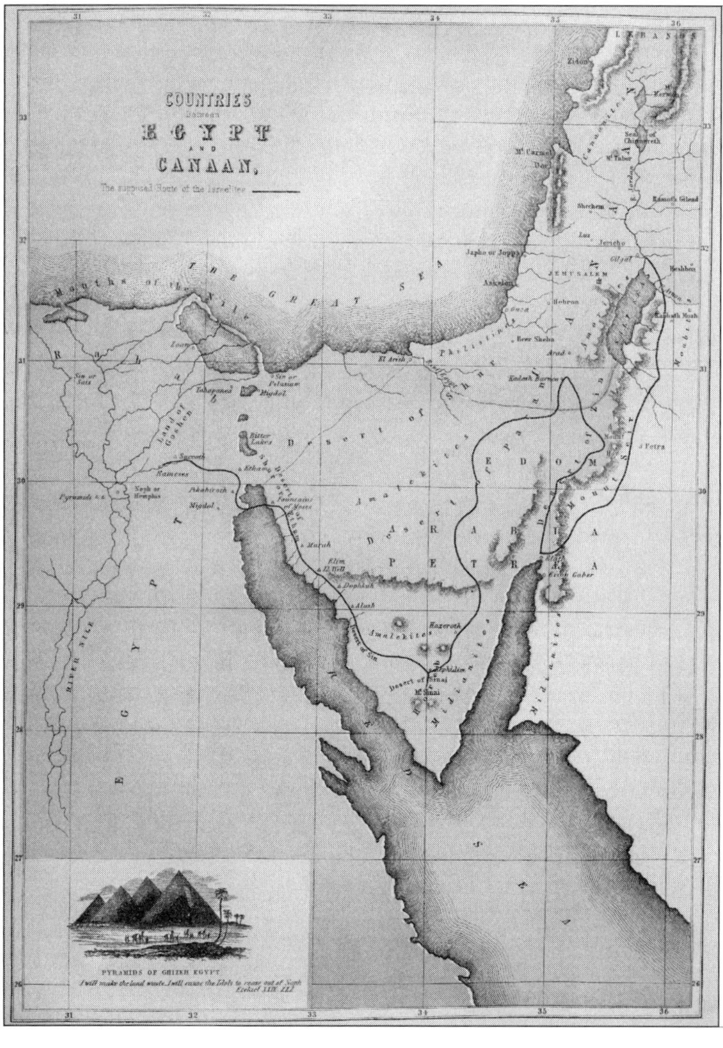

Possible Route of the Exodus

The map below tracks the possible route the Israelites may have taken from Egypt to Canaan, based on the biblical account.

Source: © Classic Image/Alamy

Nonetheless, the Exodus, which is memorialized in the festival of Passover, seems to be a turning point in Jewish thought, as the juncture at which the Israelites are regarded as having become a nation. Thus, whether factual or not, it remains a central image in Jewish law, liturgy, and practice.

Settlement, Exile, Return

After the Israelites wandered through the desert for some time, the next major event recorded in the Tanakh is the conquest and settlement of the land of Canaan. The texts chronicle the rule of the people by judges until the eventual establishment of a monarchy in Israel. Although the reign of the first king, Saul, proves to be somewhat disastrous, the two subsequent kings, David and Solomon, are considered the most beloved and successful monarchs for putting Israel on the map of the ancient Near East. David establishes Jerusalem, also known as Zion, as the capital and Solomon brings it glory by building the Temple, modelled after the Tabernacle where the presence of God was thought to dwell when the Israelites were wandering through the desert. However, after Solomon it all begins to go downhill. The rest of the book of Kings chronicles the division of the land into northern and southern kingdoms—Israel and Judah—because of disputes between Solomon's sons about succession and issues of taxation.

With a few exceptions, subsequent kings in both kingdoms lead the people astray and do not follow God's commandments, despite frequent warnings from prophets such as Amos and Hosea that divine punishment will be visited upon them for breaking the covenant. And eventually, according to the biblical story, that is what comes to pass. In 721 B.C.E. the northern kingdom of Israel is conquered by the Assyrians and the people are led off into slavery. One hundred years later in the south, King Josiah enacts a series of reforms based on a lost ancient book (believed to be the book of Deuteronomy) to bring justice back to the land, appease God, and avoid the same fate befalling his people. However, the laws are ignored and in 586 B.C.E. the Judeans too are conquered by the Babylonians. Jerusalem and the great Temple of Solomon are destroyed and the people are led off into exile.

Thus begins another major theme that runs through much of Jewish literature and liturgy: how to live in a foreign land as a distinct people and keep alive the hope of one day returning to Zion. Luckily for the Judeans, Babylon is overtaken by the Persians, and in 538 B.C.E. the Persian leader, Cyrus, enacts a declaration allowing the Judeans to return to their home and rebuild the Temple in Jerusalem. Although a good number of Jews decide to remain in Babylonia, a sizeable group returns to Judea and the Second Temple is completed by 515 B.C.E. Approximately a hundred years later, Ezra the scribe and Nehemiah, two leaders of the Babylonian Jewish community, reestablish the importance of the Torah among the returnees, enacting a series of legal innovations, including a ban on intermarriage, as a way of defining the boundaries of the new community.

Roles of Men and Women in Israelite Culture

Despite the patriarchal nature of the Bible, women figure prominently in biblical texts. Although they are mentioned less frequently than their male counterparts and hold fewer positions of leadership, the Bible does provide us with portrayals of women as prophets (Miriam, Deborah, and Hulda), judges and warriors (Deborah and Yael), and ruling queens (Jezebel, Athalia, and Esther). But even less public figures—women such as Sarah, Rebecca, Rachel, and Leah—are described as playing a significant role in the management of their households, along with their husbands. Given the Bible's ideological function, we cannot assume that these depictions provide an accurate representation of women's lives, gender relations, or the broader Israelite culture. Nevertheless, archaeological evidence does suggest that the ancient Israelites were a pioneer people, living off the land in rough terrain that would have required hard labour on the parts of both men and women (Meyers 1999, 37–38). Remains of villages suggest that households were relatively self-sufficient, with women likely serving important roles as producers of both children (more bodies meant more people contributing to the family economy) and goods (household wares and other commodities). Also, because warfare could occasionally draw the men away from the family home in these types of agrarian societies, women tended to be more involved in everyday agricultural tasks than one might expect (Meyers 1999, 37). With this in mind, one can understand the Bible's preoccupation with fertility and barrenness that we see in the narratives of many of the patriarchs. Child labour was integral for maintaining the family's supply of food, and with evidence from tombs suggesting that women's life expectancy was a full ten years shorter than that of men, the pressure was on for women to populate their households as quickly as possible.

The Second Temple Period (587 B.C.E.–70 C.E.)

In contrast to the biblical period, the Second Temple era is characterized by an outpouring from diverse literary sources that can attest to the major events of the time. By the Second Temple period, which spanned more than six hundred years, the locus of power had long since shifted from individual family units to more centralized forms of governance. During the Persian period, Jewish governors such as Nehemiah were assigned to rule in Judea, and in the absence of a monarch, members of priestly families were left in charge of most community affairs. Persian rule came to an end in Judaea in 333 B.C.E., when Alexander the Great conquered the area. This ushered in several centuries of Hellenistic influence in the region. Although up until this point the Jews had been given the freedom of self-administration by a high priest, with little interference from their foreign rulers, the landscape changed under Antiochus IV in 175 B.C.E.

The Jews had now been living under Greek rule for some time and were quite at home with many aspects of Greek language and culture, but it seems that there was a divide among the people, with some Jews more willing than others to forego Jewish practices in exchange for Greek ones. These tensions between factions of Jews—the more Hellenized versus the more traditional—reach their pinnacle when Antiochus IV intervenes in the selection of the high priest. Although the Jews regard their communal leader as being divinely appointed, in stark contrast, Antiochus sees the high priest as simply one more governor in his empire, an official he can dismiss and install at will. He sees an opportunity to profit from the political appointment of a leader for the Jews, and gives the position of high priest to the highest bidder. He replaces Onais III, whom the people regard as the legitimate high priest, with his more Hellenized brother Jason, and then he replaces Jason with the even more Hellenized Menelaus when the latter offers Antiochus more bribe money.

Sabbath: the Jewish day of rest, observed on Saturdays. The Sabbath commemorates the fact that God rested on the seventh day after creating the universe, according to the Hebrew Bible.

The Jews begin rioting against Antiochus's appointees for the priesthood, and Antiochus responds by clamping down on Jewish practice. Observance of the **Sabbath** (see "Major Jewish Festivals," below) and other festivals is banned, along with circumcision and animal sacrifices. The Temple is plundered for its gold, and images of Greek gods and forbidden animals such as pigs are sacrificed on the Temple altar. In 167 B.C.E. a family of priests known as the Hasmoneans initiates a successful revolt against both the radically Hellenized Jews and Antiochus's empire. Led by Judah the Maccabee and his brothers, the rebel faction recaptures Jerusalem and rededicates the Temple, cleansing it of foreign idols and impure animals. This rededication of the Temple is what is commemorated by the Jewish festival of Hannukah (see "Major Jewish Festivals," below).

Words

The Dead Sea Scrolls

In 1947, not far from the Dead Sea, a Bedouin boy stumbled across a series of caves containing several clay jars with portions of ancient Hebrew, Aramaic, and Greek manuscripts inside them. Essentially he had found an ancient Jewish library and the earliest surviving examples of Hebrew biblical texts that we have today. The caves also contained several texts that did not become part of the Hebrew biblical canon but were preserved in the Catholic and Protestant versions of the Bible, as well as several previously unknown texts that were peculiar to the Dead Sea sect that authored and compiled the documents. The texts, which are thought to date from 150 B.C.E. to 70 C.E., speak to the great diversity of Jewish thought and practice during the Second Temple period.

Thus, in 141 B.C.E. the rule of the Hasmonean dynasty began, and a self-governing Jewish state emerged whose leaders served as both high priests and kings of Israel. This period was characterized by civil war and deep sectarian tensions. As a result of this instability, self-rule was short-lived, and in 63 B.C.E. the Roman military leader Pompey captured Jerusalem. In 37 B.C.E. Herod the Great was installed by the Romans as king of Israel. Herod left his mark on the region through his great architectural feats, most notably expansion of the Temple in Jerusalem. Not long after Herod's death, the Romans declared Judaea to be a Roman province. It was during this time that the early Jesus movement arose. Although it would later evolve into Christianity, at the time it was only one of many factions that sought to reform the corruption plaguing

PEOPLE & PLACES

The Western Wall

The Western Wall, also known as the Wailing Wall, is today all that remains of the great Jerusalem Temple. The large rectangular stones at the base date from the time of Herod, while subsequent layers were added from the seventh century onwards. Since the early Middle Ages, Jews have been congregating to pray at this site, often coming to weep and mourn the loss of the sacred Temple that once stood there. In 1967 it was transformed by the State of Israel into an open-air synagogue under control of the Israeli Chief Rabbinate (see "Authority," below). As can be seen here, the plaza in front of the wall is sex-segregated: men pray on one side and women on the other. It is customary to leave a note with one's personal prayers in cracks of the wall and, as a sign of respect, to walk backwards when leaving the site. The wall is always open for prayer but it tends to be busiest on the Sabbath, major festivals, and especially the ninth day of Av, the day the Temple was destroyed in 70 C.E.

Source: A. Hyman Photography/Getty Images

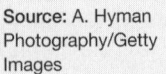

Jerusalem and the Jewish leadership. A Jewish rebellion against oppressive Roman taxation laws broke out in 66 C.E., only to be crushed in 70 C.E. by the Roman emperor Vespasian and his son Titus. Jerusalem was destroyed and the Temple was razed to the ground, leaving only the western outer wall of the complex intact. This wall remains standing today and is considered to be the most revered site for Jews worldwide.

The Rabbinic Period (70–700 C.E.)

Although Jews by this time were living in communities throughout the Roman empire, there were now two major centres of Jewish life, one concentrated in Palestine (the name given to the land of Israel by the Romans) and the other in Babylonia, where a thriving community had remained since destruction of the First Temple in 586 B.C.E.

Palestine

In Palestine, after the destruction of the Second Temple in 70 C.E., the mantle of community leadership once enjoyed by the priests was taken up by the rabbis. One of the most noteworthy rabbis of the period was Rabbi Akiva, whose humble origins as a shepherd are described in the Talmud. One story has the impoverished, non-scholarly Akiva going away to study Torah at the bidding of his wife, only to return twenty-four years later with more than 24,000 disciples (bNed 50a, Soncino Press).

A generation before Akiva, two other famous sages in first-century Palestine were Hillel and Shammai. Although they lived just before the destruction of the Second Temple, their teachings were seminal in the centuries that followed. Hillel was a poor woodcutter known for his leniency and compassion in matters of law, while Shammai was a builder with a reputation for impatience and a stricter approach to halacha. While they themselves did not argue that much, their disciples did: the Talmud reportedly contains three hundred disputes between the schools of the House of Shammai and the House of Hillel. Although Jewish practice is to follow Hillel, the rulings of Shammai were considered just and valid in his day.

With Jerusalem in tatters in the wake of 70 C.E., the rabbis eventually moved their centre of religious learning to Galilee, in northern Palestine. Relations between Rome and the Jews soon restabilized, and the leader of the Jewish community, known as the patriarch, was officially recognized by the Roman authorities. When the Jews were granted Roman citizenship along with the rest of the inhabitants of the empire, the future even looked bright.

However, in 313 Constantine became the first Christian emperor of Rome, and by 380 C.E. Christianity was the official state religion: all the subjects of the now Byzantine empire were expected to accept the tenets of the Christian faith. In the early fifth century the office of the patriarch was abolished and Jews came under further restrictions, preventing them from holding public office and building new synagogues. The notion of Jews as "Christ-killers," or collectively responsible for the death of Jesus, became entrenched in the Church during this period. Under Emperor Justinian, religious persecution intensified: decisions of the rabbinic court could be overruled by the state, public readings of the Torah could no longer occur in Hebrew, and reading of the Mishnah was outlawed.

Rule over Palestine then seesawed between the Persians and the Byzantine empire, with Jerusalem falling under the auspices of the Islamic dynasty, or caliphate, of the Umayyads in 638 C.E. It was at this point that Jews were permitted to return to Jerusalem, but by then Babylonia had long surpassed the Holy City as the centre of the Jewish world.

Babylonia

Although we have an abundance of scholarly works that explore the Greco-Roman and Byzantine context in which the Jews of Palestine lived, far less research has been done by Jewish historians on Babylonian sources, so, outside of rabbinic literature itself, we have little external documentation to ascertain the experiences of the Jewish Babylonian community. Nonetheless, we know that, just like the Jews of Palestine, whose interests were represented by the patriarch, the Jews in Babylonia had their own communal leader, known as the *exilarch*, or head of the community in exile. Sometime after the destruction of the Second Temple, it is believed that the ruling Parthians granted self-government to the Jews within their borders, thus empowering the exilarch to make official decisions on behalf of the community (Strack and Stemberger 1996, 3).

Geonim: heads of the rabbinic academies in Babylonia from approximately the sixth to eleventh centuries.

Diaspora: the Jewish world outside Israel.

In terms of religious authority, the most significant of the Babylonian rabbis was Abba Arika, known simply as Rav. Rav established his own rabbinic academy in Sura, which became the centre of Jewish intellectual life for many centuries thereafter. Much of the material in the Babylonian Talmud consists of debates between Rav and his rival Samuel, the head of the academy in Nehardea. For more than two centuries Jews lived peacefully in Babylonia, allowing the Babylonian take on Jewish law to flourish. Hence the Babylonian Talmud developed in a more sophisticated fashion than its Palestinian counterpart. By the mid-eighth century, the Babylonian academies had come to surpass those in the land of Israel.

Rabbinic Literature and Social History

Much like the Hebrew Bible, the works of rabbinic literature—the Mishnah, the Talmuds, and the volumes of the midrash—were never intended to be history books. Rabbinic sources are highly edited documents that describe the law as the rabbis understood it. Hence their texts provide a window into an idealized world: the way the rabbis hoped that people would conduct their day-to-day affairs. Consequently we find that both their laws and their incidental accounts of social relations often seem to conflict with the findings of material culture. A good example is the numerous Greek and Latin inscriptions, from synagogues throughout the Roman and Byzantine world, that attest to women being given titles such as *elder*, *mother of the synagogue*, and *priest* (Brooten 1982, 41–99). Although the Talmud prohibits women from being prayer leaders in most circumstances and denies that woman from priestly families can perform any of the priests' major liturgical functions, scholar Bernadette Brooten maintains that these were more than simply honorary titles and likely reflect women's involvement as leaders in the ancient synagogue.

Since no competing Jewish group of the period has left any major literary sources, it is often difficult to interpret what these archaeological findings may mean. However, even the rabbis' own sources can sometimes point to other, non-dominant perspectives on Jewish life and law. Although throughout the Talmud there seems to be an assumption on the part of the rabbis that women are not obligated to study Torah, there are also intriguing references to a woman named Beruriah, who is depicted as very learned in both Torah study and rabbinic precepts. She is cited as having been able to learn "300 traditions in a day from 300 masters" (bPes 62b, Soncino Press), and on several different occasions she is portrayed as correcting other men, including her husband, for their misunderstanding of a biblical verse. So, despite the rabbis' generally negative disposition toward women and the study of Torah, virtually every source associated with Beruriah attests to, and is complimentary about, her great familiarity with scripture and rabbinic interpretation.

The Medieval Period (c. 700–1800)

The Rise of the Geonim

With the ascendancy of Babylonia as the centre of Jewish life in the eighth century, the heads of the rabbinic academies, known as the **geonim**, went about clarifying matters of Jewish law for Jews both in the **Diaspora** and in the land of Israel. Responding to queries sent to them from both home and abroad, the geonim would interpret and apply the laws of the Talmud in order to give rulings in the cases that appeared before them.

Under Islamic rule, as "people of the book," Jews and Christians were given protected status. Although, as non-Muslims, Jews faced many religious restrictions similar to those they had experienced at the hands of the Byzantines, under the Abbasid dynasty such policies were not strictly enforced. As long as Jewish and Christian subjects paid a poll tax, they were able to live with a great degree of freedom (Sachar 1966, 161). The geonim, as religious leaders of the Jewish community, thrived in this context. Through their engagement with the Muslim scholars living around them, the geonim became aware of rationalist philosophy, philology, and linguistics, and these new disciplines had a profound impact on their own writings. Since Muslim interpretation of their own sacred book, the Qur'an, involved in-depth study of Arabic grammar, the geonim concluded that the key to their own religious texts might similarly lie in a better understanding of the Hebrew language. Consequently, a new emphasis on the plain or simple meaning of the biblical text, rather than the hidden or esoteric one, emerged.

This change in approach was not only due to intellectual interactions with their Muslim neighbours. The second factor that deeply influenced the work of the geonim was the emergence of the Karaites, a rival Jewish movement that favoured a more literalist approach to the biblical text. The Karaites ridiculed the rabbis' use of the midrash, rejecting rabbinic interpretations as groundless. Like the Sadducees before them, the Karaites claimed that the rabbis were favouring the oral law over the written law. The Karaites' different conception of Jewish law inevitably led to different expressions of Jewish practice. Their approach had tremendous popular appeal, as it did not require a class of scholars to interpret the law; at one point they even threatened to become the dominant power in Judaism. So the rabbis of the geonic period had no choice but to take seriously some of the Karaites' critiques of the rabbinic method; as a result we find the geonim fighting back and engaging head-on with Karaite discourse in their own work. The most prominent of the geonim to attack the Karaite philosophy was Saadia Gaon (882–942). He translated the Bible into Arabic (the day-to-day language of the Jews of Baghdad) and provided more literal and straightforward commentaries so that the sources of Talmudic thought would be more apparent and more accessible to the masses.

Saadia's day marked the pinnacle of the Babylonian academies. Soon after, their prestige waned and both the secular authority of the exilarch and the religious influence of the geonim no longer held sway with the rest of Diaspora Jewry. By the end of the tenth century the Abbasid empire, which had amassed numerous states in far-flung places, had become quite fractured, and Baghdad was beset by political turmoil. This instability was one impetus for the Jews to look outside Babylon for new opportunities. Although the Jews since biblical times had mostly been engaged in agricultural work, with a few artisans and merchants among them, beginning in the eighth century C.E. Jews found themselves concentrated mainly in urban centres. As a result, farming became less prevalent and Jews increasingly found themselves involved in commerce and finance (Grossman 2004, 2). This, in addition to their high rates of literacy, served them well over the next several centuries. Based on their successes in Babylonia, Jewish traders began moving west in search of new commercial ventures. Thus the centre of the Jewish world began to migrate toward Europe, especially Spain, Portugal, France, and Germany.

Sephardic: Jews whose ancestry and style of practice can be traced back to medieval Spain, the Mediterranean, and the Middle East.

Ashkenazi: Jews whose ancestry and style of practice can be traced back to medieval Germany and Eastern Europe.

Around this time Jews became split into two major ethnic divisions: Sephardic and Ashkenazi. **Sephardic** Jews can trace their ancestry to *Sepharad*—the countries of the Iberian peninsula (modern-day Spain and Portugal)—while **Ashkenazi** Jews trace their heritage back to those who settled in *Ashkenaz*, or Germany, between 800 and 1000 C.E. Both Sephardic and Ashkenazi Jews found much prosperity in these European locales until a series of expulsions and persecutions eventually sent them flocking to communities in North Africa and parts of Eastern Europe. Although all these Jews, regardless of geography, would have initially carried with them the laws and customs established in the Talmud by Babylonian Jewry, over time regional customs developed from different social and political circumstances. By the sixteenth century this had led to separate Ashkenazi and Sephardic codes of Jewish law, with each geographic region having its own distinct rabbinic authorities.

Sepharad

The period of Jewish settlement in Spain between approximately the late seventh century and early twelfth century is often referred to as a golden age of Jewish history. When the Moors (Muslims of mixed Arab, Berber, and Spanish descent) conquered southern Spain and Portugal, a unique period of cross-cultural exchange was ushered in and artistic, scientific, and philosophical endeavours flourished. Restrictions on Jews were lifted, and the favourable conditions allowed them to experiment with poetry and philosophy and even rise in the ranks politically. Jews in medieval Spain also served an important function as translators. As intermediaries between Muslim and Christian cultures, Spanish Jews were well positioned to translate newly arrived scientific, literary, and philosophical texts from Arabic and Greek into Hebrew. Through collaboration with Christian scholars, these Hebrew works would then be translated into Latin to facilitate their transmission to a far wider European audience.

But this age of prosperity and tolerance soon came to an end, as Christian kingdoms were waging the *Reconquista*, a battle to win back the Iberian Peninsula from the Moors. Around the same time, the Almohades, a Muslim sect with a stricter interpretation of Islamic law and practice, conquered the region in the mid-twelfth century, resulting in the forced conversion of many Jews and destruction of many synagogues and other Jewish institutions.

However, it was during this dark period that one of the greatest Jewish thinkers of all time, Moses Maimonides—also known as by the acronym Rambam (short for Rabbi Moshe ben Maimon)—was born in 1135. Forced to leave the Spanish city of Cordoba, Maimonides' family feigned conversion to Islam and moved first to Fez, Morocco, before settling in Cairo, which was then governed by a more tolerant Muslim regime. There Maimonides wrote his famous *Mishneh Torah*, a fourteen-volume codification of Jewish law, as well as the *Guide for the Perplexed,* a work that tried to reconcile Greek philosophy and Jewish law. He not only became the head of the Egyptian Jewish community but eventually served as court physician to the sultan of Egypt, Saladin.

But not all Jews travelled south during the oppressive reign of the Almohades. Some sought refuge to the north, in the re-conquered Christian regions of Spain and Portugal. But as more parts of the Iberian Peninsula fell under the control of Christians, the status of the Jews became quite dire. The crusades sweeping across Europe were certainly a factor leading to the deterioration of their position. Although the Crusades began as an effort to win back the land of Israel from Muslim control, the pope eventually gave permission for these battles to go beyond the borders of the Holy Land. Soon the Crusades and the Reconquista shared one ideology, and the Jews of Spain and Portugal became the victims of this religious fervour. By the 1300s a number of restrictions had been imposed on Spanish Jews, similar to those they had experienced in other times and places, such as being prohibited from holding public office. However, now they were also forbidden to fraternize with Christians, had to live in separate Jewish quarters in major cities, and were compelled to wear an identifying yellow badge to easily distinguish them from their Christian neighbours. They were regularly forced to endure assault, robbery, and numerous massacres.

To escape these persecutions, many Jews converted to Christianity. However, the conversions were often half-hearted, and in many instances Jews would assume the outward signs of Christianity while secretly staying true to their Jewish faith in private. These people became known as *conversos*, or "crypto-Jews." In 1477 Spain's Queen Isabella and her husband, Ferdinand, sanctioned a tribunal to root out and execute those who refused to make their conversion complete. Known as the Inquisition, the tribunal interrogated all recent converts, applying torture to obtain confessions and to compel crypto-Jews to inform on one another. Those who confessed and did penance were spared, but if it was discovered that they had relapsed, they were burned at the stake. Eventually the number of *conversos* proved to be too great; fearing that the Jews might succeed in luring Christians and other recent converts back to the practice of Judaism, in 1492 Isabella and Ferdinand issued the Edict of Expulsion, officially expelling the Jews from Spain. Many initially attempted to seek refuge in other parts of Christian Europe before moving on to places such as Turkey, North Africa, and the Middle East.

Kabbalah Beginning with the biblical book of Ezekiel, which describes the prophet's vision of God as a divine chariot, mystical texts contemplating the nature of God and how to directly experience God's majesty had long been embraced by communities of Jews. But the expulsion from Spain precipitated a crisis of faith that not only renewed Jewish interest in mystical traditions but also granted them popular appeal. From the post-biblical era through to the early medieval period, Jewish mysticism was concentrated mostly in *hekhalot* literature, texts that promoted austere practices, esoteric prayer, and meditations in order to guide the practitioner's soul on its perilous ascent through the seven heavenly realms. These mystical journeys would usually culminate in the mystic's encounter with God in his heavenly palace, or *hekhal*, in order to gain some sort of secret knowledge.

Beginning in the twelfth century, these ideas developed into a more holistic mystical system known as *Kabbalah*, from a word meaning "to receive." It was believed that the teachings of Kabbalah had been passed from teacher to student all the way back to the time of Moses, or even Adam. The centrepiece of this tradition is the Zohar. Although the text is attributed to the great second-century sage Rabbi Shimon bar Yohai, it is believed to have actually been written by the Spanish scholar Moses de Leon in the thirteenth century. Written as a line-by-line commentary on the five books of Moses, the Zohar understands the entire Torah as a code for deciphering the nature of God. In it God is envisioned as the *Ein Sof*—that which is limitless and beyond understanding. The Ein Sof manifests itself in the universe through ten *sephirot*, or emanations of energy, which contain both male and female aspects. Since this divine energy is dynamic, the actual configuration of the ten sephirot is thought to affect the fate of humanity on earth, but this is understood as a two-way street; indeed, in Kabbalistic thought, human action can affect the sense of balance within the godhead.

The more rationalist among the rabbis condemned these ideas, fearing they would lead to polytheistic beliefs, but Kabbalah continued to take hold among laypeople. The movement reached its pinnacle under Isaac Luria (1534–72), a Kabbalist who lived a century after the Spanish expulsion in the northern Palestinian town of Safed, which to this day remains a hub of Jewish mystical activity. The mystical system attributed to Luria is intricate and complex, but it resonated with the Jews of his day primarily for its ability to account for the hardship and ongoing expulsions in their lives. Lurianic Kabbalah explains the creation of the universe as follows: God contracted Godself in order to make room for the world and then put the ten emanations of the divine presence into vessels and released them into the cosmos. However, the divine light was much too powerful to be contained, and the vessels shattered, creating disharmony in the world. Accordingly it is up to humanity to initiate a tikkun olam, or repair of the world: to put back together the shattered shards of divine light that have left the world in chaos, the Kabbalist must engage in fervent study, meditation, and performance of God's commandments. Proper conduct and intentional performance of ritual will then bring on the arrival of the Messiah and end the period of Jewish exile.

Shabbetai Zvi One of the most ardent followers of Luria's teachings was Shabbetai Zvi (1626–76), a charismatic Turkish sage who got caught up in the messianic fervour of his age. Engaging in unusual behaviour from an early age, Shabbetai Zvi was banished by local rabbis from his hometown of Izmir, and once again from Salonika (considered a mystical centre in his day) for purportedly trying to conduct a wedding ceremony between himself and the Torah (Scholem 1973, 159). After wandering throughout the Ottoman empire, he eventually ended up in the Palestinian city of Gaza, where a local sage named Nathan proclaimed him the Messiah. As he played the part by riding around on horseback, news of this proclamation spread like wildfire and Shabbetai Zvi gained followers in Jewish communities far and wide, many of them making their way to Palestine to witness first-hand the end of days. Eventually his activities caught the attention of the sultan himself, who perceived him as a political threat; he was asked to choose between death and apostasy. Shabbetai Zvi chose to save himself and converted to Islam, dashing the hopes of his expectant followers. It was a devastating blow, as the Turkish mystic had been a symbol of hope for beleaguered Jews in both Sepharad and Ashkenaz. And like their brethren from the Iberian peninsula, the Jews of Ashkenaz were no strangers to misfortune.

Ashkenaz

Jewish life in medieval Ashkenaz was generally characterized by hardship, bigotry, and bloodshed. Nevertheless, one notable period of peace and affluence occurred between the ninth and eleventh centuries.

Feudalism and the Jews Although Jews had lived in this region since the days of the Roman empire, invasions by numerous Germanic tribes and the subsequent anti-Jewish policies taken up by the ruling church made it socially and economically unstable for hundreds of years. However, when Charlemagne conquered and united much of Central and Western Europe in 800 C.E., the prevailing laws of the Church were ignored or overturned; Jews flooded back into the areas along the Rhine River, seeking out new opportunities in trade and commerce. These vocations were a particularly good fit for Jews, since the feudal system was the norm in most parts of northern Europe at this time, which it made it quite difficult for them to own land.

Feudalism was a rigid system in which people had responsibilities to those above them in the hierarchy while asserting power over those below them. Land was apportioned by the monarch to feudal lords, who became heads of mini-states of their own by allowing knights and serfs to live on their land. The knights often controlled some portion of land themselves and were required to take an oath of loyalty, amass weapons, and fight on behalf of the lord to protect his property, while the serfs were lower-class residents who worked the land and paid taxes in exchange for the lord's protection.

The Jews were to a large extent outside this social organization, since they generally worked as merchants, lived in urban centres, and were exempt from military obligations. They also had their own self-sustaining economies. Jews tended to do business primarily with Jews in other towns and countries, and they would travel great distances, accumulating goods, important contacts, and valuable information from exotic locales. As a result, Jewish merchants were able to obtain more rare, high-margin goods such as silks, spices, and furs than their Christian counterparts. Such items could be afforded only by those at the top of the social hierarchy, which allowed Jews to become both prosperous and in demand by the nobility (Glick 1999, 45–47).

Generally a local charter would guarantee Jews some basic rights and outline their obligations, which often involved payments of exorbitantly high taxes to landowners or the state treasury. The outsider status of the Ashkenazi Jews was underscored by the fact that, when it came to most aspects of day-to-day life, Jewish law dictated how they conducted themselves. At this time halacha became the community touchstone in a completely unprecedented way. Since initially there was little expertise in rabbinic matters among the Jews living along the Rhine, this was another reason to stay in close contact with a vast network of other, similarly isolated Jewish communities dotted across Europe. So in many respects, the Jews of France and Germany were quite alien: socially and legally separate entities reliant more upon one another than anyone else in the highly stratified feudal societies in which they were living. Still, because of the flow of money and international goods they brought to the region, their presence was welcomed and any barriers to the flourishing of their businesses were removed.

Intellectual and Halachic Development In this environment, Jewish intellectual life also thrived. Two of the more notable rabbinic authorities of the period were Rabbi Gershom and Rabbi Shlomo Yitzhaki, who is better known by the acronym Rashi. Rabbi Gershom (c. 960–1040) established his own Talmudic academy, and scholars from all over Europe came to study under him. He is most famous for his influential modifications to Jewish law, including banning polygamy—which had been permitted according to biblical law—and requiring both husband and wife to consent in order for a divorce to be valid. Gershom's marital law reforms were quite radical and had far-reaching implications. Although, even after these changes were made, the husband remained the only party to the marriage who could initiate a divorce, the wife now at least had a bargaining chip to ensure that she was appropriately compensated should the relationship end. If these injunctions were violated a man would face excommunication, or being cut off entirely from the Jewish community. Given the precarious status of the Jews in Ashkenaz, excommunication was a very serious threat indeed: losing your entire social and economic network, with no place to take refuge, could leave you as good as dead.

While Gershom's student Rashi (1040–1105) may not have revolutionized Jewish social relations in the same way, his influence on Torah and Talmud study is just as deeply felt almost a thousand years later. His clear and concise commentaries on the entire Tanakh and most of the Babylonian Talmud became intensely popular. With his selection of the best examples of the midrash and inclusion of the plain-sense meaning of the text as well, Rashi's line-by-line commentaries seemed to be a winning combination. Eventually his work became so integral to the understanding of the text that no one, from the young pupil to the seasoned scholar, dared read either Jewish source without consulting his interpretations.

The Tide Turns: The First Crusade Towards the end of Rashi's life, the unique period of relative stability and royal favour that the Jews in the Rhine had enjoyed came to an end. With the empire once unified by Charlemagne now fragmented, the Church once again dominated social policy toward the Jews. The First Crusade to free the Holy Land began in 1096, and hordes of angry men, both knights and peasants, made their way across Europe in a murderous rage. Realizing that, in addition to the Muslims in Palestine, there were enemies of the Church much closer to home, many of the peasants made it their special mission to kill the "Christ-killers"; the Jews of the Rhineland were subjected to numerous massacres. Although bishops and archbishops did rail against these violent acts, there was no way to control the fury that had been unleashed. After the First Crusade, the Jews of Germany in particular constantly lived in fear of the next attack. Libellous accusations of child murder for Jewish ritual purposes became rampant, which further fanned the flames of anti-Jewish assaults. In the ensuing centuries Jews would have fewer and fewer rights all across Europe.

Expulsions and New Horizons Expulsion from several countries soon followed: from England in 1290, from France in 1394, and from parts of Germany in the 1400s. In some instances Jews would briefly be allowed back into these places after paying large sums of money, only to be ousted again. They were blamed for everything from bad crops to foreign invasions. The worst of the accusations was that they were somehow responsible for the Black Death, a vicious plague estimated to have killed approximately twenty-five million people across Europe between 1348 and 1350. Jews were tortured, and many falsely confessed to initiating a plot to kill Christians by poisoning wells, food, and so on. Copies of these false confessions were sent from town to town, unleashing more bloodshed among Western Europe's Jewish residents.

For the Jews of Germany and other parts of Western Europe at this time, Poland would prove to be a haven. As was the case in other European centres, the Jews had originally been welcomed into Poland to help bolster the country's economy. Although violence against Jews sometimes erupted there too, it was mild compared to what they had faced in other parts of the continent. By the end of the fifteenth century the majority of Ashkenazi Jews had migrated eastward, making Poland the new centre of European Jewish life. In the mid-sixteenth century Polish Jews were even granted self-government. Each city or town had its own assembly of elders, known as a *kahal*, that would collect taxes and oversee the management of Jewish courts, schools, and other communal institutions. The great rabbinic academies of Poland arose and **Yiddish** flourished as the primary language of Ashkenazi Jewry. The **shtetl**, a small town or village inhabited almost exclusively by Jews, also became a fixture of Jewish life at this time.

Yiddish: the language of Ashkenazi Jewry. It is a unique mixture of German, Hebrew, Aramaic, and Russian, written in Hebrew characters.

Shtetl: a Yiddish word for the small towns and villages Eastern European Jews lived in from 1600 until their destruction by the Nazis in the 1930s and '40s.

Hasidism: the Jewish piety movement that arose in Poland and the Ukraine in the 1700s. The movement was initially based on the mystical teachings of the Baal Shem Tov, but today it has splintered into more than thirty distinct sects.

Hasidism Toward the beginning of the eighteenth century, the movement of **Hasidism**, or Jewish piety, developed. Deeply influenced by Jewish mysticism, Hasidism was a response to the rigidity and elitism of the rabbinic system as it had taken expression in Poland. Rabbi Israel ben Eliezer, also known as the Baal Shem Tov, brought Judaism back to the masses by encouraging them to develop a direct relationship with the Divine. Focusing less on intensive study and the proper execution of ritual, Hasidic teachings privileged religious fervour over reason and promoted singing, meditation, and prayer as a means of separating oneself from the material world. This approach was frowned upon by the traditionalist Jews of Lithuania, who saw Judaism as a religion of Talmud study. They asserted their displeasure by referring to themselves as *Mitnagdim*, meaning "those who are opposed." But the Baal Shem Tov's teachings

Haskalah: the Jewish Enlightenment, in which traditional attitudes toward religion were challenged as Jews encountered the new scientific, philosophical, political, and cultural modes of thought that were gaining ground in Europe.

were warmly embraced by the Jews of the Ukraine, who lived in poor rural areas that were suffering tremendously as the Polish Commonwealth began to disintegrate. Hasidism remained influential in the region and eventually transcended its Polish-Russian roots. Although the Enlightenment weakened its appeal, this popular movement and philosophy retains hundreds of thousands of adherents to this day, has splintered off into more than thirty major dynasties, and is now considered one of the movements within ultra-Orthodox Judaism (see below).

By the end of the eighteenth century Poland had been subjected to numerous foreign invasions; its territory was divided up among the three neighbouring nations of Russia, Austria, and Prussia. Most Jews now found themselves subjects of the Russian empire and their residence limited to an area known as the Pale of Settlement. Although they were subject to similar restrictions as Jews had faced elsewhere, the autonomy of self-governing Jewish councils was left intact and shtetl life went on as before, despite the fact that most Jews were living in abject poverty. Although life in Russia was not easy, it would become unbearable when a wave of *pogroms*, or organized anti-Jewish riots, swept through the country in the late 1800s. Most Jews would flee to the United States, while others would try their luck in Turkish-ruled Palestine.

Over the next two hundred years, Jewish life would change radically. Although both Sephardic and Ashkenazi Jews had endured terrible persecutions, humiliations, and forced conversions since the Middle Ages, the worst atrocity yet was still to come.

The Modern Period (from c. 1800)

Enlightenment and Emancipation

While Jewish law dominated the culture of medieval Jewry, with the advent of the Enlightenment, the monopoly of the rabbis on every aspect of Jewish life ended. The Enlightenment was a period in European history when traditional institutions, customs, and values were critically reexamined. Cultural and intellectual life blossomed, along with new socio-political movements and rational and philosophical thought, and soon science prevailed over religion as the major source of authority. Given that it was an age characterized by multiple and often contradictory philosophies, there is no consensus as to when the Enlightenment actually began. However, one major turning point during this period was the French Revolution (1789–99), which abolished feudalism and the stranglehold of the Church on the populace. In its aftermath, equality was in theory granted to all the men of France, regardless of status, sect, or religion. But for the Jews who had been let back into France just over a century earlier, it was not until the rise of Napoleon that these reforms took the force of law in any meaningful way.

Although Napoleon's personal feelings toward the Jews were not necessarily positive, he seemed to see some political benefit to gaining their support throughout his empire. In every region he conquered, he overturned laws that had confined Jews to ghettoes in the poorer, run-down areas of cities, and in 1807 he recognized Judaism, along with Catholicism and Protestantism, as an official religion of France.

As a new era of tolerance toward minorities spread throughout Europe, the Jews were emancipated in other countries as well, finally receiving recognition as citizens. With citizenship came rights long denied to them, including the right to vote, to live where they wanted, to attend universities, and to pursue careers of their choosing. Although this did not snuff out lingering discrimination and bigotry, and though legal rights did not always translate into lived realities, it certainly made the status of Jews less precarious.

Moses Mendelssohn

In tandem with these developments, Judaism was undergoing an Enlightenment period of its own. Known as the **Haskalah**, from the Hebrew word for wisdom, this new movement helped to assimilate the Jews into mainstream European culture. But it also precipitated a splintering of traditional Judaism into distinct denominations and altered Jewish practice forever. The figure most closely associated with the Haskalah is Moses Mendelssohn (1729–86), a German Jewish philosopher who achieved a level of intellectual success unknown to most Jews in his day. After centuries of living in ghettos, Jews had become quite isolated and insular, and Mendelssohn recognized that his community needed to be better integrated into secular German society if they were ever to be truly accepted by their fellow Europeans. He strongly believed that a better understanding of German language and culture would open up these avenues to Yiddish-speaking Jews, allowing them to participate in German intellectual life as never before.

Since the Torah was a text routinely read by Jews, Mendelssohn saw it as an ideal vehicle for introducing the richness of High German to his community. He undertook a uniquely Jewish translation of the Hebrew Bible into German and also authored an accompanying commentary, which included traditional interpretations as well as his own insights, which he hoped would serve as a gateway to the outside world. The project was a success, and soon Jews were publishing Torahs in a variety of European languages. More literacy in these languages meant more access to new literature and new ideas, and more active involvement in the new political movements sweeping across the continent. Mendelssohn continued to work tirelessly for his community, publicly advocating for Jewish civil rights and helping to lay the groundwork for Reform Judaism.

New Denominations

The Reform Movement Many of Mendelssohn's Jewish followers revelled in their newfound intellectual freedom. Some began to see rabbinic Judaism as too limiting and instead adopted Christianity, which also had the benefit of gaining them more civil liberties. Assimilation into wider German society was alluring, so much so that of Moses Mendelssohn's six children, only two remained Jewish. A significant number of those who had dabbled in the Haskalah wished to stay loyal to their faith but believed that Judaism itself needed to be more compatible with the secular modern world. Initially these reformers were just interested in making cosmetic changes to synagogue services to make them more aesthetically pleasing and in keeping with the times. The services were shortened and prayers and sermons in German were introduced, as were musical instruments.

But soon a group of young Jewish intellectuals, who because of emancipation had enjoyed the benefits of both a university education and traditional Jewish study, proposed more fundamental modifications. Ethics were emphasized over ritual, and Jewish dietary laws and other ritual obligations were abandoned. These Jews regarded themselves as part of a religious community, not a nation, and they eschewed the idea of a return to Zion. Descriptions of miracles and hopes for the coming of a Messiah were removed from the liturgy; Judaism was regarded as a living tradition that would evolve with the times, not as a rigid set of rules that were stuck in the past. There was a move to return to the biblical text and not be bound by its Talmudic interpretations.

Reform Judaism gained in popularity and similar movements arose in both Britain (where it was known as Liberal Judaism) and the United States, where Jews from across Europe were steadily moving because of the social and economic freedoms it offered. The movement's key principles were eventually articulated in a seminal document known as the *Pittsburgh Platform* of 1885. In 1937 the *Columbus Platform* would revisit in particular the rejection of Zionism, and many of the traditions formerly deemed antiquated would be re-embraced, but in the mid-1800s the Reform movement was appealing precisely because of those breaks with the past.

In keeping with the Reform vision of modernizing the tradition, another key innovation was deeming women to be "honorary men," granting them at least in theory the same religious rights and duties as men in both the home and the synagogue. From early on in the movement's history, both boys and girls had ceremonies to mark their birth and their coming of age, and both received a religious education, but it would take until 1972 for the movement to go so far as to ordain a woman as a rabbi.

Orthodoxy Although this new approach to Judaism helped to stem the tide of conversions to Christianity, more conventional rabbis were horrified by Reform Judaism and the reckless changes it had made to thousands of years of legal thought and tradition. Frustrated by their loss of community control, traditional rabbis fought back in an attempt to prove that classical interpretations of the Torah and modernity need not be mutually exclusive. Samson Raphael Hirsch (1806–88) was the most vocal of the traditionalists; he believed that study of secular subjects and engaging in European life were not only permissible but necessary. He also believed that the Torah and Jewish law remained the ultimate authority, providing guidance on how to be a good person as well as a good Jew. Still, it was important for him to participate in the wider culture in order to help promote Torah values and transform society for the better. Both modern Orthodoxy, which envisions a synthesis of religious learning and worldly knowledge, and ultra-Orthodoxy (also known as Haredi Judaism), which believes worldly involvement should be more limited, claim Hirsch's philosophy as the basis for their respective movements.

While most modern Orthodox Jews today maintain professional and business relationships with both Jews and non-Jews, Haredi Jews generally try to remain as separate as possible from their non-Haredi neighbours. Living in small, insular communities somewhat akin to the European shtetls, they continue to speak Yiddish among themselves and reject modern Western clothing in order to create a linguistic and visual barrier between themselves and the surrounding culture, whether they are in Israel or part of the Diaspora. Many Haredi men even shun traditional forms of employment, preferring to devote their days to Torah study. This often leaves Haredi women in the unenviable position of trying to raise a family while also being the primary breadwinner. This trend has led to staggering levels of poverty among Haredi Jews, especially in Israel (Rivlin 2011, 227).

Conservative Judaism In 1845 a German rabbi named Zacharias Frankel broke away from the Reform movement, believing that his colleagues had simply strayed too far from tradition. A leading figure in the *Wissenschaften des Judentums* movement, or "science of Judaism" school, along with other German-Jewish luminaries such as Leopold Zunz, Abraham Geiger, and Heinrich Graetz, Frankel believed that the new, scholarly approaches to religion and religious texts that had arisen in secular universities should be applied to the study of Judaism. Yet he also held that halachic practices such as keeping kosher had value and that something was lost when the Hebrew language was no longer used for prayer. But he differed from Hirsch as well, asserting that halacha had always evolved to reflect the needs of the times and that it needed to continue to do so.

This middle approach between Reform and Orthodox theologies found a particularly sympathetic audience in both the United States and Canada and came to be known as Conservative Judaism. Since, like Orthodoxy, the movement regards halacha as binding, women in Conservative Judaism were originally subject to the same leadership limitations and prohibitions they had always faced with rabbinic Judaism. However, in 1972 a group of women brought forward their desires for social equality in the synagogue, and eventually women were deemed able to take on the same halachic obligations as men. This would lead to the ordination of Conservative women as rabbis in 1985. Although membership has dwindled in recent years, it was once the largest Jewish denomination among North American Jews.

Reconstructionism In the mid-twentieth century a fourth major denomination developed in the United States, based on the teachings of Mordecai Kaplan (1881–1983). Reconstructionism is the smallest of the four movements, and like Reform Judaism, it does not regard halacha as binding but rather as a series of "folkways" that each community can choose to adopt. Certain practices, such as praying in Hebrew and Torah study, are particularly valued and promoted, but generally speaking, Western notions of ethics and morality take precedence over Jewish law.

In addition to the development of separate denominations, each with their own distinct theologies and philosophies, two other major events left their mark on modern Judaism: the Holocaust and the establishment of the state of Israel.

Anti-Judaism Becomes Anti-Semitism

The rise of nationalist movements in the late 1800s generally spelled trouble for European Jews, since anyone who seemed different was regarded with suspicion as possibly thwarting the unification of the nation-state. Jews, with their foreign languages and alien customs, were regarded as being disproportionately active in finance, the press, and radical political movements such as socialism. As a result, they were suspected of conspiring to undermine the very foundations of capitalist society. In Germany, which was experiencing an economic downturn, this era of mistrust gave rise to a political party whose primary platform was to rid the country of Jews. The party referred to itself as the League for Anti-Semitism. **Anti-Semitism** was a word coined in the nineteenth century to refer to the hatred of the Jews. According to racial theories prevalent in Germany at the time, "Semites" were people of Middle Eastern origin—namely the Jews—who were inferior to the "Aryans," who were defined as being of pure Germanic or Nordic ancestry.

The League for Anti-Semitism petitioned to bar Jews from schools and universities and from holding public office. Jewish-owned businesses were boycotted and pamphlets attacking every aspect of Jewish life were disseminated throughout the country. This once again resulted in waves of violence against Jews. The Jews of Germany had gained much since emancipation, and the current of hatred inspired by the anti-Semites was a terrible setback. The influence of the League waned once several of its leaders were found guilty of forgery and theft, but the damage had already been done. Realizing that they would never be fully accepted as German citizens, many Jews left the country for greener pastures in America (Sachar 1966, 342).

Anti-Semitism: hatred of and discrimination against Jews. Anti-Semitic ideas led to the death of six million Jews under the Nazi regime between 1933 and 1945.

Zionism: the movement to establish a Jewish homeland in the biblical land of Israel.

Zionism

Around the same time, Jews throughout Europe were also getting caught up in the nationalist spirit. As conditions became increasingly hostile toward them in Germany, France, and Russia, a desire for a Jewish national homeland was ignited. As already mentioned, the hope for a return to Zion had always remained alive in much of Jewish literature. For centuries Jews had prayed facing east, toward the direction of Jerusalem, and to ensure that the holy city was never far from their minds, many had placed a decorative plaque bearing the word *mizrach*—Hebrew for "east"—on a wall in their home.

Since the days of the destruction of the Second Temple there had continued to be a Jewish presence in Israel under a succession of foreign regimes: the Romans, the Byzantines, Arab Muslims, the Crusaders, the Mamluks (Egyptian Muslims), and the Ottoman empire (Turkish Muslims). Although the major centres of Jewish intellectual life had moved elsewhere, a strong sense of religious fervour inspired some Jews to return to Israel, especially when persecutions in other places intensified. But conditions were rough, and taking into account occasional attacks by the local Arab population, in addition to rampant illness and food shortages, Jews were not flocking back to such an environment in large numbers.

Nevertheless, in the nineteenth century, the conditions for realizing this dream of returning to the land of Israel on a large scale, of bringing an end to centuries of wandering from place to place, seemed within reach. The movement became known as **Zionism**, and it was championed by a Viennese Jew named Theodor Herzl. The Zionist movement was initially opposed by Orthodox Jews, who believed that a return to the Holy Land could be possible only with the coming of the Messiah, and it was equally resisted by Reform Jews, who feared it would raise further questions in the minds of Europeans about their national loyalties. But Herzl was undeterred. Although he considered other potential sites for a Jewish colony (both Argentina and Uganda were at one point on the table), he eventually settled on the biblical land of Israel and went about raising support from Jews and non-Jews alike for the creation of a modern Jewish state. Believing that diplomacy was the key to assuring a viable Jewish homeland, Herzl met with key international figures, including the sultan of the Ottoman empire, the pope, and the leaders of Germany, Italy, Austria, and Britain, in an attempt to win their endorsements. But while Herzl worked the political end of things, other factions of Zionists, especially those from Russia with socialist leanings, were interested in a more practical approach; after Herzl's death, all efforts went into increasing the settlements of Jews in Palestine.

PERSPECTIVES

Other Conceptions of Zionism: Ahad Ha'am and Rav Kook

Zionism as a movement gained tremendous traction, and all the major thinkers of the nineteenth and early twentieth century, from philosophers to theologians, engaged with it in some way. But while Herzl represented political Zionism, there were other influential streams of Zionist thought: cultural Zionism and religious Zionism.

Cultural Zionism is primarily identified with a nineteenth-century Russian Jew named Asher Ginsburg, better known by his pen name, Ahad Ha'am. Ahad Ha'am viewed Palestine as the cultural and spiritual centre of the Jewish people and hoped that, as an ideal, it could serve to renew Jewish identity and Jewish culture, which had been badly weakened by centuries in the Diaspora. Since Jewish practice could no longer be relied upon to unify the Jews, he advocated for a secular Jewish culture rooted in the Hebrew language. While he did not oppose the idea of a Jewish state, he did warn early on of potential conflicts that could arise with the indigenous Arab population (Prior 1999, 230).

The influential Jewish thinker Martin Buber (1887–1965) was a great admirer of Ahad Ha'am's vision. Buber is most famous for his philosophical treatise *I and Thou*, which maintains that the world is divided into a series of relationships defined by language: there is I–It, which emphasizes the division between people and objects, and I–Thou, which strives for unity and commonality between subjects and allows us a glimpse of the Divine. Unlike his friend the eminent philosopher and educator Franz Rosenzweig, who was ambivalent about the role of Palestine in revitalizing Jewish spirituality, Buber was an ardent Zionist. Like Ahad Ha'am, he saw Zionism as having a spiritual and ethical basis that could renew what it meant to be Jewish in the world. Although it was a highly unpopular position at the time, Buber championed the creation of a bi-national state in Palestine, a country that could be a homeland to both Palestinians and Jews.

While both cultural and political Zionists tended to be secular, in the late nineteenth century a group of Orthodox Jews also began to promote the establishment of a modern Jewish state. At the centre of this movement was Rabbi Abraham Isaac Kook, who began to justify Jewish settlement in Israel according to Jewish law. Although it had long been understood in traditional circles that a return to Jewish self-rule in the land of Israel could be brought about only with the coming of the Messiah, and that any human attempt to hasten the process was in defiance of God's plan, Rav Kook regarded the secular Zionist movement as a tool of God for establishing a sovereign state based in Torah principles (Prior 1999, 71). While he went on to become the first chief Ashkenazi rabbi under the British and influenced many Orthodox youth to settle in Palestine in the pre-state period, he made few inroads among ultra-Orthodox factions.

To this day most ultra-Orthodox Jews who reside in Israel do not recognize the legitimacy of the state and refrain from participating in the political process. However, the religious Zionist movement remains active in contemporary Israeli life and is strongly associated with many of the Israeli settlements in the West Bank (see Map of Israel and the Palestinian Territories, page 66). Those affiliated with Gush Emunim, a more radical political faction started by Rav Kook's son, believe that all territory acquired in Israel's wars is part of God's biblical promise to the Jewish people and should not be negotiated as part of any potential peace settlement.

After the First World War, the British gained control of most of the Middle East and gave their official support to establishment of a Jewish homeland in Palestine. Jewish immigration continued to thrive, but as the number of Jews increased, the local Arab population began to worry about their future. Rioting began, and so as not to damage their relationship with the Arab world, the British reversed their position, virtually putting a stop to Jewish immigration to Palestine and declaring their intention to make Palestine an Arab-ruled state within a decade. Leadership within both the Jewish and Arab communities rejected this decision, but the limitations on Jewish immigration in particular proved to be devastating for world Jewry. This was in 1939, and the situation for Jews in Europe was about to change in a profound way.

The Holocaust

In the wake of the First World War, the economic situation in Germany was dire. Germany had been blamed as the instigator of the war, and the Treaty of Versailles required that the country disarm, give up territory, and provide monetary compensation to other European nations that had suffered losses. In this political climate, German anti-Semitism found a new foothold. In 1933 the Nazi Party, which advocated for racial purity of the German people, came to power under Adolph Hitler. Although the Roma people, gays and lesbians, communists, and the disabled were also targeted by the party's policies, all the misfortunes that had befallen Germany were attributed to the Jews. Jews were barred from most professions and were unable to own land or attend schools and universities. They were prohibited from marrying Aryans—those of so-called pure German blood—and pre-existing marriages between Jews and Aryans were annulled. Jews were stripped of all civil rights, as well as their citizenship. In 1938 a mass pogrom was undertaken: across the country, Jewish-owned shops and synagogues were destroyed. The event signified an end to most Jewish social and cultural life in Germany, and Jews began leaving en masse, many seeking refuge in other parts of Europe, since immigration to places such as Palestine, the United States, and Canada was virtually impossible at the time.

Then, in 1939, Germany invaded Poland. Not only did this precipitate the outbreak of the Second World War, it signified a shift in Nazi policy toward the Jews.

Shoah: a word meaning "calamity," the Hebrew term for referring to the Holocaust.

With the occupation of Poland, a further two million Jews fell under their administration. At this point the Nazis began rounding up Jews in ghettos and then transferring them to labour and extermination camps, where they were gassed in ovens and burned in crematoria. This new strategy was known as the "final solution" to the so-called problem of the Jews. As more and more European countries and parts of North Africa fell under Nazi control, major centres of both Ashkenazi and Sephardic life were destroyed. By the end of the Second World War, six million Jews, approximately one million of them children, had been murdered across Europe. To Jews this mass murder came to be known as the Holocaust, or **Shoah**, a Hebrew word meaning "calamity."

Establishment of the State of Israel

A significant source of hope in the post-Holocaust era was the establishment of the state of Israel in 1948. In the wake of the Second World War, after the atrocities that had befallen the Jews came to the world's attention, the United Nations voted to create a Jewish homeland in Palestine. Although this would provide a solution for the thousands of Jewish refugees rendered homeless by the Nazi war machine, it created a new refugee problem for the indigenous Palestinian Arab population, many of whom would be displaced. The original U.N.-sponsored plan included a partitioned state, with one portion of land going to the Jews and the other to the Arabs. Jerusalem, as a city holy to Jews, Muslims, and Christians, would serve as a shared capital. Dissatisfied with the way the land was to be divided, the Palestinian Arab community as well as the states in the Arab League rejected the plan; the Jewish leaders, however, were willing to accept the terms and pleased by the official recognition of a Jewish homeland that the plan granted.

When a Jewish state was declared, the governments of Lebanon, Syria, Iraq, Egypt, and Jordan invaded the country. For the state of Israel this marked the beginning of decades of conflict with the Palestinians as well as neighbouring Arab states. Numerous wars were fought over division of the territory (see below) and thousands of people were killed. While peace treaties have since been signed with Egypt and Jordan, and some of the land gained in subsequent wars has been handed back by the Israelis, the region remains mired in violence. The majority of residents, whether Israeli or Palestinian, have now accepted the necessity of a two-state solution, but negotiating the terms and boundaries of these states remains problematic. Nonetheless, several joint Israeli-Palestinian ventures focused on shared environmental issues (such as water scarcity), medical concerns, education, and dialogue provide hope for the future.

Jewish Life in Israel Since so much of Jewish spiritual life, practice, and identity was developed in the Diaspora, with the establishment of a Jewish state, Jews living in Israel had to redefine what it meant to be Jewish. For many, and especially in light of the Holocaust, the age-old Jewish rituals seemed meaningless. Many wanted to break with the past, which included abandoning Yiddish, the language of the European ghettos. Instead, Hebrew was chosen as the language of the new state, and thanks to the pioneering efforts of Eliezer Ben Yehuda, the ancient tongue once reserved for scriptural study and prayer was revived and transformed into a language of everyday speech. For these "new Jews," living in Israel and contributing to the development of a society

Map of Israel and the Palestinian Territories

In 1967 Israel went to war with Egypt, Syria, and Jordan, and in six days it was able to capture the Old City and East Jerusalem as well as the Golan Heights and the areas known as the West Bank, Gaza, and Sinai. While the Sinai and the Gaza Strip have been handed back to Egypt and the Palestinians respectively, the other areas remain in dispute. As this map illustrates, parts of the West Bank are currently under Palestinian administrative control, but this limited autonomy is complicated by large settlements of Israelis scattered throughout the area that continue to be governed by Israel. The final status of the West Bank and the Israeli settlements is to be part of a future peace agreement between Israel and the Palestinian leadership. As of 2011, these negotiations were at an impasse.

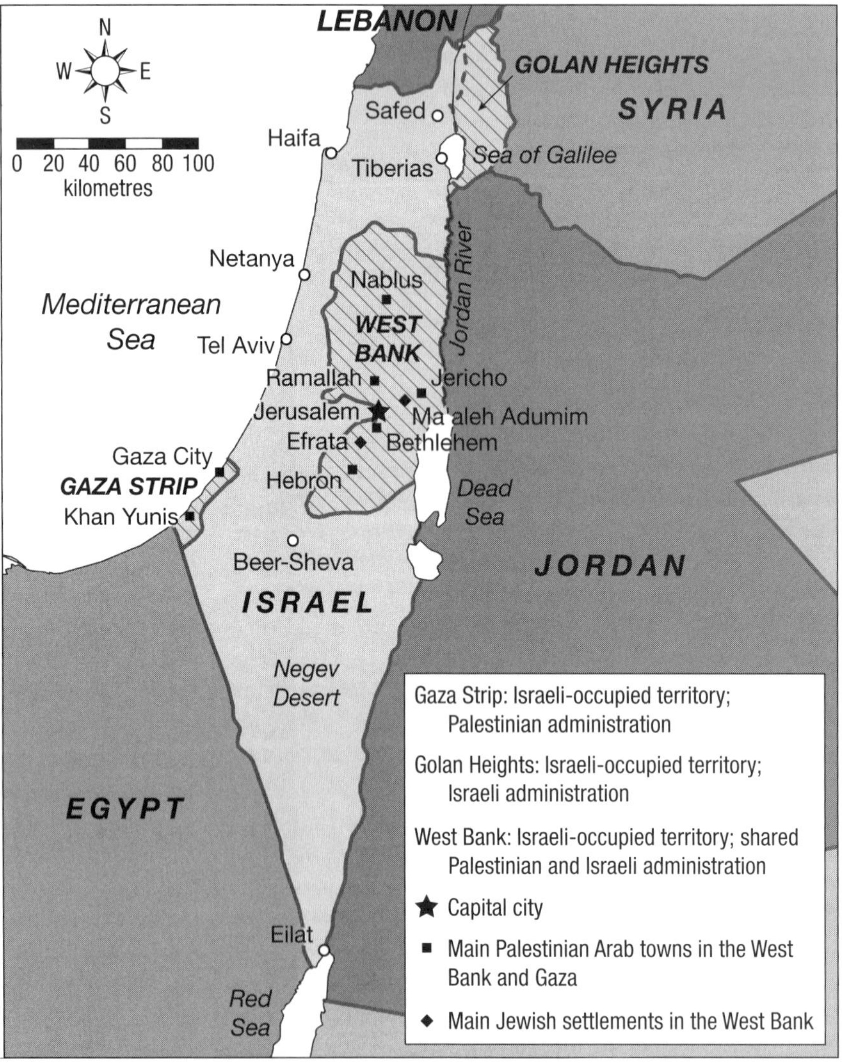

based on Jewish cultural values became the primary basis of their Jewish identity. Although the majority of the population is decidedly secular, a sizeable number of ultra-Orthodox Jews also live in Israel and have a significant voice in governing the country. As a result, all citizens, regardless of ethnicity or religion, are generally subject to a secular legal system similar to the type we have in Canada, but when it comes to matters such as marriage, divorce, death, and conversion, Orthodox halacha has the final say in the lives of Jewish citizens (see "Authority" and "Identity" below).

SPIRITUAL AND RELIGIOUS PRACTICES

Although, in theory, observance of Jewish law had always been a personal choice—since Jews were generally ostracized by the dominant culture in the places they settled—being accepted as part of the Jewish community was paramount. Historically speaking, being accepted meant adhering to the precepts of Jewish law as defined by the local ruling rabbis. However, in a post-Enlightenment Jewish world, strict adherence to Jewish practices became voluntary in a whole new way. Once Jews were granted basic rights as citizens in several countries and the rabbis of the shtetl lost their monopoly on Jewish life, many Jews began to look at their options and reassess the role these ancient traditions would have in their lives. As a result, today observance of these rituals varies. While Orthodox Jews tend to be most stringent in matters of Jewish practice, other contemporary Jews may choose to strongly embrace some practices while rejecting others.

Jewish Feminist Ritual: A Twentieth-Century Innovation

After the Enlightenment, perhaps the next major social and political trend to affect modern Jewish practice so profoundly was the feminist movement. Since the 1970s, feminist thought has left an indelible mark on Jewish practice in all the major denominations. For Jewish women who were at the forefront of the women's rights movement in the United States in particular, the dissonance between changes they were seeing in American social policy and the static nature of synagogue and Jewish institutional life was profound. Realizing that they could not limit their feminist critique to existing American socio-economic issues, a fledgling movement of Jewish feminists sought to achieve equal participation of Jewish women in all aspects of Jewish life (Hyman 2008, 224). Eventually this would translate into the development of Jewish feminist rituals, either by creating entirely new practices, such as all-women Torah readings, or by reclaiming and adapting existing traditions, such as naming ceremonies for newborn daughters. In the process, Jewish feminists have not only created new traditions but have infused old ones with a new, egalitarian ethos. In the following discussion of spiritual and religious practices, there is not one custom or institution that has not in some way been altered by Jewish feminist thought.

The Synagogue

Coming from a Greek word meaning "house of gathering," *synagogue* is of ancient origin. As the name implies, a synagogue was a venue in which the community could gather for a variety of reasons. Early sources tell us that synagogues were used for political meetings and social gatherings and as schools, courts, and hostels (Levine 1996, 430). In other words, it was not reserved for religious activities alone, although prayer, public readings of scriptures, and sermonizing most certainly took place there as well.

Today's synagogues continue in that ancient model and often double as community centres, with adjoining schools and social halls to serve all a community's needs. In smaller communities in particular, where other Jewish organizations and institutions may be scarce, the synagogue becomes the focal point for all Jewish life, whether ritual, social, or cultural. Public lectures, Hebrew classes, singles events, and youth group activities often take place within a synagogue's walls.

Public Worship

Regarding the synagogue's religious function, most communal Jewish worship does take place in the synagogue, but a synagogue is not necessary for prayer or for reading aloud from the Torah. Prayer can take place anywhere and at any time, as long as the setting does not detract from the appropriate spiritual intentions.

Minyan: the quorum of ten people required for the recitation of certain prayers.

Tallit: the prayer shawl worn in the synagogue.

Tefillin: small black leather boxes worn on the head and arm during morning prayers. The boxes contain passages from the Hebrew Bible.

There are three set times for prayer during the day: morning, afternoon, and evening services. Jews can recite their prayers in any language, although it is generally preferred that services be conducted in Hebrew, which is considered the language of holiness. Prayers typically express praise and thanksgiving to God or ask for divine mercy and forgiveness.

Words

Prayer and Spiritual Intention: A Hasidic Tale

Although Jews are expected to make use of the traditional liturgy in the siddur, a lack of literacy was never to prevent anyone from participating in public prayer, as revealed in this story about the Hasidic master the Baal Shem Tov:

Once on Yom Kippur, the Jewish Day of Judgement, an illiterate shepherd boy entered the synagogue. The boy was deeply moved by the service, but since he could not read the prayers he started to whistle, hoping to offer his haunting melody as a gift to God instead. Members of the congregation were horrified—who dared to desecrate their prayers in such a fashion? Several congregants wished to throw the boy out, but the Baal Shem Tov intervened. "You should be thanking this child," he said. "For until now, our prayers were not reaching the heavenly court. But this shepherd's whistling was so sincere, so pure, that it ascended straight to God, taking the rest of our prayers with it."

Most of the liturgy in the traditional siddur, or prayer book, can be recited on one's own, but certain prayers require a minimum of ten people, or a **minyan**, as it is called in Hebrew. In Orthodoxy it is necessary for all ten people to be men over the age of bar mitzvah (thirteen years old), whereas in the more liberal streams of Judaism, the minyan can be made up of both men and women.

Structure

There are no formal requirements as to what a synagogue should look like; in fact, the architecture of synagogues is as varied as the communities in which they are built. The prevailing architecture of the time and place is usually what determines what a synagogue will look like. Thus the synagogue in Kaifeng, China, built around 1163 C.E., resembled a Chinese temple from that period, while the synagogue in Cochin, India, retains several elements of a Hindu temple. Synagogues in Europe tended to be patterned after churches, while in Muslim-dominated lands, synagogues were often indistinguishable from mosques.

Generally speaking, though, synagogues tend to have a raised platform from which the designated prayer leader conducts the recitation of prayers, an ark where the Torah is kept, and a lamp reminiscent of the menorah, or candelabrum, that stood first in the desert Tabernacle and then in the Temple. Some traditional synagogues also include a *mehitzah*, a partition meant to separate men from women during worship, to ensure proper decorum between the sexes.

Attire

During morning prayer services, traditional men (and some women) wear *tefillin* and *tallit.* The **tallit** is a fringed four-cornered garment that is worn as a prayer shawl. The fringes, according to medieval commentators, are to serve as a constant reminder of God and God's laws. Although the tallit is traditionally worn over the shoulders, some practitioners also cover their head with the shawl. This allows them to block out all distractions and focus intently on their prayers.

Tefillin are also meant to help achieve a sense of closeness to the Divine. According to the prayer one is required to recite before putting on tefillin, they are meant to instil a sense of being bethrothed to God. Also known as *phylacteries,* from a Greek word meaning "amulet," tefillin are small black boxes connected to leather straps. They are worn on one's head and arm in a literal reading of a verse in Deuteronomy 6:8: "And you shall bind [these words] for a sign on your hand, and they shall be for frontlets between your eyes." They are meant to serve as a reminder that God led the children of Israel out of Egypt. The Shema prayer, as well as three other sets of biblical texts that refer to tefillin, are placed inside the black boxes. Like a Torah scroll, these texts are handwritten on parchment. If the texts contain even a single error or blemish, they are not considered appropriate for fulfilling the commandment.

Dress Code in Daily Life

In more traditional denominations of Judaism, modest dress is required for both men and women. What constitutes modest dress varies from community to community, but for Orthodox women this means not wearing revealing clothes such as short skirts and sleeveless or low-cut tops. It also means that married women must cover their heads, as their hair is deemed to be sexually provocative to men other than their husbands or close relatives. Many married Orthodox women wear a loose headscarf to fulfil this commandment, while others wear a wig—known as a *sheytel* in Yiddish—in order to conceal their own hair in public.

It has also become customary for Jewish men to cover their heads as an acknowledgment of God, the higher power above. While in some ultra-Orthodox communities the covering is a black or large fur hat, more common is the *kippah*, a small, round skullcap. Among Orthodox men, the kippah is worn at all times. In Conservative, Reform, and Reconstructionist communities, men as well as women may wear a kippah during prayer or when engaging in traditional study.

Major Jewish Festivals

The Jewish calendar is a lunar calendar, which means that each month follows the cycles of the moon and is about 29 or 30 days long. However, because the lunar year comprises only 354 days, as compared to the 365 days in a solar year, every few years an additional month is added to the Hebrew calendar. This ensures that the lunar calendar keeps pace with the solar calendar and Jewish festivals occur within the same season each year. This is important, since most of the key Jewish holidays correspond to significant periods in the agricultural cycle in addition to commemorating specific events in Jewish history. As an example, Passover, in addition to being a celebration of the Israelites' freedom from bondage in Egypt, also marks the spring harvest.

A day on the Hebrew calendar begins at sunset, as opposed to sunrise; hence all Jewish festivals begin in the evening. In rabbinic times the months and festivals were set according to sighting of the new moon. Reports of new-moon sightings would be evaluated in a rabbinic court; once the rabbis were satisfied that they had accurate testimonies from two reliable witnesses, official confirmation would be disseminated throughout the Jewish world. Because it often took a few days for the news to reach communities outside the land of Israel, it became a practice in the Diaspora to celebrate a holy festival over a two-day period, just to make sure that their own calculations and observations conformed with the practice of the greater Jewish community. Although eventually the calendar was fixed to avoid miscalculations, it became a custom among Diaspora Jews to continue observing the additional days. This is still the case among Orthodox and Conservative Jews living outside Israel, while Reform and Reconstructionist Jews have abandoned the practice.

The Sabbath

The Sabbath is a weekly day of rest that commences on Friday night at sunset and ends at sunset on Saturday evening. It is a commemoration of the fact that God created the universe in six days, according to the Genesis narrative, and rested on the seventh day. Keeping the Sabbath as a holy day by refraining from all work is the fourth of God's Ten Commandments.

But how does one define *work*? In a modern context, one might think that strenuous activity such as running is considered work, while operating a car or turning on a light switch, which requires little physical effort, would not be included in the prohibition. However, according to Jewish law, just the opposite is true. One can run on the Sabbath, but driving and turning on lights is forbidden. The rabbis of the Talmud determined that all activities connected with the building and operation of the Jerusalem Temple were prohibited on the Sabbath. This amounted to thirty-nine distinct categories of work: activities such as striking with a hammer, ploughing, sewing, building, sifting, baking, and lighting a fire. So *work* is not simply strenuous activity but rather deliberate activity in which something new is created. With the invention of electricity, turning on lights and driving a car came to be considered in Jewish law as similar to lighting a fire: a spark is created, which explains why they should be prohibited.

While all these various restrictions are generally observed only by more traditional Jews, even those Jews who do not regard themselves bound by halacha may participate in a traditional Sabbath meal with their families. Throughout history, Jews have tended to pull out all the stops for the Sabbath; even the poorest families would wear their finest clothes and do their best to prepare a more elaborate meal than usual to welcome the spirit of the Sabbath into their homes. Special songs and prayers are recited and two candles are lit before sundown so that there will be light and joy in the home. Other Sabbath traditions include blessing and drinking a cup of wine to add joy to the day, and serving two special braided loaves of bread, known as *challah,* in remembrance of the double portion of *manna,* a special bread-like food provided by God to the Israelites in the desert to prevent them from going hungry over the Sabbath.

Traditional Sabbath foods vary from community to community, but chicken soup—known reverently as "Jewish penicillin"—tends to be an Ashkenazi favourite, while *cholent* or *chamin*, a slow-cooked stew of beans, barley, potatoes, and meat, is a popular dish in both Sephardic and Ashkenazi homes. With the exception of cooking, which can be done according to rabbinic law on other Jewish festivals, all activities prohibited on the Sabbath are likewise prohibited for all major festivals.

Rosh Hashana

Rosh Hashana is the Jewish New Year, believed to be the day that God created the universe. Typically occurring in early fall, Rosh Hashana is celebrated over two days and marks the beginning of the ten Days of Awe, a period of reflection during which Jews are expected to seek forgiveness from one another and from God for their sins. The holiday is traditionally spent in the synagogue reciting special liturgy that speaks to God's majesty and God's capacity for forgiveness. A *shofar*, or ram's horn, is blown throughout the day to awaken worshippers to their obligation to repent for their sins. It is also a custom to eat sweet foods such as apples and honey in the hopes that one will have a sweet year.

Yom Kippur

Yom Kippur is the Jewish Day of Judgment and falls ten days after Rosh Hashana. It is the culmination of the ten Days of Awe. Since it is thought to be the day when one's deeds are weighed and evaluated, Jews spend the day fasting and praying for forgiveness from God so that they will be "inscribed in the Book of Life" for one more year. To facilitate their capacity for inner reflection and contemplation, traditional Jews not only refrain from eating and drinking but also abstain from sex, bathing, and wearing makeup or leather shoes. This is one of the four times in the year when the memorial service for the dead is read in the synagogue; it asks God to grant rest and peace to the souls of deceased relatives and those killed in persecutions of Jews through the ages.

Sukkot

Sukkah is a Hebrew word meaning "booth" or "hut." It refers to the temporary dwelling that Jews use for eight days during Sukkot, the Festival of Booths. During this holiday, which falls five days after Yom Kippur, traditional Jews try to eat, sleep, and study in the sukkah. The festival commemorates the huts in which the Israelites dwelled during their forty-year sojourn in the desert after the exodus from Egypt, but it is also a holiday of thanksgiving. To mark the harvest and thank God for the earth's bounty, Jews are commanded to gather together four plants: citron (*etrog*), closed date palm branches (*lulav*), and myrtle and willow branches (*hadass* and *arava*). Presumably chosen for their abundance and beauty at harvest time, a popular homily interprets these four species as being symbolic of four parts of the body: the citron is shaped like a heart, the date palm like a backbone, the myrtle like a mouth, and the willow like an eye. These body parts are in turn thought to represent compassion, assertiveness, and the ability to convey the teachings of Torah and perceive the inner good in everyone. As the allegory understands it, each of these elements is necessary for the proper worship of God.

Immediately following this festival is the holiday of Simchat Torah, which marks completion of the annual cycle of reading the entire Torah. It is celebrated with recitation of the final verses of Deuteronomy, followed by the opening chapters of Genesis, to illustrate that the cycle of Torah reading never truly ends. The Torah is taken out of the ark and paraded around the synagogue while congregants rise from their seats to sing and dance with it; it is not uncommon for the joyous revelry to spill out into the streets. Other customs include the carrying and waving of brightly coloured paper flags by children. These flags usually bear religious images such as the Ten Commandments, but in the recent past they have also had more nationalistic overtones, depicting scenes of Israel's military might. The origins of the flag ritual are obscure, but in North America they are often topped with apples and are thought to evoke the banners under which the twelve tribes of Israel marched in the desert.

Hannukah

Hannukah is a post-biblical holiday that marks reconsecration of the Jerusalem Temple by the Maccabees after it was plundered and made ritually impure during the oppressive reign of Antiochus IV, who prohibited many traditional Jewish observances (see "The Second Temple Period," above). According to the retelling of events in the books of the Maccabees and in the Talmud, when the Temple had once again been made pure, there was only enough oil to keep its *menorah*, a seven-branched oil lamp, lit for one day. However, miraculously, the oil lasted for eight days. As a result, Hanukkah is commemorated by lighting candles for eight days and eating oily foods such as fried potato pancakes and doughnuts.

Gambling games with spinning tops, called *dreidels*, are also commonly played at this time. The practice has a long history but its precise connection to Hanukkah is unknown. One popular explanation holds that Jews would play this spinning-top game as a ruse to obscure from the Greeks that they were actually studying Torah. Dreidels made outside Israel typically have a single Hebrew letter on each of their four sides: *nun*, *gimel*, *hay*, and *shin*. These letters stand for the Hebrew equivalent of "a great miracle happened there," alluding to the ancient miracle in the Jerusalem Temple. Since the events transpired in Israel itself, Israeli dreidels have a slightly different arrangement of letters (*nun*, *gimel*, *hay*, *pay*) to connote "a great miracle happened *here*."

Purim

Also a post-biblical holiday, the most unusual celebration of Purim commemorates events described in the book of Esther: a story of the survival of the Persian Jews after their planned extermination by the evil Haman, prime minister in the court of King Ahasuerus. Although it does not appear to correlate with any specific historical events, the story describes how Mordechai and Esther, the Jewish heroes of the story, interfere with Haman's plot and, with the help of Ahasuerus, reverse Haman's decree. The holiday is often described as the Jewish Halloween, as it is a custom to dress up and masquerade as someone else, possibly because Esther hides her Jewish identity for much of the story. It is also customary to drown out Haman's name with noisemakers when the book of Esther is read aloud in the synagogue.

Passover

As described in the introduction to this chapter, Passover is an eight-day spring festival commemorating the liberation of the Israelites from slavery in ancient Egypt. The story of the Exodus is retold on the first two nights, at a communal meal known as a seder. Some of the most prominent symbols used in telling the story are placed on a tray, or seder plate, in the centre of the table for all the participants to see. The foods on the seder plate are fixed—a shank bone, a roasted egg, a spring vegetable, a sweet paste, bitter herbs, and romaine lettuce—and each is meant to represent either freedom or slavery. In the past thirty years it has also become customary in some circles to add an orange to the seder plate, to represent women's fight for equality in Judaism. For the duration of the holiday, matzah is consumed in the place of bread and other leavened grain products (those that have come into contact with water and been allowed to rise). For Ashkenazi Jews, prohibited foods include rice, corn, and other legumes, while Sephardic Jews deem these to be permissible.

Shavuot

Shavuot commemorates the giving of the Torah on Mount Sinai and also marks the grain harvest, as well as the time when the first fruits would be brought to the Temple in Jerusalem. The holiday is celebrated by staying up all night immersed in Torah study and by eating dairy products, since, before the giving of the

Kosher: food that is fit for consumption according to Jewish law.

Torah, the Israelites were unaware of laws concerning the proper slaughter of animals.

Dietary Laws: Keeping Kosher

As you can see, food is central to the observance of many Jewish holidays. Food is not only about sustenance but also serves a symbolic function in Jewish life. Throughout history, Jews have remained distinct from their non-Jewish neighbours, in part because of their unique food restrictions and guidelines regarding food preparation.

Consider the following real-life examples of Jews "keeping kosher": a mother shopping for her family scrutinizes the label on a box of cookies before putting it in her cart, while across town a couple at a dinner party inquire whether the appetizers are made with shellfish or pork and whether the lasagne contains both meat and cheese. In our health-conscious and increasingly multicultural Canadian society, such behaviours are less conspicuous and less identifiably Jewish than they might have been at one time. Muslims, Buddhists, and Hindus, as well as ethical vegetarians, health-food junkies, and people with allergies, have similar concerns about the food they put in their mouths. Still, the intricacies of Jewish dietary restrictions are an example of the ways in which Jewish law touches on the most ordinary aspects of day-to-day living.

Eating Animals

According to the Torah, not all animals are considered **kosher**, or "fit," as the Hebrew word implies. The Torah provides a detailed list of which animals are permissible and which are forbidden for eating. For an animal to be kosher, it must have split hooves and must regurgitate its food before digesting it. According to these criteria, cows and sheep are kosher, as is their milk, while pigs and camels are not. Birds of prey such as hawks and vultures are not kosher, while chicken, ducks, pigeons, turkeys, and geese are suitable for eating, as are their eggs. Only fish that have both fins and scales are kosher, which rules out shellfish and squid. With the exception of one variety of locust that most Jews can no longer identify, insects are generally not kosher. Animals that have died from illness or have medical defects cannot be consumed.

In order for meat and poultry to be kosher, the animal must be slaughtered in a specific way by a person trained in Jewish law. The slaughtering techniques are intended to minimize the suffering of the animal as much as possible. After the animal is slaughtered, the blood, which is considered the life source of the animal, must be extracted through a salting process. If the blood has not been drained from the animal, the meat is not considered kosher.

Milk and Meat

Meat and milk products are not allowed to be eaten together. This is based on a biblical verse that prohibits the cooking of a baby goat in its mother's milk. While many explanations have been offered for this prohibition—that it is inhumane to eat a goat in the very milk that gave it life, that it shows a lack of compassion toward the mother, that this was a specific pagan practice that the Torah was seeking to outlaw—it became a custom among Jews to completely separate all dairy and meat products. This separation extended to the very plates, pots, and utensils used to cook, prepare, and eat the food. As a result, in homes and restaurants where the kosher laws are diligently observed, separate sets of dishes are kept for milk and meat products. After eating meat, it has also become obligatory to wait a designated amount of time before partaking of dairy.

Rationale for the Laws

The Torah does not provide a rationale for why certain animals are permissible and others are not. The first-century Alexandrian Jew Philo suggested that certain animals are prohibited because they possess undesirable qualities—in other words, "we are what we eat." From this perspective, Jewish dietary laws help to instil in us only the best of qualities from the animal world. Maimonides, the twelfth-century doctor-philosopher, similarly proposed that prohibited animals were unhealthy for the body. But for those who follow these commandments, the proposed explanations are not significant. For many, since eating is an activity that takes up so much of the day, the dietary laws are seen simply as a way to be mindful of what we eat, where it comes from, and how it was prepared.

This reconnection to our food can help to bring a sense of holiness into an otherwise mundane activity.

Kosher Labels Kosher certification bodies examine the ingredients used to make the food, supervise the preparation process, and inspect the processing facilities to make sure that kosher standards are maintained. Some kosher certifying agencies are quite strict while others are known to be more lenient in their understanding of what is permissible. Their labels are registered trademarks and cannot be printed on a package without explicit permission from the specific kosher certification agency (see box).

COR is the main kosher certification body of Toronto, while MK is affiliated with Montreal. The letter U within a circle is the symbol of the Orthodox Union in the United States, possibly the most widely recognized and trusted organization when it comes to matters of *kashrut*. A D next to one of these symbols means the product is dairy, while a P usually means *pareve*—the food can be consumed with either dairy or meat products.

Sources: (top to bottom) Kashruth Council of Canada; Jewish Community Council of Montreal; Orthodox Union; Kof-K.

Purity Laws

Outside of Orthodoxy, the purity laws are the least widely observed by contemporary Jews. As far back as the biblical period there has been a prohibition on having sexual relations with a woman having her period. We are not entirely sure why this is the case. Although it was a fairly common prohibition or taboo in many ancient cultures, some scholars have proposed that in ancient Israel it may have been linked to a larger understanding of death and illness. Biblically speaking, if you had recently been near a corpse or a severely ill person, or if you had expelled or been exposed to certain bodily fluids, such as semen and menstrual blood—both of which signified absence of life, or failure to make a baby—you were considered ritually impure. Impurity in this context did not mean that you were sinful, bad, or dirty in any way; rather, it might have meant simply that you had been exposed to death, and as a result were temporarily barred from the Temple of God.

Once the Temple was destroyed, the laws governing purity fell into disuse for the most part. However, since the taboo on sexual relations with a menstruating woman did not hinge on the existence of the Temple, it lingered on. According to Jewish law, a woman is required to wait until her period has ended, count an additional seven days, and then immerse herself in a ritual bath before resuming sexual relations with her husband. In Orthodox Jewish households this prohibition on sex extends to all touching between spouses, casual or otherwise, and many maintain separate beds during this time.

Attitudes toward women's menstrual "impurity" vary among Jewish feminists. Rachel Adler rejects the very notion that a woman's life-giving biological process should be associated with death, and believes that it is impossible to escape the connotations of dirt and sin inherent in the biblical understanding of menstruation (1993, 39). Other feminists prefer to focus on the spiritual possibilities offered by the *mikveh*, the ritual bath that renders the woman sexually available

Brit: the covenant that God established with the people of Israel in the Torah. One of the signs of the covenant is the *brit mila*, or circumcision, that all Jewish males undergo at eight days of age.

once more. Understanding water itself as a uniquely feminine symbol, Toronto-based rabbi Elyse Goldstein has proposed that women reclaim the mikveh as a vehicle for healing and rebirth (1993, 131). She, as well as other female rabbis, regards immersion in the mikveh as a way to mark significant events in a woman's life not already addressed by traditional Jewish rituals: for losses such as divorce or miscarriage and victories such as beating cancer, surviving domestic violence, or receiving rabbinic ordination (Hammer 2010).

Rites of Passage

Birth

Brit Mila The birth of a baby boy is commemorated with a *brit mila*, or circumcision ceremony, on the eighth day after the baby is born. This is in keeping with God's directive to Abraham in Genesis 17: 10–14 and marks the entry of the boy into the covenant with God:

> Every male among you shall be circumcised. You shall circumcise the flesh of your foreskins, and it shall be a sign of the covenant between me and you. Throughout your generations every male among you shall be circumcised when he is eight days old. . . . Any uncircumcised male who is not circumcised in the flesh of his foreskin shall be cut off from his people; he has broken my covenant. (NRSV 1993)

In the Middle Ages the circumcision ceremony was combined with naming the child, and it went from being a relatively private event to a public celebration that took place in the synagogue and was accompanied by wine and a celebratory meal. This continues to be the case today.

The circumcision is performed by a person known as a *mohel*, someone who is specially trained in the laws of brit mila. Today in Canada, the mohel often tends to be a physician as well. Traditionally the mohel is a male, although in recent years a few women have been certified by the Conservative, Reform, and Reconstructionist movements to perform the ritual.

Simchat Bat Circumcision is not required for girls, and given that it was commonly practised in many traditional societies, it is interesting that it is never even discussed as an option in classical Jewish sources. Although there are no formal requirements to mark the birth of a girl in Judaism, naming rituals for girls also go back to the Middle Ages. In the past forty years, in large part because of the impact of feminist thought on modern Judaism, the *simchat bat* ceremony, which formally welcomes the girl into the Jewish community, has become commonplace. Since Jewish law is silent on this matter, it is an opportunity for many Jewish families to create personalized rituals and prayers that reflect their hopes and dreams for their daughters. *Simchat bat* means "the joy of having a daughter."

Bar and Bat Mitzvah

The bar or bat mitzvah is the traditional coming-of-age ceremony for boys and girls. If you've heard of a bar mitzvah before, the term may conjure up images of an awkward preteen, his voice cracking as he sings before an entire community. Or maybe it makes you think of a lavish party, complete with a DJ, flashing lights, and lots of presents. While that may be the case today, the celebration has come a long way from its humble beginnings. The term *bar/bat mitzvah* simply means "son/daughter of the commandments." According to the Talmud, up to a certain age, boys and girls are regarded as not being responsible for their actions; their parents bear responsibility for all their good deeds as well as their bad ones. However, by the age of thirteen for boys and twelve for girls, children are considered mature enough to take on the obligation of fulfilling God's commandments.

Beginning in the Middle Ages, this entry into the world of Jewish law became an occasion of celebration.

Ketubah: a traditional Jewish marriage contract that stipulates a husband's religious obligations to his wife.

A boy would receive the honour of being called up to the Torah to recite the appropriate blessings and chant aloud the weekly reading in front of the whole congregation. This was often followed by a short speech directly related to the Torah reading, in which the young man could showcase what he had learned, and a celebratory meal. In some communities he might also be given his own tallit and tefillin to further underscore the fact that he was now considered an adult male according to Jewish law.

The tradition of an equivalent ceremony for girls is a much newer innovation. The first official bat mitzvah was held in 1922, when Judith Kaplan, daughter of Mordecai Kaplan, the first rabbi of the Reconstructionist movement, read aloud part of that week's Torah reading (Marcus 2004, 107). Today, in Conservative, Reform, and Reconstructionist congregations the bat mitzvah is no different from the celebration for boys. However, even in modern Orthodox and ultra-Orthodox communities the bat mitzvah is now a staple ceremony. The girl is expected to study a text of her choice, whether from the Tanakh or the prayer book, and give a lecture on it before the congregation (Marcus 2004, 115).

Marriage

Since having children is understood as an obligation according to Jewish law, and sexual relations are to occur only within licit relationships, marriage is highly encouraged in Judaism. However, marriage is not just about procreation; companionship and sexual pleasure are also understood as integral to marriage, even in traditional sources. Jewish weddings are extremely joyous occasions characterized by lots of boisterous music and frenzied dancing. In fact, it is a traditional obligation to make the bride and groom happy on their wedding day. Wedding traditions vary in each community, but traditional ceremonies tend to include two witnesses, a wedding contract known as a **ketubah**, a wedding canopy under which the ceremony takes place, at least one ring, and the breaking of a glass at the end of the ceremony.

Breaking of the Glass The rationale for breaking a glass at the end of the Jewish wedding ceremony has been the subject of much speculation. The rabbis suggested

The traditional ketubah, which dates back to Talmudic times, outlines a husband's obligations to his wife and describes how she will be financially compensated in the event of divorce. Today it has taken on a more symbolic role, characterizing the sanctity of Jewish marriage. As seen here, ketubahs have also become elaborate works of art that can be hung on the wall of the couple's home. This ketubah makes use of the classic Jewish folk art of paper-cutting. The traditional text lies at the centre of the piece, with swirling vines cut into the paper around it. Across the top and along the sides we find a verse from Jeremiah (25:10), which is traditionally sung at weddings.

Source: Ruth Stern Warzecha Gefen papercut, ketubah.com

that it is to help the celebrants recall the destruction of the Temple, while the Jewish mystics regarded it as a reminder that the world is fragmented and in need of repair. Folklorists suggest that it was adopted from Christian wedding customs and is supposed to scare away evil spirits, while anthropologists see it as a veiled allusion to the breaking of the bride's hymen, which would traditionally occur when the marriage was consummated on the wedding night. Whatever the reason, it is perhaps the most lasting image from a Jewish wedding and a moment always eagerly anticipated by the guests, as it means the celebrations can truly begin.

Death

Traditional death and bereavement practices are designed to help Jewish mourners acknowledge their loss so they can gradually return to everyday communal life. From the moment of death until burial, the body is guarded by special attendants. At one time this was done to ensure that the corpse was not stolen or desecrated; today it is simply part of paying respect to the dead. These attendants are also responsible for washing the body and wrapping the deceased in a clean white shroud. According to Jewish law, no embalming is allowed, nor are open caskets or cremation. In Israel no coffins are used, except in the case of military or state funerals. In Canada, on the other hand, the body is usually placed in a plain pine box. In either case, the body is buried as quickly as possible.

After the body is buried, family and friends gather at the home of one of the mourners for the *shiva*. Derived from the Hebrew word for seven, the shiva marks the seven days during which mourners remove themselves from regular, everyday activities. According to Jewish law, only a person who has lost a parent, spouse, sibling, or child is defined as a mourner. During the period of the shiva, mourners sit low to the ground, may tear their clothes, and are discouraged from bathing, shaving, having sex, cooking, or conducting business of any kind. A shiva is not like an Irish wake—music, dancing, and other forms of frivolity are considered inappropriate—but, depending on the circumstances surrounding the person's death, it need not be a silent, sombre event either. Traditionally, family and friends come to help comfort the mourners by preparing meals or sharing stories about the deceased. Community members will also come to participate in daily prayers and help make up a minyan so that the mourners can recite the *Kaddish*, the traditional prayer for the dead. After the shiva is over, traditional Jews may refrain from attending festive occasions and will continue to recite the Kaddish prayer daily for a full year after the person's death.

AUTHORITY

Since the destruction of the Second Temple there has been no centralized body with authority over worldwide Jewry. As indicated earlier, from approximately 500 C.E. until the 1850s, normative Judaism was a Judaism run by the rabbis. Rabbis functioned in many cases as de facto community leaders and dealt with political as well as religious matters. After the Enlightenment, many secular Jewish movements arose, as well as new religious denominations, and each developed its own institutional framework. As a result, Jewish religious authority began to splinter off in many different directions. Today rabbis are still esteemed members of the community, and for many they are the final authority on Jewish practice. Nevertheless, for others a rabbi is simply a spiritual leader who officiates at life-cycle events, and other community professionals, such as academics, teachers, counsellors, writers, artists, and politicians, may be just as influential in terms of how they understand their Judaism.

North American Leadership

Beginning in the nineteenth century, Jews came in vast numbers to seek refuge and new opportunities in America. While Europe had been the centre of Jewish life until the Second World War, after the Holocaust the United States became the new locus of Jewish leadership. Today most major Jewish institutions have their world headquarters in the United States.

Numerous secular Jewish organizations, such as United Jewish Federations of North America and B'nai Brith International, provide leadership and advocacy for Jewish communities by raising funds for Jewish education, arts, culture, social services, and community development projects. However, none of these plays any official role in religious life. Furthermore, secular organizations have numerous different mandates and different positions on key issues such as Israeli politics or dealing with anti-Semitism. Consequently, no one organization purports to represent the entire Jewish people.

Reform, Conservative, and Reconstructionist Leadership

In terms of religious leadership, the Reform, Conservative, and Reconstructionist movements all have their own rabbinical colleges. These ordain, or officially recognize, both men and women as rabbis so that they can go on to lead their own synagogue congregations or serve as community educators, military or hospital chaplains, or social service providers in the Jewish community. These rabbinical programs train their students in Jewish texts, academic biblical criticism, the history of Judaism, and Jewish practice and provide them with the vocational skills needed to provide spiritual guidance to members of their communities. Conservative rabbinical degrees focus more deeply on Jewish law. Anyone who graduates from one of these intensive five-year programs is considered qualified to be a rabbi.

Each of these denominations also has its own governing council, which sets ethical standards and guidelines for its rabbis and makes social, religious, and policy decisions on behalf of the movement. Reconstructionist and Reform laypeople are not bound by any of these decisions; Conservative Jews, on the other hand, may regard these rulings as halacha.

Orthodox Leadership

Orthodox Judaism trains prospective rabbis in seminaries known as a *yeshivot.* These students undertake a rigorous curriculum involving study of Jewish law and liturgy and spend their days poring over the Talmud and Jewish legal codes such as the Shulhan Aruch and related commentaries. Although a university degree is not a prerequisite for rabbinical study, at New York's Yeshiva University, the most widely acclaimed of modern Orthodox yeshivot, an undergraduate degree as well as the equivalent of a master's degree is required before ordination is granted.

For the majority of Orthodox laypeople, halacha as interpreted by rabbinic leadership is considered binding. Nevertheless, some rabbis are regarded as more authoritative than others. For instance, Rabbi Joseph Soleveitchik (1903–93), a former head of Yeshiva University, was one of the more pre-eminent figures of the twentieth century, while Rabbi Menachem Mendel Schneerson (1902–94), leader of the Hasidic group known as Chabad-Lubavitch, was so influential that many of his followers claim that he is the Messiah and eagerly anticipate his return to proclaim his true identity (Ehrlich 2005, 217).

Israel

In Israel only one denomination is recognized as having religious authority in matters of Jewish law, and that is Orthodoxy. Whereas in the Diaspora living according to Jewish law is essentially a personal choice, in Israel, as explained earlier, some aspects of Jewish law are incorporated into the laws of the state. This was established under British rule and accepted into law by the state of Israel in the early 1950s. The British also established the institution of two chief rabbis—one Ashkenazi and one Sephardic—appointed by the state; they have jurisdiction over personal status issues such as marriage, divorce, inheritance, burial, and conversion, as well as Jewish dietary laws, granting ordination to rabbis, overseeing holy sites such as the Western Wall, and heading rabbinical courts, where disputes over these issues are adjudicated. This encompasses quite a wide sphere of influence. In essence, if you are a Jew living in Israel, regardless of your individual beliefs, Jewish law as defined by the Chief Rabbinate will affect your most personal decisions, including, for example, how you get married.

Because marriage falls under the auspices of the Rabbinate, there is no civil marriage option in Israel, and marriages that are outlawed according to Jewish law—such as those between Jews and non-Jews and same-sex marriages—will not be performed. Similarly, only Orthodox clergy are recognized by the state as able to perform marriages, so a marriage conducted in Israel by a Reform rabbi has no official status. Nevertheless, there is a loophole: if you were married outside Israel, the state has no choice but to recognize your union. Consequently, many secular, interfaith, or same-sex couples travel abroad to tie the knot.

IDENTITY

There is perhaps no question so fraught as "Who is a Jew?" in contemporary Jewish circles. The simple answer is that traditional law considers you Jewish if you were born to a Jewish mother or if you converted to Judaism through an Orthodox-sponsored conversion process. But even that is an incomplete and problematic answer. What about a person with a Jewish father and a non-Jewish mother? And what about the legitimacy of non-Orthodox conversions? Furthermore, can one give up most Jewish traditions and still be regarded as Jewish? These questions have been answered in different ways throughout Jewish history.

Cultural Judaism

Let us deal with the last question first. Is it possible to reject all Jewish practice and continue to self-identify as Jewish? Today there are great numbers of Jews who do not keep kosher or observe the Sabbath and other festivals; who rarely, if ever, set foot in a synagogue; and who know nothing about the Torah or the Talmud, yet they still consider themselves deeply Jewish. In fact, according to *American Jewish Identity Survey 2001*, there are 5.5 million Americans who consider themselves to be Jewish, yet approximately half of these Jews define themselves as secular (Mayer, Kosmin, and Keysar 2001, 7). For these secular Jews, Judaism is more of cultural or ethnic identity than a religious one. Their Judaism is defined by their identification with Jewish history, Jewish art, music, and literature, and Jewish languages, as well as the American Jewish immigrant experience. In Israel too, many define their Jewishness by the fact that they live in Israel, speak Hebrew, and continue to eat the ethnic foods, read the books, and listen to the music that their parents brought with them from their countries of origin. And the fact that Israelis grow up with the Rabbinate defining Jewish practice may also lead many to spurn the more traditional components of religion (Dashevsky, Lazerwitz, and Tabory 2003, 257).

Identity and Israeli Immigration Laws

Given this cultural component of Jewish identity, one might be inclined to suggest that a Jew is anyone who defines himself or herself as one. But Israeli immigration policies, as well as the halachic standards employed by the Chief Rabbinate, have created narrower definitions. When the state of Israel was established, one of the first laws it enacted was the Law of Return. Since the state was in part designed as a safe haven for Jews escaping persecution, this law granted automatic citizenship to any Jewish person wishing to live there. From the perspective of the Law of Return, a Jew is defined as anyone who would have been regarded as a Jew in Nazi Germany. Hitler's policies affected not only those born to a Jewish mother and converts to Judaism but also those whose fathers were Jewish, who had even one Jewish grandparent, or who were married to a Jew, so all such people are accepted as immigrants under the Law of Return.

Whose Conversion Is It Anyway?

However, being fast-tracked under the Law of Return does not mean that you are automatically considered a Jew in other areas of Israeli law. For instance, according to the Rabbinate, being allowed into the country has no bearing on your eligibility to marry another Jew, since the Rabbinate maintains a strictly halacha-based definition of who is deemed a Jew. Prior to applying for a marriage licence, hopeful brides and grooms must prove they are Jewish by including a letter from an Orthodox rabbi attesting to that fact or establishing that they have converted. While many secular Jews born in Israel must struggle to find an Orthodox rabbi who knows them and their families well enough to provide this documentation, for converts the system is even more problematic. Under the Law of Return, a Jewish conversion in any of the major denominations is regarded as valid enough to entitle you to Israeli citizenship, but non-Orthodox conversions are not recognized by the Chief Rabbinate. To complicate matters further, in recent years the Rabbinate has been tightening its criteria, even going so far as to overturn some Orthodox conversions (Barkat 2006; Jeffay 2008).

Indeed, conceptions of who is a Jew have become more polarized in the past half-century. In 1983 the Reform movement decided to recognize people with only a Jewish father as full members of the Jewish community, to avoid alienating children of interfaith marriages. While Reform leaders saw this as a progressive step to ensure Jewish continuity in an age of assimilation, when more and more Jews were marrying non-Jewish partners, Orthodoxy and Conservative Judaism feared that this would create more divisiveness among Jews. Although by the twentieth century the different denominations did not agree on much, theologically speaking, at least until that point they had shared a historical definition of what constituted a Jew by birth. By accepting those with a Jewish father as not needing to convert if they wished to marry another Jew, the Reform movement radically reconfigured questions of Jewish identity.

RELIGIOUS DIVERSITY

Denominationalism versus Post-denominationalism

As indicated throughout this chapter, what constitutes Judaism has always been incredibly diverse, even dating back to antiquity. Jewish expressions of religiosity have never been homogeneous and today, with four major denominational movements, there is a whole range of practices and beliefs for present-day Jews to choose from. Yet for some, even the categories of Orthodox, Conservative, Reform, and Reconstructionist are stifling. Believing that contemporary Judaism has become too fractured and over-institutionalized, some modern practitioners advocate for a post-denominational Judaism and struggle to create communities and synagogues that are both traditional and egalitarian, halacha-driven and progressive, and that cater to the needs of as many Jews as possible.

Ashkenazi versus Sephardic

It is important to note that these nineteenth- and twentieth-century denominational divisions are Ashkenazi constructs, and actually quite alien to Sephardic sensibilities. Because Sephardic Jews tended to engage more with their non-Jewish neighbours throughout history, Sephardic practice slowly evolved as times changed, without necessitating the type of break with tradition that was instigated by Ashkenazi Reform leaders in Germany. Today it is virtually impossible to speak of modern Judaism without touching on the tremendous impact of the four major movements, but that is because it is Ashkenazi Judaism that predominates in most major Jewish centres.

According to political scientist Daniel Elazar, at the end of the eleventh century, Sephardic Jews comprised 97 percent of world Jewry and Ashkenazi Jews only 3 percent. However, by the end of the eighteenth century, because of improved standards of living in Christian Europe as compared to Muslim-dominated lands, Ashkenazi Jews had experienced a population explosion and outnumbered Sephardic Jews three to two. Although many more Ashkenazi Jews perished in the Holocaust, significantly reducing their numbers, as of 1992 they still comprised approximately 80 percent of Jews worldwide as compared to 20 percent for Sephardic Jews. As a result, in order to ensure that their rich history is not forgotten and their unique practices do not disappear entirely, Sephardic Jews have established their own synagogues, schools, and cultural centres.

But Sephardic Jews are not a homogenous community either. Jews from places as diverse as Persia, Yemen, Azerbaijan, Ethiopia, and India are often described as Sephardic because their practices more closely resemble those of Sephardic Jews. Styles of prayer, holiday customs, traditional foods, and clothing vary tremendously and are often a reflection of each community's country of origin and historical experiences.

THE CANADIAN CONTEXT

The Jewish community has a long history in Canada, having arrived here even prior to Canada's being recognized as a country. The first Jews fought as British army officers against the French and decided to settle in Quebec after the British declared it one of their colonies in 1763. Aaron Hart was the most prominent of these first settlers. He became a successful furrier and businessman in Trois-Rivières, and one of his sons, Ezekiel, went on to be elected as leader of the opposition in the legislature of Lower Canada in 1807. However, he was unable to assume office, as he refused to swear the oath of allegiance on a Christian Bible. It took until 1832 for Jews to be exempted from such an oath; at that time they were accepted as full British subjects in Quebec and permitted to hold public office. This was remarkable in its day, as it would be several more years before the Jews of England were granted similar rights (Schoenfeld 2001, 165).

By the time the first census was taken in Canada, in 1871, there were 1,151 Jews in Canada, settled mainly in Montreal, Toronto, and Hamilton, Ontario. During the waves of Russian pogroms in the 1880s, Eastern Europe's Jews fled for their lives, turning in great numbers to places such as the United States and Canada for safety. By the outbreak of the First World War in 1914, the Jewish population of Canada had multiplied to more than 100,000, and Jews could be found in every major city across the country (Schoenfeld 2001, 167).

Immigration Policies: None Is Too Many

Between 1907 and 1921, several periods of economic hardship resulted in a contraction of the job market and more severe limitations on Canadian immigration. Authorities clamped down on who was allowed into the country, and Chinese, Jewish, and African-American immigrants suffered most from these discriminatory new policies. The Great

Depression resulted in even further restrictions, which, combined with rampant anti-Semitism and the absence of any real refugee program, made it all but impossible for Jews hoping to escape the Nazis to find asylum in Canada. As the Jewish population rose in the early 1900s, anti-Semitism had become rampant in Canada, especially in Quebec, where the Jews were seen as a threat to the French and Catholic character of the province (Abella and Troper 2000, x). As the plight of the Jews of Europe under the Nazis became more widely known, Canada received pressure both at home and internationally to develop a refugee policy and take in its share of Jews. Nevertheless, as has been noted by political scientist Gerald Dirks, in 1938 the government of Prime Minister William Lyon Mackenzie King had an unwritten policy to keep the Jews out of Canada:

> We do not want to take too many Jews, but in the circumstances, we do not want to say so. We do not want to legitimize the Aryan mythology by introducing any formal distinction for immigration purposes between Jews and non-Jews. The practical distinction, however, has to be made and should be drawn with discretion and sympathy by the competent department, without the need to lay down a formal minute of policy. (King, quoted in Dirks 1977, 58)

Historians Irving Abella and Harold Troper have similarly illustrated that as late as 1945, when an anonymous Canadian official was asked by journalists how many Jews would be allowed to enter Canada after the war, he replied, "None is too many" (2000, xxi). The borders of most countries were closed to Jews during the years of Nazi terror, and Canada accepted fewer than 5,000 Jewish immigrants between 1933 and 1945. This is a dismal record compared to the United Kingdom, which accepted 70,000; Argentina, which took in 50,000; and the United States, which accepted 200,000 Jews (Abella and Troper 2000, xxii). In 1946 policies began to change—Canadian citizens were allowed to sponsor first-degree relatives (see "A Jewish-Canadian Tale of Immigration") and some refugees were allowed to enter the country as well—but even so, Jews were still routinely rejected by the immigration authorities. In 1948 Canada adopted a new Immigration Act, and 180,000 postwar immigrants were granted entry to Canada, among them 8,000 Jewish refugees (Abella and Troper 2000, 279). In the ensuing years, Jews entered Canada in greater numbers than ever before, and the fight against ingrained anti-Semitism and racism really began.

Jews and Canadian Public Policy

Once these new Jewish immigrants had arrived in Canada, many found that life here was not quite as free as they had hoped. Jews—along with Afro-Caribbean immigrants and French Canadians—were routinely discriminated against when it came to employment and housing opportunities, and even places of recreation such as hotels, clubs, and beaches often excluded Jews (Wyman and Rosensvieg 1996, 750). But in the postwar period the negative effects of racism on society at large were beginning to be understood by mainstream Canadians. Canada became a signatory to the

PEOPLE & PLACES

A Jewish-Canadian Tale of Immigration: Rose and Harry Mandelbaum

My own maternal grandparents came to Canada during the period of restricted immigration. Their story is not unusual and serves to illustrate some of the hurdles that Eastern European Jews in particular experienced in the postwar period.

Rose was from the cosmopolitan town of Kovno, Lithuania, and Harry was from a small shtetl in Poland called Tarlow. Rose had survived the war by escaping from a slave-labour camp and Harry was one of the 200,000 Jews who had fought in the Polish army against the Nazis.

35 percent (Robinson 2006). This represents the highest and second-highest records for Jewish day-school attendance in all of North America.

Today there are more than 364,000 Jews living in Canada, including a sizeable Sephardic population in Montreal, of mostly French-speaking Moroccan immigrants, and an Ashkenazi majority that maintains a strong connection to its Yiddish heritage through flourishing Yiddish theatres, music, films, and cultural festivals in Toronto, Montreal, and Vancouver. Having a strong sense of their Judaism as both a religious and a cultural identity, Canadian Jews have contributed to the Canadian mosaic in a variety of fields. From poet-songwriter Leonard Cohen and journalist Naomi Klein to Supreme Court Justice Rosalie Abella and HIV/AIDS activist Stephen Lewis, Canadian Jews have made their mark both in Canada and around the world.

@

JUDAISM AND THE INTERNET

A woman unsure of which Hebrew blessing is required prior to eating a jelly doughnut quickly refers to the iBlessing app on her iPhone. A teenage boy downloads a complete copy of the Hagaddah onto his laptop to help him lead his family's Passover seder. We live in a world that is bursting with technological innovation. While in the past, science and religion have had a vexed relationship, all the contemporary Jewish denominations that have embraced modernity are seeing the new opportunities that these technologies can provide.

Ultra-Orthodoxy and the Internet: Chabad.org

One organization that immediately recognized the Internet's potential for reaching vast numbers of non-practising Jews was the Chabad-Lubavitch Hasidic sect. Best known for its hospitality and learning centres all over the globe, Chabad has made exhaustive use of modern technologies to promote its programs and services, since one of its goals is to bring unaffiliated Jews back to traditional Jewish practice. Chabad began hosting its own website as early as 1988, and it was the first Jewish educational presence and virtual Jewish library on the World Wide Web (Coutin 1999). Thousands of Jewish sources have been digitized and uploaded onto their flagship site, Chabad.org, and the teachings of their now deceased spiritual leader, Menachem Mendel Schneerson, have been made available as online videos. The movement now has its own media centre that maintains more than a thousand websites, sponsors daily and weekly podcasts on the works of Maimonides and other important Jewish thinkers, and freely utilizes YouTube, Facebook, and Twitter to promote its events and fundraisers. In this regard, Chabad sets itself apart from several other ultra-Orthodox movements that actually dissuade their adherents from making use of the World Wide Web, fearing that they will encounter pornographic images and ideas prohibited by Jewish law.

Chabad was also a pioneer when it came to the now ubiquitous "Ask the Rabbi" websites, where one can seek answers to questions about Jewish law, history, and practice. A person anonymously sends in a question to a website and receives a response from a scholar or rabbi within twenty-four hours. For instance, a person may ask what forms of birth control are acceptable according to Jewish law, if a particular food item is kosher, or what Jews believe about God. While the overwhelming majority of these sites are run by Orthodox organizations, some sites allow users to pose questions to Conservative and Reform rabbis as well. Chabad has "Ask the Rabbi" services on its own site and administers two others, AskMoses.com which offers a live chat service, and thejewishwoman.org, which is run by women for women.

Authority Online

While one website (halacha.com) advertises that it has some of the most noted rabbis of our time answering questions of Jewish law, and lists their names, other sites skirt the question of authority altogether, simply indicating that they have thirty or so rabbis on staff to respond to public queries. In many cases it is up to the questioners to track down the names of the respondents and evaluate on their own whether or not the source or the response given is reliable. Indeed, authority is often in the eye of the beholder. An otherwise secular Jew may not be looking for the same type of answer as an ultra-Orthodox Jew, and each will likely be impressed by a different set of credentials. While rabbinic authority in the modern period was already decentralized, the use of the Internet has made this even more pronounced. The speed and efficiency offered by the Internet enable the questioner to pose his or her questions to numerous different rabbis at the same time and to compare the responses given. This in turn empowers the questioner to become his or her own authority in matters of Jewish law, much to the chagrin of the rabbis who operate these online forums.

The success of and high demand for "Ask the Rabbi" sites are a curious phenomenon. While in the past people would walk into their school or synagogue to speak to a flesh-and-blood being when they had a question, today Jews are more dispersed and more assimilated than ever before, and many may not have access to a rabbi in their community. Hence, for young, unaffiliated, and web-savvy Jews, the Internet is the first place they turn should they have a question about their heritage (Coutin 1999). Plus, the anonymity of the Web appeals to many people, especially if their question deals with sexual intimacy, crises of faith, or other personal matters. While one Orthodox blogger (Gelman 2009) cautions that receiving Jewish legal advice online is a poor substitute for a face-to-face encounter—in which the rabbi can pose follow-up questions and ensure that the needs of the person asking are being appropriately addressed—others see it as revolutionary that the wisdom of the sages is only a mouse-click away.

CONCLUSION

Jewish self-concepts, textual traditions, and religious practices (to return to Satlow's threefold scheme) have changed tremendously over the millennia. Beginning as a centralized tradition with worship in a single temple, Judaism is now understood as a worldwide phenomenon with multiple denominations and innumerable expressions of its core practices and beliefs. In the twenty-first century Judaism faces new challenges, such as a growing chasm between Diaspora Jews and Israelis, rising rates of anti-Semitism and assimilation, and a palpable disenchantment with the rigidity of existing denominational movements. But if there is one element that is common to Judaisms throughout the ages, it is the ability of its practitioners to adapt to new circumstances. And if the tradition's long history is any indication, it seems that Jews will likely find a way to navigate these uncharted waters and, if necessary, redefine Judaism once again.

KEY TERMS

Anti-Semitism, p. 63
Ashkenazi, p. 55
Brit, p. 74
Diaspora, p. 54
Geonim, p. 54
Halacha, p. 39
Hasidism, p. 59
Haskalah, p. 60
Ketubah, p. 75
Kosher, p. 72
Matzah, p. 31
Midrash, p. 33
Minyan, p. 68
Mishnah, p. 45
Rabbi, p. 31
Responsa, p. 48
Sabbath, p. 51
Seder, p. 31
Sephardic, p. 55
Shoah, p. 65
Shtetl, p. 59
Tallit, p. 68
Talmud, p. 32
Tefillin, p. 68
Torah, p. 32
Yiddish, p. 59
Zionism, p. 63
Zohar, p. 48

CRITICAL THINKING QUESTIONS

1. Is Judaism a religious identity or a cultural one? Or is this a false dichotomy? Explain.
2. Try to come up with your own stipulative definition or map of Judaism. Why would such a framework be useful?
3. Which do you think has had a greater impact on modern expressions of Judaism, the Enlightenment or feminism?
4. How have Canadian Jews shaped and contributed to Canadian multicultural policies? And how have these policies shaped the Jewish identity of Canadian Jews?
5. Are online "Ask the Rabbi" forums different from earlier forms of correspondence between rabbis and practitioners on Jewish legal matters? How has the Internet affected traditional Jewish authority?
6. The Tibetan leader, the Dalai Lama, once asked how the Jews managed to keep their traditions alive through thousands of years of exile. What do you think might account for the survival of Judaism over time?

RECOMMENDED READING

Abella, Irving, and Harold Troper. *None Is Too Many: Canada and the Jews of Europe, 1933–1948*. Toronto: Key Porter Books, 2000.

Baskin, Judith, ed. *Jewish Women in Historical Perspective*. Detroit, MI: Wayne State University Press, 1999.

Bauer, Yehuda, and Nili Keren. *A History of the Holocaust*. Danbury, CT: Franklin Watts, 2001.

Ben-Amos, Dan, Ellen Frankel, and Dov Noy, eds. *Folktales of the Jews*. Vol. 1, *Tales of the Sephardic Dispersion*; Vol. 2, *Tales of Eastern Europe*. Philadelphia: Jewish Publication Society, 2006.

Berlin, Adele, and Marc Zvi Brettler, eds. *The Jewish Study Bible*. New York: Oxford University Press, 2004.

Biale, Rachel. *Women and Jewish Law: The Essential Texts, Their History and Their Relevance for Today*. New York: Schocken Books, 1984.

Brym, Richard, William Shaffir, and Morton Weinfeld, eds. *The Jews in Canada*. Oxford: Oxford University Press, 2010.

Dash Moore, Deborah, ed. *American Jewish Identity Politics*. Ann Arbor: University of Michigan Press, 2008.

Ehrlich, M. Avrum. *Encyclopaedia of the Jewish Diaspora: Origins, Experiences and Culture*. Santa Barbara, CA: ABC-CLIO, 2009.

Goldberg, Harvey. *Jewish Passages: Cycles of Jewish Life*. Berkeley: University of California Press, 2003.

Neusner, Jacob. *Judaism: The Basics*. Oxford: Routledge, 2006.

Novak, David. *Law and Theology in Judaism*. Jersey City, NJ: Ktav Publishing, 1974.

Plaskow, Judith. *Standing Again at Sinai: Judaism from a Feminist Perspective*. New York: HarperOne, 1991.

Scheindlin, Raymond P. *A Short History of the Jewish People: From Legendary Times to Modern Statehood*. Oxford: Oxford University Press, 1998.

Steinsaltz, A. *The Talmud, the Steinsaltz Edition: A Reference Guide*. New York: Random House, 1989.

RECOMMENDED VIEWING

Fiddler on the Roof. Dir. Norman Jewison. Perf. Chaim Topol, Molly Picon. Cartier Productions, 1971. DVD. Based on the stories of Yiddish writer Sholem Aleichem, this musical explores the trials and tribulations of Tevye, a simple milkman living in czarist Russia who is struggling to marry off his daughters and stay true to Jewish tradition as the world around him changes rapidly.

Half the Kingdom. Dir. Roushell Goldstein and Francine Zuckerman. National Film Board of Canada, 1989. DVD. By focusing on the personal stories of seven women in Canada, Israel, and the United States, this documentary explores the changing role of women in Judaism across the denominational spectrum.

The Jazz Singer. Dir. Alan Crosland. Perf. Al Jolson, May McAvoy. Warner Bros., 1927. DVD. Centring on the show business ambitions of a cantor's son, this film portrays the tensions between traditional Jewish ways and pursuit of the American dream. The film also has the distinction of being the first "talkie."

Promises. Dir. Carlos Bolado, B. Z. Goldberg, and Justine Shapiro. Perf. Moshe Bar Am, B. Z. Goldberg, Sanabel Hassan. Independent Television Service, 2001. This documentary looks at the Israeli–Palestinian conflict through the eyes of seven children, who, although they live twenty minutes away from each other, reside in completely different worlds.

Schindler's List. Dir. Steven Spielberg. Perf. Liam Neeson, Ben Kingsley. Universal Pictures, 1993. DVD. This film tells the story of Oskar Schindler, a German businessman, who managed to rescue more than a thousand Polish Jews by employing them in his factories during the Second World War.

Soferet: A Special Scribe. Dir. Donna Zuckerbrot and Daniel Zuckerbrot. Perf. Aviel Barclay. Reel Time Images, 2005. DVD. This documentary follows the spiritual journey of Aviel Barclay, an Orthodox woman who received traditional training to become a Torah scribe, despite outcry from the Orthodox Jewish establishment that such a endeavour is reserved for men alone.

The Ten Commandments. Dir. Cecil B. DeMille. Perf. Charlton Heston, Yul Brynner. Motion Picture Associates, 1956. DVD. Although not entirely true to the biblical account, this film chronicles the story of the exodus from Egypt.

Trembling Before G–d. Dir. Sandi Simcha Dubowski. Perf. Shlomo Ashkinazy, Steve Greenberg. Cinephil, Keshet Broadcasting, 2001. DVD. A documentary about gay and lesbian Orthodox Jews trying to reconcile their faith with their sexuality.

Yentl. Dir. Barbra Streisand. Perf. Barbra Streisand, Amy Irving, Mandy Patinkin. United Artists, 1983. DVD. Based on a short story by Isaac Bashevis Singer, this musical tells the tale of a young Polish girl who disguises herself as a boy in order to gain entry into a yeshiva and pursue her love of classical Jewish text study.

USEFUL WEBSITES

Ashkenaz Foundation

The Ashkenaz Foundation hosts the largest Jewish cultural event in Canada. Its website showcases current Jewish music, art, theatre, dance, and film.

Chabad.org

Operated by the Hasidic sect Chabad-Lubavitch, this site has one of the most comprehensive libraries of Jewish texts in English translation on the World Wide Web, including the Torah, works by Maimonides, and other Hasidic sources.

From Immigration to Integration: The Canadian Jewish Experience

A joint project between Jewish advocacy organization B'nai Brith Canada and the Canadian National Archives in Ottawa, this online publication on the website of B'nai Brith Canada's Institute for International Affairs traces the history of the Canadian Jewish community from its early days to the present.

Halakhah.com

This site includes the Soncino translation of the Babylonian Talmud into English.

Institute for Global Jewish Affairs

This site posts valuable research on new trends in anti-Semitism and other developments in Jewish communities across the world.

Jewish Orthodox Feminist Alliance

An excellent online resource dealing with issues of women and Jewish law.

Judaism 101

This encyclopedic website includes nuanced information on Jewish beliefs and practices. Written primarily from an Orthodox perspective, each section is tagged as basic, intermediate, or advanced to help guide those new to Jewish concepts.

Jewish Virtual Library

Another encyclopedic website sponsored by the American-Israeli Cooperative Enterprise. With more than 13,000 entries and 6,000 photographs, it is unique in its direct access to Judaic and Hebraic treasures from the U.S. Library of Congress.

Rambi

This is the best source for scholarly articles on any topic in Jewish studies.

Ritualwell.org

Sponsored by the Reconstructionist Rabbinical College, this site is dedicated to Jewish feminist ritual and other contemporary approaches to Jewish practice.

Union for Reform Judaism

Official website of the Reform movement in North America.

United Synagogue of Conservative Judaism

Official website of the Conservative movement.

REFERENCES

Abella, Irving, and Harold Troper. 2000. *None Is Too Many: Canada and the Jews of Europe, 1933–1948.* Toronto: Key Porter Books.

Adler, Rachel. 1993. "In Your Blood, Live: Re-visions of a Theology of Purity." *Tikkun* 8, no. 1 (1993): 38–41.

———. 1998. *Engendering Judaism: An Inclusive Theology and Ethics.* Philadelphia: Jewish Publication Society.

Barkat, Amiram. 2006. "Rabbinate No Longer Recognizes Overseas Conversions" (23 May). http://www.haaretz.com (accessed 15 July 2010).

Biale, Rachel. 1984. *Women and Jewish Law: The Essential Texts, Their History and Their Relevance for Today.* New York: Schocken Books.

Brooten, Bernadette. 1982. *Women Leaders in the Ancient Synagogue.* Brown Judaic Studies Series 36. Atlanta, GA: Scholars Press.

Coutin, Talia S. 1999. "Ask the Rabbi Online" (30 November). http://www.jta.org (accessed 15 July 2010).

Dashevsky, Arnold, Bernard Lazerwitz, and Ephraim Tabory. 2003. "The Journey of the 'Straight Way' and the 'Roundabout Path': Jewish Identity in the United States and Israel." In *Handbook of the Sociology of Religion*, ed. Michelle Dillon. Cambridge: Cambridge University Press.

Dirks, Gerald E. 1977. *Canada's Refugee Policy: Indifference or Opportunism.* Montreal: McGill-Queen's University Press.

Ehrlich, Avrum. 2005. *The Messiah of Brooklyn: Understanding Lubavitch Hasidism Past and Present.* Jersey City, NJ: Ktav Publishing.

Elazar, Daniel J. 1992. "Can Sephardic Judaism Be Reconstructed?" Daniel Elazar On-line Library, Jerusalem Center for Public Affairs. http://www.jcpa.org (accessed 27 June 2010).

Fendrick, Susan. 2005. "Jewish Feminist Ritual and Brit Milah." *Sh'ma: A Journal of Jewish Responsibility* (March). http://www.ritualwell.org (accessed 15 July 2010).

Gelman, Barry. 2009. "On Line Psak: Bad Medicine" (8 December). *Morethodoxy: Exploring the Breadth, Depth and Passion of Orthodox Judaism*. http://www.morethodoxy.org (accessed 16 July 2010).

Glick, Leonard B. 1999. *Abraham's Heirs: Jews and Christians in Medieval Europe*. New York: Syracuse University Press.

Goldstein, Elyse. 1998. *ReVisions: Seeing Torah Through a Feminist Lens*. Toronto: Key Porter Books.

Grossman, Avraham. 2004. *Pious and Rebellious: Jewish Women in Medieval Europe*. Waltham, MA: Brandeis University Press.

Hammer, Jill. n.d. "Rising from the Ritual Bath." http://www.ritualwell.org (accessed 15 July 2010).

Heine, Heinrich. 1866. *The Poems of Heine*, trans. Edgar Alfred Bowring. London: Bell and Daldy.

Hyman, Paula. 2008. "Jewish Feminism Faces the American Women's Movement: Convergence and Divergence." In *American Jewish Identity Politics*, ed. Deborah Dash Moore, 221–42. Ann Arbor: University of Michigan Press.

Jacobs, Louis. 1984. *The Book of Jewish Belief*. Springfield, NJ: Behrman House.

Jeffay, Nathan. 2008. "Rabbinical Court Puts Thousands of Converts in Legal Limbo" (8 May). http://www.forward.com (accessed 16 July 2010).

Jewish People Policy Planning Institute. 2010. *Jewish People Policy Planning Institute Survey 2007*. http://www.jpppi.org.il (accessed 4 June 2010).

The JPS Tanakh: The New JPS Translation According to the Traditional Hebrew Text. 1985. Philadelphia: Jewish Publication Society of America.

Lerner, Gerda. 1986. *The Creation of Patriarchy*. New York: Oxford University Press.

Levine, Lee. 1996. "The Palestinian Synagogue Reconsidered." *Journal of Biblical Literature* 115, no. 3: 430.

Marcus, Ivan. 2004. *The Jewish Life Cycle: Rites of Passage from Biblical to Modern Times*. Seattle: University of Washington Press.

Mayer, Egon, Barry Kosmin, and Ariela Keysar. 2001. *American Jewish Identity Survey 2001*. New York: Graduate Center of the City University of New York.

Meyers, Carol. 1999. "Women and the Domestic Economy of Ancient Israel." In *Women in the Hebrew Bible*, ed. Alice Bach, 37–38. New York: Routledge.

Midrash Rabbah. 1961. Genesis, vol. 1., trans. Maurice Simon. New York: Soncino Press.

———. 1983. Ecclesiastes, trans. A. Cohen. London: *Soncino* Press.

Neusner, Jacob. 1991. *An Introduction to Judaism: A Textbook and Reader*. Louisville, KY: Westminister John Knox Press.

NRSV. 1993. *HarperCollins Study Bible: New Revised Standard Version*, ed. Wayne Meeks. HarperCollins.

Plaskow, Judith. 1995. "The Right Question Is Theological." In *On Being a Jewish Feminist*, ed. Susannah Heschel, 223–33. New York: Schocken Books.

Prior, Michael. 1999. *Zionism and the State of Israel: A Moral Inquiry*. London: Routledge.

Rivlin, Paul. 2011. *The Israeli Economy from the Foundation of the State to the 21st Century*. New York: Cambridge University Press.

Robinson, Ira. 2006. "Canadian Jewry Today: Portrait of a Community in the Process of Change" (15 September). http://www.jcpa.org (accessed 16 July 2010).

Ross, Tamar. 2004. *Expanding the Palace of Torah: Orthodoxy and Feminism*. Lebanon, NH: Brandeis University Press.

Sachar, Abram Leon. 1966. *History of the Jews*. New York: Alfred A. Knopf.

Satlow, Michael. 2006. *Creating Judaism: History, Tradition, Practice*. New York: Columbia University Press.

Schachter-Shalomi, Zalman. 1993. *Paradigm Shift: From the Jewish Renewal Teachings of Reb Zalman Schachter-Shalomi*, ed. Ellen Singer. Northvale, NJ: Jason Aronson.

Schoenfeld, Stuart. 2001. "The Religious Mosaic: A Study in Diversity." In *From Immigration to Integration: The Canadian Jewish Experience, A Millennium Edition*, ed. Ruth Klein and Frank Dimant, 165–81. Toronto: Malcom Lester.

Scholem, Gershom. 1973. *Sabbatai Sevi: The Mystical Messiah, 1626–1676*, trans. R. J. Zwi Werblowsky. Princeton, NJ: Princeton University Press.

The Soncino Talmud CD-ROM. 2000. Chicago: Soncino Press. CD-ROM.

Strack, H. L., and Gunter Stemberger. 1996. *Introduction to the Talmud and Midrash*, trans. and ed. Martin Bockmuehl. Minneapolis, MN: Fortress Press.

Tigay, Jeff. 2004. "Exodus: Introduction." In *The Jewish Study Bible*, ed. Adele Berlin and Marc Brettler, 102–7. New York: Oxford University Press.

Union for Reform Judaism. n.d. "Q & A." http://www.urj.org (accessed 16 July 2010).

Weinrib, Lorraine. 2001. "Ensuring Equality: The Role of the Community." In From Immigration to Integration: The Canadian Jewish Experience, ed. Ruth Klein and Frank Dimant, 69–92. Toronto: Malcolm Lester.

World Health Organization. n.d. "Male Circumcision for HIV Prevention." http://www.who.int (accessed 5 June 2010).

Wyman, David, and Charles Rosensveig. 1996. *The World Reacts to the Holocaust*. Baltimore, MD: Johns Hopkins University Press.

Timeline

- **c. 4 B.C.E.** Birth of Jesus.
- **c. 30 C.E.** Crucifixion and Resurrection of Jesus.
- **c. 65 C.E.** Death of Paul.
- **70 C.E.** Destruction of the Second Temple in Jerusalem.
- **313** Edict of Milan legalizes Christianity.
- **325** First Council of Nicaea.
- **380** Christianity becomes official religion of the Roman empire.
- **381** Nicene Creed finalized at Council of Constantinople.
- **c. 397** Augustine's *Confessions*.
- **451** Council of Chalcedon.
- **529** Athenian academy closed; first Benedictine monasteries established.
- **787** Second Council of Nicaea allows for the veneration of icons.
- **800** Charlemagne crowned Holy Roman Emperor by Pope Leo III.
- **870** Mission of Cyril and Methodius to the Slavonic peoples.
- **988** Russia adopts Orthodox faith.
- **1054** Break between Rome and Constantinople.
- **1095** Pope Urban II launches the Crusades.
- **1274** Thomas Aquinas's *Summa Theologica*. Bonaventure's Soul's Journey to God.
- **1416** Medieval mystic Julian of Norwich's *Revelations of Divine Love*.
- **1517** Martin Luther, German reformer, posts *The Ninety-Five Theses*.
- **1534** Henry VIII becomes head of the Church of England.
- **1536** John Calvin's *Institutes*.
- **1740s** Great Awakening in the American colonies. John Wesley launches Methodist movement in Great Britain.
- **c. 1750** The European Enlightenment.
- **1870** First Vatican Council.
- **1948** World Council of Churches founded.
- **1962–65** Second Vatican Council.
- **2000** Beginning of the third millennium of the Christian era.

CHAPTER 3

Christianity

M. Darrol Bryant

INTRODUCTION

Prologue

It is Easter Sunday, 2001. In Gimli, Manitoba, a minster of the United Church of Canada is welcoming members of her congregation to breakfast in the church hall following the **Easter** sunrise service. For years it has been the practice of their church to gather at six a.m. to celebrate the joyful message of life renewed, based on the Christian teaching of the **resurrection** of Jesus from the dead after his crucifixion. The service was held outside in the local park, where three crosses had been erected, and as the sun rose the congregation sang, "Hallelujah, hallelujah, give thanks to the Risen Christ."

In Rimouski, Quebec, the faithful have gathered at the **Roman Catholic** Saint-Germain Cathedral to celebrate the Easter Mass. Father Blanchet smiles as he welcomes the parishioners to this historic church, which was made a cathedral in 1867, the same year that Canada came into being. He remembers when the church was as full nearly every Sunday as it is today. Things have changed, and now the regular Sunday Mass sees only a handful of mostly elderly parishioners. But today is not a time for regrets; it is time to celebrate—it is Easter Sunday. It is time to unfold the order of service, of which at least some elements go back more than 1,500 years.

"He is risen! He is risen indeed!" These are the words exchanged as members of an **Orthodox** congregation in southern Saskatchewan gather for the Easter service in their onion-domed church. The prairie landscape is reminiscent of the Russian steppes from which their ancestors came more than a century ago. Yet here it is the timeless Divine Liturgy, the Orthodox name for the Sunday worship service, that draws them together. Inside, the smell of incense is strong. Their priest has just driven out from the city to their rural church. Cries of "He is risen! He is risen indeed!" ring out.

In All Saints Anglican Cathedral in Edmonton, Alberta, the **bishop**, Reverend Victoria, is preparing for the Easter Sunday service. She came to Edmonton as its bishop in 1997, although women have been ordained as priests in the Canadian Anglican Church since 1975. In the worldwide Anglican fellowship, the first ordained woman was Florence Li Tim-Oi, in Hong Kong in 1944. It had been a long journey, given the opposition to women in leadership roles. Now Bishop Victoria quietly prepares to lead worship at All Saints; soon the choir will sing "Jesus Christ Is Risen Today."

Quakers in Kitchener-Waterloo, Ontario, gather in silence on this Sunday, as every Sunday, to await the leading of the spirit. There will not be any formal or outward celebration in their meeting, but there will be an inward conviction that the spirit of Christ continues to address "that of God" within. Across the region, Evangelical, Lutheran, Baptist, Pentecostal, Church of God, Presbyterian, Mennonite, Swedenborgian, Missionary, Chinese Christian, Korean Presbyterian, Caribbean Christian, and several other Christian groups will also gather to mark Easter Sunday in their own distinctive ways.

Easter: celebration of the resurrection to new life of Jesus Christ, the most important feast day in the Christian calendar.

Resurrection: the term used in the New Testament for the events following Jesus's crucifixion and burial; for some liberal Christians, a metaphor for renewal.

Roman Catholic Church: another name for the Catholic Church, those churches that are in communion with the Bishop of Rome (the pope).

Orthodox: from the Greek *orthodoxos*, meaning "having the right opinion," a term that came to mean adherence to the creed of Nicaea; also the name for churches of eastern Christianity such as the Greek and Russian Orthodox.

Bishop: a Christian official who has oversight of churches in a certain region, a position established in Roman Catholic, Orthodox, Anglican, Lutheran, and some other Protestant churches. Bishops are only male in the Roman Catholic and Orthodox traditions but may be either male or female in Anglican/Episcopal, Lutheran, Methodist, and other Protestant bodies.

Quakers: the popular name for those belonging to the Religious Society of Friends, a Christian movement of the 1650s that grew up around the teachings of George Fox.

Mary Magdalene: an early female follower or disciple of Jesus who, according to the New Testament, was a witness to his crucifixion and the first to encounter the resurrected Christ. In some Gnostic Christian writings she is considered an Apostle.

Christian (Gregorian) calendar: a revision of the older Julian or Roman calendar, named for Pope Gregory XIII, who promulgated the new calendar in 1582. After the Middle Ages, the years following the birth of Christ were cited as Anno Domini (A.D., or "the year of our Lord") and the years preceding his birth B.C. or "before Christ." Today the years are cited as C.E. (Common Era) and B.C.E. (before the Common Era).

Words

For Christianity is the embodiment of one single truth through the ages: that death precedes birth, that birth is the fruit of death, and that the soul is precisely this power of transforming an end into a beginning by obeying a new name.

Source: Eugen Rosenstock-Huessy, *The Christian Future or the Modern Mind Outrun* (New York: Harper & Row 1966).

Many Christians believe that, after Jesus died on the cross, he was resurrected. Easter is their celebration of belief in the renewal of life as represented by Jesus's resurrection. According to the Christian story, **Mary Magdalene** and some other women who were followers of Jesus went to his tomb to anoint his dead body after he had been crucified, and found the tomb empty. Most Christians believe that this event is at the heart of the Easter story, the holiest day in the **Christian calendar**. The task here will be to explore these narratives and the beliefs that developed as Jesus's following grew and a new tradition known as Christianity evolved and spread. Sometimes, of course, historical accounts differ from those offered by Christians themselves. This is only natural and arose out of the different perspectives and goals of historians and Christians, something Scott Kline discusses in Chapter 1, on the study of religion. In what became a highly patriarchal tradition, many modern feminist theologians now emphasize the role that women played in this significant event.

Across the world, Catholic, Orthodox, and Protestant Christians, among other communities, gather to worship and share their faith in many different ways. Outwardly as diverse as the many cultures of humankind, they are united in their conviction that through Jesus, God is active in transforming the life of humanity. The more than two billion Christians form about 30 percent of the world religions. Christianity is also the most widespread of all the world's religious traditions and the most diverse. It began two thousand years ago as a movement within the Jewish world in Palestine, then part of the Roman empire. Within its first century it spread south into Africa, into the Middle East, and perhaps as far away as India. Since then it has found its way into the lives of human beings in all the cultures and nations of the world. Today the majority of Christians are no longer found in Europe and North America: Christianity has spread to the peoples of Africa, Asia, and Latin America. It is this vast and richly diverse tradition that we will explore here.

This chapter will introduce the reader to the elements of **creed**—a formal statement of Christian beliefs—spirituality, ritual, identity formation, practice, and social expressions of Christianity. These elements give the varied Christian communities their distinctive ethos and flavour, although its diversity makes understanding Christianity challenging.

First, Christianity will be examined from a cross-cultural perspective. Second, the diversity of Christianity will be highlighted, particularly in its Catholic, Orthodox, and Protestant forms. We will also stress that there are many approaches to understanding Christianity, both from believers' perspectives and those of scholars of religion. For believing Christians, Christianity is not simply a collection of narratives, beliefs, doctrines, rituals, or habits, as it might be in a scholarly approach, but is rather a way to understand the meaning of life and the unfolding of events in history. The Christian way of seeing the world evolved gradually over the first centuries of the Christian era, beginning with early Christians' attempts to understand the meaning of the life, death, and resurrection of Jesus (Smith 2005, 1–35). For Christians, this includes these beliefs:

- In the beginning, God created the world and everything in it. These words stem from the opening lines of the Hebrew Tanakh, the sacred writings of the Jewish people, which were also the sacred scripture of the first Christians.

Creed: an early statement of the Christian faith, articulating its central beliefs.

Salvation: the act of saving, rescuing, or making whole, the Christian teaching of the way in which humanity is restored to communion with God.

- The relationship between God and humanity is disrupted and broken. Humanity is not all it should be and needs to be restored to a right relationship with God.
- The story of the death and resurrection of Jesus has led to an understanding of Jesus as redeemer of humanity and restorer of the relationship between God and humanity.

This worldview provides the basic backdrop for understanding the rich diversity of thought and practice we find within Christianity over the past two millennia.

The Spiritual Quest

The spiritual quest within Christianity is a quest for wholeness, an overcoming of that which keeps humans estranged from God. The very term **salvation**, which is often used in the Christian traditions to speak of the goal of the spiritual quest, comes from the Latin *salvus,* meaning "made whole, delivered, healed." In Christianity the quest is to be restored to communion with God. Within this context we now turn to the central beliefs, sources, history, practices, and identities that characterize Christianity through the ages.

Practices

Christian Symbols

Two of the earliest symbols of Christian faith were the fish and the cross. They were found in the catacombs, the places of Christian burial in Rome.

There are several explanations for the fish as a Christian symbol. It is a rendering of the Greek alpha (α), or *a* in the Greek alphabet. Jesus Christ was referred to as the *alpha*, meaning the beginning, and the *omega*, meaning the end of human history. It was a simple image that had resonance

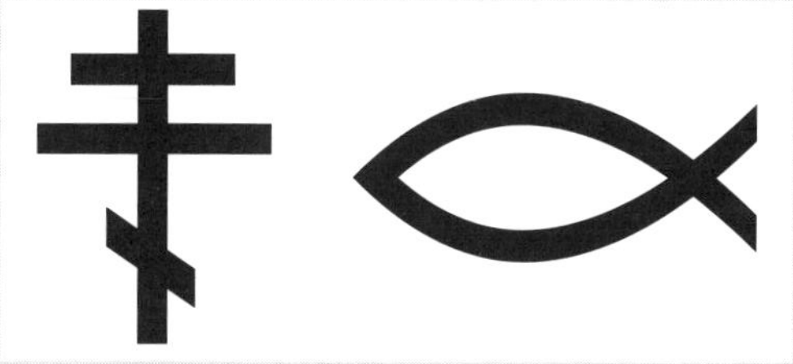

Source: Dr_Flash/Shutterstock

(continued)

with biblical stories of Jesus, who called his followers "fishers of men" (Mark 1:17), and the story of feeding many with "seven loaves and a few small fish" (Matt. 16:32ff).

Another explanation suggests that the fish was a secret sign that Christians shared during times of persecution. When meeting, one person might draw one arc of the sign in the sand and the other person would add the second arc, thus identifying their common connection with Christianity. Later it was said to be related to the Greek word for fish, *ichthys* (ΙΧΘΥΣ). The first letter, iota (Ι), is the first letter in *Iesous* (Jesus); the second is chi (Χ), the first letter in *Christos* (Christ); the third is theta (Θ), the first letter in *Theos* (God); the fourth is upsilon (Υ), the first letter in *Yios* (son); and the fifth is sigma (Σ), the first letter in *Soter* (Saviour). This gives us the acrostic ΙΧΘΥΣ, meaning "Jesus Christ, Son of God, Saviour."

Sources: Donald P Oehman/Shutterstock (left); Photos.com (right)

Late in the second century the cross also emerged as a symbol of Christianity. By the early 200s Clement of Alexandria, the head of the Christian catechetical school in Alexandria, was referring to it as a Christian symbol. It was a simple four-sided cross that had multiple resonances, recalling both Jesus's death on the cross and the four directions of the compass. It wasn't until the eleventh and twelfth centuries that the crucifix, which presents the body of Christ on the cross, began to appear above the altar in Western Catholic churches. It was in the Middle Ages that the crucifix became a popular symbol in Catholic Christianity.

The cross and the crucifix have become universal within Christianity. However, the crucifix is the preferred symbol in the Catholic and Orthodox traditions of Christianity, while the Protestant traditions prefer the empty cross as a symbol of the risen Christ.

CENTRAL BELIEFS

When one encounters the variety of communities that have emerged in the history of Christianity, it is sometimes hard to remember that Christianity emerged around the life, death, and resurrection of Jesus of Nazareth. Because the first Christians were Jews, they initially understood him to be the expected messiah, which means "anointed one," a Jewish king who would usher in a reign of peace. As the early movement developed over the first three centuries of the Christian era, many followers came to acknowledge Jesus as the **incarnate** word of God. They came to believe that he revealed the creative, redemptive, and sanctifying activity of God in history. But it was only at the Council of Nicaea in 325 that Christian communities arrived at the creed, or statement of belief, that would be foundational to worship for most Christians through the ages.

Nicene Creed

We believe in one God, the Father All Governing, creator of heaven and earth, of all things visible and invisible.
We believe in one Lord Jesus Christ, the only begotten Son of God, begotten from the Father before all time, Light from Light, true God from true God, begotten not created, of the same essence as the Father, through whom all things came into being, who for us men, and because of our salvation, came down from heaven, and was incarnate by the Holy Spirit and the Virgin Mary, and became human. He was crucified for us under Pontius Pilate, and

suffered and was buried, and rose on the third day, according to the Scriptures, and ascended to heaven, and sits on the right hand of the Father, and will come again with glory to judge the living and dead. His Kingdom shall have no end.
And in the Holy Spirit, the Lord and life-giver, who proceeds from the Father, who is worshipped and glorified together with the Father and Son, who spoke through the prophets; and in one, holy, catholic, and apostolic Church. We confess one baptism for the remission of sins. We look forward to the resurrection of the dead and the life of the world to come."

Source: *Creeds of the Churches*, ed. John Leith (Garden City, NJ: Anchor Books, 1963).

The early creeds come from the third and fourth centuries of the Christian era (Bettenson and Maunder 1999, 25–29). We know that the Nicene Creed was articulated through the first two councils of the Christian church, the Council of Nicaea in 325 and the Council of Constantinople in 381. The origin of the Apostles' Creed is uncertain, but it is generally thought to come from the third century and was widely used in the fourth and fifth centuries. These creeds embody the faith of the church and the convictions of Christians; they are typically recited in the context of worship in most Christian communities.

In recent times we have seen contemporary reformulations of these creeds. One example is the New Creed of the United Church of Canada, from 1968. It attempts to articulate the faith in terms that are gender neutral.

We are not alone,
    we live in God's world.
We believe in God:
    who has created and is creating,
    who has come in Jesus,
    the Word made flesh,
    to reconcile and make new,
    who works in us and others
    by the Spirit.
We trust in God.
We are called to be the Church:
    to celebrate God's presence,
    to live with respect in Creation,
    to love and serve others,
    to seek justice and resist evil,
    to proclaim Jesus, crucified and risen,
    our judge and our hope.
In life, in death, in life beyond death,
    God is with us.
We are not alone.
    Thanks be to God.

Source: The United Church of Canada

Incarnate: from the Greek ensarkosis (Latin *incarnatio*), meaning "made flesh." It is a Christian teaching that "the Word [*logos* in Greek] became flesh and dwelt among us" (John 1:14), meaning that Jesus Christ was the incarnate word.

Church: an assembly, congregation, or community that gathers to worship God.

Redeemer: Jesus's death on the cross is believed to have redeemed sinful humanity and restored it to a relationship with God.

The Divine

Central to the teaching of the Christian **churches** is belief in God. Christianity is the second of the three Abrahamic traditions, Judaism, Christianity, and Islam. It considers itself a monotheistic tradition, that is, a tradition that believes in one God. What distinguishes Christianity from the other Abrahamic traditions is what is known as a trinitarian understanding of God as "three in one, one in three": namely God as Father, Son, and Holy Spirit, or God as Creator, **Redeemer**, and

Bible: a collection of writings that form the sacred scripture of Christianity. There are differences among Catholics, Orthodox, and Protestants concerning the books to be included in the Bible.

Sanctifier. Christianity, like all the world's religious and spiritual traditions, affirms the reality of something beyond the mundane. Within most religious traditions this *something* has many names. It is variously called god, the sacred, the absolute, the ultimate mystery, the great spirit, or emptiness (Smith 1991). Behind and beyond these many names lies a perception of the reality of the sacred. It is generally acknowledged that the reality of God is beyond form, beyond words, beyond concepts, beyond images, beyond gender. This means that all our words are inadequate to describe the reality of that which is utterly beyond.

For Christians, God is known through divine self-disclosure, or revelation. Abrahamic traditions hold that revelation is precisely what God has done. For the Jewish traditions, Yahweh's purposes become known through creation, the Torah, and the biblical history of Israel. The Muslim traditions see Allah revealed in the gift of the Qu'ran to his messenger, the Prophet Muhammad. Christians believe that God is disclosed as redemptive love in Jesus Christ, as witnessed to in the **Bible** (see Freedmann and McClymond 2001).

Over the first three centuries of the Christian era, there were many views concerning God's revelation in Jesus and the relationship of Jesus to the one he called *Abba* (Father). Some Gnostic Christians did not believe that God was the creator of the heavens and the earth; they thought that creation was the work of a lower creator god or being called a *demiurge*. Some Christians did not believe that Jesus had died on the cross, while others thought that Jesus revealed a god other than the one God of the Jews. It was these divergent beliefs that led the church to clarify what it believed concerning God.

That clarification led to the affirmations of the historic creeds. There God is affirmed to be "one God, Maker of heaven and earth"—the first article of the creed. Later thinkers in Christianity used other terms in their efforts to unfold this affirmation of God as the creator and source of everything that is. The second article goes on to affirm a belief in "one Lord Jesus Christ, the only begotten Son of God, begotten of the Father before all worlds, Light of Light, very God of very God." Behind this affirmation lay controversies over the identity of Jesus that stemmed from the second and third centuries, which were further complicated by the affirmation of the Council of Chalcedon (451) that the person of Jesus the Christ is "fully human and fully divine." The affirmations in the creeds became fundamental to how Christians understood the revelation of God in Christ. However, they continued to explore and probe the mysteries affirmed in the creeds, giving rise to teachings that have been central to Christianity's development over time (Jenson 2002, 1–55).

PERSPECTIVES

Christians often say "God reveals Himself" or "God the Father" as if God were male. This highlights the inadequacy of language in relation to the ultimate. Many Christian churches today reject this male-dominated language for God and have begun a process of revision because they fundamentally believe that God is beyond gender, space, and time. Feminist theologians have been at the forefront of these changes, insisting that a privileging of male language, as well as male-dominated institutions and leadership, has led to a hierarchy of men over women. In some churches careful attention is given to the reading of scripture and the singing of traditional hymns, changing the masculine pronouns for God into gender-neutral terms.

Humanity and the Human Condition

Christianity, like the other great religious traditions, offers its own understanding of the human condition. It shares with biblical Judaism the root conviction that humanity is created "in the image of God, male and female he created them" (Gen. 1:27). This is part of a fundamental affirmation of the goodness of all creation that comes from God. In the conclusion of the biblical story of creation found in Genesis, we read these words: "and God saw everything that he had made, and behold, it was very good" (Gen. 1:31). This affirmation that the Creation comes from God and that it is good is shared across all the forms of Christianity.

While Christianity teaches the goodness of humanity, it also recognizes that humanity is broken. Again, all the great religious traditions recognize that human beings are not, to use a contemporary phrase, all they could be. Buddhism, for example, reminds us that life is full of suffering, while Hinduism sees that life is compromised by spiritual ignorance (Smith 1991). For Christianity, the brokenness of life arises from a turning away from God.

One finds many differing accounts within the Christian traditions of what gives rise to this turning away from God. In Christian traditions this broken human condition that estranges humans from God, neighbours, and the self is spoken of as *sin*. Some see sin as rooted in human freedom, others in pride, some in disobedience, and yet others in human self-centredness. This is a matter of continuing debate within Christianity, though all agree that there is brokenness or estrangement within humanity. The doctrine of original sin was an important development in Christian history that attempted to explain the estrangement of humanity from God.

PERSPECTIVES

The Doctrine of Original Sin

Original sin is a Christian doctrine rooted in an understanding of Adam and Eve's defiance of God in the Garden of Eden, described in Genesis 3. In the narrative, when the primordial couple, coaxed by the snake, disobeyed God's command not to eat the fruit of a designated tree, they were banished from the garden. In Christian traditions, this came to be understood not just as their own offence but also as a sin ascribed to all humanity.

This teaching did not spring from ancient Judaism, nor is it found in Islam. It is a doctrine read into Saint Paul, for example, when he writes, "By the disobedience of one man, many were made sinners" (Rom. 5:19). From this perspective, all human beings are considered to be "born in sin"—meaning inclined toward wrongdoing from birth. The notion of original sin is understood as pervading and tainting all human faculties. Christian groups differ on whether original sin is inherited genetically from the first couple or whether Adam in his misdeed simply represented all humanity.

One of the key debates in early Christian history pitted Pelagius (350–420 C.E.), who believed that every individual enters the world innocent and is then corrupted by the surrounding environment, and Saint Augustine (354–430 C.E.), who championed the idea of original sin. Augustine feared that the Pelagian view suggested humans could achieve salvation by their own efforts rather than relying on the power of God's grace, which was conveyed to the penitent because of Jesus Christ—understood as a second representative of all humanity (Adam being the first) who amends for all sin through his sacrifice on the cross. Pelagius, meanwhile, insisted that the doctrine of original sin took away humans' responsibility for their actions.

Most conservative Christian churches follow in the tradition of Augustine. More liberal approaches, such as that of theologian Matthew Fox, who posits the alternative of "original blessing" instead of original sin, follow in the line of Pelagius (Schuurman 2011).

Source: Peter Schuurman

SOURCES

Christianity emerged out of a matrix of Jewish and Middle Eastern traditions, Hellenic culture, and the society of imperial Rome.

Jewish Traditions

Central to the original matrix were the Jewish traditions. Jesus of Nazareth and the first generation of his followers were all from a Jewish world that was facing tremendous challenges. Their land had been under the control of foreigners for most of the previous four hundred years, and now they were a province of the Roman empire. It was a land that had been trodden by Jewish prophets for a millennium and where Jewish priests had conducted their rituals and sacrifices in the Temple since the time of Solomon (c. 970–30 B.C.E.). The Roman governor, Herod the Great, had begun rebuilding the Temple in c. 19 B.C.E., but the people of Palestine were still struggling to find their way. They were a fractured people in a difficult time.

Different Jewish groups—the Pharisees and Sadducees were the largest, but there were also smaller groups of Zealots, Essenes, and Herodians—were each seeking to find ways to be faithful to the Torah and to deal with the Roman occupation. Unlike many of their neighbours, the Jews believed in one god, and the name of the Holy One (Yahweh) was so holy that it did not cross the lips of pious Jews. This was also a time filled with messianic expectations, and it was in this context that a new movement was initiated by Jesus of Nazareth, a movement that sought to revitalize the Jewish community.

Hellenic Culture

The Jewish world in which Christianity began was not an isolated world. Since the time of Alexander the Great (356–323 B.C.E.), Hellenic culture had permeated the ancient world. Greek had become the *lingua franca* of the region, and the early Christian writings were in that language rather than Aramaic, the language of Jesus, or Hebrew, the language of the Jewish people. The wisdom of the Greek philosophers was widely known throughout the region, as were stories of the Greek gods and goddesses.

The caravan routes of the ancient world passed through the land of the Jews, making it a crossroads of commerce and trade. Olive groves dotted the countryside and villages were small, though Jerusalem is estimated to have had a population of 25,000 to 30,000 (some claim more). Culturally it was a diverse world, and elements from this world came to be part of the early Christian movement.

Roman Society

Imperial Rome was the dominant political power at the time of Jesus. Rome had ruled the Jewish lands since 63 B.C.E. The rebuilding of the Temple in Jerusalem that began in 19 B.C.E. under Herod the Great, who was seeking favour with the Jewish people, would continue through the time of Jesus. The Roman occupation had also brought the political practices, religion, and ideas of Roman society to the area. This added yet another layer to the world in which early Christianity began.

Middle Eastern Traditions

Other Middle Eastern traditions had influenced biblical Judaism before the emergence of Christianity. These included ancient Semitic traditions; Assyro-Babylonian traditions, including the Epic of Gilgamesh; and the Zoroastrian traditions of ancient Persia, with its teachings of the cosmic struggle of good and evil. When Christianity emerged, there were also goddess traditions from Anatolia and ancient Greece, with its splendid temple of Artemis, goddess of fertility, near Ephesus, and the traditions of Isis from Egypt. When Christianity moved beyond Jerusalem, it also encountered the mystery religions of the ancient world. These were smaller cults, such as the mysteries of Mithras and Osiris (the Egyptian god of the afterlife), whose initiation practices were shrouded in secrecy.

There is little scholarly consensus on the extent of the impact of these traditions on Christianity, but it is clear that they all influenced its development to some degree. This was the context in which Christians began to identify the sources that would shape their tradition as it unfolded in an ever-changing world (Kohn and Moore 2007, 1–72).

Oral Traditions

Little is known of the events and developments that occurred following Jesus's crucifixion and resurrection. Contemporary scholars of early Christianity tell us that stories of his life and teachings then began to circulate by word of mouth. His followers, initially dispirited, began to preach and teach what they knew about the Jesus they had known and the one they now knew as their risen Lord. Adolf von Harnack (1851–1930), a German theologian, though questioning the authenticity of doctrines that emerged in the early church, wrote in his book *What Is Christianity?*: "Whatever may have happened at the grave, and in the matter of the appearances, one thing is certain: This grave was the birthplace of the indestructible belief that death is vanquished, that there is a life eternal" (1901, 162).

Slowly these oral traditions moved beyond Jerusalem and Galilee to other places where Jesus's disciples took their message. The Apocryphal Acts of the Apostles, an early Christian writing from the second century, is filled with legends and stories of disciples taking the Christian message to other lands. We do know that with Paul, the apostle to the Gentiles (people who are not Jewish) in the 40s, these oral traditions reached across the Mediterranean world. By the 50s and 60s, some of these oral traditions had begun to take written form, perhaps in Aramaic but certainly in Greek. They would become the building blocks for the **Gospels**, the first four books of the Christian Bible, and some of the other writings included in the Bible.

The Bible

The Bible of the first Christians was the Jewish Bible, the Tanakh. It consists of three parts—the Torah (the first five books), the Prophets, and the Writings—and is a collection of writings that tells the story of the encounter of the Jewish people with their God, Yahweh. But the early Christians read it in light of their experience with Jesus of Nazareth, their Lord. Contemporary biblical scholars tell us that when the first Christians gathered, they read from the sacred writings of the Jews, recounted oral stories about Jesus, prayed, and shared a meal—the Lord's Supper—that they had learned about from the disciples.

The earliest writings that we know of in the Christian scriptures are the writings of Paul. They come from the late 40s and 50s C.E. These writings (for example, Philippians, First and Second Corinthians) are letters that Paul wrote to communities he had founded on his missionary journeys. Then there came the Gospels: Mark, the first; Matthew and Luke, from the 70s; and John, probably from the 90s. The other writings stem from the 70s and 80s. Other early Christian writings such as the Didache, the Teachings of the Apostles, and the Gospel of Thomas did not become part of what is called the Christian canon: the collection of writings considered to be reliable sources that became part of the New Testament. The twenty-seven books that make up the Christian canon were largely in place by the end of the second century. However, it wasn't until 382 that the Council of Rome listed the books of the Christian New Testament. These are the authoritative texts for the contemporary Catholic, Orthodox, and Protestant churches.

Gospel: from the Greek *euaneglion* (Latin *evangelium*, Old English *god-spell*), referring to the "good news" or "good tidings" of redemption in Jesus. It is also the name given to the first four books of the Christian New Testament.

These new writings were added to the Tanakh, or Hebrew scripture, to make up the whole of the Christian Bible. But there are variations among Catholics, Orthodox, and Protestants concerning the canon of the Old Testament. While the Protestant Bible has thirty-nine books in the Old Testament, the Catholic Bible has forty-six and the Orthodox Bible has forty-nine or fifty-one.

How scripture is understood varies. For Catholic traditions, scripture is part of the long tradition of the church and is to be seen and interpreted in that context. For the Orthodox traditions, scripture is seen in the context of the tradition and is to be interpreted in the context of the creeds. Protestant Christianity places scripture above tradition and the church; it is considered the definitive authority. Yet within each of these Christian strands, among individual Christians belonging to these traditions, among institutions, and even among church leaders, there is a great deal of diversity.

In the early twentieth century, American fundamentalism took the view that the Bible is the highest authority in the Christian life and has to be interpreted literally by the believer. This was a dramatic break with the older traditions of Christianity and provoked battles concerning scripture that are still going on, particularly among American Christians. Mormons, who consider themselves part of the Christian tradition, hold that their scripture, the Book of Mormon, is equal in authority to the Bible.

Councils

Councils were meetings of the leaders or bishops of the early Christian church to discuss issues facing the community. They became authoritative sources on matters of church practice and teaching. In Christian scripture we find an account of the first Christian council, the Council of Jerusalem. According to the Acts of the Apostles, this council was called to address the issue of whether or not Gentiles (non-Jews) were obliged to follow Jewish food laws if they became part of the new Christian community. The outcome of the meeting was that Gentiles were not obliged to observe the dietary laws once they had become Christians.

The first ecumenical (from the Greek *oikumene*, meaning "whole inhabited world") council was the Council of Nicaea in 325. Initiated by Emperor Constantine, this council gave Christianity its first shared creed, the Nicene Creed. This was later amended at the second Council of Constantinople in 381 and became the standard creed recited in the midst of Christian worship down to the present day. As a creed, it embodies the faith of the Christian community.

Christian Writers, Thinkers, and Mystics

Over the nearly two thousand years of Christian history, innumerable writers, thinkers, and mystics have contributed to the development and interpretation of Christianity. It was with Paul, the apostle to the Gentiles, that the early Christian movement began to engage those outside the Jewish world. From his missionary journeys of the 40s until his death by crucifixion in the mid-60s, Paul established *koinonias*, or churches, across the Roman world. He later wrote letters to these fledgling communities in Corinth, Ephesus, Thessalonica, Galatia, Philippi, and Colossae, as well as to the community in Rome before his visit. These letters became part of the Christian New Testament.

In addition to the writings that became part of the New Testament, there were writings beginning in the second century that addressed people both in and outside the Christian community. These writers became known as *apologists*, for their reasoned treatises concerning the Christian faith. In the mid-second century, Justin Martyr, a Greek convert to Christianity, wrote an apology addressed to the emperor and the Roman Senate pleading for a fair hearing for Christians. Origen, an Alexandrian Christian, wrote a book called *Contra Celsus*, a reply to the ridicule that the philosopher Celsus had heaped on Christians. Tertullian, who wrote in Latin, addressed Roman society and urged the toleration of Christians, even though they would not participate in the cult of the emperor or serve in the armies of Rome.

Later, Gregory of Nyssa wrote a treatise called *Not Three Gods* in an effort to clarify Christian teachings concerning God, and his elder brother, Basil the Great, wrote a liturgy that is still used in the Orthodox church to this day. Augustine wrote his *City of God* to answer charges that Christianity was responsible for the fall of Rome. These works, often referred to as the writings of the *Church Fathers*, affect the shape of Christianity for those who adopt their insights and wisdom.

Another group of writers who influenced the faith of many Christians was the *mystics*. Although mystics always insisted that words were inadequate to express their special experience of the Divine, they attempted to give people some sense of what had happened to them. Though there are mystical elements in all Christian writings, the first great mystical treatises came from Pseudo-Dionysius, a late-fifth-century figure. He wrote *On Divine Names*, *Mystical Theology*, and *Celestial Hierarchy*—works that pointed to the deeper mystery of existence. The Middle Ages witnessed a flowering of mystical writings from women, such as Hildegard of Bingen, Mechthild of Magdeburg, Margery Kempe, Catherine of Siena, Teresa of Avila, and Julian of Norwich. Julian's *Revelations of Divine Love* speak of God as "our Mother," and Teresa of Avila's *Interior Castle* sparked reform of her religious order of nuns, the Carmelites. The mystical tradition continued into the twentieth century with writings such as Thomas Merton's *The Seven Storey Mountain* and Father Bede Griffiths' *The Marriage of East and West*.

Writings of Reformers

It is important to acknowledge the writings of the reformers—those who sought to change or alter the Christianity they knew in their own time. Calls for reform have been an aspect of Christian writing from the beginning, but the major reform writers were those who founded new religious orders within Christianity (e.g., Benedictines, Franciscans, Dominicans) and new denominations in the Christian world (e.g., Lutheranism, Reformed, Methodism). Earlier writings were foundational for these new innovations in the Christian world. For example, Benedict of Nursia (480–547), the founding figure of Western monasticism, wrote his Rule of Saint Benedict after he had founded some monastic communities. During the Reformation period, the writings of Martin Luther (1483–1546)—beginning with *The Ninety-Five Theses* and on to *The Freedom of the Christian* and his translation of the Bible into German—would shape Lutheranism down to the present day. The same can be said for the writings of John Calvin, especially his *Institutes of the Christian Religion*, which shaped Reformed churches, and for Menno Simons, the Catholic priest and writer who became the leader of the Mennonites, the Dutch Anabaptists who bear his name.

Over the course of Christianity's two-thousand-year history, innumerable sources have influenced the unfolding life of Christianity. This will become more obvious as we turn now to the story of Christianity through the ages.

HISTORY

The World at the Birth of Jesus

As we have already noted, Christianity originated in the first century and grew to become the world's largest religious tradition. Here we will unfold something of that story from its beginnings in Palestine, then a province of the Roman Empire at the eastern end of the Mediterranean. This region was also a crossroads for caravans headed north from Africa and south with traders from the north and from more distant parts of Asia. It was a world vastly different from that of the twenty-first century. Travel was on foot or by horse or camel, or by boat if you were near the water. There were no modern means of communication to link one place to another. You could write letters on parchment, but they had to be carried and delivered by hand, taking weeks, months, or even years to arrive. Most human beings would never travel more than a few miles from where they were born. It was a world very different from our own.

This was a world dominated in the West by imperial Rome, but within its boundaries were some older civilizations. In northeast Africa was the Egyptian civilization, which was more than three thousand years old. Alexandria, on the Mediterranean coast of Egypt, was probably the most cosmopolitan city of the time. In Asia Minor was the Hellenic, or Greek, culture that since the time of Alexander the Great had permeated the known world as far as the borders of ancient India. Athens was still the heartland of its classical culture, and there we encounter the thought of Plato, Aristotle, and the great Greek philosophers. Out on the eastern edges of the Roman world were the Parthian and Scythian worlds, and beyond them the ancient civilizations of Central Asia, India, and China. The great Silk Road that began in Antioch—where the followers of Jesus were first called Christians—was just north of Palestine and ran all the way to China, a journey that took years to complete.

It was a world in which there were no churches, though there were temples dedicated to the many gods and goddesses of the Greek and Roman religions. Near Ephesus (modern-day Turkey) was a temple of Artemis, the Greek goddess known as Diana to the Romans, that was one of the seven wonders of the ancient world. Temples to the Roman gods were also being built in Palestine during these times. Jesus's people, the Jewish people, had one temple. It was in Jerusalem, a two- or three-day walk from Jesus's village in Galilee to the north. It had been recently rebuilt and was dedicated to Yahweh, the god of the Israelites. Unlike other temples, there was no image in the Jewish Temple. The Jews believed there was only one God (that is, they were monotheists) and that God could not be represented by an image. There were also synagogues, places for Jews to assemble for prayer and study, although they were not originally places of worship (Kohn and Moore 2007, 45–92).

In other parts of the ancient world were other kinds of religious practice and belief. There were followers of the Indian religions in India; the *chiao*, or teachings, in China; and Buddhism, which had recently moved out of India into Central Asia and would follow the Silk Road into China. Many Persians followed the ways of Zoroaster, and there were also the mystery religions and the manifold tribal religions of the ancient world. While there were differences of belief and practice across this world, there was also a shared assumption. That shared conviction was that the visible world of everyday was enfolded in a larger, invisible world of spirit. It was into such a world that Jesus of Nazareth was born in about 4 B.C.E.

Jesus in History

Little is known of the historical Jesus. Christian scriptures, which cannot be read simply as a historical record, tell us that he grew up in Nazareth, a small village in Galilee two or three days' walk from Jerusalem. According to the early Christian writings, he was born to Mary and Joseph in Bethlehem, near Jerusalem. Later, when Jesus began his ministry, he was baptized by his cousin, John the Baptist, in the River Jordan. According to the writer of the Gospel of Luke, he began his ministry when he was about thirty years old, following a time of prayer alone in the wilderness. He then began teaching in the synagogues and the countryside of Galilee. When he returned to Nazareth, he went to the synagogue, where he read from the prophet Isaiah. His reading included these words: "The Spirit of the Lord is upon me ... he has anointed me to preach good news to the poor ... to proclaim release to the captive ... sight to the blind ... liberty [to] those who are oppressed ...." And when he had finished reading, he said, "Today this scripture has been fulfilled ..." (Luke 4: 16–21).

Over the next one to three years, Jesus gathered a group of followers as he travelled the countryside teaching and, according to New Testament writers, healing the sick. He spoke, they said, as one who had authority. He often told stories and parables and he urged people to change their lives; at times he withdrew from public to pray. He referred to God by the familiar term *Abba*, or Father, and summarized his teachings as love of God and one's neighbour. At the end of this time he travelled to Jerusalem, where he was arrested and put to death by the Roman authorities. Mary Magdalene and other early women followers of Jesus took spices to anoint his body but, according to New Testament sources, when they reached the tomb, they found it empty. Later some of his followers claimed to have encountered Jesus on the road to Emmaus, a village a short distance from Jerusalem.

The sources that we have for the historical Jesus are limited to the early Christian writings, especially those that came to be part of the Christian New Testament. Consequently, we cannot really know where Jesus was born, when he started his ministry, or all the things that he said or did. There are also other sources, for example, a couple of references in a writing of Josephus (c. 37–100), a Jewish writer and author of *Antiquities of the Jews*. Josephus simply notes in passing that there was "a wise man, Jesus ... a doer of wonderful works" whom Pilate had "condemned to the cross." But then he appeared to them—"those that loved him" is Josephus's phrase—after three days. He also noted that "the tribe of Christians named for him are not extinct to this day."

All the early Christian writings come from a time after Jesus's death and they share the conviction that Jesus had risen after he was crucified. How did the early Christian writings that became part of the Christian canon—the New Testament—portray Jesus of Nazareth?

Jesus in the Canonical Gospels

Throughout his ministry of teaching and healing, people wondered who Jesus was. The early Christian writings known as the Gospels—the books of Matthew, Mark, Luke, and John—call him by many names, including "Teacher," "Jesus of Nazareth," and "the Son of Man." Each gives a distinctive portrait of Jesus of Nazareth. According to contemporary scholarship, there is a great deal of uncertainty about the identity of the authors of the Gospels.

The Gospel of Mark

Mark's gospel, considered to be the earliest, presents Jesus as a mysterious figure who preaches, teaches, and heals the sick in Galilee. He gathers a small band of followers around him. They recognize him as the Messiah but he tells them to tell no one. He then goes up to Jerusalem, where he is betrayed, arrested, and executed in the manner reserved for opponents of imperial Rome: by crucifixion. Mark's gospel ends with Mary Magdalene and the other women discovering the empty tomb. In Mark, then, Jesus is portrayed as the suffering "Son of Man," the one who suffers for the coming of God's reign in human affairs.

The Gospel of Matthew

In Matthew we have a different portrait. It opens with a genealogy that places Jesus in a lineage that goes back to the Jewish king David and then all the way back to Abraham. Matthew presents the story of Jesus's miraculous birth in Bethlehem. After being baptized by his cousin, John the Baptist, Jesus retires into the wilderness to pray. He then goes "about all Galilee, teaching ... and preaching the gospel of the kingdom and healing every disease and infirmity." Like Moses of the Israelites, who led the exodus from Egypt and received the Law on Mount Sinai, Jesus is presented as teaching a new way to fulfil God's will and law, the way of righteousness. Jesus's way is outlined in the Sermon on the Mount (Matt. 5–7) and includes a new commandment: "to love the enemy and to do good to those who oppose you." In Matthew's gospel, Jesus is also characterized as challenging tradition by healing on the Sabbath and eating with outcasts and sinners.

The Gospel of Luke

Luke's portrait of Jesus is found in two volumes, the Gospel According to Luke and the Acts of the Apostles. While contemporary biblical scholars are not in agreement as to the actual authorship of these works, they appear to have been written for a non-Jewish audience. Here Jesus is portrayed as a liberator of the oppressed and a friend to the disadvantaged. When he announces his intentions in his home synagogue in Nazareth, he says that his purpose is "to set at liberty those who are oppressed." It is in Luke's versions that readers come to learn about the Good Samaritan and the Good Shepherd, figures that readers of the Gospels have loved through the ages.

Though born in humble circumstances, Luke's Jesus is the son of God, central to the story of salvation that is unfolding in human history. While things do not appear to be going in the right direction, Jesus's death on the cross turns out to be essential, and his death is presented as not the end of the story. In Luke's gospel Jesus tells his disciples that "it is written that Christ should suffer and on the third day rise from the dead and that repentance and the forgiveness of sins should be preached to all nations" (Luke 24:46).

In Luke's second volume, Acts of the Apostles, he continues to unfold the story of salvation, a new chapter in God's dealing with the world. According to Acts, sometime after Jesus's ascension to heaven, the disciples receive the gift of the Holy Spirit, which allows them to begin to preach the story of Jesus in public. This then leads to the founding of a new community of believers. Luke calls the early Christians followers of "the way," which is understood as revealed in the life, acts, and teachings of Jesus of Nazareth that his followers emulated.

The Gospel of John

The fourth portrait of Jesus comes from the Gospel of John. It is the latest of the Gospels, probably written at the end of the first century. It discloses a very different Jesus, with no historical lineage or birth story to introduce him. Rather, John uses a Greek philosophical term referring to cosmic reason, *logos* (word). Christ is presented as the one who "in the beginning was the Word and the Word was with God, and the Word was God ... in him was life and the light of men ... And the Word became flesh and dwelt among us, full of grace and beauty" (John 1:1–4, 14). Contemporary scholars regard the opening to John's gospel as a hymn.

John has Jesus's ministry unfolding over three years, with numerous trips between Galilee and Jerusalem. All the events of that ministry disclose Jesus as "the light," John's central metaphor for Jesus. Jesus is presented as bringing a truth that shines in the darkness and reveals the truth or wisdom of God. In this gospel are the famous "I am" passages: "I am the bread of life"; "I am the light of the world"; "I am the way, the truth, and the life"; "I am the resurrection and the life." In John's gospel, Jesus also continually reminds his hearers that he was "sent by the Father" as the embodied word of God. The connection between the embodied word and God is so profound that the writer of the gospel even has Jesus say, "I and the Father are one" (John 10:30). Many biblical scholars see in these statements the early community's belief in Jesus's divine authority rather than a faithful rendering of his own words.

The horror of the crucifixion of Jesus becomes in John a "lifting up," a glorifying of God, a disclosure of the light illuminating the darkness. This lifting up, or exaltation, is also a part of John's resurrection story. Again it is Mary Magdalene who first discovers the empty tomb and first sees Jesus and calls him *rabboni* (teacher). For John, Jesus is the risen word that then appears to the disciples (Neufeld 2007, 56–79).

It is a multi-faceted portrait of Jesus that emerges in the canonical gospels. After the death of Jesus's first followers, it was these writings, along with the other twenty-three books of the Christian New Testament, that became the witness that is foundational for Christianity. It is important, however, to remember that these writings emerged over the first hundred years after Jesus's death. They did not receive canonical status until the fourth century.

PERSPECTIVES

Biblical Scholarship: The Jesus Seminar

There is a great deal of diversity (and dissent) within biblical scholarship, particularly with regard to traditional and liberal approaches, as to the authorship of the gospels and other New Testament books, the miracles, and the actual sayings of Jesus in the gospels. For some fundamentalist Christian scholars, the Bible is divinely inspired and must be read literally. Liberal approaches that developed after the Age of Enlightenment in the late eighteenth century, including biblical criticism, do not consider the Bible to be a collection of factual statements but instead as narratives reflecting their writers' and the early community's beliefs. These approaches are undeterred by notions of the correctness of church doctrine or biblical inerrancy. Jesus's miracles, for instance, are largely understood as metaphorical narratives pointing to the greatness of God.

The Jesus Seminar, founded in 1985 by two biblical scholars, Robert Funk and John Dominic Crossan, has grown into a group of about 150 scholars who gather to reconstruct the life, actions, and words of the historical Jesus. They have concluded that many sayings attributed to Jesus were in fact later additions. The findings of the Seminar have drawn both support and harsh criticism from other biblical scholars and clergy.

Paul, Apostle to the Gentiles

Though Christianity began as a movement within Judaism, it soon began to spread to the Gentile world. A central figure in that development was Saul of Tarsus (c. 5 B.C.E.–67 C.E.), who later came to be known as Paul, the apostle to the Gentiles. Saul was a Pharisee—a member of a prominent sect that observed Jewish law strictly—from Tarsus (in modern-day Turkey), and he was a strong opponent of the followers of Jesus. There are varied versions of the events surrounding what is known as Saul's conversion story. The writer of the Acts of the Apostles tells us that while on his way to Damascus, Saul had an experience that utterly changed the direction of his life. Acts notes that he heard a voice saying, "Saul, Saul, why do you persecute me?" When Saul inquired, "Who are you, Lord?" The answer was, "I am Jesus, whom you are persecuting" (Acts 9: 3ff). Paul's own account is simply that he "received a revelation of Jesus Christ … when God … was pleased to reveal his son to me, so that I might proclaim him among the Gentiles."

Paul saw himself as having received a commission to become a follower of Jesus, and he became a great missionary responsible for establishing churches in urban centres across the ancient world. Paul's letters to these churches, in places such as Corinth, Philippi, Thessalonica, and Ephesus, in the 40s and 50s are the oldest writings included in the Christian scripture. He also wrote to the Christians in Rome, and it was in Rome that Paul, after twenty

Words

Paul's Social Vision of the Christian Message

Writing to the Christians in Galatia, a community that Paul had established on his missionary journeys, he articulates his radical social vision of Christianity:

"… in Christ Jesus you are all sons of God through faith. … For as many of you as were baptized into Christ have put on Christ. There is neither Jew nor Greek, there is neither slave nor free, there is neither male nor female; for you are all one in Christ Jesus" (Gal. 3: 26–28).

years of missionary work, is believed to have died as a Christian martyr.

From an Outlaw Religion to the Religion of the Empire

In 64 C.E. a fire destroyed large sections of Rome. Emperor Nero, whose actions surrounding the fire came to be highly criticized, was looking for a scapegoat. He found it in the obscure Jewish group that was just beginning to be known as Christians. There were rumours that they talked about a new kingdom and a new lord—an affront to the ruling political leaders, who assumed this meant that the followers were not being loyal to Nero's empire. They seemed suspicious, so they were blamed for the fire and brutally persecuted. Later they would be charged with atheism for their failure to observe the cult of the emperor. This became the first persecution of early Christians.

When troubles in Palestine led to the destruction of the Temple in Jerusalem in 70, anything associated with the Jewish people was held suspect. It was not until Constantine's Edict of Milan in 313 that Christianity would be legalized and the periodic waves of persecution come to an end. Over those 250 years, Christianity took root in the towns and cities of the ancient world, including among groups of women in the upper echelons of Roman society. Catechetical schools were founded in Alexandria and Antioch, and communities of Christians were established in Corinth, Ephesus, Damascus, and Carthage, in North Africa.

The Roman policy of scapegoating Christians and persecuting them for their faith and for their failure to observe the cult of the emperor eventually backfired. Over time the martyr emerged as the exemplary Christian, the one who in the face of persecution went calmly to his or her death rather than renounce the Christian faith. This led to more rather than fewer followers of the Christian message, yet persecution continued into the early fourth century.

PEOPLE & PLACES

The Martyrdom of Perpetua

The story of the martyrdom of Perpetua was known across the Christian world. She was arrested and imprisoned in Carthage for the simple reason that she was a Christian and refused to participate in the cult of the emperor. She was a young woman who had a nursing child, and her father pleaded with her to renounce her faith. She answered that she could not be "anything else than what I am, a Christian." When Hilarion, the Roman governor, asked her to offer sacrifice for the emperor's welfare, she replied, "I will not; I am a Christian." She was "condemned to the beasts" and calmly met her death in the public arena (Malone 2000, 102–17).

Christian Apologists

In the midst of this periodic local persecution, in the second and third centuries Christians began arguing about their beliefs as they sought to gain respect from their Roman and Greek critics. The apologists, a group of Christian thinkers, emerged to address these issues (Frend 1984, 229–57). In the mid-second century Justin Martyr addressed the Roman authorities, pleading for a fair hearing. Answering charges that the Christians practised cannibalism, he explained that it was a ritual practice to consume the "body and blood of Christ." He was, however, ignored and put to death. Later, Origen took issue with those who presented Christianity as an example of lower-class absurdity in his *Contra Celsus* ("Against Celsus"), aimed at a famous philosopher who had ridiculed Christianity.

While the apologists held firmly to the conviction that Jesus had opened up a new way to be in relation to God, and that God had raised Jesus from the dead after he was crucified, they were uncertain how to explain the relationship of the Christ to God. Some thought that Jesus had come to have a special relationship with God when he was baptized by John in the River Jordan. Others thought he was a special creation of God from the time of his birth. And some thought that when Jesus had lived on earth, he *was* God and that the heavens had been empty. Others thought the mystery couldn't be explained and simply had to be believed. These debates were to continue for a considerable period.

PEOPLE & PLACES

Justin Martyr, the First Christian Apologist

Justin Martyr (c. 100–165) was a Greek convert to Christianity and a philosopher. He addressed his *First Apology*, or defence of the Christian faith, to the Roman emperor and the Senate, answering charges that Christians were atheists and cannibals. It explained that Christians believed that Jesus the Christ fulfilled the universal longing for truth and he also explained what it was that Christians practised. It includes these words:

To the Emperor Titus ... Augustus Caesar ... to the Senate and the whole Roman people—on behalf of men of every nation who are unjustly hated and reviled, I, Justin, the son of Pricus and grandson of Bacchius ... in Syria Palestrina ... have drawn up this plea and petition.

... Reason requires that those who are truly pious and philosophers should honor and cherish the truth alone, scorning merely to follow the opinions of the ancients, if they are worthless ... to speak and do what is right, though death should take him away. So do you, since you are called pious and philosophers and guardians of justice and lovers of truth, at least give us a hearing?

What sound-minded man will not admit that we [Christians] are not godless, since we worship the Fashioner of the universe, declaring him, as we have been taught, to have no need of blood and libations and incense, but praising him by the word of prayer and thanksgiving for all that he has give us ... that Jesus Christ alone was really begotten as Son of God, being his Word and First-Begotten and Power, and becoming man by his will he taught us these things for the reconciliation and restoration of the human race.

We have been taught that Christ is the first-begotten of God and have previously testified that he is the Logos [Eternal Reason] of which every race of man partakes. Those who lived in accordance with reason are Christians, even though they were called godless, such as, among the Greeks, Socrates and Heraclitus.... But those who so live now, are Christians fearless and unperturbed ...

[Concerning Christian rites and practices, Justin wrote:] On the day called Sunday there is a meeting in one place of those who live in cities or the country. There ... the memoirs of the apostles or the writings of the prophets are read ... the president in a discourse then urges us to the imitation of these noble things. Then we stand together and offer prayers.... Then bread and wine and water is brought and distributed to all there and a collection is taken ... to take care of the orphans and widows and those who are in want ... and the strangers ... (Justin Martyr, *First Apology*, in Kerr 1978, 20–25).

Source: Justin Martyr, "Apology: Plea for a Fair Hearing," Hugh T. Kerr, first published in *Early Christian Fathers* (Volume I in the Library of Christian Classics, Westminster). Used by permission of Westminster John Knox Press. www.wjkbooks.com.

At the same time, great efforts were being made to clarify the teachings of those who were called the Apostles, men who had known Jesus personally. This came to include Paul, who also believed that he had met Jesus on the road to Damascus. Summaries of the teachings of the Apostles, called *regulae fidei* ("rules of faith"), came to be written and collected. The thinkers expressed things in their own words, but they all realized that their Christian faith was built upon a three-articled faith: a faith in God the Father, "the Creator

> PEOPLE & PLACES
>
> **Irenaeus (c. 130–202), Bishop of Lyons**
>
> Born near the Black Sea, educated in Rome, and a Christian bishop in Gaul (modern France), Irenaeus articulated this rule of faith (*regula fidei*) during his conflict with a group known as Gnostic Christians:
>
> The church, although scattered over the whole world even to its extremities, received from the Apostles and their disciples the faith in one God, the Father Almighty, Maker of heaven and earth, the seas and all that in them is ... Christ Jesus, the Son of God, who became incarnate for our salvation, and in the holy spirit, who by the prophets proclaimed the dispensations, the advents ... the passion and resurrection from the dead ... this kerygma and this faith the church ... diligently observes, as if it occupied one house, and believes as it had but one mind ....
>
> Irenaeus also said, "Christ became what we are so that we could become as he is."
>
> **Source:** *Perversions of the Heretic,* first published as *The Treatise of Irenaeus of Lugdunum Against the Heresies* in Early Christian Classics, trans. and ed. by F. R. Montgomery Hitchcock by SPCK in 1916.

of Heaven and Earth"; in God the Son, "His Son our Lord"; and in God the Holy Spirit, "the Lord and Giver of Life." The relationship between each of these articles of faith, however, remained a mystery.

Despite these continuing debates within Christianity, the exemplary courage of the early Christian martyrs and their ongoing missionary activity turned more and more people toward the Christian faith. When the Roman emperor Diocletian (244–305) launched an empire-wide persecution of Christians in 303, calling them "God-worshipers," it was to be the last persecution. While some renounced their faith, many others died: 3,000 to 4,000 is the best estimate. A struggle for dominance followed the death of Diocletian, and Constantine became one of two new rulers of a divided empire. He reigned from 306 to 337, becoming the sole emperor after 324. Constantine, together with Emperor Licinius, who ruled in the east, issued the Edict of Milan in 313. It legalized Christianity and restored the property of churches to the bishops. The situation for Christianity was dramatically altered. No longer an outlaw religion, it became by 380 the official religion of the Roman empire. Christianity would come to be centred in Constantinople, where Constantine had moved the capital in 325, for hundreds of years.

Councils, Thinkers, Monks, and the Christian Church (325–1000)

The changes that came with Emperor Constantine's linking Christianity to the political realm could not have been anticipated. Christian communities suddenly became state-supported institutions. Constantine seems to have recognized that the growing Christian world could be an important source of order and stability across the Roman world, and the church welcomed its new-found social position and prominence. The bishops of major centres of Christianity—Rome, Alexandria, Antioch, and Constantinople—began to gain enhanced stature. By the end of Constantine's reign in 337, he was regarded as a Christian emperor, something that would have been inconceivable for former generations, particularly those who remembered the earlier persecutions of Christians (Frend 1984, 474ff).

Constantine, however, began to discover that there was a great deal of disagreement in the Christian world with regard to what exactly Christians believed and practised. Was God the creator of the world? Some Christians said no, others said yes. What was the relationship between God and Jesus Christ? There were many views. What was the Holy Spirit? Constantine called a gathering of leaders of the church to address these issues, leading to the formation of a new institution called a council.

Councils

In 325 Constantine invited the bishops of the church to gather at his summer residence in Nicaea. When the 318 bishops had gathered, their debates came to focus on the curious question of whether or not there was a time when Jesus Christ was not. It seemed crucial to those in attendance to define a right, or orthodox, understanding of the relationship between Jesus and God. One group, led by Athanasius, a bishop from Alexandria, insisted that the fatherhood of God was eternal and thus God's son was also eternal. The Arians, or those sympathetic to Arius, a popular priest from Alexandria, argued that only God was eternal and that the incarnate *logos* (word of God)—that is, Jesus—was a special creation of God. They seemed to suggest that there had been a time when the Son was not. Athanasius won the debates, with only two bishops supporting Arius in the end.

The result was the Creed of Nicaea, or Nicene Creed (see pages 92–93), the first attempt to articulate the shared faith of the Christian church. It affirmed that God was the creator of the world. This was a crucial affirmation that signified a less pronounced voice for Gnostic Christians, who believed that the world was created by a demiurge, a being understood as responsible for the creation of the material world but subordinate to God. The creed also affirmed that Jesus Christ was the son of God and "very God of very God," and that the Holy Spirit was "the Lord and Giver of Life." Gnostic Christianity and other movements that held alternative beliefs were being moved increasingly to the margins of Christianity.

The council also settled some practical issues such as the date of Easter: Christians would use the solar calendar rather than the moon-based Jewish calendar. It also issued some rules on common practices, including a prohibition on self-castration (a practice that some early apologists viewed as an expression of Christian chastity), usury among priests, and kneeling during the liturgy.

Later councils were initiated mainly by bishops from the leading Christian communities in Rome and Constantinople. Over the next four centuries there were six more ecumenical councils—Constantinople I, Ephesus, Chalcedon, Constantinople II and III, and Nicaea II—as well as numerous local councils seeking to resolve issues of faith and practice for Christians. The last of these, the second Council of Nicaea, addressed the issue of icons. There were those who opposed icons, or holy images, on the grounds that people were worshipping images when worship should be offered only to God; they were known as *iconoclasts*. The council decided that it was permissible to venerate icons but not to worship them. One of the arguments in favour of icons was that without them, the illiterate masses would have no access to the teachings of scripture.

This was also a time that began to see a growing gap between the way that Christian faith was understood in the western, Latin-speaking regions of the Holy Roman Empire and its eastern, Greek-speaking counterpart.

The Cappadocian Fathers

In the era between the first council at Nicaea (325) and the second, at Constantinople (381), a group known as the Cappadocian Fathers—the brothers Basil the Great and Gregory of Nazianzus and Gregory of Nyssa—rose to prominence. Their name stemmed from their origins in Cappadocia, a Christian region in modern-day Turkey. Between the first and second councils these men helped to clarify Christian teachings. Immensely influential, they became known as *apophatic* thinkers, that is, those who acknowledge that God is ineffable, or beyond words and concepts. Thus language is understood as always inadequate to the truth and reality of God. It was a kind of thinking sometimes called the *via negativa*, or negative way. Gregory of Nyssa would say that Christians did not "believe in three gods," as some people assumed when they heard the Christian teaching about the Father, Son, and Holy Spirit. Rather, he said, God is one but is revealed and known in Christian experience as Father and Son and Holy Spirit. It was a way of thinking that acknowledged paradox and mystery (Gregorios 1988, 1ff).

Augustine of Hippo

Born into a religiously mixed family in Thagaste in North Africa, Augustine (354–430) came to be regarded as the central thinker of the Latin-speaking west. Augustine was thirty when he became a

Christian after sampling other philosophies and outlooks. He had been a Manichean, following a teaching that centred on the eternal rivalry between good and evil in the universe, before becoming a neo-Platonist. It was from the neo-Platonists that Augustine learned to think about God in spiritual rather than material terms. Then, as a young rhetorician attached to the Roman court in Milan, Augustine underwent a dramatic conversion to Christianity. It was the culmination of a long spiritual journey. He abandoned his career and, with his illegitimate son Adeodatus ("gift of god"), returned to North Africa to found a religious community, where his reputation as a holy seeker grew. When he went to the nearby town of Hippo to attend church, he was seized by the parishioners, who brought him to the bishop and insisted that he be made a priest. He was duly ordained as a priest, and when the bishop died, Augustine became the new bishop of Hippo.

His reputation grew because of two books, *The Confessions* and *The City of God.* His *Confessions* is an autobiographical account of his journey toward the Christian faith. It opens with the famous words "The soul is restless until it comes to rest in God." Augustine then recounts his journey through infancy, childhood, and adolescence into young adulthood. He writes of jealousy in infanthood, rivalry in childhood, peer pressure and desire in adolescence, and competition and self-advancement in young adulthood. Yet, Augustine argued, beneath it all was a constant longing for God. It is only upon finally turning to God that one comes home to oneself.

In the *City of God,* Augustine responds to the charge that the fall of Rome in 410 was a consequence of the Romans' abandonment of their pagan gods for Christianity. Augustine argues that since the City of Man—that is, all human societies—is rooted in self-love, it must be impermanent. Societies rise and they fall, since they are subject to the imperfection of human beings in time. In time only limited justice and peace are achieved. Only the City of God, grounded in the love of God and God's justice, is forever. But the City of God is only anticipated in time; it is fulfilled in eternity. While Christians should support the quest for justice and peace in human society, they must also recognize the limitations of such a quest.

Words

Augustine

From *The Confessions**

... man desires to praise thee, for he is a part of thy creation ... thou has made us for thyself and restless is our heart until it comes to rest in thee.... (Augustine 1998, 52)

I wish now to review in memory my past wickedness ... not because I love them, but that I might love thee, O my God ... the world so often forgets thee, its Creator and falls in love with thy creature instead of thee. (54)

[At the moment of Augustine's conversion] I was weeping in the most bitter contrition of my heart, when suddenly I heard the voice of a boy or girl ... "pick it up, read it." I ceased weeping and began ... to think whether it was usual for children ... to sing such a song ... I got to my feet [thinking] this was a divine command to open the Bible and read the first passage I should light upon ... "not in drunkenness ... not in chambering and wantonness, not in strife and envying, but put on the Lord Jesus Christ ..." I wanted to read no further, nor did I need to. For instantly ... there was infused in my heart something like the light of full certainty and all the gloom of doubt vanished away. (58)

From *The City of God*†

... I have taken upon myself the task of defending the glorious City of God against those who prefer their own gods to the Founder of that city. I treat it both as it exists in this world of time ... living by faith, and as it stands in the security of its everlasting seat. (Augustine 1972, 5)

The experience of mankind in general, as far as God's people is concerned, is comparable to the experience of the individual man. There is

(continued)

a process of education through the epochs of a people's history, as through the successive stages of a man's life, designed to raise them from the temporal and the visible to an apprehension of the eternal and the invisible. (392)

The peace of the body ... is a tempering of the component parts in duly ordered proportion; the peace of the irrational soul is a duly ordered repose of the appetites; the peace of the rational soul is the duly ordered agreement of cognition and action. The peace of body and soul is the duly ordered life and health of a living creature; peace between mortal man and God is an ordered obedience, in faith; ... peace between men is an ordered agreement of mind with mind; the peace of a home is the ordered agreement among those who live together ...; the peace of the heavenly City is a perfectly ordered and perfectly harmonious fellowship in the enjoyment of God, and a mutual fellowship in God.... (870)

St. Augustine Confessions, trans. Henry Chadwick (Oxford University Press, 1998).

†*The City of God*, ed. David Knowles (Penguin Books).

With Augustine, Christian thought began moving in a direction that was more focused on the moral and social dimensions of Christianity than on the mystical elements that were more evident in eastern Christianity.

Monks and Monasticism

This period also saw the emergence of the monastic traditions of Christianity. They grew out of the ascetic practices of the Desert Fathers, men such as Saint Anthony (c. 251–356) in Egypt who went into the desert to live lives of strict ascetic and spiritual discipline, practices they felt could lead to union with God. These monks of the 200s gave rise to new monastic practices in the 300s and 400s that have endured down to the present day. In the east the *Rule of Saint Basil* came to dominate the communal monastic forms. Basil the Great, bishop of Caesarea, established his monastery in about 350; he opposed the extreme asceticism of hermit monks living in seclusion. Basil emphasized the founding of communities devoted to prayer and work. Even before 350, his older sister, Macrina, had begun establishing monasteries.

In the west, Benedict of Nursia's (480–527) *Rule of Saint Benedict* (c. 510) led to an enduring form of monastic life. Benedictine monasteries were organized around eight periods of communal prayer, known as the *horarium*. These periods of communal prayer structured a daily life that also included work and study. Every day the monks would pray the *horarium,* study spiritual and devotional literature, and engage in manual work in the monastery fields, in the kitchen, or in the *scriptorium* copying manuscripts. There was no private property, and the monks took vows of obedience, celibacy, and poverty (Frend 1984, 881–83). The Benedictine way proved to be very successful, and within a century there were Benedictine monasteries across the western Christian world. As the so-called Dark Ages descended on the West, monastic traditions kept alive the culture and learning of the ancient world. Later, during the time of Charlemagne (c. 800), the Benedictines became involved in education.

Crusades, Schoolmen, and Mystics in Medieval Christianity, 1000–1500

Shortly after the beginning of the new millennium of the Christian era, leaders of the western church sought to impose their dominance on the eastern church. The result was the "Great Schism," which split Christianity into the western, Catholic church and the eastern, Orthodox church—a rupture that endured throughout the new millennium, despite short-lived efforts to heal the breach at the Council of Florence (1439). The Great Schism was largely a consequence of the papacy's seeking to extend its authority.

Pope Gregory VII (1073–85) issued his *Dictatus Papae* in 1075, which claimed that the Roman church was founded by God alone and that the Roman pontiff alone could rightfully be called universal. This was later called the Papal Revolution, and it had enormous consequences for the life of medieval Christians. While contributing to the split between eastern and western Christianity, it also fuelled conflict between popes and kings as they jockeyed for power.

Gregory, like some other popes of the period, was influenced by the reforms at Cluny, in France, that had revitalized monastic traditions. This was also a time that saw the emergence of new institutions (universities and mendicant orders) and new thinkers (schoolmen and mystics) that would reshape Christianity in the medieval period. It would also give rise to the Crusades.

The Crusades

The Crusades were a series of nine military initiatives launched by the popes from 1095 until 1272. The first was initiated by Pope Urban II in 1095. It was in part a response to a request for assistance from the Byzantine emperor in Constantinople, but it was also undertaken to wrest the Holy Land from the control of "infidels" (unbelievers). The infidels were identified as the Muslims who had controlled Jerusalem and the ancient lands of Palestine since 638. In 1099 the Crusaders took Jerusalem, slaughtering Muslims, Jews, and Christians. The city was recaptured in 1187 by the Muslims under Salah ad-Din (Saladin), who recognized the rights of all faiths to religious worship in Jerusalem.

There were eight subsequent failed attempts to take Jerusalem. Additional crusades were waged in Europe against pagan Slavs and the Russian Orthodox in Russia, against Cathars—Christians in France who were regarded as heretical—and others. The Crusades were a blot on medieval Christianity. They were also the final wedge in the Great Schism between eastern and western Christianity, particularly the Fourth Crusade in 1204, when Constantinople, the centre of the eastern church, was pillaged.

Words

An account of the sack of Constantinople from Nicetas Choniates, the Byzantine historian and imperial secretary:

> How shall I begin to tell of the deeds wrought by these nefarious men! Alas, the images [icons], which ought to have been adored, were trodden under foot! Alas, the relics of the holy martyrs were thrown into unclean places! Then was seen what one shudders to hear, namely, the divine body and blood of Christ was spilled upon the ground or thrown about. They snatched the precious reliquaries, thrust into their bosoms the ornaments which these contained, and used the broken remnants for pans and drinking cups—precursors of Anti-Christ, authors and heralds of his nefarious deeds which we momentarily expect. Manifestly, indeed, by that race then, just as formerly, Christ was robbed and insulted and His garments were divided by lot; only one thing was lacking, that His side, pierced by a spear, should pour rivers of divine blood on the ground.
>
> Nor can the violation of the Great Church [Hagia Sophia] be listened to with equanimity. For the sacred altar, formed of all kinds of precious materials and admired by the whole world, was broken into bits and distributed among the soldiers, as was all the other sacred wealth of so great and infinite splendor....
>
> No one was without a share in the grief. In the alleys, in the streets, in the temples, complaints, weeping, lamentations, grief, the groaning of men, the shrieks of women, wounds, rape, captivity, the separation of those most closely united. Nobles wandered about ignominiously, those of venerable age in tears, the rich in poverty. Thus it was in the streets, on the corners, in the temple, in the dens, for no place remained unassailed or defended the suppliants. All places everywhere were filled full of all kinds of crime. Oh, immortal God, how great the afflictions of the men, bow great the distress! (Nicetas 1912, 15–16)

Source: *Nicetas Choniates: The Sack of Constantinople* (1904), D. C. Munro, tr., Translations and Reprints from the Original Sources of European History, Series 1, Vol. 3:1 (rev. ed.) (Philadelphia: University of Pennsylvania Press, 1912).

Mendicant Orders

The medieval period also saw the rise of mendicant orders. These were religious orders that embraced poverty, depending for support upon the charity of local populations, and sought to enhance the life of lay Christians. The most famous of the mendicant orders, the Franciscans, was founded by Saint Francis of Assisi (1181–1226), who was known for his love of all creation and for his strict asceticism. The only writing attributed to Francis is his "Canticle to the Sun," which celebrates creation, including Brother Sun, Sister Moon, Mother Earth, and Sister Water. While praying in a local church in Assisi, a hill town in central Italy, Francis felt called by Christ to "repair" the church, which he understood as a call for spiritual renewal of the Christianity of his day. He embraced a life of poverty and taught and preached—even to the birds, it is said. The number of his followers grew quickly; they were known for their joyous singing as they preached the gospel of Jesus to the people of Umbria. Tradition holds that late in his life Francis received the *stigmata*, the wounds of Christ, on his own body. One of his followers, Bonaventure (1221–74), wrote a *Life of Saint Francis* and also *The Soul's Journey to God,* a seven-stage account. *The Soul's Journey* is one of the classics of medieval spirituality.

The Dominicans were another mendicant order who were known as preachers. They were followers of Dominic, a Spanish priest. The Dominicans sought to renew the church by teaching and preaching among the poor and among the Albigensians, a growing Christian religious group that was considered heretical. Dominicans later became known for their contributions to a newly founded institution of the medieval world, the university.

Schoolmen

Schoolmen was the name given to teachers in the universities that began to emerge in the European Christian world. Thomas Aquinas (1225–74), perhaps the greatest of the schoolmen, was a Dominican, as was the great medieval mystic Meister Eckhart. These new schools of higher education began to spring up across Europe: in Bologna in 1088, Paris (1150), Oxford (1167), Salamanca (1218), and Coimbra (1290). They were influenced by the schools of Cordoba in Muslim Spain that had brought the ancient learning of Greece to Europe in the 900s, and by the cathedral schools run by religious orders. These new universities taught law, rhetoric, logic, mathematics, music, and astronomy. It was in this milieu that medieval scholars such as Thomas Aquinas, who taught at the University of Paris, inaugurated what he understood as a new science: theology, a novel approach to the study of God (from the Latin *theos*). He believed that there were two sources for knowledge of God: reason and revelation. In his *Summa Theologica,* Thomas sought to order that knowledge in a disciplined and orderly way. His was an intellectual journey toward God (Gilson 1956, 6–13).

Medieval Women Mystics

Within the monasteries and nunneries of medieval Christianity, both men and women were seeking to chart the spiritual journey to God. The approach to God of the medieval women mystics grew out of their visionary experience, their practice of prayer, and their learning. Hildegard of Bingen (1098–1179) was one of these remarkable women. She corresponded with popes and kings, composed music, painted her visions, and founded communities in Bingen and Eibingen. Her writings include *Scivias* ("Know the Ways of the Lord") and the *Book of Divine Works*. These visionary works focus on a creation suffused with divine presence and the inner spiritual connection between the human microcosm and the divine macrocosm.

Hildegard spoke of the divine in terms drawn from the natural world. Once, for example, she described the soul as "the green life force of the flesh." Here is her vision of the origin of life:

> I, the highest and fiery power, have kindled every spark of life . . . with wisdom I have rightly put the universe in order. I, the fiery life of divine essence, am aflame beyond the beauty of the meadows, I gleam in the waters, and I burn in the sun, moon, and stars. . . . I awaken everything to life. The air lives by turning green and being in bloom . . . the waters flow as if alive. . . . I remain hidden in every kind of reality as a fiery power. I am life . . . I am also Reason . . . I breathe life into everything. . . . For I am life who and entire . . . for this life is God. (Hildegard 1987, 10–11)

For Hildegard this was a vision of the universality of Christ, the vital life force in everything that is.

Another remarkable woman mystic, Julian of Norwich (1342–1416), wrote near the end of the medieval period. Little is known of her historically except that she is called Julian of Norwich because she lived in a small hut, or anchorage, attached to the cathedral in Norwich, England. In the fourteenth century the population of Europe was being decimated by the Black Plague. When Julian was thirty she became very ill, and it was during this illness that she experienced her "shewings" that became the substance of her book *Showings or Revelations of Divine Love*. This work is widely regarded as the most profound of all medieval mystical texts. It enjoyed a resurgence of interest in the twentieth century because of its assertion that God is "our Mother."

Words

God Is Our Mother

For all mankind which will be saved by the sweet Incarnation and the Passion of Christ, for he is the head and we are his members....

I contemplated the work of all the blessed Trinity [and] I saw and understood that the high might of the Trinity is our Father, and the deep wisdom of the Trinity is our Mother, and the great love of the Trinity is our Lord.... I saw these three properties: the property of the fatherhood ... the motherhood ... and the lordship in one God.

In our Father ... we have our being, and in our Mother of mercy we have our reforming and restoring ... and through the Holy Spirit ... we are fulfilled.

So Jesus Christ ... is our true Mother. As truly as God is our Father, so truly is God our Mother ... and so Jesus is our true Mother in nature by our first creation, and he is our true Mother in grace by his taking our created nature. All the lovely works and all the sweet loving offices of beloved motherhood are appropriated to the second person....

This fair lovely word "mother" is so sweet and kind in itself that it cannot truly be said of anyone or to anyone except of him who is the true Mother of life and of all things. To the property of motherhood belong nature, love, wisdom and knowledge, and this is God.

Source: Julian of Norwich, in *Showings* (Revelations of Divine Love) (New York: Paulist Press, 1978).

Protest, Reform, and Renewal: An Era of Reform, 1500–1750

In 1517 an Augustinian monk and professor at the new university at Wittenberg, Martin Luther (1483–1546), initiated a movement that would fracture the unity of western Christianity. It was later called the Reformation, and it gave rise to several new forms of Protestant Christianity. The movement began as an invitation to an academic debate about the practice of selling indulgences—promises that souls in purgatory would be forgiven their sins—and spiralled into reforms that changed the face of Christianity in the West and contributed to the rise of the modern age.

The 1500s were a century of reforms that gave rise not only to new Protestant traditions—Lutheran, Reformed, Anabaptist, and Anglican—but also to a renewed Catholic tradition following the Council of Trent (1545–63). It was a movement of reaction to the widespread corruption of the late medieval church and it led to changes in the patterns of authority, liturgy, teaching, and moral life of western Christianity.

Voices of Protestant Reform: Lutheran, Reformed, Anabaptist, and Anglican

The Lutheran Way: *Sola Fidei*, or Faith Alone
Martin Luther is popularly known as the German priest who confronted the Roman Catholic Church by nailing his "Disputation of Martin Luther on the Power and Efficacy of Indulgences" (later known as the *Ninety-Five Theses*) on the door of the castle church in Wittenburg in 1517. The actual nailing of the document to the door is disputed by historians, but whether it was nailed or not, copies were almost immediately printed and dispersed. Historians further maintain that Luther's "Disputation" was in fact a scholarly and thoughtful objection to certain practices, an appeal to the Pope's authority rather than a confrontation with the church, at least at that point in his career.

The reforms initiated by Martin Luther centred on his understanding of faith as the way to a living, vital relationship to God. Luther believed that Christians were mistaken in their belief that it was their good works that earned them God's favour rather than realizing that, in Jesus Christ, God had already extended gracious love toward all. It was this truth, Luther insisted, that Christians needed to open themselves to receive in faith. Faith, however, was not to be turned into another way of earning God's favour. Living faith, said Luther, is a gift and a grace; faith and good works must be rightly ordered. And for Luther, faith preceded good works, not the other way around. Faith was also be understood as "God's work in us." Luther believed that in the life, death, and resurrection of Jesus, God had opened the way to being made one with God. This he understood as a disclosure of God's love for human beings, a revelation of grace and a source of radical trust in the grace of God.

Words

Luther's "Introduction to Paul's Letter to the Romans" in his translation of the Bible into German clarifies his view of faith:

> Faith is not what some people think it is. Their human dream is a delusion.... Faith is God's work in us that changes us and gives us new birth from God. It kills the Old Adam and makes us completely different people. It changes our hearts, our spirits, our thoughts, and all our powers. It brings the Holy Spirit with it. Yes, it is a living, creative, active, and powerful thing, this faith. Faith cannot help doing good works constantly.
>
> Faith is a living, bold trust in God's grace. ... Such confidence and knowledge of God's grace makes you happy, joyful, and bold in your relationship to God and all creatures. The Holy Spirit makes all this happen through faith. Because of it, you freely, willingly, and joyfully do good to everyone.... It is just as impossible to separate faith and works as it is to separate heat and light from fire.

Source: Dr. Martin Luther's *Vermischte Deutsche Schriften*, ed. Johann K. Irmischer, vol. 63 (Erlangen: Heyder and Zimmer, 1854).

Luther's teachings found resonance among some of his contemporaries but led to conflict with church authorities; he was excommunicated in 1521. Some of the German princes, led by Frederick the Wise (1463–1525), Prince of Saxony, supported him. Luther thus found himself at the forefront of changes that led to new forms of Christianity.

The Reformed Way The spirit of reform ignited by Martin Luther began to influence religious life across Europe. In the 1520s it was especially notable in Zurich and Geneva, Switzerland, and gave rise to what historians would later call the Reformed churches. In Zurich, the great Catholic humanist Ulrich Zwingli (1484–1531), educated in the new learning of the time and influenced by Luther and Erasmus, began to challenge what he perceived as superstitious elements in Christianity. He felt that obedience to the will of God mediated through scripture was the central issue, and that renewed attention to scripture could purify the church and society.

In Geneva, Jean Calvin (1509–64), having fled his native France, came to lead the Reform movement in the 1530s, when he published the first edition of his *Institutes of the Christian Religion.* It grew to be a huge two-volume work that offered systematic exposition of a newly reformed faith. Calvin accepted justification by faith as the central teaching of scripture and of the Protestant movement. He became known for his emphasis on the sovereignty of God. For Calvin, the entirety of wisdom consisted of two parts: knowledge of God and of oneself.

Calvin's *Institutes* was divided into four sections. They dealt with knowledge of God the Creator, knowledge of Christ the Redeemer, the manner of receiving grace (the life of the believer), and the external means by which humanity is drawn into communion with Christ. The latter was Calvin's way of speaking about the church and, surprisingly, the magistrate, or political ruler. According to him, the magistrate was obliged to support the Christian religion. Calvinism spread beyond Geneva to parts of Germany, France, Holland, England, and Scotland, where it led to the founding of the Presbyterian denomination.

The Anabaptist Way Another reformed pathway was opened in Zurich by those who rejected the ritual of infant baptism that was practised throughout the Christian church. They came to be known as Anabaptists, meaning those who are baptized again as adults. They shared Zwingli's commitment to scripture and could not find any warrant for the practice of infant baptism in the Bible. They insisted that baptism was a ritual that should instead come after one's personal decision to follow the way of Christ. In 1527 Felix Manz in Zurich was the first of many Anabaptists put to death for their beliefs, but over the next decade the Anabaptist movement grew. Menno Simons, a former Catholic priest who had converted to the Anabaptist way, emerged as one of its great leaders in Holland.

The Anglican Way In 1534, King Henry VIII (1491–1547) compelled the English Parliament to pass the Act of Supremacy, making the sovereign "the only Supreme head on earth of the Church in England." This political act transferred authority over the church in England from the Pope to the monarch. A series of acts known as "the dissolution of the monasteries" (1536–41) followed, allowing the Crown to take ownership of monastic and church properties in England. There was considerable turmoil until the reign of Elizabeth I, who brought stability to the English situation. What is remarkable about Anglicanism is that it maintained both Catholic and Reformed traditions under one roof.

Reform in the Catholic Tradition

There was also a spirit of renewal in the Catholic world. Erasmus of Rotterdam (1466–1536) championed the new learning of his time and sought renewal of the moral life of Catholic Christianity. He was initially sympathetic toward Luther but broke with him when he saw that Luther's reforms were going to break the unity of the church.

In 1540, Ignatius of Loyola (1491–1556) founded a new religious order based on his profound insights into the processes of spiritual transformation. His order was known as the Society of Jesus, also called the Jesuits. Members of this order underwent a long process of education in the spiritual life, centred on Ignatius's *Spiritual Exercises*. Deeply opposed to Protestantism, they became leaders in education and in missionary work. Early Jesuits took their Christian message to the Americas, India, and China.

The Spanish Catholic reformer and theologian Teresa of Avila (1515–82) renewed her Carmelite order through her book *The Interior Castle,* a practical guide to a life of prayer that was intended to lead to union with God. Carmelite nunneries continue to be guided by the life of prayer and meditation taught by Teresa of Avila.

The Council of Trent The Catholic Church's response to the Protestant Reformation was the Council of Trent (1545–63). The council clarified Catholic teaching in relation to scripture and tradition, enhanced the education of priests, standardized the liturgy in a form that would remain constant until the Second Vatican Council (1962–65), and led to a revised Catholic breviary. The breviary includes regulations for the celebration of Mass, the official daily prayers of the church.

Discovering the New World: Christianity and Colonization

Just prior to the outbreak of the Reformation, Christopher Columbus, a lay Franciscan and Italian sea captain sailing under the Spanish flag, discovered the lands of the Americas in 1492. After reaching islands in the Caribbean he returned to Spain, where he was greeted as a hero. He returned to the Americas in 1493, 1498, and 1502. Columbus initiated Europe's exploitative relationship with the new lands of the Americas, which saw as much as a third to a half of the Indigenous population dead of disease and warfare within a century and a half. Soon Spanish conquistadors had captured the lands of the Aztecs in Central America (Hernando Cortes in 1521) and the Inca empire of Peru (Francisco Pizarro in 1531). The Spanish established hegemony from the present-day American southwest through Mexico, Central America, and all of South America, except for Brazil, which was claimed by the Portuguese.

Bartolome de las Casas (1484–1566) represented the small minority of Catholics who protested against the Spanish treatment of Indigenous peoples. His father had sailed with Columbus and was given lands in modern-day Cuba. After de las Casas saw the treatment the Native people received, he returned to Spain, became a Dominican, and spent the rest of his life seeking to change Spanish ways in the New World. In his book *The Only Way,* he argued for the dignity of societies of Indigenous people—some of those societies, he said, had exceeded those of Europe—and spoke against their enforced conversion. He spent his life seeking to have the lands of the Inca restored to their people.

Christianity and colonialism came to be closely intertwined because Christianity, in both its Catholic and Protestant forms, was the religion of European colonial powers. When Columbus encountered Indigenous people on his 1492 voyage, he remarked that they were all friendly. He then went on to say, "they ought to make good and skilled servants, for they repeat very quickly whatever we say to them. I think they can very easily be made Christians, for they seem to have no religion" (Fuson 1992, 75–77). These would prove to be fateful words for the Indigenous peoples of North America.

By and large, explorers and colonists were supported and blessed by their Christian leaders and churches, who viewed them as instrumental in bringing the truths of Christianity to the nations being conquered. Missionaries, like the colonists, came to spread the superiority of Christianity and European civilization and practices. They believed that expansion of these western frontiers and conversion of the world to Christianity were intended by divine providence. Missionaries often monopolized education within the colonies, founding schools in order to shape the minds of children, some of whom were forced to attend Christian or, later, government schools, and eventually training conquered peoples as ministers and missionaries.

Reforming the Reformers

Within a generation of the beginnings of the Protestant movements there came efforts to reform the reformers. The Protestant reformers had proclaimed the doctrine of a "priesthood of believers." This teaching sought to overturn the medieval view that divided Christians into the religious—that is, monks and nuns and priests—and lay Christians. It challenged the view that the religious could achieve a higher level of union with God than ordinary people. The doctrine of the priesthood of all believers meant that all believers had direct access to God through Christ: access to God did not have to be through an intermediary, understood as either the priesthood or the church. This teaching introduced a democratic element into Christianity and profoundly enhanced the status of lay Christians.

Puritans The 1550s saw the emergence of the Puritan movement among English Christians. They were English Protestants who had taken refuge on the Continent during efforts to restore the Catholic Church as the official church of England. Influenced by the teachings of Calvin, they returned to England after Elizabeth I renewed the Act of Supremacy in 1559. The Puritans were determined to extend reform within the church and the world, and so they became known as "worldly reformers." They were a diffuse group that gave rise to many dissenters against the Anglican establishment. They saw Christ—not the pope or the sovereign—as the head of the church, opposed vestments and "popish elements," and sought congregational (less hierarchical) structures of authority. They saw themselves as visible saints, people who had experienced "new birth" and now lived a righteous life.

Puritans established the Massachusetts Bay Colony in 1630 and came to have a large impact on colonial American life. The great Jonathan Edwards (1703–58), for example, was at the forefront of changes in Christianity in the American colonies in the 1730s and '40s. The Puritans disrupted English politics and society during the time of Oliver Cromwell, who became Lord Protector of England in the 1650s after dethroning the king. Another group they influenced was the Religious Society of Friends, also known as Quakers. This movement began in England in the 1640s, led by the reformer George Fox. Fox taught that "there is that of God in everyone." When the Friends met on Sundays, they sat in silence. There was no clergy; those gathered simply waited to be moved by the spirit. If they were so moved, they would share their "leading," as they called it, with the other Friends.

Pietists The Pietist movement among Lutherans in Germany was another movement meant to transform the lives of ordinary Christians. Philipp Jakob Spener (1635–1705), regarded as the founder of Pietism, encouraged lay Christians to meet together in small groups to read the Bible. He argued that the Bible was the living Word and addressed the everyday concerns of human beings. Christians should help one another discern the meaning of that living Word for their lives, he said; in this they did not need to depend on their ministers. He reminded his hearers that devotion and a vital faith in the living Christ were at the heart of the Christianity. Vital faith was not to centre on doctrine but to focus on living in a loving and charitable way. This movement, like other lay-oriented movements in Protestant Christianity, crossed denominational lines.

Methodists In the mid-1700s, John Wesley (1703–91) initiated the Methodist movement, which would have a huge impact on English-speaking Christianity in England, the United States, and later many other parts of the world. Wesley was an Anglican priest who was inspired by Jonathan Edwards's *A Faithful Narrative of the Surprising Work of God*, an account of the Connecticut River Valley Awakening of the 1730s in the American colonies, and began to preach along the highways and byways of England. Wesley believed that all Christians were loved by God and called to a life of holiness. Moreover, he was persuaded that the spirit of God was at work in the human heart to root out pride, self-will, and anger. He taught that Christians were not only justified, as Luther had taught, but that they were also being inwardly transformed in the image of Christ. This transformation was called *sanctification*, or what Wesley called "Christian perfection." As pride, self-will, and anger were being overcome by the Spirit, then, according to Wesley, Christians were becoming more like Christ. Christian perfection was for Wesley another name for holiness. Wesley thus democratized Christian spirituality, for he made it open to everyone to attain holiness.

From the European Enlightenment to a Global Christianity, 1750–2000

Revivalism in America

As the European Enlightenment was beginning in Europe, the American colonies were going through a series of events known as the Great Awakening. From 1740 to 1750, the preaching of revivalists was transforming the colonial landscape. Benjamin Franklin, a prosperous Philadelphia publisher, recounted his experience of going to hear the English Calvinist George Whitefield preaching in the town square. Although initially skeptical of what he would hear, he was so moved by Whitefield's exhortations that when a collection box for an orphanage in Georgia was passed through the massive crowd, he too emptied his pockets.

The Great Awakening emphasized the transforming work of the spirit of God in the lives of individuals and society. It was leading to "new birth" and promised the renewal of society. Yet thinkers such as Jonathan Edwards, the great colonial American Puritan who was already engaging Enlightenment figures such as Locke and Newton, warned that this new emphasis was being threatened by hubris, or pride and self-interest. Nonetheless, the Great Awakening prepared the way for the coming transformation of life in colonial America that resulted in the founding of the American republic.

The European Enlightenment

Meanwhile, the European Enlightenment was unfolding in a different way. As a movement of the intellectual world—new thinking about science, governance, and society—it gave rise to an outlook that challenged the dominance of Christianity in social life. This is reflected in thinkers such as John Locke in England, Voltaire in France, and later Immanuel Kant in Germany. Locke argued for a social contract against the right of rulers. Voltaire used his acerbic wit to lampoon what he considered to be superstition and priest-craft while championing reason against revelation. Kant saw humanity shaking off the shackles of tradition and claiming its own autonomy. It was an "age of reason" that questioned religion as it embraced the new empirical sciences and began to remake society in its own (human) image.

Many Protestant Christians welcomed the new thinking, with its emphasis on human rights, its recognition of social pluralism, and its support for new democratic initiatives. But there were also many Christians who were suspicious of the naturalistic philosophical assumptions of the new age and its seemingly wholesale rejection of tradition. Many felt that God was being eclipsed by reason. This was especially so in the French Revolution. The new republic took over all church lands in December 1789—supporters of the revolution saw Roman Catholicism as part of the *ancien régime* that needed to be swept away. In 1793–94 there were attempts to replace the Catholic way in France with a cult of reason, including enthroning the goddess of reason in the Cathedral of Notre Dame.

Around the same time, the Second Great Awakening unfolded in the newly formed United States in the early 1800s. It gave rise to many restorationist movements such as the Disciples of Christ, the Mormons, and the Seventh-Day Adventists. These were groups that sought to return to an earlier form of Christianity. The most radical were the Mormons with their new scripture, the Book of Mormon. Their leader, Joseph Smith, was killed by a mob, but the group continued under the leadership of Brigham Young and settled in Utah. The forms of American Christianity were multiplying several-fold.

Modern Christian Thinkers

While many religious leaders carried on without addressing the new intellectual currents of the Enlightenment, there were those who did address the challenge of modernity. Friedrich Schleiermacher (1768–1834) believed that the Enlightenment figures had failed to grasp the true nature of religion. In his famous *On Religion: Speeches to Its Cultured Despisers*, Schleiermacher posited that religion was neither primarily about thinking or belief, as some Enlightenment thinkers assumed, nor primarily about morality, as others assumed. It was, according to him, rooted in something prior to thinking, believing, or willing. It was a sense or "feeling of absolute dependence" that Schleiermacher regarded as the touchstone of religious life. He went on to write *Christian Faith*, which is widely regarded as the beginning of modern theology. It sought to find a way of accommodating Christian faith to the new intellectual and cultural traditions of modernity.

In the nineteenth century, John Henry Newman (1801–90) was a leading figure in the Tractarian movement among Anglican Christians that investigated the beginnings of doctrinal development in Christianity. His studies eventually led him to join the Catholic Church and rise in its ranks. Cardinal Newman later wrote on the development of doctrine; he opposed the teaching on papal infallibility that was declared at the First Vatican Council in 1869–70.

On the European continent, Søren Kierkegaard (1813–55) was forging an approach to the Christian faith that came to be known as Christian existentialism. It centred on struggles with anxiety and despair within a life of faith. Kierkegaard thought that conventional Christianity was too shallow and moralistic to address these challenges. The life of faith was, according to him, the most difficult thing in the world. Much of Kierkegaard's thought is based on the New Testament passage Philippians 2:12, where Christians are called to "continue to work out your salvation with fear and trembling." In his book *Fear and Trembling*, he imagined the struggle, the fear, and the dread that Abraham must have experienced when he believed he had been commanded by God to sacrifice his son Isaac on Mount Moriah (Gen. 22: 1–19). This, said Kierkegaard, was an example of the life of faith—not a life of boring convention but a life of inward struggle. He did not dwell on the joyous outcome—according to the Genesis story, God stopped Abraham from sacrificing his son—but rather focused on the inward journey of Abraham's life. In Kierkegaard's view that is the place where faith is won or lost. True faith is a struggle to become a whole human being.

Responses to the Industrial Revolution

The Industrial Revolution transformed England. Urbanization and the introduction of the factory system created large populations of men and women who were struggling to survive. When George Williams (1821–1905) went to London in the 1840s, he was appalled by the conditions for young working men in London and, together with his friends, founded the Young Men's Christian Association (YMCA). Seeking to put Christian principles into practice, it grew to be a global movement with more than forty-five million members in 2000. The aim of the YMCA was to build a "healthy spirit, mind, and body."

Later, in the 1850s, Emma Roberts (1818–77) initiated a prayer union for young women, and Mary Jane Kinnard (1816–88) opened a hostel and training institute for young women struggling with the exploitation of the industrial world. These would grow into the Young Women's Christian Association (YWCA), which would become the largest women's network for social change in the world.

Another response to the plight of the urban poor was the creation of the Salvation Army in 1865 by Methodist minister William Booth (1829–1912) and his wife, Catherine (1829–90). Organized along military lines, the Army was a conservative evangelical movement dedicated to addressing the needs of the poor. Working among the poor and destitute, it grew to be the world's largest charitable organization and now has a presence in more than 120 countries.

Women in Social Reform

During the nineteenth century, Christian social reform movements continued to develop. For example, the Abolitionist movement to end slavery, which began in the 1830s, was a by-product of the Second Great Awakening, the American Christian revival movement. Women took leading roles in these social movements. For example, Harriet Beecher Stowe, a Quaker, wrote the anti-slavery novel *Uncle Tom's Cabin* (published in 1852) and was involved in forming the Underground Railroad, which helped slaves escape to Canada.

The 1848 Seneca Falls Convention in Seneca Falls, New York, initiated by Lucretia Mott (1793–80), another Quaker, led to a movement for women's rights, including the right to vote. She was joined by Elizabeth Cady Stanton (1815–1902), who later became the principal author of the *Woman's Bible* (1895, 1898). Later, the Social Gospel movement included women such as Jane Addams (1860–1935) and Ellen Gates Star (1859–1940), the founders of Hull House in Chicago, the first settlement house that addressed the needs of recent immigrants.

Many other women were also active social reformers throughout the nineteenth century, and these courageous women began to challenge the endemic patriarchy of the Christian traditions. There were also efforts to reform the economic system of capitalism, the prison system, and other social institutions.

A Dawning Ecumenical Age

In 1893, the World's Parliament of Religions held in Chicago marked the beginning of changes in relations among the world's religions. Drawing representatives from across the religious world, this meeting introduced the Christian West to the other great traditions of religious life. Swami Vivekananda, a Hindu guru, electrified the audience as he spoke of the greatness of Hinduism and of all the world's religious traditions. The Ceylonese (Sri Lankan) Buddhist Anagarika Dharmapala chastised the Christian world for its attitudes toward other faiths. The great American historian of Christianity Philip Schaff saw the gathering as the beginning of a "new epoch in the history of religion." In 1895 the World Student Christian Federation was founded to build new relations across the divisions of the Christian world.

Pentecostal movement: a twentieth-century charismatic form of Christianity that emphasizes "baptism in the spirit" and has grown rapidly around the world.

Early in the twentieth century a new strand of charismatic Christianity was born in the **Pentecostal movement**. It had multiple origins, but one of the best known is the Azusa Street Pentecostal revival in Los Angeles in 1905. It was led by William J. Seymour, an African-American preacher, and centred on ecstatic spiritual experiences that included baptism in the spirit and glossolalia, or speaking in tongues. Since then it has become the fastest-growing Christian church worldwide.

When the World Mission Congress was held in Edinburgh in 1910, there was evidence of a movement that sought to build new relations among the warring factions of Christianity. After four hundred years of polemics, a new spirit of respect and cooperation, largely among Protestant Christians, was beginning to stir. In 1948 the World Council of Churches (WCC) was founded. Within a decade it had brought together most of the Protestant and Orthodox world into one ecumenical fellowship. This movement was initially resisted by the Catholic Church. It wasn't until after two World Wars that the Second Vatican Council (1962–65), initiated by Pope John XXIII, brought the Catholic Church into this new ecumenical age. Besides opening the church to the new spirit of modernity, Vatican II's *Nostra Aetate* (Declaration on the Relation of the Church to Non-Christian Religions) called for "dialogue and co-operation" with other traditions. Though not officially part of the WCC, the Vatican has participants on some of its commissions.

In 1965 Pope Paul VI and Patriarch Athenagoras of Constantinople met and nullified the mutual excommunications of 1054. This led to better relations between the Catholic and Orthodox leaders but it did not end the continuing tensions between the two communities. The work of reconciliation continued, and in 1991 Pope John Paul II declared that "the Catholic Church and the Orthodox are two lungs within the same Body." During his time as pope, John Paul was able to establish new relations with Orthodox churches of the east.

In the late 1960s and early '70s, the Vatican and the WCC launched initiatives of dialogue with people of other faiths, which was sometimes called a wider ecumenism. Now known as interfaith encounter and dialogue, these efforts marked a significant development in the history of Christianity (Phan 1990, 3ff). One consequence of dialogue with peoples of other faiths has been a growing recognition of the need for a renewed and revitalized Christianity, one that can address the challenges of antireligious secularism and the social crises generated by the new world order.

The Third Millennium

Christianity now finds itself entering its third millennium at a time when the world faces challenges of global scope. The environmental crisis and global warming, the growing gap between the rich and the poor, a world population of more than six billion human beings, the desertification of northern Africa, the pollution of the oceans, women's movements for equal dignity—the litany of challenges facing the world and Christianity is seemingly without end. While church attendance dropped dramatically in most Western countries in the 1960s in the face of aggressive secularism, there was also a growing interest in other forms of religion, spirituality, and new religious movements. Moreover, Pentecostal Christianity has spread across the globe, and Christianity has experienced significant growth in Africa and some parts of Asia. At the same time there has also been a resurgence of Islam. It remains to be seen how Christians will deal with this ever-changing world (McManners 2001).

SPIRITUAL AND RELIGIOUS PRACTICES

Christian spiritual and religious practices are rich and varied across the many streams of Christianity. Central to those spiritual and religious practices is the Christian church. But what is the church? Church buildings may take the form of soaring stone cathedrals, modern suburban mega-churches, storefront meeting places, mud huts, or the modest brick or wooden buildings that dot the North American landscape. These are the buildings that house many of these spiritual and religious practices, but many Christians understand the church more in religious and spiritual terms. Some see it as the "mystical body of Christ" or, as the early creeds say, "one holy, catholic, and apostolic church," or as a *koinonia* (community) gathered in the name Jesus. The buildings may be small and simple or soaring and elaborate. All are consecrated places where people gather to pursue religious—in worship, prayer, music, and celebration—and spiritual ends.

The central spiritual and religious practices of Christianity grow out of the life and ministry of Jesus of Nazareth, and later an understanding of the resurrection of Jesus from the dead, as the gateway to knowing God. The Gospel of Matthew recounts the story of Jesus being challenged to identify the greatest commandment. Jesus replied that it was "to love God with all your heart . . . all your soul, and all your mind . . . and . . . You shall love your neighbor as yourself. On these two commandments depends all the law and the prophets" (Matt. 22:36–40). While love of God and neighbour summarizes Jesus's teaching, the stories recounted in the early Christian writings known as the gospels give us glimpses of his life and practice. Central to that life was prayer and the meal that Jesus shared with his disciples before his crucifixion; it was this meal, known as the Last Supper, that became the centrepiece of Christian worship.

Worship in Early Christianity

The early Christian writings contain some hints about worship among the Christians. They gathered in homes or synagogues (Jewish places of assembly or houses of prayer), where they prayed, sang psalms, and shared a sacred meal based on the last supper that Jesus shared with his disciples during the Jewish Passover. These gatherings were also an occasion for instruction in the new faith

Religion in Quebec society has played a central role since the early days of New France in the seventeenth century. The spread of Catholicism throughout the Americas played an important role in the growth of what was originally a French and then a British colony. The Catholic Church wielded considerable presence and authority in Quebec, building monasteries, abbeys, and churches in both urban and rural areas. They remain evidence of the religious and cultural heritage of Quebec. Traditional institutions and values came to be questioned in the 1960s, a period of radical modernization in Quebec called the Quiet Revolution. The influence of the Catholic Church has waned significantly since that time, and Quebec's falling birthrate is evidence of this weakening impact.

Source: © Barrett & MacKay/All Canada Photos/CORBIS

and the new order that they believed God had initiated with the resurrection. In the second-century writing the Didache, there is a recommendation that Christians say the **Lord's Prayer** three times a day and whenever they gather, as well as a commentary on the Lord's Supper that was celebrated. Justin Martyr, writing in the middle of the second century, describes the early practice in Rome:

> ... on the day called Sunday there is a meeting ... the memoirs of the apostles or the writings of the prophets are read ... the president in a discourse then urges us to the imitation of these noble things. Then we all stand together and offer prayers ... bread and wine and water is brought and distributed to all there ... a collection is taken ... to take care of the orphans and widows and those who are in want on account of sickness or any other cause.... (Justin Martyr* 1978, 26)

Lord's Prayer: the prayer of Jesus found in the New Testament that begins "Our Father, who art in Heaven," the most widely recited prayer in the Christian traditions.

With the institution of Christianity as the religion of the state in the fourth century came the building of churches as places of public worship.

* Justin Martyr, *Apology: Plea for a Fair Hearing* in Hugh T. Kerr, *Early Christian Fathers* (Vol I in the Library of Christian Classics, Westminister) John Knox Press

Eucharist: one of the central rituals of Christianity. Known as the Eucharist by Catholic and Orthodox churches and Protestants of the high liturgical traditions, it is popularly called Mass among Catholics, while most Protestants prefer the terms Lord's Supper or Holy Communion.

Christian Worship

Since Christianity's beginnings there has been a coming together of the community in public or corporate worship. Worship is a gathering in the presence of the sacred. Within the Christian tradition, worship is a corporate action employing words, gestures, song, silence, and prayer to recapitulate the central Christian story.

Worship in Catholic Christianity

Worship in the Catholic traditions is centred in the **Eucharist** (from a Greek term meaning "thanksgiving"), a celebration that grew out of Jesus's last meal with his disciples, the Last Supper. The gathering to worship is popularly called the Mass, and it is a celebration in word, gesture, and action of the mystery of Jesus Christ. Following the Council of Trent in the 1500s, identical services in Latin were held in Catholic churches across the world. After Vatican II there were revisions to the liturgy of the Eucharist, and the use of vernacular languages rather than Latin was introduced (although some contemporary Catholic congregations have again begun to celebrate Mass in Latin).

As people enter a Catholic church, they typically dip a finger in what is considered to be holy water and make the sign of the cross upon their body. Then, as they approach where they will sit, they kneel in the direction of the altar, where the sacrament (understood as the consecrated host, or Christ's body and blood) is kept, again making the sign of the cross. Before taking their seat, they kneel to pray. The service begins as the priest enters the church holding up the scripture as he walks behind the cross-bearer leading the procession. Also in the procession are others involved in the service, such as altar boys and girls and priests who will assist in the service. When they reach the altar, the cross and the scripture are set in their places and the invocation "In the name of the Father, Son, and Holy Spirit" is intoned. The Mass has begun.

PEOPLE & PLACES

Visiting a Greek Orthodox Church in Canada

Before writing this account of worship in Orthodox Christianity, I attended a service of Divine Liturgy in my community. As I opened the door to the church, I could smell incense. Immediately inside—in the area called the narthex—were two icons, or holy images. The parishioners went to them, bowed and kissed them, crossed themselves, and then went into the nave, the main area of the church in front of the sanctuary. Children were held up by their mothers to kiss the icons. Traditionally the congregation would stand in the nave during the Divine Liturgy, but many Orthodox churches in the West have adopted pews for seating. (When I attended a Russian Orthodox church in Moscow, we stood for three hours.)

On the walls of the local Orthodox church were rows of colourful icons. At the front of the church, a wooden iconostasis (screen) separated the sanctuary from the nave. The iconostasis had a central door and two side doors, and on the screen were images of the angel Gabriel, the apostles, saints, the "mystical meal of Christ," Mary, and Jesus Christ. Above the sanctuary and visible to the congregation was a large blue and red painting of the *theotokos* (mother of God) with the baby Jesus. At the very top of the wall was a small image of Christ *Pantocrator*, or Christ as ruler of the universe.

When I had found my seat, I offered my prayers, then picked up the book containing the Divine Liturgy of Saint John Chrysostom (347–407), the liturgy that is followed across the Greek Orthodox world and in many of the other Orthodox churches. The service began with a procession through the nave into the sanctuary. The Divine Liturgy was sung or chanted in Greek, with an occasional phrase in English. When the priest spoke to the congregation during the service of the Word, he spoke in English. Structurally, the service, like the Mass, was composed of two parts: the liturgy of the Word and the liturgy of the Eucharist, which is called the liturgy of the faithful. Prayers, actions, processions, sound, and silence were woven into a moving performance.

A procession also marked the Eucharist as the bread and wine were brought forward while prayers of praise and thanksgiving were recited and liturgical gestures enacted. There was a sharing of the consecrated bread that included even the very small children, since they had been baptized and *chrismated* (the Orthodox term for confirmation). All those who have been baptized and chrismated are expected to be frequent recipients of the "divine mysteries," with the Eucharist being understood as the central divine mystery. At the dismissal, the priest intoned, "Let us go forth in peace ...."

Following introductory rites that include the act of penitence, the Kyrie, the Gloria, and prayers, the service turns to the liturgy of the Word and the liturgy of the Eucharist. The liturgy of the Word includes readings from scripture, a brief homily or sermon, recitation of the creed, and the prayers of the faithful. This is followed by the liturgy of the Eucharist, the high point of the Mass. Here the elements—the bread and the wine—are brought forward by members of the congregation to be consecrated by the priest before the communion rite. During the consecration, prayers are intoned and the words from the Last Supper of Jesus and his disciples are spoken: "This is my Body, given for you. This is my Blood, given for you." The consecrated elements are then lifted up and presented to the congregation. This action of consecration, which reenacts Christ's sacrifice, is the dramatic high point of the liturgy of the Eucharist. Then the bread and wine are distributed to the congregation, with members coming forward to receive them, then returning to their seats to pray until everyone is served.

The service concludes with a blessing that enjoins all to love and serve God in their everyday life. Though this order of service may include some local elements—such as drums and African music in Africa or the incense and flowers of south India in Kerala—the Mass has the same structure and form across the Catholic world.

Worship in Orthodox Christianity

Worship in the Orthodox traditions is known as the Divine Liturgy. The term *liturgy* comes from the Greek *leitourgia,* meaning "a public work of the people." In Orthodox churches the Greek phrase *basileia tou theou*—"the kingdom (or reign) of God"—is written over the entrance. It is believed that upon entering the consecrated space of the *ecclesia*, or church, one is truly entering God's kingdom.

Sacrament: an outward sign of an invisible grace.

Orthodox services engage the whole person and invoking all the senses. According to Orthodox thinkers, the Divine Liturgy, especially the Eucharist, is the vision and the image of true human life as God created it and intended it to become.

Worship in Protestant Christianity

Worship in the Protestant traditions is extremely varied. It ranges from what are called the "high" liturgical traditions of Anglicans and Lutherans to the "low" liturgical, or plain, services of the Reformed traditions to the silence of Quaker gatherings. When western Christianity broke up into Catholic and Protestant ways in the 1500s, Anglicans created a Book of Common Prayer that is still followed. Lutherans slightly revised the traditional Catholic service, positioning proclamation of the word (scripture reading, preaching, and hymns) as the centrepiece of worship. Reformed traditions rejected the idea of worship as a **sacramental** activity and instead built their version around prayer, reading of the scriptures, and the sermon. No longer was the Eucharist or Mass central to every worship service, as it had been in the Catholic and Orthodox traditions. In the Protestant traditions the emphasis was instead on prayer, proclamation, preaching, and hymn singing.

Among Protestants there is a wide range of teachings concerning the Eucharist or, in the terminology most Protestants use, the Lord's Supper or Holy Communion. Anglicans and Lutherans have retained a sacramental understanding of the Eucharist.

Practices

The Lord's Prayer

A major practice of Christianity is prayer, which is understood as central to the spiritual and religious practices of the Christian tradition. The Lord's Prayer is the most common prayer.

Our Father, who art in Heaven,
Hallowed be Thy Name.
Thy Kingdom come, Thy will be done, on earth as it is in heaven.
Give us this day our daily bread
And forgive us our trespasses, as we forgive those who trespass against us,
And lead us not into temptation, but deliver us from evil.
[The Catholic version, found in the Gospel of Matthew, ends here.]
For thine is the kingdom, and the power, and the glory
Forever and ever. Amen
[In the Orthodox tradition, the following four lines that end the Lord's prayer are recited only by the priest:]
For thine is the kingdom, and the power, and the glory of the Father and of the Son and of the Holy Spirit
Now and ever and unto the age of ages.

When the early Christian community gathered, they said this prayer, which was seen as a prayerful summary of Jesus's message. During Christianity's later development, more elaborate forms of worship came to be included, but this prayer has always been present. Some liberal Christian churches are changing the gendered language of the Lord's Prayer by beginning with "Our loving God" or "Our Mother and Father."

Church year: a division of the calendar into seasons punctuated by holidays ("holy days") and festivals that mark crucial moments in the life of Christ. It begins with Advent, the four Sundays leading up to Christmas.

Advent: the beginning season of the Christian liturgical year, the four Sundays leading up to Christmas.

Many Reformed and Protestant groups such as Congregationalists, Presbyterians, and Baptists understand the Lord's Supper as a memorial event. Among Protestants there is also a wide range of practice in the celebration of the Lord's Supper. They see it as authorized by scripture and required to be observed by Christians, but they reject many doctrines that grew up around the practice. Among Anglicans and Lutherans, the Lord's Supper may be celebrated weekly, monthly, or quarterly. Among other Protestants, it is done monthly, quarterly, semi-annually, or annually.

In many Pentecostal and some Evangelical Protestant churches, the emphasis falls on joyful singing, preaching or proclamation, and prayer (including, in some Pentecostal services, "speaking in tongues"). One might attend a Jamaican Pentecostal service comprising mainly singing, accompanied by tambourines and guitars, and brief, enthusiastic messages from the pastor and others moved by the spirit. In some African-American churches there is much praising of God, spirited gospel singing and other music, dramatic preaching, and much participation by the congregation.

The Church Year: Christian Festivals and Celebrations

Christianity has its own calendar with which to mark seasons and festivals of the **church year**. In those churches that observe this calendar, the liturgical cycle begins with **Advent**, the season leading up to Christmas and the birth of Christ. The purpose of the church-year calendar is to lead the community on a spiritual journey reenacting the Christian narrative. It begins in late autumn by anticipating the coming of Jesus (Advent), then moves on to the birth and recognition of Jesus (Christmas and Epiphany). The journey with Christ continues during Lent, a time of fasting and spiritual renewal, the entry into Jerusalem, and the events leading up to Jesus's death on the cross, followed by the joy of Easter in the spring, based on the belief in the resurrection of Christ. Pentecost, the gift of the Holy Spirit, and the Sundays of ordinary time follow as the mission of Christ is lived out in the world. The cycle covers the entire year and then begins again. Eastern Christianity follows a similar pattern through the life, death, and resurrection of Christ.

The more liturgical Protestant churches continue the traditions of the church year with some variations. The less liturgical Protestant churches are much looser about following the church year but still celebrate Christmas and Easter. The ecumenical movement within Christianity in the twentieth and twenty-first centuries saw a renewal of interest in the cycle and has sought to coordinate the practices of Protestants.

Christmas is a Christian festival that celebrates the birth of Jesus. The date of Christmas as December 25 was not established until the fifth century, and it was not then the major feast day that it would become. **Epiphany** (January 6) was more widely celebrated as the manifestation of the divine in human form. Christmas grew to be a more important festival in the medieval period, although it was only in the nineteenth century that Christmas trees were introduced. Christmas has since become a commercial extravaganza and that is mixed up with many other cultural practices today. For example, it is celebrated in Japan with Santa Claus and gift-giving, but there is no mention of the birth of Christ.

Lent (*quadragesima* in Latin, meaning "fortieth") is a period of prayer and fasting in the Church year that begins in February and leads up to Easter, the central festival of Christianity. In Catholic communities (and in a less boisterous way among Orthodox Christians) it is preceded by Carnival, a time of festivities, masquerade, merrymaking, and public parades. The most famous carnival is held annually in Brazil, which has the largest Catholic population of any country in the world. Another famous carnival is Mardi Gras, held in New Orleans, Louisiana. Quebec City also has its own, more modest carnival every year.

Epiphany: a Christian feast celebrating the Divine incarnated in Jesus; in Western churches, traditionally celebrated on January 6, commemorating the Magi finding the infant Jesus. Eastern churches celebrate Epiphany on January 19, commemorating Jesus's baptism by John the Baptist.

Christian Rituals and Sacraments

Rites of Passage

"Rite of passage" is an anthropological phrase used to describe rituals that mark the transition from one stage of life to another. In early societies the central rite of passage was the initiation rite that marked the transition from childhood to adulthood. Christianity developed its own ritual practices, practices that drew upon the traditions of its Jewish forebears and the mystery traditions of the ancient world. Some of these ritual practices came to be known among Catholic Christians as *sacraments*. As noted earlier, a sacrament is defined as "an outward sign of an invisible grace." This means that the actions, gestures, and words of the ritual (the outward sign) serve to convey God's invisible love and grace to the recipient. Among Orthodox Christians, these rituals are called *mysteries*. Protestant Christians vary in their understandings of ritual practice. While they were not created as rites of passage following the stages of a human life, there is a parallel between Christian sacraments and rituals and the life cycle.

Catholic Sacraments, Orthodox Mysteries, Protestant Rites

There are seven sacraments in the Catholic and Orthodox traditions. While Orthodox Christians acknowledge the same seven major rituals as the Catholic tradition, this number is not fixed; there may be other ritual actions that also serve to bring one closer to God. The seven sacraments are baptism, confirmation, the Eucharist, holy orders, marriage, penance, and anointing of the sick. There is a link between these sacraments and important moments in the life cycle. *Baptism*, for instance, becomes one's entrance into the church. It is an initiation ritual that incorporates the infant into the death and resurrection of Christ, an act that, according to Catholic teaching, wipes away sin.

Confirmation is also an initiation ritual, coming later in one's life to confirm and strengthen one in the faith. Among Protestant Christians, confirmation usually occurs in the teenage years and is accompanied by instruction in the Christian faith. It signifies one's assuming of the responsibilities of an adult within the church, so in that respect it parallels initiation rites that mark the passage from childhood to adulthood. However, in the Catholic tradition, the rite of confirmation comes much earlier and signals full participation in the life of the church. Among the Orthodox the rite is called *chrismation*, as it involves anointing with chrism, a holy or consecrated oil also known as myrrh, and it follows immediately after baptism.

The sacraments of *marriage* and *holy orders* can be seen as related to adult vocation or calling, either to marriage and family life or to the religious life and priesthood. Marriage is a sacred bond and in the Catholic tradition is considered inviolable. The sacrament of marriage conveys the grace necessary to sustain a couple throughout their lifetimes.

There is a wide variety of rites and practices among Protestant Christians. While Anglicans and Lutherans retain the term *sacrament*, they have generally reduced the number from seven to two: baptism and the *Eucharist*. Lutherans regard baptism and the Eucharist as sacraments but reject the Catholic doctrine of transubstantiation, a belief that during the ritual of the Mass, the bread and wine are changed, in substance, into the flesh and blood of Christ. Other Protestant Christian traditions regard the Lord's Supper and baptism as central Christian rites but reject sacramental understandings of their significance. Many Protestant traditions regard the Lord's Supper as a memorial rite, a remembrance of Christ's death and resurrection. For some, in the rituals associated with communion, congregational members renew their covenant with God and with each other. The sacraments, mysteries, and rituals of baptism, marriage, and death rituals are discussed in greater detail below.

Baptism Baptism, as mentioned above, is an initiatory rite: it marks one's entry into the church and the Christian journey to God. It is a spiritual cleansing and initiation into the faith of the community, performed in the name of God the Creator, Redeemer, and Sanctifier or God as Father, Son, and Holy Spirit. It is regarded as a sacrament among Catholic, Orthodox, Anglican, and Lutheran traditions. In most other Protestant groups—Reformed, Presbyterian, Methodist, Congregational, and the United Church—baptism is regarded as a ritual but does not have the same symbolic significance as do sacraments. Some Christian groups, such as some Quakers, do not practise baptism.

Those traditions that consider baptism a sacrament practise infant baptism. Churches that regard baptism as a rite practise either infant baptism or, in the case of Anabaptists, Baptists, and Pentecostals, adult or what is called "believers' baptism." Here baptism is regarded as an outward ritual that follows a deliberate inward decision to follow the message of Jesus.

Marriage Marriage in Christian traditions is generally understood as the coming together of a man and a woman in the holy state of matrimony. It is considered a sacrament in the Catholic tradition, being likened to the relationship of Christ and the church. Many of the Protestant traditions regard marriage as a covenant, modelled on the covenantal relationship between God and humanity.

In the Catholic and Protestant churches, the man and the woman marry each other through an exchange of vows, with the priest or minister and congregation acting as witnesses to their promises to one another. The priest or minister then pronounces a blessing on the marriage. In the Orthodox churches it is the priest who marries the couple. Marriage is regarded across the many traditions of Christianity as a sacred and lifelong bond. In many jurisdictions the minister or priest also acts as an agent of the state to make marriage legally binding.

In recent decades there has emerged the issue of same-sex marriage. This was—and still is—strongly resisted by the majority of Christian traditions. However, in jurisdictions such as Canada where same-sex marriages have been legalized, some churches, such as the "affirming congregations" of the United Church of Canada and some community churches, now perform blessing ceremonies for same-sex couples.

Divorce Divorce, or dissolution of the marriage bond, is not permitted in the Catholic Church. There are, however, many Catholics, especially in North America, who are divorced. How is this possible? The answer is that they have had their marriage bond dissolved by civil authorities rather than through church courts or canon law. Catholics can, however, have a marriage annulled through church courts based on canon law, but such annulments are difficult to attain since they are not granted on psychological or personal grounds. Traditionally, Catholics who have been divorced in civil courts are encouraged to participate in Catholic worship services but not permitted to take part in the Eucharist. However, this is changing, and some divorced Catholics do receive communion. The Orthodox tradition is similar to the Catholic Church's in that it does not allow divorce.

Most Protestant churches allow divorce. In most cases, this means that they recognize divorces granted by civil courts. Legal marriages are marriages conducted by the state or its agents, which in many jurisdictions include the clergy. Thus divorce becomes a civil rather than an ecclesiastical matter. Protestant churches also allow divorced parties to remarry.

Funerals Funerals are rites or ceremonies conducted on the occasion of the death of a person. All branches of Christianity conduct funerals. Seen in the context of rites of passage, funerals mark the transition of a human being from being among the living to being among the dead. The funeral service is a structured way to honour the life of the one who has died and to assuage the grief of those who mourn. There are many diverse beliefs within Christianity about life after death. The Nicene Creed, the most widely used symbol of Christian belief, says simply, "we look forward to the resurrection of the dead and the life of the world to come." All else is speculation.

Christian Spiritual Practices

Reading the Bible

A spiritual practice that emerged out of the Protestant reforms of the 1500s was devotional reading of the Bible. This was a practice that grew out of the emphasis among the Protestant reformers that the Bible was the primary source of authority in the life of a Christian. *Sola Scriptura*, or "scripture alone," became one of the slogans of the Reformation.

In order to read the Bible spiritually and devotionally, it was necessary to have a portable text. This was made possible by the emergence of a new technology, the printing press, invented by Johannes Gutenberg (1398–1468). Prior to this time, the Bible was a huge text copied by hand and bound in large folios that took two people to lift. It wasn't until the 1600s that printed versions of the Bible emerged that could be easily carried and owned by families. The other barrier was that laypeople were often illiterate. It was only the educated who could read and write and knew Latin well enough to read the Bible. However, reformers such as Martin Luther and John Wycliffe (c. 1320–87) translated the Bible into the vernacular languages. Wycliffe was the first to translate the Bible into English; Luther was the first to translate it into German. As the Bible was translated into vernacular languages, it became more widely read.

Later Protestant movements such as Pietism in the 1600s and the Methodists in the 1700s encouraged the practice of small groups gathering to read scripture together. In these circles the Bible was approached not as an ancient text but as the living word that addressed the current situation of the believing community. Jakob Spener, the Lutheran pastor who founded Pietism, encouraged people to gather in groups of twelve to read the Bible and help one another interpret its relevance to their current needs. Personal devotional reading was also encouraged.

Prayer

There is a great deal of diversity in the practice of prayer within Christianity. While virtually all Christians pray and share the Lord's Prayer, the many streams of Christianity have developed their own characteristic forms. Within the Catholic and Orthodox traditions, set prayers are incorporated into the Mass and the Divine Liturgy. But there are also forms of prayer that developed within the monastic traditions. While Protestants rejected monasticism, they too developed their own practices of prayer.

Prayer and Meditation in the Monastic Traditions
The idea of a life dedicated wholly to prayer and spiritual discipline first emerged among Egyptian Christians in the third century who became known as the Desert Fathers. One of those early ascetics was Anthony the Great (c. 251–356). The legend is that upon hearing these words from the Gospel of Matthew: "Go sell what you have, give to the poor . . . and come, follow me" (19:21), Anthony did just that. He went into the desert wilderness to follow Christ. He and other early monks lived a solitary life and through prayer, meditation, and ascetic disciplines cultivated a practice that led to God. The spirituality of the Desert Fathers inspired monastic developments in both eastern and western Christianity.

Mount Athos, on a peninsula surrounded by the Aegean Sea in Macedonia, Greece, has been a centre of Eastern Orthodoxy since 963 C.E. Often called the "Holy Mountain," the peninsula—classed as a semi-autonomous monastic republic—is populated by twenty Eastern Orthodox monasteries, including Russian, Serbian, Bulgarian, and Romanian religious houses. Daily schedules within the monasteries include prayer (communal or private), communal dining, work (with specific duties for each monk), and rest. During religious celebrations that include long vigils, the schedules are changed accordingly. Although land-linked, Mount Athos is accessible only by a single boat, the *St. Eshpigmenitis*. Only men over eighteen years of age are welcome to visit or to live on Mount Athos; Eastern Orthodox adherents are given precedence. Women have been barred from the "Holy Mountain" since the eleventh century, as they are considered to be barriers to the monks' spiritual progress and enlightenment.

Source: © Alain Keler/Sygma/CORBIS

Benedict of Nursia (480–547) developed a form of monastic life that became characteristic of Catholic Christianity. Benedict's rule is built around eight periods of communal prayer each and every day. It begins with *vigil* at two a.m., *lauds* at daybreak, *prime* at six a.m., *tierce* at 9 a.m., *sext* at noon, *nones* at three p.m., *vespers* at sundown, and *compline* at dark. This cycle of daily prayer builds remembrance of God into the very fabric of the day and the life of the monks. Prayers during these periods are often sung or chanted.

Benedictines also practise a form of meditation known as contemplation. They incorporate manual work into their daily lives—tending the fields, maintaining the monastery, working in the kitchen—alongside the study of spiritual literature. It has proved to be an immensely successful form of monastic life in the West. Other religious orders—Franciscans, Dominicans, and the followers of Teresa of Avila—also developed their own distinctive monastic traditions and practices of prayer.

The Jesus Prayer Within the Orthodox monasteries there developed what came to be called the "Jesus Prayer" or the "Prayer of the Heart." This practice had ancient roots but it received its classic form in the teachings of Gregory Palamas (1296–1359), a monk at the famous Orthodox monastery of Mount Athos, founded in the fourth century. This method of prayer followed Saint Paul's admonition to "pray without ceasing"; it involved repetition of the words "Lord Jesus Christ, have mercy on me, a sinner." It was to be practised, Gregory taught, in conjunction with participation in the Divine Liturgy, and with an attitude of humility.

A well-known anonymous classic of Russian spirituality, *The Way of the Pilgrim,* recounts a journey into the practice of the Jesus Prayer. Following the advice of a monk, the author began to repeat the words of the prayer several hundred and then thousands of times a day. The practice came to be integrated with his breathing in and breathing out. First done out loud, it gradually became a silent, inner repetition of the phrase. This had a profound and transformative impact on the anonymous pilgrim, as it led him into a deeper love for his fellow human beings and his god. Prayer, he realized, was both communion with God and an awakening to the spiritual powers within.

Spontaneous or Free Prayer In some Protestant traditions, especially among American Baptists and some Methodists, comes the tradition of spontaneous or free prayer. This is the recitation of prayer during worship that is not written or set, but rather a personal and spontaneous prayer from the heart. These prayers come at standard places in the worship service, usually at the beginning, before the sermon, and toward the end of the service. It is central to Quakers and Pentecostals, who believe that the Holy Spirit moves us to prayer and sometimes even supplies the words.

Marian Devotion A widespread practice among Catholic and Orthodox Christians is devotion to Mary, the mother of Jesus. It developed in early Christianity and at the Council of Ephesus (451) when Mary was given the title *theotokos*, a Greek word meaning "god-bearer." The term is usually translated into Latin as *mater dei* and into English as Mother of God. In Orthodox Christianity the term *theotokos* has been retained; it is included in the Divine Liturgy and in the iconography of the church.

Marian devotion grew to have a pervasive role in Catholic practice and spirituality. Mary's titles grew to include, besides Mother of God, the Blessed Virgin, the Holy Mother, and many others. This devotional practice was especially important in medieval Catholic life, when many churches, such as Notre Dame ("Our Lady"), were named in honour of Mary. Some medieval theologians even referred to Mary as the *mediatrix* or the *co-redemptrix* along with Christ. The saying of the rosary—a set of prayers using a string of beads—as an act of devotion became especially popular in late medieval times and continues today. Contemporary Marian shrines include those of Lourdes (1858) in France, Fatima (1917) in Portugal, and Medugorje (1981) in the former Yugoslavia. Although the shrines at Lourdes and Fatima are recognized by the Catholic Church, the shrine at Medugorje has not received official approval, though it is visited by tens of thousands pilgrims every year.

In Protestant Christianity Marian devotion has virtually disappeared, although it is still found among some Anglo-Catholic Anglicans and to a lesser degree among some Lutherans. On the whole, Protestant Christianity rejected the practice as infringing on the worship due to God alone and Christ alone as mediator.

PEOPLE & PLACES

Pilgrimage to Assisi

When I was in Assisi, Italy, in the 1970s I found myself in the midst of a pilgrimage. Pilgrims had walked from various places in Europe to visit the home of Saint Francis, the remarkable thirteenth-century monk. They were coming down from the hill on which Assisi is located to a church, Santa Maria degli Angeli, in the valley below. I joined them for the six-kilometre hike. Along the way some sang, some carried banners—including a group that had walked from Germany—others visited, and some maintained silence. After we entered the huge church, a special service unfolded: prayers were recited and hymns were sung. Later, visiting with some Franciscans back in Assisi, I learned that the blessing at the end of the service had included an indulgence (a reduction of punishment on earth for sins already forgiven) for participation in the pilgrimage.

Pilgrimage: a spiritual journey to a site considered holy.

Pilgrimage

Pilgrimage is a practice found in all of the world's religious traditions, including Christianity. The English word *pilgrimage* comes from the Latin *peregrinus*, meaning "wandering over a distance." It was common for Jewish people to make a yearly pilgrimage to the Temple in Jerusalem. The practice of pilgrimage continued among Christians but to sites connected to the life of Jesus. It became a more widespread practice during the time of Constantine and his successors, when churches were built in Jerusalem and in other places where significant events in the life of Jesus had occurred. For example, when a church was built in Bethlehem in the fourth century to mark the place of Jesus's birth, it became a place of pilgrimage. Later pilgrimages included sites associated with Christian martyrs, saints, or holy persons, or where appearances of Mary had been reported.

The motives for pilgrimage are many and varied. Some undertake a pilgrimage to fulfil a vow, others to gain spiritual benefits, and yet others to receive forgiveness for a wrong done or seek healing of an illness.

The Camino de Santiago ("way of Saint James") is a series of pilgrimage routes across Europe that lead to the cathedral of Santiago de Compostela in northwest Spain. Originating in the ninth century, it became the most popular pilgrimage site in medieval Europe. In

Liberation theology: a contemporary movement that began in Latin America in the 1960s and has since spread to Africa and Asia, which sees the core of Christian teaching as liberation from oppressive social and political structures and a hope for a more just society.

the twentieth century it experienced a great revival of interest, and now thousands take part in this journey. There are numerous websites devoted to the Santiago de Compostela pilgrimage.

Christian pilgrimage sites are found all across Europe, in the Middle East, and around the world. The shrine of Our Lady of Guadalupe in Mexico is visited by tens of thousands of pilgrims every year. Sometimes it is said that the church itself has been on a pilgrimage as it has developed throughout history.

AUTHORITY

There is no single pattern of authority across the Christian traditions. Authority in Christianity ranges from the hierarchically structured patterns found in the Catholic traditions to the Quakers, who acknowledge no other authority than "that of God in everyone." Moreover, as in all religious traditions, the issues of authority, identity, and diversity in Christianity are intertwined.

Human beings, like all creatures, are born into a world of infinite scope and grandeur, into families and societies. Most find themselves included in religious events from infancy. They thus grow up in particular communities where they encounter many voices of authority. These include the voices of parents, the extended family, and religious leaders, as well as the manifold voices of society. The voices also include the particular community of faith in which they are raised. For the one-third of humanity that makes up the Christian demographic, that community might include a local parish or church that could be Catholic or Methodist or Russian Orthodox or Church of Christ in Africa or the Thomas Christians of Kerala, in India. Authority within these diverse contexts unfolds in particular and nuanced ways, even though they share patterns of authority in the Christian context.

The question of authority is linked to the diversity one finds in Christianity. Consider the following four scenarios.

Scenario I Juan grew up in a Catholic family in Colombia. He was an altar boy and a faithful participant in the life of the church. When he went to university, he wondered if he had a vocation to the priesthood. He studied philosophy and took courses in theology and then decided to enter a seminary. During his studies, he learned about the new **liberation theology** of Latin America. He saw the need for identification with the poor in their struggle for a better life, and it moved him deeply. He also knew about the criticism directed at liberation theology by the Vatican and papal authorities, which made him feel conflicted. He spoke with his spiritual advisor, who urged him to pray about the matter. Juan finally decided to leave the seminary because he did not want to feel in conflict with the authorities in the church, even though he believed that liberation theology was in line with the teachings of Jesus. As a layperson he continued to practise liberation theology by getting involved with a group of Catholics and Protestants working with communities across Latin America to further the aims of liberation for the poor and oppressed.

Scenario II Freya was born in communist East Germany in the early 1950s. Her family was Lutheran, but it was a difficult time for the church. Under pressure from the state authorities, the Lutheran Church sought to find its way with integrity in the new socialist world. As a teenager, Freya often felt conflicted. Some of her friends embraced the new youth groups initiated by the secular state, while she was drawn to the ways of her church. State atheism was the norm and faith in God was considered a hangover from the past. It was difficult, but she persisted. Freya didn't oppose socialism but she did disagree with atheism. She found voices in the church that helped her negotiate her way into adulthood, and she continued in her connection to the church even though it meant walking carefully in relation to state authorities.

Scenario III George was born into a Syrian Orthodox community in Kerala, on the southwest coast of India, that was also called the Thomas Christians. They held firmly to the conviction that Jesus's disciple Thomas had come to India and laid the foundations of their community. As a young boy, George had playmates who were Christians, Hindus, and Muslims. This wasn't surprising, since Kerala was 40 percent Hindu, 30 percent Muslim, and 30 percent Christian, and these communities had lived side by side for centuries. He later said that the only persecution his community had experienced was from other Christians, especially from Catholics when the Portuguese arrived in India in the 1500s. When the Portuguese Christians encountered the Thomas Christians, they denied their Christianity because they knew nothing about the pope in Rome. But some of the Thomas Christians persisted, and they remain a vibrant strand of Indian Christianity today. George grew up in the multi-faith context of Kerala and later married and became a priest in his Syrian Orthodox Church.

Scenario IV When Sarah goes to her Quaker meeting on the First Day, as Sunday is called, she enters the meeting place and takes her seat in the circle, quietly nodding at the others who have gathered. The community sits in silence, waiting to be led by the Spirit. Some mornings they spend the entire hour in silence. Sometimes one of the Quakers feels led by the Spirit to share with others an experience, a prayer, or a song—a "leading," in Quaker parlance. At the end of an hour, two elders stand and shake hands, thus ending the service. Then there are introductions of visitors, announcements, and, if necessary, a brief business meeting. This is often followed by tea or coffee. This has been Sarah's practice since her parents brought her to a "meeting" when she was a young girl. She is proud of her Quaker heritage and especially its pacifism and opposition to war.

Embodied in these stories are different patterns of authority as they are found in the context of different traditions of Christianity. Dictionaries often define *authority* as the power to enforce laws, exact obedience, or to command, determine, or judge. These definitions emphasize the legal and institutional dimensions of authority but do not address the nature of moral authority or authority in the spiritual realm. It is the realm of moral and spiritual authority that we encounter in the religious traditions of humankind.

In a religious context, authority has to do with what the community of believers and practitioners regard as trustworthy, reliable, and authoritative in relation to Christian ways, or the teachings, practices, and traditions of Christianity. Every religious tradition has persons who exercise authority within the community of faith. It needs to be emphasized that authority is always relational: it is a relationship within a community. One always need to ask, authority for whom? in what community or social group? according to whom? The pope has authority within the Catholic world, but to those outside the Catholic world he is just another voice, though one that carries the weight of being head of the largest body of Christians in the world. For non-Catholic Christians, his voice may have some spiritual authority but no institutional or legal authority.

Within the Christian traditions, then, one encounters several levels and kinds of authority, ranging from the charismatic authority of its founder to the authority of scripture and tradition, from the institutional authority of the church to the authority of conscience. These overlapping types of authority may also, from time to time, come in conflict with one another (Keelan 2006, 33ff).

Charismatic Authority

In the Christian scriptures, Jesus is often characterized as one who "spoke with authority." What does this mean? We know virtually nothing of Jesus beyond what is found in the early Christian writings that became the New Testament. There he is presented as one who often spoke in parables, stories, or short aphorisms. He invited people to "follow him" and he spoke of God's kingdom; he urged his listeners to be peacemakers and to love their enemies. For some, his words had the ring of truth. These were words that carried what scholars call *charismatic authority*, a persuasiveness that rested in Jesus's exemplary character and behaviour. This authority was not due to a position he held in the legal or political structures of his society, or to some inherited status or any institutional position. It was, as it were, the voice of moral and spiritual authority.

Apostolic Authority

Apostolic authority refers to an understanding of the charismatic authority of Jesus passed on to his followers. It was a spiritual passing from one generation to another, a process seen in other religious traditions as well. As people responded to the charismatic authority of Jesus's life and teaching, they began to build shared memories across generations that were the beginning of oral and lived traditions.

Apostolic succession: the passing on of spiritual power or blessing from teacher to follower, from one generation to the next.

To use a term from the German sociologist Max Weber, over the following generations Jesus's charismatic authority went through a process of "routinization." What Weber meant was that the community that had grown up around Jesus developed patterns of behaviour, practice, and authority that sustained the community beyond Jesus's death. It is this process that we see at work when we look to the authority of the apostles, the Bible, and the traditions of early Christianity.

Biblical Authority

Christians acknowledge the authority of the Bible, just as Hindus, Muslims, and Buddhists acknowledge their own sacred writings. The Bible is regarded as a trustworthy source for Christian life and practice and for wisdom concerning God. Christians have all kinds of teachings and theories concerning the meaning of the authority of scripture. The most common teaching is that the Bible is the inspired word of God.

The Bible is the principal written authority among Christians for their knowledge about God, Jesus, and the beliefs and practices of early Christianity. Protestant Christians affirm that the Bible stands above all other authorities—including the authority of tradition and the church—in relation to the Christian life. But Orthodox Christians see the Bible as part of tradition, to be read and interpreted in relation to the creeds and tradition. Catholic Christians see the Bible as not having an independent authority; instead it is to be interpreted in the context of tradition and the creeds by the *magisterium*, the bishops of the Church. Pentecostal Christianity has a high regard for the Bible but adds the living experience of the Spirit, especially in relation to baptism in the Spirit and glossalalia, or ecstatic utterance, as a mark of authentic Christianity. There is great variety among Pentecostals, but they tend, like American fundamentalists and some Evangelical Christians, to a literalistic reading of scripture.

Apostolic Succession

Orthodox and Catholic churches, along with some Protestant communities, acknowledge the continuing authority of the apostles through a teaching known as **apostolic succession**. They believe that there is an unbroken line of succession from Jesus's apostles down to present-day priests, bishops, and patriarchs. The apostles passed their authority on to their successors through "laying on of hands," a practice that later became a ritual of consecration. It is difficult to establish this historically, but it is part of the official teachings of the Catholic, Orthodox, Anglican, and some Lutheran traditions. Other Protestant traditions have the office of bishop but it does not rest on the principle of apostolic succession. Bishops are appointed, elected, or chosen by lot. The scope of their authority also varies across the traditions of Christianity.

Authority of the Church

Christians acknowledge the authority of the church as embodied in their Christian leaders. While there is a range of patterns of organizational structures, this is an embodied and institutionalized authority that is based on position or office.

The most centralized pattern of authority is found in the Catholic Church. There, final authority in matters of faith and in the life of the institutional church rests in the pope, the supreme pontiff. Beneath the pope are cardinals, bishops, and priests. In the context of the local parish, the priest is central. In this tradition, local priests are assigned to particular parishes by their bishops.

In the Orthodox traditions the authority of tradition is diffused throughout hierarchical but autonomous national churches. A degree of precedence is given to the patriarch of Constantinople, but that title is more honorary than institutional. Each of the Orthodox traditions has its own patriarch, who is the highest authority for that particular Orthodox community, whether it is in Greece, Russia, or Romania, for example.

Protestant churches have diverse patterns of authority ranging from the more hierarchical forms of church governance found in the Anglican and Lutheran traditions to the congregational policies of the Congregational and Pentecostal traditions.

Authority of Conscience

In Christianity, *conscience* is understood as the faculty of discerning goodness in the individual human being. Many Christians believe that one should never act contrary to the demands of one's conscience. But there is a wide range of views within Christianity concerning the relationship of the authority of conscience to other forms of authority within the Christian community. Some take conscience as the inner voice in an individualistic way, while others insist that the voice of conscience must be resonant with the discernment of the larger community or with tradition. A continuing challenge to Christians is how to weigh the several voices of authority in relation to the immediate issues that confront one, and one's community of faith.

The Crisis of Authority in Contemporary Christianity

The past five centuries have witnessed a relentless series of challenges to the authority of the church. Some have perceived this as a crisis of authority within contemporary Christianity, a crisis that has arisen from multiple sources. First there were challenges to the authority of the medieval Catholic Church from within Christianity itself, challenges that gave rise to the new Protestant traditions. Then

PERSPECTIVES

Contemporary Christian Reform Movements

Liberation Theology

The term *liberation theology* originated in South America with Catholic theologians Leonardo Boff and Gustavo Gutierrez, among others. They took the position that encountering the God of the Bible meant moving beyond academic theologizing to live the gospel in a radical way, by living with and for the poorest and most marginalized in society. Boff developed a theology of the "preferential option for the poor," which was built on Luke 6:20: "Blessed are the poor, for theirs is the Kingdom of God." At its core, liberation theology proposes that God is always and everywhere on the side of the poor and the oppressed and marginalized. Theologians included an analysis and critique of traditional formulations of global power and its structures—including their own church's attitude to the poor, its riches, and its hierarchy—for legitimizing an unjust world order and thereby contributing to the poverty of the many. The emphasis of liberation theology is on orthopraxis rather than orthodoxy. Christians are called to immerse themselves in the lives and concerns of the poor and to work for the liberation of the oppressed from whatever binds them. Since its origination in South America, liberation theologies have developed worldwide, focusing on the power structures and specific needs of the poor in each particular region.

Feminist Theology

In the nineteenth century, women such as Lucretia Mott and Elizabeth Cady Stanton criticized the way the Bible was used to uphold male-dominated social structures. For Christian feminists, this has continued to be a central theme in their work of reform. Feminist theologians in the 1960s and 1970s began examining how male bias has skewed theological understandings of God, nature, doctrines, and history. The authority of the Bible was challenged, given that the "official canon" was put in place by male leaders of the church. Male language, for example, led to women's subordination in society at large and particularly in the Christian church, even more particularly with regard to women's leadership roles in the church. Mary Daly, a feminist theologian, has argued famously, "If God is male, then the male is God!" (Daly 1973, 19). Increasingly, feminist theologians have begun realizing that issues of race, sexuality, sexual orientation, class, ethnicity, and economics must also be addressed through their developing theologies. They thereby acknowledge that *all* systems of domination must be challenged to ensure justice and freedom for all, and this includes a critique of white feminist privilege.

came the intellectual challenges of the European Enlightenment, which, in the name of reason, questioned the authority of revelation. Yet another challenge has come from modern biblical studies that question traditional teachings concerning scripture. The growth of democratic traditions in the modern world has challenged the authoritarianism within Christian traditions, and the emergence of feminism has challenged the paternalistic or patriarchal elements of Christian authority.

The responses on the part of Christianity to these challenges have varied across the Catholic, Orthodox, and Protestant worlds. The denominations of Protestantism incorporated more democratic procedures into the life of their denominations as they elected governing authorities within their own communities and enhanced the role of congregations in the appointment of pastors. In contrast, the Catholic and Orthodox traditions staunchly reaffirmed traditional practices.

There was wide acceptance of modern approaches to the study of scripture among the mainline Protestant churches until the fundamentalist reaction in American Protestantism occurred at the beginning of the twentieth century. Fundamentalist Christians have insisted on a literal interpretation of scripture while the mainline churches acknowledge a more differentiated approach, creating an ongoing debate on this matter within the Protestant world. The Catholic Church initially resisted modern approaches to the study of scripture, but it has shifted its position in recent decades.

The Second Vatican Council was a major breakthrough for the Catholic Church in relation to the challenges of modernity. The council acknowledged the reality of pluralism within modern societies, affirmed religious freedom, redefined the church as "the people of God," and called for dialogue with other traditions. Many hoped that this new spirit would lead to a significant shift in the patterns of authority within the church, but that has yet to occur. Rather, we have seen tensions between pro-Vatican II elements and their opponents within the Catholic world. The election of Pope Benedict XVI in 2005 was widely regarded as a victory for the conservative elements in Catholic Christianity.

At the heart of the current crisis of authority within Christianity are the issues of human sexuality, the ordination of women, and gay sexuality. When, for example, the 1968 papal encyclical *Humanae Vitae* ("On Human Life") reaffirmed traditional Catholic teachings on human sexuality and reproduction, the response among many Catholics in North America and Europe was to widely and silently either dismiss or ignore it. Most of these Catholics did not leave the church, nor did they protest. They simply decided to follow their own beliefs and ignore the teachings of the church. It would appear that in this case some Catholics heeded the authority of conscience over the authority of the church.

The recent sexual abuse scandals in the Catholic Church have again raised the question of authority within the church, especially since the hierarchy has been revealed as colluding in covering up these grave offences. How can one trust authorities who have acted in ways contrary to their own teachings? The scandal is compounded when these are authorities who claim to speak on behalf of Christ.

There is also considerable dismay among Catholics in relation to the issues of women's ordination and homosexuality. Mainline Protestant churches have moved to ordain women, and in some cases the majority of persons being ordained in a given year are women. The issue of homosexuality is also on the agenda, and while some denominations have accepted homosexuals and same-sex marriage or unions, others remain adamant in their opposition. These issues within contemporary Christianity are unlikely to be resolved in the near future.

IDENTITY

The question of identity—who is a Christian?—is important, complex, and multidimensional. It has social (outer), psychological (inner), historical (past), and future dimensions. Imagine, if you will, the following scenarios. They are fictional, but based on the lives of real people I have known. They explore the complex issue of identity, of how Christians understand themselves. They reveal how intertwined the social and the personal dimensions of religious identity are. All these people are devout Christians, seeking to be faithful to the teachings of their community of faith, seeking to live their faith in daily life.

Christian Identity: Six Scenarios

Scenario I Claire is now in her eighties. She rises at seven a.m. in order to make it to morning mass at the parish she has been part of for more than fifty years. On her way she thinks about her family, now scattered across the United States. And she thinks of the tasks that await her this week. She will spend two afternoons at the library where she volunteers; she especially likes reading to the children. She will also help out at the food kitchen on two other days. She reminds herself that she will have to make time to visit the Sisters of St. Joseph, some of whom taught her children decades ago.

As she enters the church, Claire crosses herself and makes her way to the pew. She kneels and crosses herself again, then offers her prayers. The Mass unfolds with its familiar rhythms, the service comforting and sustaining her as it always has. She has always been a Catholic. Even though she married a Protestant—an unusual act sixty years ago—and is often critical of the hierarchy, especially for its failure to ordain women as priests, being part of this church and this faith has always sustained her life. "One can't let the failures of the church get in the way of one's relationship to God" is something Claire often says. Prayer has become second nature and is never far from her lips; the sacraments have been her guides. She has been a good Catholic.

Scenario II Mary is thirty-five and lives in Kenya with her husband and five children. Every day is a struggle, but Mary is filled with joy: she loves her family and God. She is part of the "People of Love," the popular name given to her Church of Christ in Africa. Her family converted to Christianity when the East African Revival blazed through her tribe in the 1950s. The preaching and praying, but especially the singing, had brought them in contact with this movement. The Church of Christ began when Anglican authorities told some priests to end their involvement in the revival movement. Instead, many left the Anglicans and started their own, independent church.

Mary's children will all go to the little school run by the church while she spends most of her day picking tea in the green hills outside town. Her husband, Gilbert, has already gone to fish in Lake Victoria. He is fortunate to have work. Throughout the day Mary looks forward to the evening, when people gather at her church to pray and sing. Being part of the "People of Love" gives her great sustenance.

Scenario III Hi, my name is Marc. I am in high school, and my days are filled with thoughts of soccer and girls. I am also going to confirmation classes. My parents want me to be confirmed but I have a lot of questions about this Christian thing. After class last week, I went to visit the pastor and I shared with him some of my doubts and questions. I was surprised by his response. Pastor Johnson was great—he said that having questions was normal, part of maturing and growing up. Wow, I was so relieved. Danny told me that his pastor just got angry with him when he told him about his doubts. Next time I see my pastor, I'm going to talk to him about girls and sex. I'm confused. I don't know if I'm going to go through with this confirmation thing, but I know that if I do I want it to be my decision.

Scenario IV Brother Jonas rises early—he wants to greet the coming of the new day; he remembers Saint Francis's "Canticle to the Sun." He joins his Franciscan community at seven a.m. for prayers and hymns as they celebrate Mass. Then his day takes him to a local school to share with the students his decision to become a brother and follow the path of Saint Francis. In the afternoon he helps out at a drug addiction centre and homeless shelter. It is difficult work, but service to all living beings was central to Saint Francis's message. He taught, following Jesus's example, that it was in serving neighbours and loving strangers that Christians love and serve God. Though Jonas has found some things difficult—especially giving up his girlfriend—he also feels fulfilled in his Franciscan life.

Scenario V As David heads for his barn, he is worried about rumours he has heard that Canada might be sending troops to Afghanistan. He knows this will be a challenging issue for his conservative Mennonite community: they have been pacifists since the beginning of their history, early in the sixteenth century. Following Jesus, especially the Sermon on the Mount, is often difficult in the midst of a world ruled by love of power and money. He is grateful that his community has sustained him. He also knows that the wider world looks askance at his community's rejection of many aspects of modern life. As he enters the barn, the cows stir and some moo, knowing they are about to be fed.

Old Order Mennonites are part of the Anabaptist ("rebaptized") Mennonite movement that began in Switzerland in the sixteenth century. They were distinct from both Catholics and the Lutheran and Reformed Protestants. Anabaptists believed that only adults should be baptized, adhered to a strict interpretation of Jesus's Sermon on the Mount (Matt. 5–7), and rejected many traditional practices such as taking oaths, serving in the army, wearing a wedding ring, or participating in any form of secular government. Mennonites experienced both political and religious persecution and were forced to live in remote areas of Europe. After coming to Canada and the United States, the Old Order split from the larger Mennonite church in the late nineteenth century. Old Order Mennonites continue to use the German language in their meeting houses and homes. Above all, they emphasize remaining free from "the world," including many modern conveniences and technology such as the automobile, preferring to use horses and buggies. They have settled in various parts of Pennsylvania, Virginia, Ohio, Indiana, and Ontario.

Source: © Nik Wheeler/CORBIS

Scenario VI It is five a.m. as Ae-cha ("Loving Daughter") makes her way to the large Pentecostal church in Seoul. Every morning, several hundred gather for prayer at five thirty. They pray, sometimes with eyes filled with tears as they address their heavenly Father. These are tears of both joy and sadness, signs of the presence of the Spirit. Ae-cha became a Christian while she was in college, where she was "baptized in the Spirit." She has recently married Du-ho, but he is too caught up in his new job to come to church every day. She prays for him too. Prayers are said aloud and in unison, all praying in their own words but together. After an hour, she returns home to fix breakfast for her husband before heading off to work.

Each of these scenarios touches on the issue of identity, the ways in which people understand their lives as Christians. One's religious identity is simultaneously a personal and a social journey as it is formed in the context of one's community of faith, that complex of teaching, practice, and ritual that makes up the many forms of Christianity. At the same time, each person puts that shared faith and way together in his or her own manner, giving it a personal stamp, whether one is a Methodist, an Anglican, a Catholic, Russian Orthodox, or a Thomas Christian.

These scenarios give us three insights about Christian identity. First, the quest for identity is a personal journey.

Second, it involves a community of faith. And third, identity is not fixed but evolves over time. While the scenarios above focus on the personal dimensions of the search for a Christian self-understanding or identity, they also point to the social aspects of one's identity. Christian identity is not only personal but also communal. It unfolds in the company of others and is a function of the type of Christianity that is encountered. The scenarios above are set in relation to particular traditions of Christianity, ranging from Catholic to Mennonite, African Christian to Pentecostal, but now we want to explore various paths to God found in the Christian tradition. There are three different ways of conceiving the Christian journey to God. These ways to God are paths that shape the social dimensions of the quest for Christian identity (Bramadat and Seljak 2005).

CONTEMPORARY DIVERSITY WITHIN CHRISTIANITY

As indicated earlier, Christianity is not only the largest family of religious traditions in the world in a numerical sense but also the most diverse. There are literally more than 35,000 different groups that claim the label *Christian* for themselves. Those several thousand different churches, denominations, sects, and groups can be broken down into three broad categories: Catholic, Orthodox, and Protestant. However, within each of these categories there is considerable diversity.

The Catholic tradition can be defined as churches that are in communion with the pope in Rome. Of the more than 2 billion people in the family of Christian traditions, approximately 1.2 billion are Catholic Christians. Included in this number are groups such as the roughly 4 million Ukrainian Greek Catholics and the Maronite Catholics. Ukrainian Greek Catholics have their own distinctive liturgy, and the Maronites hold some views that are unique to their tradition. Other groups fall into the Catholic category but are not in communion with Rome.

The Orthodox tradition also contains diversity. There are approximately 250 million Orthodox Christians around the world. They are subdivided into the Eastern Orthodox churches, including the Russian, Greek, and Romanian Orthodox churches, among others, and the Oriental Orthodox churches, including the Coptic, Ethiopian, and Syrian Orthodox churches. The Eastern Orthodox churches accept the first seven ecumenical councils, but the Oriental Orthodox churches accept only the first three ecumenical councils.

Protestant Christianity, with around 700 million adherents, is the second-largest group within Christianity. Given that Pentecostal churches appear to be experiencing significant growth, it is difficult to know the exact numbers. Protestants have a shared commitment to the centrality of scripture and the historic creed of Nicaea but add their own additional creeds and confessions. The forms of church governance vary widely across the Protestant traditions. The largest groupings are the various strands of Pentecostal Christianity (200 to 500 million), Anglican (82 million), Baptist (105 million), Lutheran (87 million), Methodist (75 million), and Reformed (75 million).

There are also innumerable smaller groups under the Protestant heading, such as the Anabaptists (1.5 million), Kimbanguists—the Church of Christ on Earth by his Special Envoy Simon Kimbangu—(5.5 million), and Disciples of Christ/Churches of Christ (5.5 million). Many of the smaller groups included here are independent African churches such as the Church of Christ in Africa. The Christian population of Africa has grown to over 300 million since the end of colonialism in the 1960s.

Diversity in Teaching and Theology

The core convictions of Christianity are embodied in its three-articled faith in God the Creator, Redeemer, and Sanctifier. However, while Anglicanism emphasizes the centrality of worship, Lutherans place more emphasis on the teaching of justification by faith. But what is held in common is more than what differentiates. Throughout the history of Protestantism there has been a tendency to emphasize the truth of one community of faith and to deny the validity or plausibility of another. This continues today, although there are some indications of movement beyond these polemics in an age of ecumenism.

THE CANADIAN CONTEXT

There is hardly a town or city in Canada that doesn't have a Christian church. This is evident in the number of church buildings that can be found from the smallest of towns or villages to the major cities across the country. According to the 2001 census, 77 percent of Canada's population is Christian, 43 percent identifying as Catholic, 29 percent as Protestant, and 1.7 percent as Orthodox, with the remaining 3.5 percent representing other forms of Christianity. Christianity's values and habits are woven into the history and cultural life of the country. In recent decades, with changes to exclusionary immigration policies, Canada has become more multi-religious, just as it has become more multicultural. At the same time, an increasingly secular emphasis in Canadian life has altered the place of Christianity in Canadian society.

Here we want to look at the story of Christianity in Canada's history. The European discovery of North America marks the beginning of a Christian presence in these lands. For the first three centuries of European presence, the dominant exchange was with the Indigenous peoples of Canada.

European Discovery and Settlement

Although settlements in Newfoundland were established by the Norsemen around 1000 C.E., it has been customary to credit the European discovery of Canada to John Cabot (c. 1455–98) in 1497. Like Christopher Columbus, Cabot was an Italian, although his voyages were financed by the English. He set sail from Bristol in May 1497 and landed somewhere in North America, the most likely places being Newfoundland or Cape Breton Island. He returned to England in August and the British acknowledged his discoveries. Cabot set out on a second voyage in 1498 but was never heard from again. His reports of abundant fish stocks in the North Atlantic began to bring fishing fleets to the coasts of the Newfoundland in the early 1500s.

However, it was the voyages of the French seafarer Jacques Cartier (1491–1557) that led to a European presence in the lands that became known as Canada. Cartier explored the coast of Newfoundland in 1534, encountered the Mi'kmaq people, sailed into the St. Lawrence River, and landed on the Gaspé Peninsula, where he planted a ten-foot cross bearing the words "Long Live the King of France." Through this act he took possession of the "Country of Canadas" for the French. It was at this spot, it is believed, that the first Catholic mass in Canada was celebrated, with the St. Lawrence Iroquois looking on. Cartier took two of Chief Donnacona's sons back with him to France, but he was in Canada again in 1535. But, as with the English, it was not until the 1600s that France would establish permanent settlements.

In 1605 Samuel Champlain founded the first permanent settlement in Canada, known as Port Royal (now Annapolis), in Nova Scotia. In 1608 he established Quebec City and became the first governor of New France. With Champlain came the French *voyageurs* who began exploring the vast interior of North America. In 1634 Jean Nicollet travelled as far as the Great Lakes, and in 1682 the Sieur de La Salle explored the length of the Mississippi to the Gulf of Mexico, claiming it for the French. There also came missionaries from different Catholic orders—Récollets, Jesuits, and Ursulines—who sought to convert the Indigenous peoples to their own French Catholicism.

English exploration and settlement in North America began lower down on the Atlantic seaboard. The first English settlement was at Jamestown in Virginia in 1607. In 1610 the short-lived fishing port of Cuper's Cove was founded in Newfoundland. It was to Ferryland, on Conception Bay in Newfoundland, that Erasmus Stourton (1603–58) came in the 1620s. He is believed to be the first Church of England clergyman in Canada. The Hudson's Bay Company was established in 1670, and this commercial venture brought traders into lands claimed by the British who began to establish relations with the Indigenous peoples in what is now northern Ontario and into the west. But the number of English-speaking people in Canada remained minuscule—only a few thousand—until late in the 1700s.

New France and Encounters with Native Peoples

One of the first Jesuit missionaries to arrive in New France was Jean de Brébeuf (1593–1649). He came in 1625 and journeyed into the lands of the Huron, an Indigenous people who lived in what is now Ontario, near Georgian Bay, part of Lake Huron. Like his Jesuit forebears in China in the early 1500s, Brébeuf spent several years living with Native people and learning their language, including writing the first Huron dictionary. Despite his best efforts, he was not very successful in his efforts to convert them. There was continual conflict between the Huron and Iroquois

PEOPLE & PLACES

Residential Schools

Full scale efforts to "civilize" Aboriginal peoples did not begin until British hegemony was established in 1812. In time, the government resolved to fully commit to Indian residential schools. The state and the churches collaborated in the efforts to "civilize" Indians in order to solve the "Indian problem." In 1889, the Indian Affairs Department was created and Indian agents were dispatched to Aboriginal communities. These agents would threaten to withhold money from Aboriginal parents if they did not send their children to school. Parents were even imprisoned if they resisted schooling their children. Indian agents prepared lists of children to be taken from reserves and organized round ups at the commencement of the school year. (United Nations Economic and Social Council 2010, 4)

It wasn't until 1986 that the United Church of Canada apologized for its role in imposing European culture on Native peoples. In 2008 the prime minister of Canada issued an official apology for the treatment of Native peoples in residential schools. A U.S. Senate resolution calling for an apology to the Native peoples of the United States was introduced in 2004 but has yet to be passed.

Source: United Nations, Economic and Social Council (2010) "Indigenous Peoples and Boarding Schools: A Comparative Study," Permanent Forum on Indigenous Issues, Ninth Session

peoples, and contact with Europeans also brought disease and illness. When a smallpox epidemic hit the Huron community, many blamed the Black Robes, as the Jesuit missionaries were called. In 1649 the Huron massacred the Jesuit missionaries.

Brébeuf wrote a hymn for the Huron called "Jesus, He Is Born." It began, "Have courage, you who are human beings; Jesus, he is born. The *okie* [evil] spirit who enslaved us has fled.... Jesus is born." The hymn was revised in 1926 as the "Huron Carol" and is still sung in Canadian churches. In its modern form, it opens: "'Twas in the moon of wintertime when all the birds had fled/That mighty Gitchi Manitou sent angel choirs instead.... Within a lodge of broken bark the tender babe was found/A ragged robe of rabbit skin enwrapped his beauty round.... Jesus your king is born ...."

Women in New France

Often overlooked in the history of Christianity, women were pivotal to the story of Christianity in New France, especially as educators and founders of key institutions. Marie de l'Incarnation (née Marie Guyard, 1599–1672) came to New France in 1639 and was the founder and first superior of the Ursuline congregation in Canada. The Ursuline order, founded in Italy in the 1500s, centred on the education of girls and care of the sick. In Quebec the new convent was responsible for the education of Indigenous converts to Catholic Christianity. Later this community established the first hospital in Canada. Marie de l'Incarnation learned the languages of the Indigenous people and wrote devotional literature for her students. She was beatified (recognized as a saint) by Pope John Paul II in 1980.

Another important French-Canadian woman from this period was Sister Marie Morin (1649–1730). Educated by the Ursulines in Quebec City, she joined the Religious Hospitallers of Ville-Marie in Montreal. There she took her final vows in 1671, becoming the first Canadian-born member of a religious order. She excelled in her work at the Hôtel-Dieu (St. Joseph) hospital and in 1693 became its superior. Her work on the history of the hospital became an important source for understanding this period.

Marguerite Bourgeoys (1620–1700) sailed for New France in 1653, and in 1658 she founded her first school. On return trips to France she gathered other women for her work in New France and in 1670 founded the Congrégation de Notre Dame de Montréal. She saw her institution grow and established further schools. In 1693 she stepped down as head of the congregation and turned it over to Marie Barbier de l'Assomption (1663–1739), the first member of her congregation to be born in Montreal. By 1700 there were

16,000 French-speaking inhabitants of New France but probably no more than 2,500 English-speaking residents of lands claimed by the British.

The Seven Years' War, 1756–1763

The Seven Years' War, known in the United States as the French and Indian Wars, influenced the balance of French (Catholic) and English (Protestant) power in Canada. While the population of New France continued to grow, English settlement was mainly further south, in the American colonies. Tensions between France and Great Britain led to repercussions in North America. The Treaty of Utrecht in 1713 had ceded French lands in Canada, known as Acadia, to the British. Though the British had demanded and received an oath of loyalty from the Acadians, they were nervous that they might remain loyal to the French. In 1755 the British attacked the French fort of Beauséjour in modern-day New Brunswick and then expelled six to seven thousand Acadians to France and the lower American colonies. This was known as the Great Upheaval among the Acadians, and it was to mark Catholic–Protestant relations in Canada for generations.

In 1750 France claimed lands stretching from Labrador across to the Great Lakes and from the St. Lawrence down through the Mississippi Basin to Louisiana and Florida. Britain claimed lands from Nova Scotia down the Atlantic coast to Florida and inland, as well as the area around Hudson's Bay. But when the British sought to move across the Alleghany Mountains into the west, they encountered Indigenous peoples—mainly Iroquois—and the French. The first conflict of the Seven Years' War was around Pittsburgh, in western Pennsylvania. In 1759 the British sailed up the St. Lawrence and laid siege to Quebec, at length winning the decisive Battle of the Plains of Abraham.

These events had religious overtones, as they pitted the Catholic French against the Protestant English. The 1763 Treaty of Paris ending the conflict gave Britain control over the whole of eastern North America but it granted French Catholics continued practice of their faith. The Quebec Act of 1774 recognized French law in Quebec, the Catholic religion, and the French language. In the midst of the conflict were the Indigenous peoples, whose traditional lands were increasingly being taken from them. Their spiritual traditions were largely ignored, denigrated, and later outlawed.

The American War of Independence

In 1775 conflict between the American colonies and Great Britain broke out, with major effects on the population of Canada. In 1776 the Continental Congress proclaimed the Declaration of Independence, but the war would continue until the signing of the Treaty of Paris in 1783. During the war, many British Loyalists left the American colonies for Canada. After the war, boatloads of Loyalists were taken from New York and Boston to the Maritimes, especially Nova Scotia and New Brunswick. Estimates vary, but from 40,000 to 60,000 Loyalists came to Canada during the war and in 1783–84, an estimated 30,000 to Nova Scotia and New Brunswick, 4,000 to 5,000 to Quebec, and 8,000 to 10,000 to Ontario. This migration included hundreds of black Loyalists, who were promised new lands in Nova Scotia. The influx more than doubled Canada's population and increased the number of English-speaking people in Canada. It also changed the religious composition of the country, as now the numbers of Protestants—Anglicans, Puritans, Congregationalists, Baptists, and Lutherans—had swelled.

Awakening in the Maritimes

In 1776 the Congregationalist John Henry Alline (1748–84) initiated a revival movement that had an enduring impact on religious life in the Maritimes. Born in Rhode Island, he and his family had moved with others to Nova Scotia in the 1760s. Alline had a life-transforming experience of the "redeeming love of God" in his mid-twenties. It gave him a mission: to preach and revive the faltering faith of his contemporaries, especially those from the American colonies who were moving into Nova Scotia. He was a fervent and effective preacher; he also wrote hundreds of hymns, and his gatherings were marked by singing. Soon new congregations were springing up. Alline crisscrossed Nova Scotia (which then included New Brunswick and Prince Edward Island), preaching his New Light doctrine. He was opposed by many, especially those who thought revivals unseemly. But in less than a decade Alline touched the hearts of many before dying of tuberculosis. His hymns are still sung in Baptist churches of the Maritimes.

Anglicans and Methodists in Upper Canada

Two men of religion played pivotal roles in nineteenth-century Upper Canada (now Ontario). John Strachan (1778–1867) emigrated to Canada from his native Scotland in 1799 as a tutor for a family in Kingston. Later he became the first Anglican bishop of Toronto. Adolphus Egerton Ryerson (1803–82) was born into a United Empire Loyalist family that had left the American colonies for Canada during the War of Independence. Though raised an Anglican, Ryerson followed his mother at eighteen to become a Methodist preacher. The conflicts between Strachan and Ryerson mirrored the religious situation in Upper Canada, which was largely Protestant in the south even though there were pockets and growing numbers of Catholics.

Throughout their long and distinguished careers, the two men crossed swords on many issues during Upper Canada's development in the nineteenth century. Those issues included religious liberty, clergy reserves (lands set aside to generate money for the Church of England), and education. Strachan was ordained in the Anglican Church in 1803 and became the first Anglican bishop of Toronto in 1839. In Cornwall, he founded the Cornwall Grammar School, which quickly became known as the best school in Upper Canada. Strachan had also become part of the Family Compact, a group of conservative figures who were very influential in business and government. He championed establishment of the Church of England as the official church of Canada, but was unsuccessful. He also argued that the clergy reserves should be given only to clergy of the Church of England. Though Strachan had been raised a Presbyterian, he was generally dismissive of other Protestant Christians, suspecting them of harbouring republican sentiments.

Ryerson argued against Strachan's ideas, insisting on separation of church and state and that the clergy reserves should be sold to provide income for non-denominational (but still Christian) public education in Upper Canada. Ryerson eventually won, and he also championed religious liberty for Methodists, Baptists, and other Protestant groups. Both men played significant roles in the establishment of educational institutions in Canada. Ryerson led the efforts to create a public school system in Ontario, using his experience as a Methodist circuit preacher in the service of public education, travelling across Upper Canada to convince the settlers of his ideas.

Both men played roles in the founding of the University of Toronto in 1850. Strachan had received a charter for King's College in 1827 after his move to York, as Toronto was then known. He had been influential in persuading James McGill, a member of a prominent Montreal mercantile family and a relative by marriage, to leave part of his estate to found a university, which led to the establishment of McGill University in Montreal. Bishop Strachan also championed a university for Toronto, but with only Church of England clergy as teachers. Ryerson, who had become chief superintendent of education in 1844, opposed Strachan and oversaw the founding of the secular University of Toronto in 1850. In the early 1840s he had also been a principal of Victoria College, which later federated with the University of Toronto, while Strachan was instrumental in establishing Trinity College at the University (Henderson 1969, 68ff)

Though Strachan lost his bid to see the Church of England established in Canada, he did see it grow to become a self-governing and self-sustaining church in Upper Canada. Ryerson helped to secure recognition of his own Methodist Episcopal denomination and other Protestant traditions in Upper Canada. Each in his own way exemplified a view of Christianity that assumed responsibility for the building of public institutions.

Catholic Quebec

Catholic Lower Canada was influenced more by events in France than those unfolding in the American War of Independence. The Catholic Church in Lower Canada had seen the end of the dream of New France in the mid-1700s, but the church had been given a degree of latitude in what would later become the province of Quebec. It seized the opportunity to lay down a parish system across Quebec that would endure until the mid-twentieth century. In the meantime, Catholic churches dotted the landscape and dominated the society, at least outside Montreal. During the 1800s, Quebec Catholics were strongly influenced by the Ultramontanists, supporters of the pope against the antireligious faction of the French Revolution. Deeply engaged in its political life, the Catholic Church was central to Quebec until the 1960s. Then a period of rapid social change and modernization known as the Quiet Revolution wholly transformed Quebec society. The long and close relationship between the Catholic Church and the government of Quebec was broken, leading to a newly secular era.

Christianity on the Prairies

It was not until the British North America Act of 1867 created the Dominion of Canada that attention began to turn toward what would become the prairie provinces. Settlers there were few. Native peoples and Métis—people of mixed Indigenous and European, largely French, background—were the majority. Scots and English from Ontario were beginning to move into the Red River Settlement, an area occupied by French and Métis people around St. Boniface and Winnipeg. And the new Canadian government was seeking to extend its authority there in the late 1860s and '70s, giving rise to a tragic chapter in Canadian history.

The Métis People From the early days of European presence in Canada, children had been born from liaisons between Europeans, especially French fur traders, and the Indigenous people. Some were born from temporary relationships, others from married couples. By the early 1800s there was a sizable population of Métis people across Canada, but especially on the prairies in what would become Manitoba and Saskatchewan. They were mainly hunters and trappers, but over time small settled trading communities were also established. The Métis were mostly Catholic and French-speaking but were also exposed to Indigenous religious traditions. They were often in conflict with the Hudson's Bay Company, which had a monopoly on trade in the northwest. Often regarded with disdain by others, the Métis are now recognized in Canadian law as a First Nations people.

The Red River Resistance/Rebellion In the 1860s there were intense negotiations to end the monopoly of the Hudson's Bay Company and to transfer sovereignty to Canada. In 1868 Louis Riel, a Métis, returned to St. Boniface (now part of Winnipeg) after studying for the priesthood in Montreal and law in St. Paul, Minnesota. He quickly became involved

Louis Riel (1844–85), a Métis (of mixed North American Aboriginal and European ancestry) politician and founder of Manitoba, was born in Red River. Raised as a devout Catholic, Riel studied for the priesthood at the Collège de Montréal but dropped out of the seminary just months before his ordination and returned to the Red River area. Highly educated and fully bilingual, he quickly emerged as a leader of the Métis. In 1869–70 he led a struggle known as the Red River Rebellion to form a provisional government seeking protection for Métis rights; this eventually led to Manitoba's becoming a province. During the agitation, Riel had an Ontario man, Thomas Scott, executed; fearing retribution, he fled to the United States. Even though a fugitive, he was elected to Parliament, though he was never able to take his seat in the House of Commons. After an absence of fifteen years, a delegation of Métis asked him to return to Canada. Believing that he had a prophetic mission to lead his people, Riel ended his exile and led an uprising in 1885 that escalated into a military mission against the government of Canada. He was arrested, tried, and, despite numerous appeals, executed on a charge of high treason. Riel has been understood as both a messianic figure and a political hero. His unconventional religious views aligned religion and politics in his attempt to seek justice for the Métis people of Western Canada.

Source: © The Canadian Press

in the disputes surrounding the pending transfer of lands to Canada. He championed the cause of the Métis, insisting that the issue of land for his people be addressed. He emerged as the Métis spokesman and was heading a provisional government by 1869. His views shaped the negotiated agreement that led to Manitoba's entrance into Confederation. But in 1870 Riel badly handled the case of Thomas Scott, who was tried for treason and executed. Though elected to the Canadian Parliament—three times—he was unable to take his seat because of the Scott affair.

In the mid-1870s, when visiting Washington, D.C., Riel became convinced that he was divinely mandated to lead the Métis. He went to Montana, where he married and became a teacher. In 1885, Gabriel Dumont and other Métis leaders from Canada went to Riel and persuaded him to return to lead them in what came to be called the Northwest Rebellion. The rebellion had some initial successes but was defeated at Batoche in Saskatchewan. Riel was arrested and taken to Regina, where he was tried and executed despite his eloquent testimony concerning his people, bringing to an end his tragic story. He remains a heroic figure among the Métis.

Social Passion on the Prairies In the 1880s, the prairie lands of western Canada began to be settled by immigrants from around the world, and they brought with them their religious traditions. Although immigration laws favoured those from the British empire, they also came from Russia and the Ukraine, bringing Orthodox traditions as well as Mennonite and Doukhobor beliefs. Immigrants from Germany brought their Lutheran and Catholic traditions, while Lutherans also came from Iceland and the Scandinavian countries. Later, Mormons from the United States trickled northward into the Prairies and into British Columbia. Chinese religions and Buddhism came with the Chinese workers who built the railroads in the west. English immigrants arrived in British Columbia with their Anglican ways, and near the end of the 1800s, a small number of Sikhs arrived from India. The religious landscape of western Canada was a patchwork in which the many Christian traditions adapted to the challenges of the land and the climate.

Change on the Prairies In 1902 J. S. Woodsworth (1874–1942) became the minister of Grace Church in Winnipeg. Like his father, he was a Methodist minister. He had returned to Winnipeg after studying in Toronto and Oxford, where he had become especially interested in social welfare work. In Winnipeg Woodsworth began working in the poor immigrant community of North Winnipeg and teaching a **social gospel**, one intended to realize, said Woodsworth, "the Kingdom of God here and now." He questioned the relevance of a Christianity focused on individual conversion and the afterlife, seeking to shift its focus in Canada to social reform.

Social gospel: a movement within Protestant Christianity beginning in the nineteenth century that sought to recover and apply Christian principles to social institutions and practices to create a just society.

Woodsworth worked as the superintendent of the All People's Mission from 1907 to 1913. He published his classic *Strangers Within Our Gates* in 1909 and *Our Neighbour* in 1911, outlining the social reforms he sought. In 1913 he became head of the Canadian Welfare League and travelled across the Prairies investigating social issues. A pacifist during the First World War, he resigned from the ministry in 1918. He then continued his work for social welfare in the political realm. In 1921 he was elected member of Parliament for Winnipeg North as a representative of the Independent Labour Party, retaining the seat until his death (Allen 1971, 103ff). Throughout the 1920s and '30s, Woodsworth continued to champion the cause of workers, farmers, and immigrants. He was active in the Christian Student Movement and a driving force in the founding of the Co-operative Commonwealth Federation (CCF), a social democratic political party. Woodsworth was determined give a distinctly Canadian face to socialism and a social democratic face to Canadian Christianity.

A very different face was given to Christianity in Alberta, through the work of William "Bible Bill" Aberhart (1878–1943). Born in Perth County, Ontario, he was raised in the Presbyterian Church and became a devout believer in his teenage years. Always drawn to the prophetic teachings of Christian scripture, he had hoped to study for the Presbyterian ministry. Instead, after earning a degree from Queen's University, he became a teacher. He moved to Calgary in 1910, where he was a principal and educator. He had studied the dispensationalist teachings of Cyrus Scofield

(1843–1921), an American fundamentalist and author of the Scofield Bible. Scofield focused on the prophetic materials and believed that between creation and the final judgment there would be seven dispensations, or ways in which God related to humanity. He argued that humanity was now in the final dispensation, which would lead to Christ's return and a "thousand-year millennium." Aberhart shared these views.

In addition to his educational work, in 1918 Aberhart began teaching classes in biblical prophecy that grew year by year. By 1925 his Sunday sermons that focused on prophecy were being broadcast on the radio to a growing audience. When the Great Depression came, Aberhart initially tried to persuade the United Farmers of Alberta of his schemes. Failing in those efforts, he helped found the Social Credit Party, which was based partly on the monetary theories of C. H. Douglas, a British engineer. The new party stormed to power in 1935 and would remain in power until 1971. The preachings of "Bible Bill" left a legacy of biblical literalism and fundamentalism among many prairie Christians.

In Saskatchewan, the Scottish-born Baptist minister T. C. "Tommy" Douglas (1904–86) moved in a wholly opposite direction. He became involved in the CCF, and as premier of Saskatchewan from 1944 to 1961, he led the first democratic socialist government in Canada. He would later serve in the federal parliament and was a champion of universally accessible health care. Douglas is typical of liberal Christian thought that has made a significant contribution to Canadian society.

Women Reformers

Women continued to play a vital role in the unfolding story of Christianity in Canada. Out on the Prairies, Nellie McClung (1873–1951) was a leading social reformer who championed the rights of women. A schoolteacher in rural Manitoba, she joined the Women's Christian Temperance Union (WCTU) and the suffrage movement. Her efforts led to women's gaining the right to vote in the prairie provinces and British Columbia in 1916. She was also part of the new social gospel movement. A member of the newly formed United Church of Canada in 1925, she urged the appointment of women ministers (it would not happen until 1936). In Edmonton she joined Emily Murphy (1868–1933), a prominent Anglican writer, journalist, and magistrate, and three others in the famous "Persons Case" of 1929 that saw women recognized under the law as "persons." McClung continued her outspoken advocacy for women in the church and society until her death.

Writer, social activist, and feminist Nellie L. McClung (1873–1951) is celebrated as one of the main figures who brought woman suffrage, temperance, and ordination of women to the forefront of Canadian society. She combined deeply held Christian beliefs with political activism, and as a dynamic speaker she preached the gospel of feminist activism and social transformation. She believed that it was God's intention for women and men to be treated equally, with dignity and respect.

Source: Toronto Star Archives/GetStock.com

First Ordained Woman in Canada Lydia Emélie Gruchy (1894–1992) was born and raised near Paris, France, before her family emigrated to Saskatchewan in 1913. When her brother died in the First World War, Lydia decided to become a minister. She went to St. Andrew's College in Saskatoon and graduated with top honours. In 1926 she applied for ordination in the new United Church, but was refused. While working as a minister's lay assistant, she persisted in applying for ordination until, in 1936, she was ordained at St. Andrew's United Church in Moose Jaw. She continued her ministry until 1962.

Born out of the social gospel movement in the early twentieth century, the United Church of Canada became the largest Protestant Christian body in the country. In 1925 it brought together Methodists,

Congregationalists, and roughly two-thirds of the Presbyterians in Canada into one denomination. Known for its inclusiveness, the United Church was not only the first major Christian body to ordain women but also led the way in many other reforms within Canadian Christianity. It was the United Church that in 1986 offered the first formal apology to First Nations people for imposing European culture on them. In 1998 the United Church also apologized for the pain and suffering that its involvement in residential schools had brought to many of Canada's Native peoples.

Ecumenical Christianity

Relations between the different branches of Christianity had been polemical and acrimonious since the time of the Reformation. That same fractious spirit also pervaded relations between Protestant groups, each insisting that their way was the best way. That stance carried over into Christianity throughout Canada. But in the late nineteenth and early twentieth centuries, largely initiated by North American Christians, efforts began to build a spirit of cooperation among Christian bodies. Principal George Monro Grant of Queen's University in Kingston, Ontario, attended the Parliament of the World's Religions in Chicago in 1893. On the Prairies, in Ontario, and in Nova Scotia, the ecumenical spirit led to formation of the United Church of Canada, but it wasn't until after the Second World War that a new ecumenical spirit spread throughout Canadian Christianity.

Ninety Protestant and Orthodox churches came together in Amsterdam to create the World Council of Churches (WCC) in 1948. The WCC has since grown to 349 churches, representing 560 million Christians worldwide. Though the Catholic Church is not a member, it has worked cooperatively with the WCC on its Faith and Order Commission and in development activities. Canada had already created its own Canadian Council of Churches in 1944, and in the late 1940s the Canadian Council of Christians and Jews was established.

The Changing Face of Canadian Christianity

In the 1960s and '70s, movements for social change had an impact on the religious life of Canada as it met the challenges posed by separatism in Quebec, immigration, First Nations peoples, the increasingly multicultural Canadian mosaic, the women's movement, and demands for a more just society. There was also a growing secular mentality. Elements of Canadian Christianity responded positively to the new challenges, seeking to redress past wrongs and to find creative solutions to current issues. The growing ecumenical spirit signalled a more hopeful future. At the same time, however, secularism has led to a dramatic downward shift in church-going among Canadians, and Christian churches have become sites of an ongoing struggle between more liberal and more conservative factions (Bramadat and Seljak 2005, 120ff).

One of the most significant transitions has been in the situation of women within Canadian Christianity. The 1970s and '80s saw growing numbers of women being ordained as ministers in the United Church of Canada and the first ordinations of women in the Anglican, Lutheran, Presbyterian, Mennonite, and many other Protestant denominations. Since then women have become Anglican and Lutheran bishops, Presbyterian and United Church moderators (elected leaders of the church as a whole), as well as professors in seminaries and theological schools across Canada. By 2000 half or more of the student population of many seminaries in Canada were women. This phenomenon has challenged in significant ways the patriarchy endemic in Christianity.

There are also movements for change in the status of women within the Roman Catholic world, despite the Vatican's reaffirmation of its view that priests must be men. The sharp decline in the numbers of vocations (the call to the religious life) in the western Catholic world has seen more and more laywomen assuming responsibilities in Catholic parishes and Catholic educational settings in Canada. There are also growing numbers of women theologians and theological educators. In 2005 nine women were ordained as priests in the Catholic Church by a group of what the Vatican saw as renegade bishops, in a ceremony held in the Thousand Islands of the St. Lawrence River. The church declared the ordinations invalid, but the event is indicative of the determination of Catholic women to redress the exclusionary teachings of the Vatican.

Christianity in Canada Today

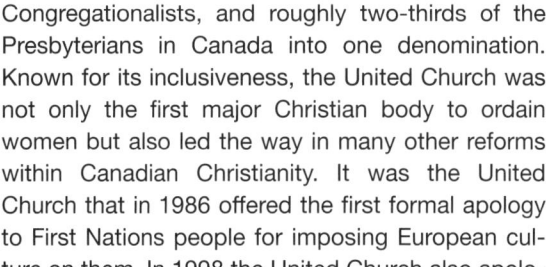

Over the past 500 years Canadian Christianity has forged its own distinctive way. It is neither the same as European Christianity, with its national churches, nor is it American Christianity, with its vaunted separation of church and state. Canadian Christianity is more attuned to the Canadian values of "peace, order, and good government" than the U.S. values of "life, liberty, and the pursuit of happiness." Many churches in Canada are more communal than individual in their emphasis, more public than private in their orientation, more intellectual than experimental in their ethos, and more sober than emotional in their expression. Canadian Christian expressions have resisted the melting-pot mentality of our southern neighbours as Canadians have forged their own multi-religious mosaic.

The 2001 census provided a snapshot of that current mosaic. As noted earlier, 76 percent of Canadians identified themselves as Christians. Of those, 43 percent were Roman Catholic, 29 percent Protestant, 1.7 percent Orthodox, and 3.3 percent other Protestant or Christian. Sixteen percent said they had no religion. The Canadian mosaic has expanded beyond the varieties of Christianity and its growing secular contingent to include populations of Muslims (2 percent), Jews (1.1 percent), Buddhists (1 percent), Hindus (1 percent), and Sikhs (0.9 percent). Canadian Christianity has welcomed the increasing presence of peoples from the world's other great religious traditions by establishing interfaith officers and dialogue programs. Christian traditions in Canada continue to evolve in the twenty-first century.

CHRISTIANITY AND THE INTERNET

Scholars of religion have only just begun to investigate the impact of the Internet on the study of the religious traditions of humankind. Entering terms such as *Christian* or *Christianity*, *Catholic* or *Orthodox*, leads to millions of results with some potential relevance to the student interested in the study of Christianity. What are we to make of this new technology and this avalanche of information? Who are these many voices claiming to offer information on Christianity? On which traditions of Christianity do sites offer information? How do we know which sites to trust and which to avoid? These are both exciting and difficult questions, especially for individuals who may have little knowledge of Christianity.

There is no denying that the Internet is changing the way in which human beings share information and communicate across our world. This is particularly the case for younger generations, who adapt easily to this new media. The virtual world is becoming for many the real world. The great Canadian media guru Marshall McLuhan taught us that "the medium is the message." That is, every medium embodies it own message; media are not neutral technologies that we then fill with content. McLuhan spent his life probing the nature of the new electronic media, but he died just as the Internet was coming on stream. It now seems that he was prescient in giving us the phrase "global village."

Christians have clearly embraced this new technology. Sites have been established by every official church in the Christian world and by a wide range of individuals and groups claiming to speak in the name of Christianity. In January 2009 Pope Benedict XVI, the leader of more than a billion Catholics, launched his own dedicated channel on YouTube, and there are official websites for all the denominations of Christianity. Vast numbers of people are seeking to create virtual Christian communities. But there are also innumerable websites created by individuals and groups who purport to provide information about Christianity that are dubious and completely unreliable. One of the challenging issues facing any user of the Internet is learning to differentiate between sites that are legitimate and responsible and those that in the name of Christianity are laced with offensive opinions that are those of the site creators alone.

One of the most important aspects of the new virtual world is the growth of social networking. There are now sites such as the United Church of Canada's WonderCafe (www.wondercafe.ca), which draws 100,000 visitors a month to discuss "spiritual topics, moral issues, and the big questions of life." Some Christian sites specialize in faith and the arts or serve a network of Christians in science; other offer Christian dating services. Christian

Forums (www.christianforums.com) claims more than 250,000 members; its declared purpose is to "discuss faith and encourage each other." There is also the Catholic Message Board, which describes itself as "defenders of the Catholic faith" and includes a section called "The Pub" that has "Saint Guinness" as its patron saint. There is another site called God Discussion, "for seekers who don't go to church." Sites such as Catholic Answers claim more than 200,000 members, and there are innumerable Christian chat rooms—Pentecostal, Orthodox, Catholic, Evangelical, fundamentalist—and also chat rooms that poke fun at fundamentalists and support their own brand of belief or non-belief. The Internet has come to play a significant role in the development of a new Christian global, albeit virtual, village.

CONCLUSIONS

Christianity and the Future

At the outset of this chapter on Christianity, the learning objectives outlined addressed coming to an understanding of both global and local Christianity. The rich diversity of Christianity and its many streams of practice and belief, alongside the traditions that Christians hold in common, have come to the fore. So too have those elements that give the many forms of Christianity their own distinctive ethos and flavour.

As Christianity enters its third millennium, it is clear that over the past hundred years it has undergone significant changes, particularly as a result of globalization. Globalization is a highly complex notion that cannot be confined to a single definition or theme, but it is perhaps best understood as "a set of social processes (economic, political, cultural, technological, and ecological) that create ... and intensify worldwide social interdependencies and exchanges while at the same time fostering in people a growing awareness of deepening connections between the local and the distant" (Steger 2004, 8–13). An important dimension of globalization that affects the very character of Christianity as it has been known for millennia has to do with changes in the demographics and geography of global Christianity. In the global North (Europe and North America), the numbers of those calling themselves Christians has fallen dramatically, while Christianity in the global South has increased significantly. Similarly, while the numbers of European and North American Catholic priests have shown a rapid decline, ordinations of priests from the global South have been increasing.

Shifts in power dynamics between the Christian North and South have already led to new configurations of denominations and movements, Christian practices, beliefs, and theological formulations. Notions such as a "post-Christian West" and a dominant "Christian South" will have significant implications for the future of Christianity. The recent controversy over same-sex marriage in the Anglican Church is a case in point. While gay marriage is widely supported in many Western societies, it is vehemently opposed by many Anglican bodies in Asia and Africa. Numerous Anglican bishops have broken communion with the worldwide church as a result of what they see as attitudes and practices that are incompatible with scripture.

Clearly the challenges and differences are significant, but so too are the similarities between Christians. New technologies, as we have noted, are making communication between global Christians more feasible, easier, and faster. Understanding unique cultural differences and highlighting similarities based on age-old Christian creeds and practices, through interaction and communication, will be an important dimension of the future of Christianity. It is some ways reminiscent of Saint Augustine's City of God:

> ... this heavenly city, then, while it sojourns on earth, calls citizens out of all nations, and gathers together a society of pilgrims of all languages, not scrupling about diversities in the manners, laws, and institutions whereby earthly peace is secured and maintained, but recognizing that, however various these are, they all tend to one and the same end of earthy peace. (Augustine 1871, 317)

Readers are encouraged to continue to explore, examine critically, and research the varied and multiple concepts, terms, practices, and beliefs in order to come to a deeper understanding of Christian traditions.

KEY TERMS

Advent, p. 122
Apostolic succession, p. 130
Bible, p. 94
Bishop, p. 89
Christian (Gregorian) calendar, p. 90
Church, p. 93
Church year, p. 122
Creed, p. 91
Easter, p. 89
Epiphany, p. 123
Eucharist, p. 120
Gospel, p. 97
Incarnate, p. 92
Liberation theology, p. 128
Lord's Prayer, p. 119
Mary Magdalene, p. 90
Orthodox, p. 89
Pentecostal movement, p. 117
Pilgrimage, p. 127
Quakers, p. 89
Redeemer, p. 93
Resurrection, p. 89
Roman Catholic, p. 89
Sacrament, p. 121
Salvation, p. 91
Social gospel, p. 141

CRITICAL THINKING QUESTIONS

1. What in Christianity is continuous with its parent tradition, Judaism, and what is discontinuous?
2. Some Christians regard the acceptance of Christianity by Constantine as a great victory, while others regard it as the fall of Christianity. Why these different views?
3. What were the issues that led to the "Great Schism" between eastern and western Christianity in 1054?
4. What was the first Bible of Christianity? How did the Bible develop over time?
5. What are ecumenical Christianity and "the wider ecumenism"?
6. How should Christians relate to people of other faiths?

RECOMMENDED READING

Abbot, Walter M., ed. *The Documents of Vatican II*. New York: America Press, 1966.

Abhishiktananda [Henri Le Saux]. *Saccidananda: A Christian Approach to Advatic Experiences*, rev. ed. Delhi: ISPCK, 1998.

Berry, Thomas. *The Dream of the Earth*. San Francisco: Sierra Club Books, 1988.

Bonaventure. *The Soul's Journey into God*. New York: Paulist Press, 1978.

Bonhoeffer, Dietrich. *The Cost of Discipleship*. New York: Touchstone, 1995.

Bryant, M. Darrol. *Religion in a New Key*. Kitchener, ON: Pandora Press, 2001.

Bryant, M. Darrol, and S. A. Ali. *Muslim–Christian Dialogue: Promise and Problems*. (St. Paul, MN: Paragon House, 1998.

Cunliffe-Jones, Hubert, ed. *A History of Christian Doctrine*. Philadelphia: Fortress Press, 1978.

Fairweather, A. M., ed. *St. Thomas Aquinas on Nature and Grace*. Philadelphia: Westminster Press, 1954.

Freedman, David Noel, and Michael J. McClymond, eds. *The Rivers of Paradise: Moses, Buddha, Confucius, Jesus and Muhammad as Religious Founders*. Grand Rapids, MI: Wm. B. Eerdmans, 2001.

Frend, W. H. C. *The Rise of Christianity*. Philadelphia: Fortress Press, 1984.

Griffiths, Bede, ed. *Universal Wisdom: A Journey Through the Sacred Wisdom of the World*. London: HarperCollins Font, 1994.

Hildegard of Bingen. *Book of Divine Works*, ed. Matthew Fox. Santa Fe, NM: Bear, 1987.

Levitt Kohn, Risa, and Rebecca Moore. *A Portable God: The Origin of Judaism and Christianity*. Lanham, MD: Rowman and Littlefield, 2007.

Luther, Martin. *Martin Luther: Selections from His Writings*, ed. John Dillenberger. New York: Anchor Books, 1962.

Palmer, Martin. *The Jesus Sutras: Rediscovering the Lost Scrolls of Taoist Christianity*. New York: Ballantine, 2001.

Raimundo Panikkar, *The Trinity and the Religious Experience of Man* (London: Darton, Longman, and Todd, 1973).

Richardson, Herbert W. *Towards an American Theology*. New York: Harper & Row, 1967.

Rosenstock-Huessy, Eugen. *The Christian Future, or the Modern Mind Outrun*. New York: Harper & Row, 1966.

Smith, Huston. *The Soul of Christianity: Restoring the Great Tradition*. San Francisco: Harper SanFrancisco, 2005.

Snyder, C. Arnold. *Following in the Footsteps of Christ: The Anabaptist Tradition*. Maryknoll, NY: Orbis Books, 2004.

RECOMMENDED VIEWING

Documentaries

Christianity: The First Two Thousand Years. Narr. Ossie Davis, Ruby Dee. Prod. Bram Roos, *Studio*, A&E, 1998 (updated 2000). Disc 1 details the first thousand years and Disk 2 focuses on the second thousand years.

Saints and Sinners: Six Volumes. Acorn Media, 1997. VHS; 6 programs, approx. 60 minutes each. Explores the history, roles, culture, and politics of the papacy; produced with the cooperation of the Vatican.

The Protestant Revolution. This four-part series gives an overview of the birth and development of Protestantism as an important and powerful engine of economic, social, and sexual change for 500 years. Presenting commentary from many of today's notable religious leaders and scholars, the series profiles numerous Protestant historical figures and factions.

Friends of God: The Evangelical Movement in America. HBO, 2007. DVD (ISBN 978-1-4213-6573-2), 58 minutes. Examines the diversity of evangelical Christianity through interviews with important evangelists, educators, activists, and ordinary members of congregations.

The Education of Shelby Knox: Sex, Lies and Education. Dir. Marion Lipschutz and Rose Rosenblatt. PBS, 2005. 76 minutes. An important documentary about a fifteen-year-old Southern Baptist girl who is transformed into an ardent liberal Christian feminist fighting for gay rights and sex education in conservative Lubbock, Texas.

For the Cause. Dir. Rodolphe Caron. Productions Appalaches, National Film Board of Canada, 2011. 53 minutes. An important film highlighting the ongoing history of the Canadian Notre Dame du Sacré Cœur community of nuns that gives voice to their dedication to justice and education alongside their call for a larger role for women in the Catholic Church.

Hip 2B Holy. Dir. Karen Pinker. Narr. Kevin Newman. 90th Parallel, 2009. 60 minutes. A news documentary about the contemporary Christian evangelical movement in Canada. Much of the film is focused on Connexus Community Church in Barrie, Ontario, where services are held in a local multiplex movie theatre and the Internet and video on demand are used to reach its congregation.

Feature Films

Black Robe. Dir. Bruce Beresford. Perf. Lothaire Bluteau, Aden Young. Alliance Communications and Téléfilm Canada, 1991. A film based on Brian Moore's novel of the same name set in seventeenth-century Canada, where a French Jesuit priest, Father Laforgue, and a companion travel through the wilderness of Quebec escorted by First Nations guides. The film chronicles Father Laforgue's inner struggles of faith as he strives to bring salvation to the Native people.

Of Gods and Men. Dir. Xavier Beauvois. Perf. Lambert Wilson, Michael Lonsdale, Olivier Rabourdin. Why Not Productions, Armada Films, and France 3 Cinéma, 2010. 122 minutes. A stunning exploration of a monastic Christian community in a Muslim world.

The Mission. Dir. Roland Joffé. Perf. Robert De Niro, Jeremy Irons. Warner Brothers Pictures, 1986. 125 minutes. A moving account of a Jesuit mission in Latin America caught in the political conflicts of the 1600s.

Bonhoeffer: Agent of Grace. Dir. Martin Doblmeier. Perf. Ulrich Tukur, Johanna Klante, Robert Joy. First Run Features and Journey Films, 2003. A film about the life of Dietrich Bonhoffer, a German Christian who opposed Hitler.

Jesus of Montreal. Dir. Denys Arcand. Perf. Lothaire Bluteau, Catherine Wilkening, Johanne-Marie Tremblay. Centre National de la Cinématographie (CNC) and Communication, 1989. 118 minutes. A group of actors produce an unorthodox play that brings opposition from the Catholic Church; set in Montreal.

USEFUL WEBSITES

British Broadcasting Corporation

A highly regarded site with accurate information on many religions, including Christianity. Its account of Christianity is good, though simplified. The section on subdivisions is centred on the different forms of Christianity found in Great Britain rather than the world. It defines religion in terms of beliefs.

Global Anabaptist Mennonite Encyclopedia

An excellent source of information on Anabaptist Mennonite traditions (Amish, Mennonite, Hutterite, and Brethren in Christ). It is an online version of an encyclopedia written by scholars of these traditions in the 1990s.

OrthodoxWiki

An unofficial website of the Orthodox community in the Wikipedia format, containing more than 3,000 entries. Articles are written in an accessible style and are generally accurate. The site has excellent graphics of Orthodox saints.

Vatican

The official website of the Catholic Church is a mine of information on the Catholic tradition. It is an excellent source for historical information on the official documents of the tradition.

Evangelical Lutheran Church in America

This is the website of the largest Lutheran body in the United States, which has more than five million members. It is well organized and presents information on the current activities of the denomination.

Indian Christianity

Christianity is claimed to have been in India since the arrival of Saint Thomas in 52 C.E. This website is one of the better sites on Indian Christianity but leaves much to be desired, as it presents a tangled and confusing story. The Wikipedia page on Christianity in India is currently the best source for information on this subject.

Internet Sacred Text Archive

This website claims to be the most accessed site of its kind and the largest freely available archive of online books about religion, mythology, folklore, and the esoteric. It contains an extensive section on Christianity that includes the Bible (including the Vulgate Bible, its Latin translation) as well as the works of classic Christian writers from the West and many texts from esoteric and theosophical Christian writers.

REFERENCES

Allen, Richard. 1971. *The Social Passion: Religion and Social Reform in Canada*. Toronto: University of Toronto Press.

Augustine of Hippo. 1871. *The City of God*, ed. Marcus Dods. Vol. 2. Edinburgh: T. and T. Clark.

———. 1972. *The City of God*, ed. David Knowles. Hammondsworth, UK: Penguin Books.

———. 1998. *Confessions*, trans. Henry Chadwick. Oxford: Oxford University Press.

Bettenson, Henry, and Chris Maunder, eds. 1999. *Documents of the Christian Church*. Oxford: Oxford University Press.

Bramadat, Paul, and David Seljak, eds. 2005. *Religion and Ethnicity in Canada*. Toronto: Pearson Longman.

Daly, Mary. 1973. *Beyond God the Father: Toward a Philosophy of Women's Liberation*. Boston: Beacon Press.

Frend, W. H. C. 1984. *The Rise of Christianity*. Philadelphia: Fortress Press.

Fuson, Robert H., ed. 1992. *The Log of Christopher Columbus*. Camden, ME: International Marine.

Gilson, Etienne. 1956. *The Christian Philosophy of St. Thomas Aquinas*. New York: Random House.

Gregorios, Paulos Mar. 1988. *Cosmic Man: The Divine Presence. The Theology of St. Gregory of Nyssa*. New York: Paragon Press.

Harnack, Adolf von. 1901. "What Is Christianity?" [*das Wesen des Christentums*], 5th ed. http://www.sacred-texts.com/chr/sus/chap36.htm#text1.

Henderson, John, ed. 1969. *John Strachan: Documents and Opinions*. Toronto: McClelland and Stewart.

Hildegard of Bingen. 1987. *Book of Divine Works*, ed. Matthew Fox. Santa Fe, NM: Bear.

Irenaeus. 1978. "Against Heresies." In *Readings in Christian Thought*, ed. Hugh Kerr. Nashville, TN: Abingdon.

Jenson, Robert W. 2002. *The Triune Identity: God According to the Gospel*. Eugene, OR: Wipf and Stock.

Johnson, Todd M. 2010. "Globalization, Christian Identity, and Frontier Missions." *International Journal of Frontier Missiology* 27, no. 4 (Winter): 165–69.

Julian of Norwich. 1978. *Showings*, trans. Edmund Colledge and James Walsh. Toronto: Paulist Press.

Justin Martyr. 1978. "Apology." In *Readings in Christian Thought*, ed. Hugh Kerr. Nashville, TN: Abingdon.

Keelan, Downton R. 2006. *Authority in the Church: An Ecumenical Reflection*. Lanham, MD: University Press of America.

Kerr, Hugh, ed. 1978. *Readings in Christian Thought*. Nashville, TN: Abingdon.

Levitt Kohn, Risa, and Rebecca Moore. 2007. *A Portable God: The Origin of Judaism and Christianity*. Lanham, MD: Rowman and Littlefield.

Luther, Martin. 1854. "Definition of Faith: An Excerpt from 'An Introduction to St. Paul's Letter to the Romans.'" In *Luther's German Bible of 1522*, trans. Robert E. Smith, ed. Johann K. Irmischer. Vol. 63, 124–25. Erlangen: Heyder and Zimmer. http://www.iclnet.org/pub/resources/text/wittenberg/luther/luther-faith.txt (accessed 3 May 2010).

Malone, Mary. 2000. *Women and Christianity*. Ottawa: Novalis.

McManners, John, ed. 2001. *The Oxford Illustrated History of Christianity*. Oxford: Oxford University Press.

Neufeld, Thomas R. Yoder. 2007. *Recovering Jesus: The Witness of the New Testament*. Grand Rapids, MI: Brazos Press.

Nicetas Choniates. 1912. *Translations and Reprints from the Original Sources of European History*, trans. D. C. Munro, rev. ed. Series 1, vol. 3, no. 1. Philadelphia: University of Pennsylvania Press. http://www.fordham.edu/halsall/source/choniates1.html.

Phan, Peter. 1990. *Christianity and the Wider Ecumenism.* New York: Paragon House.

Richardson, C. C., ed. 1953. "Didache: The Teaching on the Twelve Apostles." In *Early Christian Fathers,* 161–79. Philadelphia: Westminster Press.

Rosenstock-Huessy, Eugen. 1966. *The Christian Future, or the Modern Mind Outrun.* New York: Harper & Row.

Smith, Huston. 1991. *The World's Religions: Our Great Wisdom Traditions.* New York: HarperCollins.

———. 2005. *The Soul of Christianity: Restoring the Great Tradition.* New York: HarperCollins.

Steger, Manfred B. 2004. *Globalization: A Very Short Introduction.* Oxford: Oxford University Press.

Tillich, Paul. 1951. *The Protestant Era.* Chicago: University of Chicago Press.

United Church of Canada. "A New Creed." www.united-church.ca/beliefs/creed (accessed 11 March 2010).

United Nations Economic and Social Council. 2010. "Indigenous Peoples and Boarding Schools: A Comparative Study." Permanent Forum on Indigenous Issues, ninth session. http://www.un.org/esa/socdev/unpfii/documents/E%20C.19%202010%2011.DOC.

Timeline

- **610** First revelation received by the Prophet Muhammad.
- **622** Hijrah and the beginning of the Islamic calendar.
- **632** Death of the Prophet Muhammad.
- **632–661** Age of the Rashidun, the golden age of religious ideals.
- **661–750** Umayyad (Sunni) dynasty; capital in Damascus.
- **680** Umayyad army under Yazid (Muawiyyah's son) kills Hussein.
  Andalusia (Spain) remained Umayyad from 756 until the Reconquista in 1492.
- **750-1258** Abbasid (Sunni) dynasty; capital in Baghdad.
  Known as the political/cultural Golden Age of Islam.
- **909-1171** Fatimid dynasty (Shi'ite Ismaili); Capital in Cairo.
- **1038–1307** Seljuks (Sunni) control eastern Abbasid lands of Iran, Iraq, and Central Asia.
  Ayyubids (Sunni) rule western Abbasid lands of Syria, Anatolia, and Egypt.
- **1095** Pope Urban II calls for the first Christian crusade.
- **1258** Mongols destroy Baghdad.
- **1250–1517** Mamluks (former Abbasid "slave guard"); capital in Cairo.
- **1340** Black Death decimates populace of North Africa.
- **1501–1732** Safavid dynasty (Shi'ite Twelvers); capital in Tabriz, then Qazvin, then Isfahan.
- **1526–1858** Mughals (Sunni) dynasty; capital in Agra; British depose last emperor.
- **1517–1924** Ottoman (Sunni) dynasty; capital in Istanbul; dissolution of caliphate in 1924.
- **1947** Pakistan established as an Islamic state.
- **1965** Immigration reform in Canada and the U.S.: Muslims allowed to settle in North America in greater numbers.
- **1979** Iranian revolution: Islamic Republic of Iran established under leadership of Shii'te cleric Ayatollah Khomeini.
- **2001** Al-Qaeda terrorist attacks in New York City and Washington, DC, lead to U.S. invasions of Afghanistan and Iraq.
- **2007** United Nations celebrates Sufi poet Rumi's 800th birthday, declaring 2007 the International Year of Rumi.

CHAPTER 4

Islam

Meena Sharify-Funk and William Rory Dickson

INTRODUCTION

The Al-Rashid mosque, constructed in 1938, was Canada's first mosque. Originally located at 101 Street and 108 Avenue, Edmonton, Alberta, it was moved a few blocks in 1946 and today is preserved at Fort Edmonton Park.

Sources: City of Edmonton Archives A98-55 (left), Rod Macleod (right).

The word **Islam** means "surrender" or "submission." It is derived from the Arabic root *sa-li-ma*, which has the general meaning of "safety from harm." The Arabic word for peace, *salaam*, is also derived from this trilateral root. In the context of religion, *al-Islam* means "the submission to the will of God." A Muslim, then, is a follower of Islam, one who submits to God's will.

Muslims have been a part of the Canadian story since its inception. In 1871 Canada's first national census showed thirteen Muslims (Karim 2002, 263). In the 1880s Arab immigrants began arriving in greater numbers from Ottoman Syria. Most were Christian, though some Muslims also arrived from this region, which included Syria, Jordan, Palestine, and Lebanon. Most Arabs and Muslims settled in eastern cities such as Kingston, Montreal, London, and Toronto. Others set out westward for the prairies, where they made their living as peddlers, fur traders, farmers, and shop owners. It was the children of these pioneering Arab immigrants who would build Canada's first mosque, or Muslim place of worship.

In many Muslim communities the local mosque is not just a place of worship but also a centre of community life. Wedding ceremonies, funerals, holiday celebrations, classes on

Islam: submission to the will of God (Allah).

religion, and sometimes sports all take place within the local mosque. For Muslims living on the prairies, their desire to build a mosque was also a desire to build a community centre where their culture could be lived and passed on to their children.

In 1938 a small group of Muslim women organized the building of the Al-Rashid mosque in Edmonton, Alberta. There were fewer than 700 Muslims in Alberta in the 1930s, but despite their small numbers, these persistent prairie women raised funds for Canada's first mosque by canvassing shops on Jasper Avenue, getting contributions from shop owners of all faiths, including Jews and Christians. The women were led by Hilwi Hamdon, who was known for her "vibrant personality" and commitment to the project. She was able to secure from Edmonton's mayor, John Fry, a plot of land on which to build the mosque. The women then got a Ukrainian-Canadian builder, Mike Drewoth, to build them "a place to pray" (Lorenz 1998, 30). His influence was apparent in the mosque's resemblance to a Ukrainian or Russian Orthodox church, with its onion-shaped domes and hexagonal minarets. This architectural synthesis reflects a long history of Muslims and Christians sharing designs for houses of worship. As just one example, the third-holiest site in Islam, the Dome of the Rock in Jerusalem, was built in 685 C.E. in the style of a Byzantine *martyrium*, or church housing sacred relics (Jenkins 2008, 192–93).

On 12 December 1938, a noted translator of the Qur'an into English, Abdullah Yusuf Ali, attended the dedication of the Al-Rashid mosque, along with the mayor of Edmonton and I. F. Shaker, the Arab Christian mayor of Hanna, Alberta (Lorenz 1998, 31). The mosque would serve Arab immigrants in the area until a new, larger Al-Rashid mosque was built in 1982. In 1990 the original mosque was moved to Fort Edmonton as a heritage building, and today the new Al-Rashid mosque serves a growing Muslim community in Edmonton. This community now numbers in the tens of thousands and includes Muslims from around the world as well as local converts.

The story of Canada's first mosque tells how people of diverse faiths and ethnicities came together to build a "place to pray" for Alberta's small but resilient Muslim community. The story also highlights the important contributions that Muslim women have made to the establishment of their faith in North America: Canada's first mosque was the result of the determined efforts of a small group of women.

Throughout this chapter we will highlight the diversity inherent in Islam's history and practice and amongst Muslims in Canada today. As the story of Canada's first mosque illustrates, Muslims have established themselves as a faith and a community in interaction with others. We will see that Islam is a faith woven of many strands, some of which are tied to other peoples and religions. In this chapter we will explore the historical development of Islam: how it emerged from Arabia and spread throughout the Middle East, Africa, Asia, and eventually to the West. Then, as we consider Islamic practice and culture, we will encounter some of the diverse ways in which Islam is lived, gaining an understanding of different approaches to Islamic theology, law, and spirituality and the ways in which Muslims live their religion in everyday life. Here we explore what Scott T. Kline describes as the "discourses, practices, and communities" that together constitute a religion. Finally we will explore the history of Muslims in Canada and consider some important issues facing Canadian Muslims.

Despite the diversity of Muslim peoples and the many different ways in which Muslims practise their faith, they are united by the core beliefs of the Islamic tradition. Three core beliefs that all Muslims share are monotheism, prophecy, and moral accountability.

CENTRAL BELIEFS

Monotheism

Monotheism is a term used to describe the exclusive belief in one God. It derives from the Greek words *mono*, meaning "one," and *theos*, meaning "god." Like Jews and Christians, Muslims believe that there is only one God, the creator of the world and humanity. Also like Jews and Christians, Muslims believe in a God who is all-powerful and all-knowing as well as merciful and loving. The Arabic name for God is **Allah**, which means literally "the god" (*al-ilah*). Arabic-speaking Christians (for example, Syrian Orthodox or Roman Catholic) and Jews also use the name *Allah* to refer to God.

The scripture of Islam, the **Qur'an**, declares that Muslims worship the God of Abraham. All three monotheistic religions refer back to Abraham as the father of their faith. This is why Judaism, Christianity, and Islam are sometimes referred to as the Abrahamic religions. Muslims believe that the revelation given to Muhammad in the Qur'an restores the original, universal monotheism of Abraham. Highlighting what all three Abrahamic faiths share, the Qur'an addresses Jews and Christians as "people of the book" (**Ahl al-Kitab**), acknowledging that Jews and Christians too have received a legitimate revelation from God: "Say: People of the Book, let us arrive at a statement that is common to us all: we worship God alone, we ascribe no partner to Him; and none of us takes others beside God as lords" (3:64).

In Arabic the principle of God's oneness is known as **tawhid**, a word meaning "to make one." By accepting faith in the one God, Muslims reject what the Qur'an deems to be the one unforgivable sin: **shirk**, or associating any partners with God. Like the Torah, which states, "Hear, O Israel, the Lord our God is one Lord" (Deut. 6:4), the Qur'an states, "Your God is one, so devote yourselves to Him" (22:34). For Muslims the oneness of God is the central belief around which all else revolves.

Allah: the Arabic name for God, derived from *al* (the) *ilah* (god).

Qur'an: literally "recitation," the sacred scripture of Islam, believed to have been revealed by God to the Prophet Muhammad through the Archangel Gabriel

Ahl al-Kitab: "people of the book," a reference mostly to Jews and Christians.

Tawhid: monotheism, or the worship of one God, from "to make one."

Shirk: to associate partners with the one God (Allah).

Prophecy

How does one come to know God and His will for human life? Muslims believe that God intervenes in human history, selecting particularly righteous people to whom to convey His guidance. The Qur'an affirms that God sent prophets to all peoples, to every nation; in fact, one Islamic tradition states that God has sent 124,000 prophets since the beginning of humanity (Murata and Chittick 1994, 342). According to tradition, Adam was both the first man and the first prophet, whereas Muhammad was the last prophet sent to humanity and is described as the "Seal of the Prophets." The Prophet Muhammad was born in Mecca, a centre of trade and pilgrimage in the western part of the Arabian Peninsula, in 570 C.E. Though previous prophets were sent to particular peoples, the Prophet Muhammad is believed by Muslims to have been sent to all of humanity, bringing them God's final revelation, the Qur'an.

Muslims believe that Muhammad was a special type of prophet: a messenger. Whereas some prophets are sent with a narrow mandate to warn a particular people against wrongdoing and offer moral guidance, messengers constitute a special type of prophet who brings a sacred law and revelation that has universal validity for a period of time. The Qur'an describes five such messengers, known as the "prophets of firm resolve": Noah, Abraham, Moses, Jesus, and Muhammad. Muslims believe that a messenger is like a mirror with no defects that perfectly reflects the light of God's revelation to people. Not all prophets are messengers, as not all bring a revelation or law, but all messengers are prophets in that they are commissioned by God to warn and guide people.

The Qur'an names a variety of prophets, including Adam, Noah, Abraham, Jacob, Joseph, Moses, David, Solomon, and Jesus. In fact, the Qur'an mentions Moses more than any other figure: one finds his whole story, including his confrontation with Pharaoh and how he led his people out of slavery in Egypt. An entire chapter of the Qur'an is devoted to the story of Mary, the mother of Jesus. Unlike Christians, Muslims do not believe that Jesus is the son of God or God incarnate. However, Muslims do believe that Jesus is the Messiah, and that he will return before the end of time.

Moral Accountability

Prophets and messengers are sent to guide people to the truth, but also to warn them of punishment if they fail to heed guidance and commit acts of evil and injustice. Like Jews, Christians, and other people of faith, Muslims believe that we live in a profoundly just universe. Though

Fitrah: the innate goodness of human nature.

Tawbah: to turn toward God in repentance.

we may not see this justice fulfilled on earth, according to the Qur'an, at the end of time all humanity will be raised from death and brought before God to account for their actions while alive. This day is called the Day of Resurrection and Judgment. The Qur'an describes how those who had faith and did good deeds will be rewarded with Paradise: a realm of bliss, happiness, and pleasure lasting for all eternity. Those who rejected faith and whose evil deeds outweighed their good ones will be punished in Hell: a realm of perpetual pain and suffering. The urgency of the Qur'an's reminder to people of their moral accountability is due to this finality—on the Day of Judgment there will be no time for repentance and no more time to make up for lost opportunities. One's fate will be determined for all of eternity.

Muslims believe that all people are born in a state of original purity or naturalness, known as **fitrah**. The fitrah is the original human disposition, the state in which people were created. In this original, primordial state, people naturally acknowledge the reality of the one true God and incline toward goodness. However, people become conditioned by their social contexts to believe many different things, and their original nature is corrupted. Muslims believe the teachings of Islam allow humans to restore their original state of goodness and recognition of their Lord and Creator. This recognition of or turning toward God is called in the Qur'an **tawbah**, a word that literally means "to turn around." Sometimes translated as "repentance," tawbah is the human movement away from falsehood and injustice toward God and beautiful character traits. For Sufis, the mystics of Islam, tawbah is the first step on the seeker's spiritual ascent to God.

Islam's Sacred Book: The Qur'an

We have mentioned the Qur'an already in this introduction, but what exactly is it? The Qur'an is the sacred scripture of Islam, in the form of a book slightly shorter than the Christian New Testament. For Muslims, the Qur'an is God's final guidance to humanity, authored by God and revealed to the last prophet, Muhammad. According to tradition, Gabriel, the angel of revelation, was sent by God to recite the revelations of the Qur'an to Muhammad over a twenty-three-year period, beginning when Muhammad was forty years old. Referring to this process, the Qur'an states: "The Trustworthy Spirit has brought it down to your heart" (26:194).

The Qur'an consists of 114 chapters arranged roughly by decreasing length, with the longer chapters at the beginning of the text and the shorter chapters at the end. Each chapter has a set number of verses. When citing the Qur'an, scholars refer first to the chapter and then the verse number. For example, the quotation above refers to verse 194 of chapter 26. Resembling parts of both the Old and New Testaments, the Qur'an warns of the Day of Judgment, exhorts Muslims to charity, kindness, and justice, and recounts stories of the prophets of old. The Qur'an further contains commandments and prohibitions from which Islamic law is derived. If there is one theme to draw from the text, it is undoubtedly the overwhelming reality of God, who simultaneously transcends all thought and imagination and yet whose signs are found in the world and in the human soul:

> And there are many signs in the heavens and in the earth that they pass by and give no heed to. (12:105)
> We will show them Our signs on the horizons and in their own souls, until it becomes clear to them that this is the truth. (41:53)

The first revelations were made in Mecca over twelve years and the final ones in Medina over eleven years, until the Prophet's death in 632 C.E. The chapters revealed in Mecca tend to be much shorter in length than those revealed in Medina, and they are mostly found at the end of the written Qur'an. As these chapters were revealed in Mecca, they are known as the Meccan chapters; they are also usually divided into early and later Meccan chapters. The earlier Meccan chapters focus primarily on existential and personal issues, whereas the later Meccan chapters cover more extended discussions of sacred history and stories of prophets known in Judeo-Christian traditions (Sells 1999, 14).

The Medinan chapters contain mostly legalistic and instructive verses, which became fundamental to the organization and regulation of Muslim life in all its different spheres. The Medinan chapters reflect Muhammad's new position as a political, economic, social, and military leader, and so they address a wider range of societal, historical, and legal issues. In particular these chapters introduce laws to govern the Muslim community with regard to marriage, commerce and finance, international relations, and war and peace.

The first verse of the Qur'an revealed to the Prophet Muhammad begins with the word *iqra*, which means "read" or "recite." *Iqra* is the imperative form of the root *qara'a*, which refers to reading or reciting, and *Qur'an* comes from the same root, meaning literally "recitation." The significance of the Qur'an as a recitation connotes the importance of Arabic orality: the tradition of experiencing the word of God through the human voice speaking the classical Arabic language. The shared knowledge of Qur'anic Arabic brings together Muslims from diverse countries and backgrounds. For Muslims the Qur'an is first experienced in Arabic, even by those who are not native Arabic speakers. In Qur'anic schools children memorize chapters and verses of the Qur'an in order to recite them aloud.

The Qur'an began as something that was recited: a living, dynamic account of God's will for humanity. Initially the followers of Muhammad would memorize the verses as they were revealed, and some would write them down. By the time the revelation was complete, some of Muhammad's followers had memorized the entire Qur'an. The text was transmitted orally until, according to early Muslim historians, an official written copy was produced at the behest of 'Uthman, the third ruler of the Muslim community following Muhammad's death (Rippin 2001, 29).

Muslims believe that the Qur'an is literally the word of God. In this sense the Qur'an is not directly analogous to the Christian Bible but rather to Christ as *logos*, or the divine word (Nasr 2002, 23). Most Jews and Christians acknowledge that their scripture may have been composed by a number of authors over a long period of time, under divine inspiration but not necessarily from the direct speech of God (Sells 1999, 15). Muslims, however, view the Qur'an as a direct revelation to Muhammad through the agency of the archangel Gabriel.

Considering Muslim belief in the Qur'an as *logos*, or the divine word manifest in text, it is not surprising that Muslim scribes would want to beautify the divine word in writing. Indeed, calligraphy emerged as one of the earliest expressions of Islamic art and civilization. In traditional Muslim contexts calligraphy is further associated with good character, heart, and mind (Nasr 1987, 19). A person's writing is seen as expressing that person's inner state: beautiful writing reflects a beautiful soul. Calligraphy is not found just in copies of the Qur'an, however, but also bedecks mosques and palaces, beautifying the names of God, the Prophet, and verses of scripture in the Arabic language.

Every day devout Muslims recite the Qur'an in their prayers, which are performed five times daily. Each cycle of prayer begins with the very first chapter, or *surah*, of the Qur'an, which is known as *al-Fatiha*, "the opening." This short chapter is also referred to as the "mother of the book" or "the key." Like the Lord's Prayer in the Christian tradition, the Fatiha has seven lines:

Bismillaah ar-Rahman ar-Raheem
Al hamdu lillaahi rabil 'alameen
Ar-Rahman ir-Raheem Maaliki yaumid Deen
Iyyaaka na'buddu wa iyaaka nasta'een
Ihidinas siraatal mustaqeem
Siraatal ladheena an'amta' alaihim
Ghairil maghduubi 'alayhim wa la daaleen
Aameen

In the name of God, the infinitely
Compassionate and Merciful.
Praise be to God, Lord of all the worlds.
The Compassionate, the Merciful. Ruler on
the Day of Reckoning.
You alone do we worship, and You alone do
we ask for help.
Guide us on the straight path,
the path of those who have received your
grace;
not the path of those who have brought down
wrath, nor of those who wander astray.

Source: Translation by Kabir Helminski

The Qur'an permeates Muslim life, not only in prayers but also on the radio and television, and in public in most Muslim countries. Those who recite the Qur'an

Jahiliyyah: the pre-Islamic age of ignorance in Arabia.

Illuminated manuscript version of surah al-Fatiha
Source: Meena Sharify-Funk

with particular skill and grace gain fame in the Muslim world for their ability to bring Islam's sacred scripture to life. The Qur'an is further woven throughout classical Islamic literature and poetry. Sufism's great poet of love, Jalaluddin Rumi (d. 1273) was the best-selling poet in America in the late 1990s (Lewis 2008, 1), and he refers to Qur'anic verses and themes throughout his works. It is fair to say that the imagery of the Qur'an has shaped the landscape of Muslim minds and imaginations for centuries, to a degree rarely paralleled in the history of religions.

MUSLIM HISTORY

Pre-Islamic Arabia

Muslims refer to pre-Islamic Arabia as the age of **jahiliyyah**. The Arabic word *jahiliyyah* means "ignorance," and for Muslims it means the age of ignorance before the advent of Islam. The Muslim community emerged in seventh-century Arabia into a region dominated by ancient civilizations, empires, cultures, ethnic groups, and religions. Although there were still traces of Mesopotamian civilization and culture in the Tigris and Euphrates valleys—now modern-day Iraq—two powerful civilizations and empires dominated the region: the Byzantine empire (from the Greco-Roman tradition) and the Sassanian dynasty (from the Persian/Iranian tradition).

At the time of the Prophet Muhammad's birth in 570, the Byzantines occupied the lands of Aleppo and Damascus, Alexandria and the Nile Valley, and parts of southern Europe, including southern Spain. Their capital was based in Constantinople (later Istanbul, under the Ottomans) and Eastern Christianity was their official religion. During this period the Sassanians occupied Iran, Iraq, and the lands of Central Asia. Their capital was Ctesiphon, located near the Tigris River. The official religion of the Sassanians was Zoroastrianism, but some Persians followed other religions, including Christianity and Buddhism in eastern Iran.

For more than nine hundred years, the ebb and flow of conflict between these empires influenced trade as well as relations with the inhabitants of a large but marginal area of the Middle East known as the Arabian Peninsula. It was because of Arabia's desert environment that the inhabitants had to adopt a nomadic pastoral way of life to survive. The inhabitants were known as Arabs, or fully nomadic pastoralists (*arab* actually means "nomad").

Although Arabia was a land of aridity and nomadic people, its geographical position made it a trading crossroads between Asia, Africa, and Europe. In particular, the scattered oases located in central and eastern Arabia—an area known as the Hijaz—became dynamic settled trading communities for commerce and knowledge exchange. Three notable communities in this area were Yathrib (later known as Medina), Taif, and Mecca. Of these three, Mecca became the most prosperous, being at a crossroads of two old trade routes: between Yemen and Syria and Transjordan (the Hijaz Road) and between the Red Sea and Yemen and Iraq (the Najd Road) (Hodgson 1974, 154). Not only was it a booming trading city, it also was a city of poetry and pilgrimage.

Both in pre-Islamic and Islamic times poetry functioned as an eloquent means for expressing all the vicissitudes of human life. The power of the word and poetical composition created a means of purveying collective values and aspirations together with a pursuit through which individuals could attain honour. From the Hijaz through Mesopotamia, the rich diversity of the Arabic language empowered the poet, leading to his many responsibilities: as a narrator of legendary stories, as a vagabond wandering the desert in search of lost love and treasure, and, most important, as a transmitter of tradition and culture who mediated between the tribes.

During the jahaliyyah period, the **Ka'aba** was dedicated to deities that had been imported into Arabia via different traditions, though the common belief in Mecca suggested that it had originally been dedicated to al-Lah, the high god of the Arabs. According to the Qur'an (2:127–29 and 3:96–97), the Ka'aba was built by the prophets Abraham and Ishmael. Mecca was chosen as the Ka'aba's site because a spring is said to have appeared when Hagar and her son Ishmael were abandoned in the desert and had exhausted the water given to them by Abraham. Hagar then cast herself to and fro between the two hills of Safa and Marwa in order to find water for Ishmael. God heard the cry of Ishmael and water gushed forth, making the sound *zam zam*. This sacred spring hence became the Well of Zamzam, which is still used in various Muslim rituals during the hajj pilgrimage. Muslim tradition holds that Zamzam was forgotten but later rediscovered by 'Abd al-Muttalib, the grandfather of Muhammad ibn Abdallah, later known as the Prophet Muhammad. Muhammad was born in Mecca, into the tribe of the Quraysh and the clan of Hashem.

The Quraysh were the most prominent tribe of Mecca. The duties of this tribe included maintaining the Ka'aba, providing water and food to its pilgrims, leading tribal meetings, and proclaiming war. All Arabs, whether settled or nomadic, were organized into tribes, which were units conceived as descent groups. It was from these that Arabs derived security, rather than from a state or empire. Men within a tribe were mutually obligated to defend one another, and women were protected as dependants.

The Life of the Prophet Muhammad

The Prophet Muhammad's life can be divided into two main phases, the Meccan (570–622 C.E.) and the Medinan (622–632 C.E.). Muhammad was born in 570 and his parents' death left him an orphan at the age of six. He was brought up by his grandfather and then his uncle, Abu Talib, who was a successful trader. Under such influences, Muhammad, though a shepherd in his youth, gradually became a business agent, engaging in commerce. His reputation for trustworthiness encouraged Khadijah, a successful businesswoman, to hire him. She was a widow who was known for her nobility, intelligence, and wealth.

Ka'aba: the house of God, the sacred sanctuary and pilgrimage site in Mecca believed to have been built by Adam and later rebuilt by Abraham and his son Ishmael.

According to Muslim tradition, because of Muhammad's honesty, sincerity, and integrity, when he was twenty-five years old, Khadijah offered him marriage and she became his first wife. Around the age of thirty he started to take spiritual retreats. At this time small groups of Arabs would engage in meditation and contemplation. Known as Hunafa, they were Arab monotheists who traced their practice to Abraham. Abu Talib, Muhammad's uncle, was known for taking a month off each year for prayer and contemplation in the caves near Mecca. Consequently, some scholars of Islam have claimed that Muhammad was following in the tradition of Abu Talib and his ancestors.

At the age of forty, in 610, the second part of the Meccan phase began. During a retreat in a cave named Hira, on the mountain now known as Jabal an-Nur (Mountain of Light), Muhammad experienced his first revelation of the divine message that would become the Qur'an. This first revelation can be found in chapter 96, verses 1–5:

> Read! In the Name of the Lord who created,
> He created man from a clinging form.
> Read! Your Lord is the Most Bountiful One
> Who taught by the pen.
> Taught man what he did not know.

Hijra: the migration of Muhammad and his followers from Mecca to Medina in 622, the beginning of the Islamic calendar.

Muhajirun: emigrants from Mecca to Medina who were the first converts to Islam.

Ummah: a Muslim community.

This revelation and others to follow have been described by early Muslim biographers as a set of words that were imprinted on Muhammad's mind and heart. This first revelatory event is labelled by the Qur'an in chapter 97 as "The Night of Destiny/Power." (It is important to note here that the vast bulk of material on the Prophet's life comes from early Muslim biographers, who clearly provide an insider's, or emic, perspective on the events surrounding Muhammad's emergence as the founder of a religion.) Biographers also state that Muhammad at first thought he was going mad. Arab tradition held that spirits known as *jinns* could possess souls, and Muhammad thought he might be possessed. Reportedly he was about to throw himself over the mountainside when the Archangel Gabriel appeared in all directions and reassured him that he was indeed a prophet.

When Muhammad shared these revelations, a small community of followers emerged. Many of these early followers were said to come from the ranks of the poor; the aristocratic Quraysh not only refused to accept Muhammad as a prophet but greeted him with fierce opposition. They saw him as a threat to their privileged way of life. They feared that if Muhammad won large numbers of followers he could eventually convert his religious power into political power and dominate the city. They also saw Muhammad's attack on their pagan gods as leading to a loss of profitable trade. According to traditional narratives, the Quraysh ridiculed Muhammad increasingly and subjected some of his followers to stoning and beatings. In 616 the abuse from the Quraysh became so severe that Muhammad advised a group of his followers to escape to Christian Abyssinia (modern Ethiopia), where they were granted refuge by the Abyssinian king.

Muhammad's uncle Abu Talib did not convert to Islam, though he did maintain a special relationship with Muhammad and defended him until his death in 619. That year was later known as the Year of Sorrow, as it marked two important events: the death of Muhammad's uncle and protector and the death of his wife and confidante, Khadijah. With the passing of Abu Talib, Muhammad's protection from his clan vanished, and emerging conspiracies to assassinate him became more prevalent. These two factors encouraged him to leave Mecca and seek refuge somewhere else.

At first he went to Taif, but he was ridiculed and insulted by the people there and forced to return to Mecca. At this point fate came to Muhammad's rescue. A group of pilgrims from Yathrib, who had heard Muhammad preach and were impressed, asked him to come to their city. At the time (622 C.E.), Yathrib was being torn apart by a feud among various tribes who lived there, and an arbitrator was needed to bring peace. Muhammad accepted the invitation and encouraged his followers to go to Yathrib ahead of him. A few weeks later the Prophet himself fled from Mecca. The flight from Mecca to Yathrib is known as the **hijra**. *Hijra* in Arabic means "migration," and the seventy Meccan Muslims who emigrated to Yathrib ahead of Muhammad became known as the **muhajirun**—"emigrants" or "early converts."

In Yathrib, scholars point out, the Prophet Muhammad began to construct around himself and his followers a larger community of Muslim believers, which became known as the **ummah**. Arabs who had been members of the feuding tribes gradually submitted to the commands of God as revealed through the Qur'an. This substitution of faith for blood ties made it possible to suppress old tribal rivalries and gave rise to a revolutionary political unity. Consequently, Yathrib, the heart of the new community of Islam, or ummah, became known as Madinat al-Nabi ("the city of the Prophet") or simply Medina ("the city"). The migration to Medina not only marked the beginning of a new phase in the Prophet Muhammad's life but also the establishment of the first year of the Islamic era. (The Islamic calendar is based upon the cycles of the moon rather than those of the sun, as is our Western Gregorian calendar.)

From 622 onward the Prophet Muhammad's role changed drastically. While in Mecca he had been merely a spiritual seeker and the religious leader of a small group, somewhat in the tradition of earlier Hebrew prophets such as Ezekiel and Ezra. But once settled in Medina he played new and more powerful roles: he became a religious and political leader, a social advisor, and a revolutionary. This period also marked the beginning of a new form of political activity. The political conflict shifted from the Quraysh protecting their religion and economic privilege by oppressing Muslims in Mecca to a conflict between two cities, Mecca and Medina. The Meccans were trying to maintain their regional economic dominance while the Muslims of Medina aspired, on the one hand, to challenge the Meccans from afar and, on the other hand, to fight for survival. For instance, some Muslims tried to provoke the Meccans with small raids on their caravans to the north (itself an Arab tribal tradition). In response, the Meccans organized massive campaigns using tribal alliances against the Muslims, leading to three famous battles.

In 628 Muhammad set out on a pilgrimage to Mecca with 1,400 of his followers. The Meccans, hearing of this, sent out 200 horsemen to stop them. Fighting almost erupted, but the two sides agreed to a ten-year truce and that the Muslims would return to Medina, on the condition that they could come to Mecca the following year. In 629 Muhammad led 2,000 Muslims on the promised pilgrimage to the Ka'aba, but subsequent clashes between Muslims and Meccans ended the truce. It wasn't until 630 that Muhammad finally marched on Mecca to settle the issue, with a force of 10,000 troops. By this time Mecca had been weakened by the loss of many of its leading men in battles against the Muslims and consequent dissensions over leadership of the city, so Muhammad met hardly any resistance when he entered Mecca. One of the first actions he performed was to destroy the pagan idols that filled the holy Ka'aba. Mecca became the spiritual centre of Islam and Medina its political capital. In the twenty-two years of his prophethood, Muhammad had created a synthesis of the Judeo-Christian tradition of a single God and a latent Arabian sense of nationalism. The Arabs found in this synthesis a cause in which they could finally unite.

As leader of the developing Muslim community, the Prophet eventually married a number of women. For many Westerners it is hard to understand why Muhammad took nine wives after the death of Khadijah. Muslim historians document that many of his marriages were motivated primarily by political or moral reasons—some of his wives were widows of his lieutenants killed fighting for Islam, while others were daughters of important leaders of allied Arab tribes. One of his favourite wives was Aishah, the daughter of Abu Bakr.

As stated in the biographies, in the sixty-third year of his life and the tenth year of the new era of Islam (632), Muhammad fell ill. He spoke of his death to Aishah and then asked permission from his wives to move into her dwelling. One last time he staggered into the mosque and gave what is known as his farewell speech, and then he returned to Aishah's house, where he passed away. As the word of Muhammad's death spread through Medina, his followers were swept by shock and on the verge of panic. In the confusion, Abu Bakr is reported to have said this famous line: "Whichever of you worships Muhammad, know that Muhammad is dead. But whichever of you worships God, know that God is alive and does not die" (Lings 1983, 342). Then he quoted a verse from the Qur'an (3:144): "Muhammad is only a messenger before whom many messengers have been and gone. If he died or was killed, would you revert to your old ways?"

Khalifah: "vice-regent of God" or leader of the Muslim state.

The Age of the Rashidun: The Four Righteous Khalifahs (632–661)

The period of the Prophet Muhammad and the subsequent time of the Rashidun—"the Four Righteous Leaders"—is seen by Muslims as a golden age of religious ideals, a time when corrupt empires were humbled and a way was cleared for the preaching of Islam. A more fine-grained view reveals that this was also a time of great political intrigue, when Muslims had suddenly inherited power and were left without the guidance and leadership of the Prophet.

Like many other religious traditions when the religion becomes a powerful political force, the followers of this religion had to determine who would lead the community and what they would do with all that power. After 632, Islam embarked on an era of change and expansion that transformed it from a small religious community into an ever-growing powerful political empire. But even as this new state was expanding with unparalleled speed, it was also being torn apart by internal dissension and sporadic violence. One of the main problems to emerge after the Prophet's death was the issue of who would succeed him as the leader of the fast-growing ummah and what type of leadership should replace him. Consequently, the main question that emerged at this time was who would become the first **khalifah**. In Arabic *khalifah* means

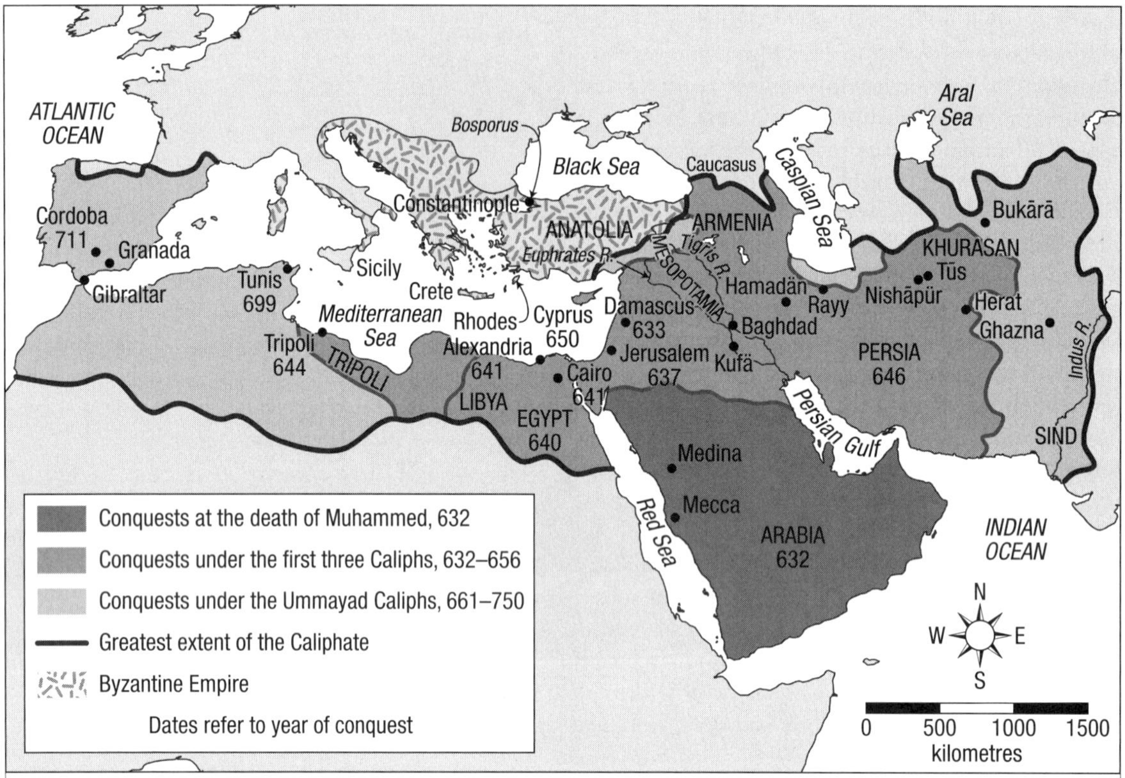

The Early Conquests

Source: A Brief History of Islam, Tamara Sonn and Mary Williamsburg. © 2004 Blackwell Publishing Ltd. Reproduced with permission of Blackwell Publishing Ltd.

"vice-regent of God," but in the context of Muslim leadership, the khalifah is the ruler of the Muslim state (it is sometimes written as *caliph*).

In the great confusion and panic over who was to succeed the Prophet Muhammad, two distinct groups emerged. One group, which would later become known as Sunni Muslims, swore allegiance to Muhammad's father-in-law, Abu Bakr, whom they felt should be the first khalifah. Another group, which would become known as Shi'ite Muslims, believed that the successor should be a descendant of the Prophet, and that such a leader was Ali ibn Abu Talib. According to Sunni tradition, the election of Abu Bakr as khalifah was to reconcile a growing division between the ansar, or later converts, and the muhajirun, the early converts. However, according to Shi'ite tradition, the election of Abu Bakr was carried out in haste, one reason being that Ali was not present at the meetings, since it was the duty of the Prophet's family to bury the Prophet properly. To this day, Shi'ite Muslims claim that Ali was unjustly passed over as righteous khalifah, and Sunni Muslims believe that Abu Bakr ushered in the age of the Rashidun.

The first khalifah, according to Sunni Muslims, was Abu Bakr. He had been a close companion of the Prophet and was a born diplomat with a vast knowledge of the tribes and politics of the Arabian Peninsula. Like Muhammad, he was of Quraysh origin. He was also a rich merchant and one of the earliest converts, and is known to have replaced the Prophet as the imam leading prayers during the Prophet's last illness.

At the time of the Prophet's death, Muslim authority had extended to encompass most of the Hijaz and its prominent cities, as well as areas of northeastern Arabia. Consequently, these cities were securely incorporated into the emerging Islamic empires. Abu Bakr inaugurated his leadership by sending an expedition into Byzantine Syria, an action that some believe the Prophet planned before his death. This act was courageous and risky, for many tribes considered their membership in the ummah to have expired when the Prophet died, and they no longer wanted to support Muslim leadership financially. Essentially they did not want to pay taxes to Medina, the political capital of Islam. Some tribes rejected membership altogether by raising up prophets or messengers of their own.

As a result, a period of strife broke out among the desert Arabs, with many rebellions that Abu Bakr was forced to deal with. These rebellions were known as **ridda**, translated as "apostasy"—the notion that there were Muslims who were rejecting Islam. The ridda wars were part of the first stage of Arab expansion in the Arabian Peninsula, while the expeditions and campaigns to Syria were part of Arab expansion outside the Arab domain.

Two years later, Abu Bakr, on his deathbed, designated Umar bin al-Khattab to be his successor and second khalifah after the Prophet Muhammad. Umar is remembered in Muslim tradition as the epitome of the stern, uncompromising, incorruptible ruler, as well as for his generosity and compassion to the Ahl al-Kitab ("the people of the book," especially Jews and Christians). Like Abu Bakr, he also possessed practical ability. While directing the Islamic conquests of Iran, Iraq, Syria, and Egypt, Umar developed a variety of societal innovations. He established a system of equitable wealth distribution, created a *pax Islamica* wherein peace between Muslims was the rule, and established a treaty with the patriarch of Jerusalem by which Christians were protected under Muslim rule at the cost of a poll tax, which later became known as the **dhimmi** clause.

During his rule, Umar took Jerusalem in 638 and then engaged the Persians in a series of battles that led to the downfall of the Sassanian empire in 641. By 644 he had occupied most of the Byzantine and Sassanian lands. However, in the same year Umar was assassinated by a Persian slave of the governor of Medina. On his deathbed, he appointed a tribal council to elect a new khalifah from two candidates, Uthman bin Affan and Ali ibn Abu Talib. As noted by biographers of early Islam, the council offered the position to Ali on the condition that he continue the policies of his predecessor, namely continued predominance of the Quraysh tribe over the Muslim community. Ali refused because he believed that the continued predominance of the Quraysh was dividing the ummah between the aristocracy and the ansar, or later converts. As a result, Uthman was chosen.

Ridda: apostasy, or turning away from a religion.

Dhimmi: the protection of non-Muslim people under Muslim rule.

Uthman was a Meccan merchant who supported the Quraysh aristocracy, having been raised in one of the most influential Meccan clans, the Umayyah. During his reign (644–56) Muslim expansion continued. In the west there were expeditions to Nubia and North Africa. Muslims developed naval power in the Mediterranean under the governor of Syria and Egypt. In the east, permanent settlements of Muslims were established, especially in Iran. Despite this expansion, Uthman is best-known for authorizing compilation of a single definitive version of the Qur'an, based on the memories of the companions of Muhammad and the early Muslim community; this is the version reputedly still used by Muslims. Historians note that Uthman had six good years of leadership and six bad years. The six bad years began around 650–51, when problems began to increase and discontents called Uthman's authority into question. Shortly after harshly opposing a group of Muslims who were protesting his rule, Uthman was assassinated in 656.

Even though Ali ibn Abu Talib was immediately acknowledged in Medina as the fourth khalifah, with no known opposition, he inherited growing problems of dissension amongst Muslims. Ali was a cousin of the Prophet Muhammad and married to the Prophet's favourite daughter, Fatima. As with Abu Bakr and Umar, there are fascinating legends about Ali from both Sunni and Shi'ite biographers. Because of these stories Ali has been given many titles, including Sword of Allah, Asad Allah (Lion of God), and Dhu'l-Fiqar (Possessor of a Two-Edged Sword). He was reputed to be a man of heroic courage and a seeker of reconciliation and peace, as well as an accomplished intellectual—there is a tradition that the Prophet Muhammad proclaimed, "I am the City of Knowledge and Ali is its Gate." In his story as related by many Islamic scholars, it is hard to find a discipline that Ali had not mastered; he

Fitnah: civil discord.

Kufic: refers to a form of Arabic calligraphy that was developed in Kufa, Iraq.

seems to have delved into a whole range of subjects such as jurisprudence, rhetoric, philosophy, mathematics, logic, astronomy, medicine, and history. Ali is further reputed to have founded the study of rhetoric and Arabic syntax, as well as the **Kufic** form of Arabic calligraphy.

Politically, the largest opposition to Ali was from late converts to Islam from the Quraysh tribe, who challenged him at the beginning of his reign in order to preserve their predominant position in the ummah. This movement was influenced by one particular individual: Aishah, the Prophet's youngest wife. In order to remain in power, the Quraysh ansar sought out support in Iraq from the inhabitants of the city of Basra. Ali, in reaction, then found support in Kufa. A famous battle ensued, known as the Battle of the Camel, in which Aishah was the leader of the Quraysh. This battle was the first in a civil war among Muslims, marking the opening of the gates of **fitnah**, or civil discord, which later became the basis for many political theories in Islam. Even though the Kufans and the followers of Ali won the battle, his authority was accepted only in Iraq and Egypt. Ali's strongest opposition still came from the Quraysh, this time from Syria. The governor of Syria, Muawiyyah, was a member of the Umayyad clan and a strong leader of the Quraysh.

Biographers state that Muawiyyah refused to acknowledge Ali as khalifah until Ali had punished the murderers of Uthman. Ali then tried to form a coalition of Kufans strong enough to coerce Muawiyyah into accepting his authority. The response to his efforts was not favourable, and in 657 Ali confronted Muawiyyah's forces at Siffu. However, the ensuing battle halted when the Syrian Muslims placed leaves from the Qur'an on their spears and appealed for arbitration. Ali agreed, and arbitrators were chosen by both groups; they then decided that arbitration would begin after one year on neutral ground. This agreement weakened Ali's position with the ummah and created doubts about his leadership, which resulted in disintegration of his coalition. A group of Ali's fighters abandoned the army, believing that he should not have agreed to the arbitration; they were called Kharijites, from the Arabic for "they had gone out."

In 661 Ali was assassinated by one of the Kharijites. This brought to an end the era of the Rashidun—the "Four Righteous Khalifahs"—as well as the golden age of religious ideals (610–661). However, it would give rise to a golden age of political and cultural, as well as intellectual, ideals (661–1258).

A Brief History of Islamic Civilizations and Empires

The Umayyads, the Abbasids, and the Fatimids

The reign of the Umayyads began with Muawiyyah in 661 and ended thirteen khalifahs later in 750, with Marwan II. The name *Umayyad* comes from the family name of a clan descended from Umayya ibn Abd Ash-Shams of the Meccan Quraysh tribe. Muawiyyah, known as "the Arab Caesar," had been governor of Syria, appointed by the third of the Rashidun khalifas, Uthman, who was a relative.

After Ali was assassinated, his sons Hassan and Hussein followed in their father's leadership role. Hassan was elected the fifth khalifah in Medina, but he was forced to abdicate his caliphate by Muawiyyah, who became the sixth khalifah and the first ruler of the Umayyad dynasty—the dynasty of the first official Muslim empire. Hassan did not live to see Muawiyyah's death, for he too was assassinated, in 669.

Before Muawiyyah died, in 680, he forced some of the prominent companions of Muhammad in Mecca to swear allegiance to his son Yazid. Some companions and their sons did not want to swear allegiance to Yazid, and one of them was the Prophet Muhammad's other grandson, Hussein. After denying allegiance to Yazid, Hussein fled Medina to take refuge in Mecca. It was from Mecca that he was invited to go to Kufa, in Iraq, where he was promised support by the growing Shi'ite community there. The Arabic word *shi'a* means "organization," "party," "faction," or "partisan." It comes form the Arabic root *shia'a*, "to adhere to." In the context of Islam, *shi'a*, or Shi'ite, means those who believed that Ali ibn Abu Talib was the legitimate successor of the Prophet.

Hussein left Mecca to lead a revolt against Muawiyyah in Iraq, under the assumption that he would be helped by people from Kufah, but in the end they betrayed Hussein by providing no assistance. Muawiyyah responded by sending his son Yazid with more than 500 troops, who brutally murdered Hussein and most of his family. This horrific event is central for all Shi'ite Muslims. To many scholars of Islam, it is comparable to Christ's crucifixion in that it evokes powerful emotions of guilt and anger at the betrayal of Hussein by the Kufans.

The Umayyads of Damascus (661–750) and Al-Andalus (756–1492) Under Muawiyyah as sixth khalifah, the political capital of the Muslim ummah moved from Medina to Damascus. Influenced by their particular Arab background, a distinctive Islamic culture began taking form under the fourteen Umayyad khalifahs who reigned in Damascus from 661 to 750. Arabic became the official language of the administration, replacing Greek and Persian in the conquered territories. The first Islamic currency—gold dinars and silver dirhams bearing Qur'anic statements—was minted to replace Byzantine and Persian currency. The Umayyads are also known for building elaborate desert palaces and beautiful mosques, such as the Umayyad Mosque in Damascus, Syria. They maintained a talented military force as well that led successful conquests in Central Asia, India, North Africa, and Spain.

The Court of Lions in the Alhambra Palace of Granada, Spain. The Alhambra Palace represents the heights of Arab/Muslim architecture in Spain. It was completed under the Nasrid dynasty in the fourteenth century, during the twilight years of Muslim rule in Spain.

Source: Irina Korshunova/Shutterstock

Because of the Umayyads' privileging of Arabs, the people of newly conquered non-Arab territories were seen as having no tribal affiliation and were thus regarded as lacking status and protection. Non-Arabs had to hire Arabs for protection. This bias toward Arabs, combined with the Umayyads' harsh rule (especially toward the emerging Shi'ite Muslim community), became a factor in their downfall. Face with both growing resentment among non-Arab subjects and internal dissent in the office of the khalifah, the Umayyads became weakened. They were defeated by another emerging dynasty, the Abbasids, in a battle at the Zab River in 750.

After the battle, the Abbasids sought out and killed the Umayyad princes. However, one prince escaped persecution: Abd ar-Rahman ibn Muawiyyah, who later became known as "the Falcon of the Quraysh." After fleeing Damascus for North Africa in 750, Abd ar-Rahman convinced an army of Syrian loyalists, Yemenites, and Andalusian Berbers to help him take over al-Andalus (Spain) in 756. There he founded the Umayyad caliphate of al-Andalus and made Cordoba his capital. This Umayyad caliphate became known in Europe as the "Moorish conquest" and the era of Muslim medieval Spain. It is interesting to note that, in opposition to the Abbasids of Baghdad and the emerging power of the Fatimids of Cairo, Abd ar-Rahman's grandson, Abd ar-Rahman III, claimed the caliphate and took the title of khalifah in 929.

The Umayyads of Spain turned out to be very different from the Umayyads of Damascus. One main difference was their length of rule: the Umayyads of Damascus reigned only from 661 to 750, whereas the Umayyads of al-Andalus lasted about 800 years, from 756 to 1492. Another characteristic that set apart the Umayyads of al-Andalus from those of Damascus was their culture of tolerance. The Abrahamic faiths coexisted peacefully in al-Andalus; for the first time under a caliphate, Jews and Christians were appointed to high offices, becoming foreign ministers and advisors. As well, al-Andalus attained unprecedented prosperity and excelled in cultivation of the arts and sciences, particularly poetry and philosophy.

As al-Andalus developed into an intercultural as well as an intellectual centre, so too did Iraq under the Abbasid dynasty and Egypt with the coming of the Fatimids. These three locations became world centres for scholarship, science, and a remarkable encyclopedic effort to collect, translate, and synthesize all the existing sources of human knowledge, from Egyptian, Babylonian, Indian, Greek, Iranian, and Chinese cultures. As many scholars hold, Muslim intellectual developments between the mid-eighth and mid-fourteenth centuries laid the groundwork for the Renaissance in Europe.

The Abbasids (750–1258) The Abbasid dynasty, known as the second dynasty and empire of Islam, succeeded the Umayyads of Damascus in 750. This dynasty lasted only until the coming of the Mongols in 1258. If the Umayyads were like desert kings, the Abbasids were more like an international world order. Under the Abbasids, Persian non-Arab culture and knowledge were fused with Muslim culture and politics. This shift from purely Arab conquest was symbolized in the transfer of capitals from Damascus to Baghdad.

The Abbasid dynasty was founded by Abu al-Abbas as-Saffah, who was related to the Prophet Muhammad through al-Abbas, Muhammad's uncle. This familial connection to the Prophet's family helped to rally Shi'ite support, as well as aid from a prominent Persian family that had been influenced by Shi'ite Islam, known as the Barmecides. Over several generations, the Barmecides' administrative skills as viziers (ministers) in the region of today's Iraq helped the Abbasids cultivate a flowering Arab-Persian Islamic civilization that is known to this day for its significant cultural, scientific, and literary achievements.

Of the thirty-seven Abbasid khalifahs, the most famous was the fifth khalifah, Harun ar-Rashid (764–809)—his name in Arabic means "Aaron the Rightly Guided"—who reigned during the peak of the Abbasid empire (his reign and court life are immortalized in the famous "Arabian Nights"). He was known for establishing diplomatic relations with Charlemagne and with the emperor of China. His reign also marked the height of Abbasid military conquests and territorial acquisition; his caliphate extended from the boundaries of India and Central Asia to Egypt and North Africa.

At the end of Harun's life he divided the empire between his two sons, al-Amin, who received the western portion, and al-Ma'mun, who received the east. Neither being satisfied with only half, the brothers soon fought a brief but bloody civil war over the succession, which ended with al-Ma'mun coming to power. Besides being a fierce warrior, al-Ma'mun was a great intellect who wanted to make Baghdad an international centre for learning. In doing so he created the famous Bayt al-Hikmah, or House of Wisdom, an intellectual centre that included a library, a translation bureau, and a school that encouraged scholars from all over the world to come to debate and learn.

PEOPLE & PLACES

Muslim Inventions and Contributions to Science

Beginning in the ninth century C.E., Muslims have made substantial contributions to a variety of intellectual and scientific disciplines. Here are some examples:

Astronomy

Muslin astronomers corrected and synthesized earlier astronomical data and theories such as the Ptolemaic model, leading to the heliocentric thinking of Copernicus. They further developed astronomical instruments, including the astrolabe, the quadrant, and celestial globes.

Chemistry

Chemists invented laboratory instruments such as the crucible, the alembic, and the retort. They also discovered sulphuric acid and nitric acid and created the first periodic table.

Engineering

Engineers invented the first waterwheels and windmills. Notably, they also created the fountain pen that held ink in a reservoir and, as with modern pens, fed the ink into the nib by a combination of gravity and capillary action.

(Continued)

Mathematics
Muslims mathematicians translated and commented on the works of Euclid, Archimedes, Apollonius, Aristotle, and Ptolemy. They also founded algebra, algorithms, and the idea of decimal factors.

Medicine
Az-Zahrawi, a surgeon in tenth-century Islamic Spain, developed techniques for treating wounds, setting bones, and removing arrows. He also developed the science of anesthesia, using opium and alcohol mixtures, and created more than 200 medical instruments, most of which have served as prototypes for modern medical instruments such as scalpels, bone saws, and forceps. Muslim physicians also developed hollow needles to remove cataracts from eyes with a technique still used today.

Trade and Industry
Muslim travellers introduced new fruits to Europe such as apricots, figs, dates, and oranges. Coffee was grown in Yemen and traded from the town of Mocha, which gave its name to a type of high-quality coffee. Because it was an Islamic ritual to bathe and wash before prayer, Muslims originated a general recipe for shampoo—vegetable oils, sodium hydroxide, and aromatic oils such as orange, rose, or thyme—that eventually reached England and that we still use today. The modern *cheque* comes from the Arabic *saqq*, a written vow to pay for goods upon delivery, instituted to avoid transporting money across dangerous terrain. Major Islamic cities were connected by an efficient postal service, and in 1150 the Sultan of Baghdad began a postal service that used carrier pigeons.

Rationalists and Traditionalists in Islamic Theology

Kalam: systematic theology, "the study of divine speech."

Sunnah: literally, "trodden path," referring to the lifestyle or way of the Prophet Muhammad.

'Ulema: scholars of Islam.

The period between the eighth and eleventh centuries was a time of great dynamism and transfusion of multiple knowledge systems, as well as a time of unprecedented decisions and guidelines for the future of the Islamic empire. This intellectual ferment gave rise to schools of law in which theology was considered to be part of the process of Islamic jurisprudence.

Theology in Arabic is **kalam**, which literally means "speech" and, in the context of Islam, "the study of divine speech." Some Muslim scholars connect the use of this word with the Greek word *logos*, which means both "living word" and "logic." Muslim theologians speculated about the nature of God and of the divine Qur'anic commandments upon which the acts of Muslims were to be modelled. Theological debate was discouraged by the first generations of Muslims, and there remains some ambivalence within the Sunni tradition toward systematic theology. The early ethos is reflected in the maxim that one should believe the Qur'an's descriptions of God's acts and attributes "without asking how."

For example, the Qur'an describes God as seated on His throne. Rather than speculate on whether this is a metaphor for God's power or whether the description is to be taken literally, Imam Malik (d. 795), the founder of the Maliki school of jurisprudence, famously said that God's establishment over the throne is known, the *how* of His establishment is unknown (that is, inconceivable), and that even asking "how" is a reprehensible innovation in religion (Fakhry 1999, xix). The best approach, according to many, is to take the Qur'an and the **Sunnah** (the way of the Prophet Muhammad) at face value, imbibing their message without delving into difficult questions on the nature of God, revelation, and unseen spiritual realities; questions that have no simple answers; and questions that can potentially lead the believer down a path of confusion and unbelief—or cause fighting and sectarian splits amongst Muslims as they enter into disagreements over the exact meaning of difficult theological terms.

Despite their early opposition to theological dispute, as Muslims encountered the Greek philosophical tradition and developed a greater awareness of Jewish and Christian theologies, pressing theological questions began to be raised. Many **'ulema**, or scholars of Islam,

Qadar: divine predestination.

Hadith: written reports of the Prophet's sayings and actions.

saw it as a communal obligation to provide coherent answers in order to safeguard the community from confusion, dissension, and heresy (Fakhry 1999, xx). Most scholars agree that the first philosophical issue that led to theological controversy was the question of free will and predestination, or **qadar** (Fakhry 1999, xx). It is around this issue that we see the emergence of the first theological schools of thought: the rationalist (Mutazilite) school and the traditionalist (Hanbalite) school.

Mutazilites, Hanbalites, and Asharites Early Muslim rationalists belonged to the Mutazilite theological school, an approach that came to prominence under the Abbasid khalifah al-Ma'mun. Mutazilites emphasized the inherent rationality of revelation, and hence the necessity of reason for understanding revelation: it is only through reason that we can appreciate the truth of revelation and have faith in God, so reason is therefore primary.

The traditionalists were followers of Ahmad Ibn Hanbal (d. 855), the founder of the Hanbali school of law (the most conservative of the four Sunni legal schools) and a noted student of **hadith**, or prophetic traditions. The "traditionalist" label comes from their emphasis on the study of prophetic traditions. Hanbalites took a more literal approach to revelation than Mutazilites, and they sought to affirm the Qur'an and the Sunnah to the letter. They believed that the religious truth conveyed in the Qur'an could not be limited by human reason; in other words, according to

PEOPLE & PLACES

Some Famous Muslim Philosophers

al-Kindi—born in Kufah, Iraq, around 801, an advisor to the Abbasid khalifahs who wrote more than 270 treatises, of which only seventy have survived. These works contributed to the development many fields, including mathematics, astronomy, chemistry, music theory, theology, and philosophy. He is best known for being the first Muslim to examine Islam and the Qur'an through a philosophical lens, drawing from Hellenistic sources and in particular the works of Aristotle. In the Muslim world, his work earned him the distinction of being called the first Muslim philosopher; in Europe he was known as "the philosopher of the Arabs."

al-Farabi—born in Farabi, Turkey, in 870, and further developed al-Kindi's thought. He became known for his insight into Greek philosophy and his amazing talent for explaining it to an Islamic audience. Among his main contributions to Muslim philosophy are his arguments for harmonizing the opinions of Plato and Aristotle, for the inherent unity of Islam and philosophy, and for a theory of the intellect. His work earned him the designation "Second Master" (Aristotle being the first).

Ibn Sina—known in the West as Avicenna. Ibn Sina was born near Bukhara in 980 and wrote the very influential treatise *Kitab al-Shifa* ("The Book of Healing"), which was a compendium of logic, geometry, arithmetic, astronomy, music, natural science, and metaphysics. This treatise would remain the basis for teaching medicine in both the Muslim world and Europe until the seventeenth century. It was from this work that Ibn Sina gained a reputation that equalled the Greek scholars of medicine such as Hippocrates and Galen, earning him the title "Prince of Physicians" in Europe and the Muslim world.

Ibn Rushd—known in the West as Averroes. Ibn Rushd was born in 1126 in Cordoba, Andalusia (Muslim medieval Spain), where he studied philosophy, law, linguistics, and medicine. He also worked under the khalifah, Amir Abu Yaqub, who asked him to write a commentary on Aristotle. This work became known as *Tahafut at-Tahafut* ("The Incoherence of Incoherence") and made Ibn Rushd famous as "the first and last great Aristotelian in Islam." It also influenced some of the greatest medieval philosophers, including Moses Maimonides, Albert the Great, Saint Thomas Aquinas, and Roger Bacon. Latin Averroists would remain influential in Europe until the fifteenth century.

Hanbalites, rational thought was incapable of wholly understanding the Qur'an and the Sunnah.

Regarding the relationship between human free will and divine predestination (qadar), Mutazilites tended to emphasize the reality of free will. As Mutazilite theologians emphasized God's rationality and justice, they argued that it would be contrary to God's justice for Him to predestine people to do bad deeds and then punish them for what they had no control over; that would be irrational. If God is truly just and rational—the position that Mutazilites based their theology on—then people must be free to choose good or evil and rightfully earn the consequences of their choice. For Hanbalites, what God does, even if it seems irrational or unjust to us, is by definition good. In terms of free will, God is the only creator; hence humans cannot be deemed to be the creators of their deeds and hence free will is essentially limited. Although this may appear to lead to injustice, since people's bad deeds are created by God and they may be predestined for Hell as a result, God's actions are good by definition, whether we can rationally understand how this is so or not. God determines what is good, and it is up to us to follow what He deems to be good. For Mutazilites, however, God reveals the sacred law because it is inherently good and rational. We, as humans endowed with reason, can rationally appreciate the goodness of God's revelation and understand its reasons; we do not need to simply accept it as good based on the fact that it is revelation. This fundamental difference in orientation between rationalists and traditionalists can be presented this way: Mutazilites say *God reveals what is good*, and Hanbalites say *What God reveals is good.*

Elements of these two schools came together with the Asharites. This school of thought eventually became the foremost theological school in Sunni Islam and is seen by many as representative of Sunni orthodoxy. The status of Asharites as orthodox Sunnis was cemented under the Seljuk dynasty, when they established a standardized system of Islamic theological colleges teaching Asharite theology. The Asharites formed a "qualified traditionalist" school that emerged out of the Mutazilites. Hence, with the Asharites we have a theological school that in some senses synthesizes the traditionalism of the Hanbalites and the rationalism of the Mutazilites. Like Hanbalites, Asharites emphasize God's omnipotence and sovereignty over creation: God creates all causes and acts, so secondary causes are ultimately illusory. Also, God's moral decrees and religious prescriptions are final, defining what is good, and humans are incapable of using reason to decipher them. However, unlike the Hanbalites, the Asharites allowed for some rational, metaphorical interpretation of scripture.

Jihad: struggle in the path of God against one's own evil inclinations and against corruption and oppression in the world.

The Sufis: Islam's Mystics

Sufism is Islam's mystical tradition, a spiritual path based on the Qur'an and the practice and teachings of the Prophet Muhammad. Some Sufis understand Sufism as an ancient wisdom tradition that predates Islam, though Islam is thought to have revived and anchored this tradition. From the life and teachings of Muhammad, Sufis trace their way most frequently through the Prophet's cousin and son-in-law Ali ibn Abi Talib. Ali is an icon of spirituality and courage for most Muslims, and Sufis in particular respect Ali as the gate or door to prophetic knowledge.

As Islam shifted from being a new, marginalized Arabian religious movement to a multicultural and wide-ranging empire under the Umayyads, those devoted to the spiritual life began to stand out against the immense wealth and power of the young Muslim community. Exemplary here is Hasan al-Basri, known as "the patriarch of Muslim mysticism" (Schimmel 1975, 30). Hasan al-Basri is representative of the early ascetic movement in that he was world-rejecting and focused on fear of God, sadness, abstinence, repentance, obeying God's commandments, and facing the day of reckoning. For al-Basri, as among other early ascetics, government was equated with evil, worldliness, and the crass pursuit of wealth and power. Sufism in this early stage was predominantly a countercultural, anti-government (ideally, not necessarily politically), and world-renouncing movement.

Sufis seek not paradise in the next life but closeness to God in this life. There is one considerable obstacle to knowing God, and that is the self. Sufis seek first to master the self. The Sufi novice needs to discipline the desires and motivations of the self; this stage of struggling to master or discipline oneself is often referred to by Sufis as the *jihad-al-akbar*, or the greatest *jihad*. In Arabic, **jihad**

PEOPLE & PLACES

The Historical Development of Sufism in Islam: Some Personalities

Rabi'a al-'Adawiyyah (d. 801)—a female saint of Basra, Iraq, who emphasized selfless love and devotion to God "neither for the reward of Paradise nor for fear of Hell, for only God can satisfy the longing of the soul."

al-Junayd (d. 910)—a leading "sober" Sufi who lived in Baghdad, Iraq, and emphasized knowledge of God and conformity with the practice of the community. "The truthful one is changed forty times in one day, but the hypocrite stays in one state for forty years."

al-Hallaj* (d. 922)—a famous "intoxicated" Sufi who was martyred for his ecstatic utterance *Ana al-Haqq* ("I am the Truth"). "Love is to stand before your Beloved, stripped naked of all attributes, so that His qualities become your qualities."

Abu Hamid Muhammad al-Ghazali (d. 1111)— a pivotal Islamic thinker who reconciled Sufi currents of Islam with more exoteric streams of thought. He sought Sufi training after success as a scholar in Baghdad gave way to self-doubt and disillusionment, giving up his privileges for ten years of seeking and then returning to write such works as "Revival of the Religious Sciences." "Your heart is a polished mirror. You must wipe it clean of the veil of dust that has gathered upon it, because it is destined to reflect the light of divine secrets."

Abd al-Qadir al-Jilani* (d. 1166)—a major Sufi saint of Baghdad, Iraq, remembered as a reviver of Islam. Thousands are said to have gathered to hear his public sermons, which emphasized fulfilment of religious duties and interiorization of faith. He founded the Qadiri Sufi order and his sayings are compiled in works such as "Revelations of the Unseen." "The search has no final finding. Knowledge of God is without end."

Muhyi ad-Din Ibn al-'Arabi† (d. 1240)—an Andalusian-born Sufi whose voluminous theosophical writings (approximately 500 works, including "Bezels of Wisdom" and "Meccan Openings") covered the spectrum of Islamic thought. He developed the idea of *wahdat al-wujud* (the unity of existence), which provided a basis for subsequent flowerings of Sufi thought and practice, and gave expression to Sufi universalism by proclaiming, "I follow the religion of love; whosesoever its camels turn, it is my religion and faith." He travelled widely in the Muslim world, eventually settling in Damascus, Syria. "Everything engendered in existence is Imagination–but in fact it is Reality. Whoever understands this truth has grasped the mysteries of the Way."

Mu'in al-Din Chishti* (d. 1236)—a major Sufi saint of India and founder of the Chishtiyya Sufi order who introduced music and poetry to spiritual practices. "The qualities that endear a human to God are river-like generosity, sun-like affection, and earth-like hospitality."

Jalal al-Din al-Rumi* (d. 1273)—perhaps the most famous Sufi in the West, known for his ecstatic, lyrical Persian poems and for the "whirling dervishes" of the Mawlawiyya order, which he founded. He was born in Khorasan but fled the Mongol invasions with his father, eventually settling in Konya, in what is now Turkey. "Love calls—everywhere and always. We're sky bound. Are you coming?"

* Timothy Freke, *The Wisdom of the Sufi Sages* (VT: Charles E. Tuttle Co., 1998).
† Muhammad Isa Waley, *Sufism: The Alchemy of the Heart* (San Francisco: Chronicle Books, 1993).

means to struggle. For Sufis, the greatest jihad is not the struggle against injustice on earth but rather the struggle against one's own negative inclinations, which are the inner source of outer injustice. After this initial stage of struggling against one's unruly desires, the Sufi can then access the heart, and it is through the heart that one comes to know God. The heart's means of drawing near to God is love, and hence Sufism is sometimes referred to as "the path of love."

The Sufi emphasis on love, ecstasy, and the transrational nature of spiritual knowledge lent itself well to poetry, which blossomed in a number of languages spoken by Muslims, including Persian, Arabic, Turkish, and Urdu. Sufi poetry permeates Muslim cultures to this day. Rumi's works, for example, are revered as some of the best in the canon of classical Persian poetry, and many Persian speakers can quote lines from his *Mathnawi*. Yunus Emre's celebrated Turkish poetry continues to inspire the search for truth beyond form:

> I've forgotten religion and piety.
> What if there's a doctrine deeper than religion?
> The works of those who leave the faith are blasphemy.
> What about a blasphemy deeper than faith?
> (Emre* 1989, 64)

The Andalusian Sufi metaphysician Ibn 'Arabi wrote a famous collection of odes in Arabic titled *The Interpreter of Desires*. Because it was filled with erotic imagery, the jurists of his time accused Ibn 'Arabi of obscenity. He responded by providing an in-depth commentary on his poetry, revealing the metaphysics of oneness that its imagery expressed and demonstrating the spiritual intent of Sufi poetry, despite its sometimes shocking imagery.

Even though these different schools of thought brought about a time of intense transmission and transformation of intellectual knowledge, they also created a time of great division and dissension. Because of emerging tensions in the region of Baghdad, the successor to al-Ma'mun, al-Mu'tasim, moved the Abbasid capital to Samarra, 60 kilometres north of Baghdad. This defensive move foreshadowed the political decline of the Abbasids: al-Mu'tasim gave too much power to a unit of Turkish guards who became known as the Seljuks, and they began to exercise their own rule over succeeding Abbasid khalifas. Consequently, several mini-dynasties emerged that fragmented the power of the Abbasid caliphate, ultimately leading to their downfall.

The Fatimids of Egypt (909–1171) Another dynasty, and one that became a political and intellectual rival to the Abbasids and the Umayyads of al-Andalus, was the Fatimids of Egypt. The name *Fatimid* reflects their claim to be descended from the Prophet through his daughter Fatima. The Fatimids were an Ismaili dynasty that gained power over parts of North Africa and in 969 established the city of al-Qahirah, meaning "the victorious"—today's Cairo.

The Ismaili Fatimids in particular are known for their many cultural achievements. One of their greatest was the founding of al-Azhar, the oldest Islamic university in the Muslim world. It was originally an institution for teaching Muslims about Ismaili history and doctrines. Because it became known as a prominent training centre it threatened Abbasid authority and eventually forced the emerging Seljuks to create their own schools. This then led to the *madrasah* system, a chain of Muslim universities across the Middle East, South Asia, and Southeast Asia.

The rhythm of the Fatimid history was very similar to that of the Abbasids in that there was great political fragmentation. The main division for the Fatimids came at the end of their rule, between the Nizaris and the Mustalis. The predominant branch is the Nizaris, who believe that there has been a living Imam since the time of Ismail. In contemporary times, this living Imam has been given the title *Aga Khan*.

Mini-Dynasties: Seljuks, Ayyubids, and Mamluks In the Abbasid empire there was a period of great political and religious consolidation and then a period of great fragmentation of political order, with breakout military factions and ultimately power divisions that led to the creation of mini-dynasties. Each of these mini-dynasties maintained the Abbasid khalifah as a figurehead while controlling its region of the empire. Three prominent mini-dynasties were the Seljuks, the Ayyubids, and the Mamluks.

In early Abbasid period, Turks were known for serving in the Muslim armies and prized for their skill as mounted archers. However, they were also seen as slaves. Historians claim that many Turkic tribes would sell their boys to Muslim leaders and then those slaves would be trained in the arts of war. Eventually they would become *ghazis*, or border warriors, for Islam, guarding the north-eastern boundaries against non-Muslim Turks. These *ghazis* became very powerful and were one of the main causes of the Abbasid empire's fragmentation into mini-dynasties.

* Yunus Emre, *The Drop That Became the Sea: Lyric Poems*, translated by Kabir Helminski and Refik Algan. Originally published by Threshold Books, 1986.

One of these mini-dynasties was the Seljuks, a Turkic Sunni people who entered into military service with the Abbasid empire and succeeded in seizing for themselves the eastern Abbasid lands of Iran, Iraq, and Central Asia. Their first leader was Toghrul Beg (1038–1194), who was the first Muslim political leader to assume the title *sultan*. The Seljuks were responsible for the "turkification" of Anatolia, which would later become Turkey. They restored Sunni rule over southwest Asia, and their great admiration for Persian culture and poetry spread that culture throughout the lands they ruled. The Seljuks also helped develop a madrasah school system for training Sunni 'ulema in Islamic law, in order to compete with the Shi'ite Fatimids. Finally, Seljuk forces weakened the Byzantine empire in Anatolia, setting the stage for later Ottoman advances.

Another mini-dynasty that emerged under the Abbasid caliphate was the Ayyubids. They were a Sunni dynasty founded by Salah ad-Din al-Ayyubi (known in the West as Saladin) that reigned from 1169 to 1260 over the regions from Syria to Egypt. Salah ad-Din, a Kurdish general, was a great heroic figure who directed a series of wars against the Crusader kingdoms in Syria and Jerusalem. It was in 1175 that Salah ad-Din took Damascus, declared himself an independent sovereign, and was recognized by the Abbasid khalifahs. He then consolidated his empire, which extended into Anatolia and Syria. In doing so he created a united kingdom surrounding the Crusader states. Such positioning

PEOPLE & PLACES

Salah ad-Din

A statue of Salah ad-Din on horseback in Damascus, Syria.

Source: © Michael Nicholson/CORBIS

Salah ad-Din's tolerance toward the Crusaders reflected that of Umar, the second khalifah. Upon entering Jerusalem in 638, Umar had met with the Greek patriarch of the Christian Church. Invited by the Patriarch to pray in the Church of the Holy Sepulchre, Umar refused, expressing concern that, should he pray in the church, future generations of Muslims would want to convert the holy Christian site into a mosque. Umar felt strongly that sites in Jerusalem that were holy to Christians must be preserved, and hence he prayed outside the church. To this day a dedicated mosque stands on the spot where Umar prayed near the Church of the Holy Sepulchre.

Salah ad-Din was reportedly frequently moved to tears by the sight of human suffering. It is said that a Frankish woman approached him in great distress, her daughter having been taken by Muslim soldiers. Salah ad-Din immediately ordered that the child be found, and she was soon located and returned to her mother. Such stories of chivalry and goodwill institutionalized Salah ad-Din as a Muslim hero in Europe (Armstrong 1988, 240).

made it easy for him to recover Jerusalem for the Muslims in 1187.

After Salah ad-Din's death in 1193, the Ayyubids reigned in the regions of Egypt, Syria, and the Hijaz. After the Ayyubids took over Cairo, al-Azhar was turned into a Sunni institution, which it still is today. Like all previous dynasties, the Ayyubid dynasty also came to end, weakened especially by attacks from the Mongols to the east and the Mamluks to the west.

When the Mongols destroyed Baghdad in 1258, they also put to death the Abbasid khalifah, al-Musta'sim. However, another force, this time from the west, stopped the Mongols in Baghdad in 1259—the Mamluks. The Arabic word *mamluk* means "one owned by another," or slave. The Mamluks were originally a military corps made up of non-Muslim slaves taken from lands beyond Islamic domains (Turkmenistan, the Circassian region, and Mongolia) who were converted to Islam at a young age. Both the Fatimids and the Ayyubids depended on the Mamluks as the backbone of their armies. However, in 1254 the Mamluks revolted against the last Ayyubid sultan, killing him and making their first sultan, Aybak, marry the stepmother of the murdered ruler.

The most celebrated Mamluk sultan was Baybars, who, after defeating the Mongols in Baghdad, took the uncle of al-Musta'sim—known as al-Mustansir—to Cairo in 1260 and installed him there as khalifah. This act legitimized Baybars' own rule as sultan and continued the line of the Abbasid caliphate. Mustansir was killed a year later in an unsuccessful attempt to take back Baghdad from the Mongols. However, the line of the al-Abbas continued through the rule of the Mamluks until 1517.

Baybars is also known for being the first sultan to maintain all four schools of law in his domains on an equal footing; this practice would inspire the Turks later on. One reason the Mamluks remained in power for close to 300 years was that they were a military and political force that was not prone to fragmentation. However, in 1517, the Mamluks, lacking firearms and cannons, were no match for the growing military power of the Ottomans, the first "gunpowder empire."

Ottomans, Safavids, and Mughals

The Ottomans (1517–1924) With such technological power, it was easy for the Ottoman sultan Selim I to conquer Cairo and incorporate it into the expanding Ottoman Empire. By defeating the Mamluks, the Ottomans could lay claim to the office of the caliphate. The last Abbasid khalifah, Mutawakkil III, who was recognized by the Mamluks as their khalifah, ceded the rights of the caliphate to Selim I and the Ottomans in 1517.

The Ottomans, also known as Osmanlis, were a clan of the Ghuzz, a branch of Turks who were descended from the chieftain of a principality in Asia Minor in the thirteenth century. In 1357 this clan, having already taken control of western Anatolia, began a series of conquests that brought Macedonia, Serbia, and Bulgaria under their power.

After many failed attempts to seize Constantinople, the Ottomans finally succeeded in 1453, under the leadership of the Ottoman sultan Mehmet II, known as Mehmet the Conqueror. He earned this title by conquering not only Constantinople but also the Balkans. Besides his skill as a military strategist and being credited with designing some of finest Ottoman cannons, Mehmet was also known for his superior language skills: he knew Turkish, Persian, Arabic, Greek, and Latin. These skills would come in handy in relations with peoples who had been conquered, especially Byzantine populations. He is known for extending protection under Islamic law to the Christian churches and monasteries, and ultimately to the Orthodox Church.

It was Mehmet's victory in seizing Constantinople that opened the way for other Ottoman sultans, such as Selim I in his conquest of the Mamluks of Egypt in 1517, and for the Ottoman caliphate to reach its highest point with Sulayman the Magnificent. Under Sulayman's reign the Ottomans conducted successful military campaigns in Europe and the Middle East, besieging Vienna, annexing Hungary, advancing through Persia, and gaining control of the Hijaz in Arabia. The Ottomans formed the largest Muslim empire and one of the longest-surviving empires in history, being officially dissolved only in 1924.

The Safavids of Persia (1501–1732) Another Muslim empire to challenge the Ottomans from the east was the Safavid empire of Persia. This dynasty originated with Ishaq Safi ad-Din (d. 1334), who was a prominent leader of a Sufi order called the Safavi. This order was associated with Twelver Shi'ism, and most of its followers were of Turkic origin. The first Safavid *shah*, or king (a Persian title used instead of *sultan*), was Ismail, a descendant of Safi-ad-Din who made Ithna 'Ashariyyah, or Twelver Imam Shi'ism, the official state religion. This decision was made in order to rally support from the Shi'a, the predominant community in Persia, as well as to establish a counterweight to Sunni legitimacy.

At first the Ottomans were the greatest threat to Safavid rule, but when the Ottomans became increasingly preoccupied with expansion into Europe, Shah Abbas I (known as "the Great Shah" of the Safavids) made peace with them. Abbas I was also known for changing the official language of the courts from Turkish to Persian. Such diplomacy, as well as other achievements in arts and commerce, made Abbas I's reign the peak of the Safavid dynasty.

The Mughals of Medieval India (1526–1858) The Mughals are a celebrated Muslim dynasty of medieval India, noted for their outstanding cultural achievements in the arts, architecture, music, and literature, all of which blended elements from Persia and India. The name *Mughal* is simply a phonetic form of *Mongol* adapted from the Persian language and Arabic script.

The Mughal Empire was founded by Babur, a descendant of Timur (a great Turkoman prince and ruler in Samarkand) on his father's side and of Jenghiz Khan (leader of the Mongols) on his mother's side. Babur became the ruler of Transoxiana after conquering Samarkand at the age of fourteen. However, after losing control of both regions, he ventured into Afghanistan, seizing Kabul and then Qandahar. In 1526 he defeated the sultan of Delhi and established his own capital at Agra.

Babur's grandson Akbar became one the most famous Mughals of all time. Emperor Akbar (1556–1605) ruled over the greatest extension of the Mughal empire, comprising most of northern India and Afghanistan. He is best known for creating a syncretist religion called *din i-ilahi* ("the religion of God"), a mixture of several religions that he was acquainted with, including Islam, Hinduism, and Christianity. Hindus in particular played an important role in Akbar's government. Following Akbar's fifty-year reign came the rules of Jahangir (1605–27), Shah Jahan (1628–58), and Awrangzeb (1658–1707). Jahangir and Shah Jahan continued with Akbar's ambitious plans for expansion and his holistic policy toward religion, also encouraging court patronage of the arts. Shah Jahan in particular is probably best remembered as the builder of the Taj Mahal, a mausoleum for his favourite wife.

Awrangzeb deposed his father, Shah Jahan, and seized the throne. He is known as the most zealous Muslim of the Mughal emperors. Though his reign was part of the golden age of the Mughals, when their power extended over most of South Asia, many historians believe that it was he who brought about the Mughals' decline in the region. The main reason for this was Awrangzeb's position on Islamic law. Abandoning his predecessors' liberal, syncretistic religious edicts, he brought in a more conservative understanding that enforced Islamic law as the only system of law in the region. This act earned the distrust and anger of his Hindu subjects and officials, creating divisions between the Muslim and non-Muslim populations. After Awrangzeb, the Mughal dynasty continued to decline until 1858, when the British deposed the last Mughal emperor for allegedly complying with an act of mutiny.

The Age of Colonization and Modernity

Whereas in Europe the coming of the modern age is associated primarily with the intellectual discoveries and social dynamism of the Renaissance and the Enlightenment, the same period brings different associations to mind in traditionally Muslim lands. For Muslims, the advent of modernity meant the beginning of colonization rather than emancipation, as virtually all Muslim territories had fallen under European occupation and imperial administration by the end of the First World War. Political subjugation to countries such as England and France marked a great historical as well as existential rupture and created a fundamental change in the basic terms of reference for Muslim culture and politics. Muslims found themselves entering a new era with a historically unfamiliar subordinate status; they were now being forced to "catch up," to reform, to undertake adjustments in all areas of life—political, legal, economic, intellectual, and social.

Because colonization represented a basic "failure" of traditional Muslim paradigms for understanding the world and organizing social and political life, responses were coloured by a process of deep communal introspection and an effort to differentiate between what is essential in historical Islam and what might have contributed to the stagnation that allowed Europe to surpass the Islamic world. Across the Muslim world, thinkers found themselves asking similar questions: Why had Muslims failed to keep up with Europe in the domains of science, technology, and politics? Was there something in the way that traditional Muslim leaders understood Islam that blocked intellectual progress? Given that Islam provides guidance for all areas of life and not just for worship, what deficits in Muslim understanding and practice had led to the current impasse? What aspects of European innovation were complementary to Islamic faith, and which "modern" ways of knowing, being, and doing were incompatible with Islamic values and norms? Efforts to answer such questions naturally led in several different directions—from secularism, reformism, and revivalism to reassertion of traditional authority—and stoked heated contestation over the most "authentic" as well as realistic responses to the new Muslim predicament.

Reformist thinkers such as Jamal al-Din al-Afghani (d. 1897) were critical of traditional Muslim political and religious authorities and called for Muslims to embrace European science, technology, and forms of government. Al-Afghani believed this was the only way to revive Islamic civilization in the face of European domination. Muhammad 'Abduh (d. 1905) and later Rashid Rida (d. 1935) would take up Afghani's cause, disseminating his ideas in Egypt and throughout the Middle East (Hourani 1983).

In contrast to reformists who wanted to modernize Islam, Muslim revivalists sought to make modernity Islamic. In other words, Islamic revivalists agreed with al-Afghani that Muslims needed to embrace modern science and technology. However, they rejected calls to reform Islam along rational lines and wanted instead to employ modern means toward Islamic ends. This led to the powerful idea of an Islamic state. The two key theorists of the Islamic state were Sayyid Qutb (d. 1966) and Abul Ala Maududi (d. 1979). Groups such as the Ikhwan al-Muslimeen, or Muslim Brotherhood, in Egypt and the Jama'at-i-Islami in South Asia seek to apply Qutb and Maududi's theories and make Muslim societies and states more religious. Some radical followers of Qutb have used violence in the hopes of bringing about an Islamic state.

The twentieth century saw the emergence of revivalist movements as a real political force in many parts of the Muslim world, represented most strikingly by Iran's 1979 Islamic revolution. Although revivalist movements are often characterized as reactionary and anti-modern, scholars such as Olivier Roy (2004) have noted that such movements contribute to the modernization of Muslim societies, by reformulating Islamic norms and practices in ways that fit with current economic, technological, and political models.

Traditionalists, unlike both reformists and revivalists, who embraced many elements of modernity, remain critical of modern developments and seek primarily to preserve traditional ways of life and religion, to the extent possible within the shifting political landscapes of the modern world. Traditionalist perspectives were and continue to be found amongst many Muslim jurists and theologians, as well as among the leadership of many Sufi orders.

Even with the official end of the colonial era during the second half of the twentieth century, Muslim societies remained deeply preoccupied with debates about religious identity, cultural authenticity, and religious as well as political authority. New states underpinned by modern nationalist ideologies have attempted to establish new forms of cooperation with traditional religious authorities and institutions, but the persistent underperformance of these states—not to mention the problem of autocracy, which has too often constricted associational life and confined civic space to the mosque—has kept the colonial-era questions alive and has helped give birth to modern Islamic movements that challenge traditional authority by asserting new interpretive tendencies of a reformist and/or revivalist character. These movements, from the Egyptian Muslim Brotherhood to the Progressive Muslim Union of North America, differ profoundly in their answers to fundamental questions about how Islamic norms should be configured in relation to a Western society distinguished by individualism, secularism, women's empowerment, consumerism, and numerous other trends.

MUSLIM CULTURE AND PRACTICE

Religious Diversity

The most historically significant division in the Muslim community is between Sunni and Shi'ite Muslims, a split that began after the Prophet's death

Ijtihad: independent juristic reasoning.

in 632 and crystallized into two distinct Islamic sects by the tenth century.

The initial division between Sunni and Shi'ite Muslims began over the question of who would lead the Muslim community following the death of the Prophet Muhammad. The division developed further over the early centuries of Islam as alternate conceptions of religious authority formed. For Sunnis, political and religious authority were divided from one another following the period of the Rashidun (632–61). The caliphate retained legitimate political authority to rule over Muslims, whereas the 'ulema, or scholars of the law, retained religious authority. For some Sunnis the Sufi saints were also inheritors of the Prophet's spiritual authority, sharing in something of his purity and insight. In medieval Sunni societies, then, the caliphate represented political authority while the scholars and Sufi saints represented religious authority.

Shi'ite Muslims believed that spiritual and political authority were integrated in the person of the Imam. Whereas Sunnis use the term *imam* to refer simply to a leader of congregational prayer, Shi'ites use the term *Imam* to refer to the infallible leader appointed by God to guide the Muslim community. For Shi'ite Muslims, the spiritual and political authority of the Prophet was inherited by members of his family and their descendants, who were the imams of their generation. Unlike Sunni Muslims, who believe that the first three khalifahs of the community—Abu Bakr, Umar, and Uthman—were righteous legitimate successors to the Prophet, Shi'ites believe that Ali, the Prophet's cousin and son-in-law, was the rightful heir of Prophetic authority and the first Imam. The word *Shi'ites* literally means "party": the first Shi'ite were the "party of Ali," or *shi'at Ali*, who emerged in support of Ali as caliph following the assassination of Uthman in 656 (Halm 2004, 1). For Shi'ite, Ali's sacred right to leadership was inherited by his sons Hussein and Hassan. They also believe that Ali, Hussein, and Hassan, and later descendants of the Prophet through their bloodline, inherited the divine right to guide the Muslim community as Imams, free from sin and infallible in their religious judgments.

The largest Shi'ite sect, the Twelvers (Ithna 'Ashariyyah), are thus named because they believe that the line of Imams ended with the twelfth Imam, Muhammad al-Mahdi. He is believed to have been hidden by God in 874 and is expected to return to be amongst people near the end of time. In the twelfth Imam's absence, the foremost legal scholars, referred to as *ayatollahs* (meaning "sign of God"), retain the Imam's authority. This authority is expressed in the capacity of the foremost ayatollahs to make **ijtihad**, or independent juristic reasoning in applying the law to new circumstances. As will be discussed later in this chapter, Twelver Shi'ites further developed their own legal school, the Jafari school of legal thought. Although they share a great deal with Sunnis, Twelver Shi'ites differ in small details regarding Muslim rituals. For example, Shi'as add statements in honour of Ali—such as "*Aliyyu waliyyu Allah*" ("Ali is the friend/saint of God")—to the call to prayer. A notable legal difference that distinguishes Twelver Shi'ites from Sunnis is that they permit temporary marriages, which are automatically terminated at the end of an agreed period.

Although Twelver Shi'ites are the largest Shi'ite group, there are other significant Shi'ites communities, such as the Zaydis and Ismailis. The Zaydis emerged as followers of Hussein's grandson Zayd, who rose against the Umayyad caliph Abd al-Malik in 740 (Halm 2004, 202). Unlike other Shi'ites, Zaydis accept the caliphates of Abu Bakr and Umar. Zaydis developed their own legal school and system of theological thought, and they are found today in parts of Yemen. The Ismailis spilt with Twelver Shi'ites over which son was the rightful successor to the sixth Imam, Jafar as-Sadiq (d. 765). Whereas Twelver Shi'ites came to accept the appointment of as-Siddiq's younger son, Musa al-Kazim, as Imam, the Ismailis held that the imamate should continue through as-Siddiq's eldest son, Isma'il. Ismailis, though numerically small today, played an important role in Islamic history, philosophy, and spirituality. As previously mentioned, under the Ismaili Fatimid caliphate in Cairo, Egypt, Ismaili thought developed significantly and spread throughout much of the Muslim world. Unlike Twelver Shi'ites, Ismailis believe that the imamate continues to this day with the current leader of the Ismailis, the Aga Khan.

Sunnah and Hadith

After the Qur'an, the second most important sacred source in Islam is the Sunnah. The Arabic word *sunnah* literally means "trodden path," and more generally refers to a person's lifestyle or habitual practice. In the context of Islam, the Sunnah refers to both the lifestyle of the Prophet Muhammad and that of the early Muslim communities of Mecca and Medina.

If the Qur'an provides ideal guidance for Muslims to live in accordance with God's will and command, the Prophet Muhammad's behaviour in words and deeds provides the best guide to implement the Qur'anic commands in everyday life. Therefore, the ideal lifestyle for a Muslim to observe is the way of the Prophet: how he organized his life spiritually, economically, intellectually, socially, politically—in all spheres. In short, Muslims seek to emulate the way and practice of the Prophet Muhammad, as he is the best example of how to live the teachings of the Qur'an. This is why the majority of Muslims describe themselves as Sunni, "the people of the Sunnah" (it is important to note that Shi'a Muslims also follow the Sunnah). The Sunnah of the Prophet includes not only his actions but also his sayings, and the actions of others to which he gave silent approval or tacit consent.

How do Muslims access the Sunnah? The Sunnah is recorded in the **hadith**, which literally means "story" or "report." In the context of Islam, hadith are written reports about what the Prophet said and did. According to one tradition, the idea of recording and collecting the hadith occurred to the second khalifah, Umar ibn Khattab. However, it was not until three hundred years after the Prophet's death that the codification process of the hadith formed definitive collections. Starting in the ninth century, scholars of hadith developed criteria to determine the authenticity of reports about the Prophet. These scholars analyzed the content of hadith texts in light of the Qur'an and evaluated the trustworthiness of the transmitters of the hadith. Each hadith has an *isnad*, or chain of transmission, going back to the Prophet. If any one of the transmitters in the chain is thought to be unreliable, perhaps because of a reputation for poor memory or lying, or if it is deemed historically unlikely that one transmitter in the chain

PEOPLE & PLACES

Muhaddithat: Women Scholars of Hadith

Contemporary Hadith scholar Mohammad Akram Nadwi's groundbreaking encyclopedia (more than forty volumes long) documents more than 8,000 women scholars of hadith (*muhaddithat*) dating back over 1,400 years. Although in the late medieval period women scholars of hadith and Islamic jurisprudence were becoming increasingly rare, this was not the way things always had been. Muslim women played unparalleled roles in the formation of the Islamic religious sciences, three of whom will be discussed here.

Aishah (d. 680)—the Prophet's favourite wife after Khadijah, and by far the most famous and important figure in the early development of hadith and Islamic law. She narrated 2,210 hadiths, of which 297 are in the *sahihs* (compilations of authentic hadiths) of al-Bukhari and Muslim; the chains of narration that begin with Aishah are consistently regarded as the most reliable. The six key principles that were later used by jurists in the art of hadith critique were devised and used by Aishah. They included checking a hadith against the Qur'an; against another, stronger hadith; against the Sunnah; against the context in which it was uttered; and against the difficulty of acting on it, as well as checking it for misinterpretation of its meaning (Nadwi 2007, 239–44).

Hafsah bint Sirin (d. 742)—a great muhaddithah and jurist and a former slave girl who had memorized the Qur'an by the age of twelve and became renowned for her beautiful Qur'anic recitation. Hafsah made the best of the learning opportunities presented to her by her master Anas ibn Malik—from whom she received her hadiths—and became one of the leading scholars of her time.

(*Continued*)

According to some, she is considered superior in her scholarship even to the renowned Hasan al-Basri (Nadwi 2007, 101).

Karimah bint Ahmad ibn Muhammad ibn Hatim al-Marwazziyah (d. 1083)—the most famous muhaddithah to teach in Mecca; people, including several prestigious imams, travelled from afar to hear her hadith narrations. She herself travelled extensively from her original home in Kushmihan in pursuit of knowledge, to Isfahan, Jerusalem, and then Mecca, where she eventually settled. She adhered strictly to the practice of maintaining authenticity of texts by insisting they be compared with the originals, and was thus respected for her accuracy and attention to detail in narration (Nadwi 2007, 57).

Source: Muhammad AkramNadwi, *al-Muhaddithat: The Women Scholars in Islam* (Oxford: Interface Publications, 2007)

Shari'ah: sacred law as revealed in the Qur'an and the Sunnah.

could have met the next, a hadith may be deemed to be weak or of dubious authenticity.

The Sunnah of the Prophet forms the ideal way of life for Muslims, functioning as a pattern of behaviour and manners that Muslims strive to imitate in their daily lives. The hadith collections provide written accounts of the Prophet's behaviour in remarkable detail, including his hairstyle, what foods he preferred, how he sat and ate, and how he interacted with his wives. For example, following the Prophet's example, Muslims eat with their right hands, avoid foods that he disliked, and wear colours he is reported to have worn frequently. Besides functioning as a pattern of life that unites Muslim practice around the world, the hadith, as the written record of the Prophet's Sunnah, are the second most important source of Islamic law, *shari'ah*.

Islamic Law: Shari'ah

The word *shari'ah* literally means "path," and in pre-Islamic Arabia it was used to refer to a path leading to a source of water. In Islam, **shari'ah** refers to the sacred law, the divine balance that Muslims are to uphold and live by. In basic terms, the shari'ah is a code of duties and principles according to which women and men should structure their lives. Besides the Qur'an and the Sunnah, the shari'ah is traditionally thought to have two other sources: qiyas and ijma.

Qiyas is analogical reasoning. This is used when a new circumstance arises that is not addressed in the Qur'an or the Sunnah or dealt with by previous jurists. Take, for instance, the question of whether it is permissible for Muslims to perform the salat (daily prayer) in a car or on an airplane. As these are inventions of the twentieth century, Muslims had no guidance on whether or not they could pray in these new forms of transportation. However, using qiyas, Muslim jurists determined that, because the Prophet prayed supererogatory prayers while riding a camel, Muslims can perform the prayer in a car, train, bus, or airplane, as these are analogous modes of transportation. Hence, although cars and trains are not mentioned in the hadith, something similar or analogous to them is: a camel. A ruling can thus be derived from such reports through analogical reasoning.

Ijma literally means "consensus," and within Islamic law it refers to the consensus of Muslim jurists on a particular issue. If it can be demonstrated that all the jurists of a particular generation of Muslims agreed upon an issue, that agreement in and of itself functions as a proof or determination of the law. As can be imagined, demonstrating the universal agreement of jurists is a difficult thing to do, and *ijma* as a result is rarely used as a legal proof, despite its acknowledged validity as a principle (Kamali 2003, 248). The famous jurist al-Shafi'i held that ijma functioned as a proof for the five pillars of the faith: the basic practices of Islam were so widely affirmed as authentic by the early jurists that their very unanimity functioned in this case as a binding consensus. Ijma is rarely invoked outside foundational practices and beliefs.

Some Muslim jurists include custom as a further source of law. This does not refer to an individual's custom but to the custom of a collectivity, to cultural practices and traditions (Kamali 2003, 369). Cultural customs that do not contravene the shari'ah are to be upheld within a court of law; as long as a people's customary practice does not go against God's commands, it can be acknowledged legally. In this sense Islam is not meant to replace a people's culture but rather to refine it in light of the Qur'an. Cultural practices that do not contradict Qur'anic principles are to be respected and valued for their role in shaping and integrating a people's collective life.

Legal Interpretive Traditions

The shari'ah is the divine law that guides Muslim life, as revealed in the Qur'an and the Sunnah. The efforts of jurists to implement the shari'ah practically is known as **fiqh**, or Islamic jurisprudence. The word fiqh means "understanding" and refers to juristic efforts to understand and implement God's commands. The discipline of fiqh has traditionally been carried out within schools of legal thought. During the seventh, eight, and ninth centuries a number of legal schools formed around particularly pious and learned scholars of Islamic law. Students came from around the Muslim world to study with famed jurists in centres such as Medina in Arabia and Kufa in Iraq. Some of these students spent years learning the methodology of a particular jurist, which they then transmitted to others, leading to the formation of a school of legal thought, or *madhab*. Most of these jurisprudential schools died out, leaving only four accepted by Sunnis as orthodox: the Hanafi, Maliki, Shafi'i, and Hanbali, each named after its founder Twelver Shi'as follow the Jafari legal school, which was founded by the sixth Shi'a Imam, Jafar al-Siddiq (d. 765).

Throughout history Muslim empires lent official support and patronage to legal schools, establishing their rulings as normative in different regions of the Muslim world. Furthermore, Muslim missionaries transmitted not only the core beliefs of Islam but also the school of law in which they practised the religion. This has led to the present state of affairs, whereby the surviving legal schools dominate in certain geographical regions.

Fiqh: Islamic jurisprudence.

The Hanafi School The Hanafi madhab is the oldest and the most widespread of the four Sunni legal schools. It is based on the teachings of Abu Hanifah (d. 768), a Persian scholar who lived in Kufa, Iraq. The scholars of Kufa and Basra made liberal use of reason in their legal rulings and so were referred to as "the people of reason" (Kamali 1999, 112). Schooled in this method, Abu Hanifah emphasized the role of qiyas, or analogical reasoning, in jurisprudence. Most Sunni Muslims in the Indian subcontinent and Central Asia, as well as Iraq, Syria, and Turkey, follow the Hanafi school of law. Perhaps because of its flexibility, the Hanafi school was favoured by many Islamic dynasties, including the Ottomans. Ottoman patronage of the Hanafi school in particular helped establish it as the most widely followed.

The Maliki School Besides Kufa, the other early centre of Islamic legal thought was Medina, the city of the Prophet in Arabia. Whereas the scholars in Iraq were known as the people of reason, the scholars of Medina were "the people of tradition." In contrast to the Iraqi use of reason, scholars in Medina relied more exclusively on the hadith to arrive at legal rulings. Malik ibn Anas (d. 795) was the most famous scholar of Medina and the founder of the Maliki school. Although based on a traditionalist methodology, the Maliki school developed a number of quite flexible legal principles, making it one of the more versatile schools of Islamic law (Kamali 1999, 113). Maliki scholars emphasize the importance of public benefit in the law. Legal rulings can be changed if it can be shown that they cause harm, because the law exists to benefit people. The Maliki school is found predominantly in North Africa, in countries such as Morocco, Tunisia, and Algeria.

The Shafi'i School Muhammad ibn Idris al-Shafi'i (d. 820) was a prominent traditionalist and student of Malik. Founder of the Shafi'i school, he attempted to reconcile the approaches of reason and tradition and create a more systematic legal methodology (Kamali 1999, 114). After studying with Malik for ten years in Medina, al-Shafi'i spent time in Iraq, engaging in debate with one of Abu Hanifah's top students, al-Shaybani (d. 805). Following his time in Iraq, al-Shafi'i worked to preserve the traditionalist approach while addressing the arguments of al-Shaybani and the people of reason.

Fatwa: formal legal opinion, or ruling of Islamic law

The result was his groundbreaking *Risala*, the first systematic articulation of the sources of Islamic law. With this work, Shafi'i is credited with completing the development of methodology in Sunni law. Most Muslims in Indonesia and Malaysia, as well as in East Africa, follow the Shafi'i school, and it is also found in parts of the Middle East.

The Hanbali School Shafi'is student Ahmad ibn Hanbal (d. 855) taught in Baghdad and attempted to base his methodology solely on the Qur'an and the hadith, developing the most conservative of the four legal schools. Many Sunnis revere ibn Hanbal for his courage in standing up to the khalifah al-Ma'mun, who attempted to enforce the belief that the Qur'an was not eternal but created by God. Ibn Hanbal suffered imprisonment and torture for maintaining the uncreated nature of the Qur'an (that is, as God's eternal word), a position that would later become orthodox for Sunni Muslims. The Hanbali school inspired some of the most conservative Muslim personalities and schools of thought. For example, Ibn Taymiyyah (d. 1328) was a famous Hanbali jurist who sought to purify Sunni Islam by purging it of Sufi and Shi'ite influences, as well as Jewish and Christian elements. Although the Hanbali school had almost died out by the eighteenth century, much of its drive toward purifying Sunni Islam was revived by Ibn 'Abd al-Wahhab (d. 1792) in the Arabian peninsula. Conservative Wahhabi doctrines continue to form the basic approach of the religious establishment in Saudi Arabia.

The Jafari School Jafar al-Siddiq (d. 765), founder of the Jafari school of thought, was one of Medina's leading scholars and is credited with mastering numerous fields of learning, including law, theology, philosophy, and astronomy. Revered as the sixth Imam by Shi'ite Muslims, al-Siddiq is respected by Sunnis as a pious and knowledgeable figure of early Islamic history, and as a teacher of Abu Hanifah and Malik. Sunni–Shi'ite divisions had not yet crystallized in the eighth century, and later Sunni and Shi'ite authors both revered al-Sadiq as a wise Muslim teacher. However, Shi'ite built upon his intellectual legacy to develop the Jafari school of legal thought. The Jafari school was based on wide-ranging hadith literature collected by the early Shi'ite imams. Though sharing much with the Sunni legal schools, Jafari jurisprudence gives authority to the Shi'ite imams and restricts juristic efforts such as ijtihad to applying the rulings of the imams to new situations.

Although followers of the various legal schools have at times been in conflict with one another, many 'ulema believe that the diversity of schools is a blessing. Each acts as a unique resource of legal thought for Muslims to draw upon in interpreting Islam's sacred sources, the Qur'an and the Sunnah.

Islamic Legal Categories

Traditional fiqh texts divide the law into two main categories: devotional matters and civil transactions. Devotional laws precisely delineate what acts of worship Muslims are to perform and how they are to perform them. Such laws provide Muslims with guidance on how to pray, at what times, when to give *zakat* (charity) and how much to give, when to fast, and what to fast from, and they outline the actions necessary for the pilgrimage to Mecca to be acceptable to God. The schools of law agree on most matters related to devotional practice, though there are small but noticeable differences between them. These include slight differences in the performance of the daily prayer, which Muslims from different parts of the world may notice when praying together. Civil laws, in contrast, regulate social practices and relations. These laws provide rules for commerce, marriage, and family inheritance. It is in regard to civil laws that most jurisprudential differences occur (Kamali 1999, 110).

When making a ruling of Islamic law (**fatwa**), Muslim jurists place a particular action within one of five categories. In theory, any conceivable human action will fall within one of the following five legal categories:

- **Obligatory:** an obligatory act is one that God requires. People are at risk of God's punishment if they fail to perform the act but rewarded if they do. The daily prayer is an action that falls within this category.
- **Recommended:** an act that is rewarded by God if performed but does not entail punishment if missed. Such acts include charity, extra prayers, and fasting outside of the month of Ramadan.

- **Permissible:** actions neither condemned nor mandated by the shari'ah for which neither God's reward nor punishment need be anticipated. Most human actions fall within the category of permissible.
- **Disliked:** actions that are not prohibited though they are to be avoided if possible. One is not punished for disliked actions but is rewarded if they are avoided. Divorce is an example of an act that is permissible but disliked.
- **Prohibited:** actions explicitly forbidden by law that entail legal sanction and divine punishment. Actions that fall within this category of Islamic law include murder, adultery, theft, and intoxication.

Ijtihad

Ijtihad is derived from the root *jahada*, and it literally means "striving" or "self-exertion." Technically ijtihad is the striving made by a jurist to determine the rules of Islamic law based on evidence supplied by the source texts, the Qu'ran and the Sunnah. The individual who performs ijtihad is a *mujtahid*. It is important to note that a mujtahid's ruling is an inference deemed probable based on the sources. Ijtihad is not written in stone, and a particular mujtahid's conclusion can be challenged by another mujtahid also deemed qualified to infer rulings from the sources of the law.

Muslim understandings of the term *ijtihad* derive from the story of Mu'adh ibn Jabal, a story recorded in Abu Dawud's hadith collection. The Prophet Muhammad sent Mu'adh ibn Jabal as a delegate to the region of Yemen. As Mu'adh was leaving for Yemen, the Prophet asked him what the criteria were for administering the region to which he was being sent as deputy. Mu'adh replied, "The Qur'an." The Prophet asked, "And if you find nothing?" Mu'adh replied, "The Sunnah." The Prophet again asked, "And if you find nothing?" Mu'az stated, "Then I will exert myself [*ajtahidu*] to form my own judgment and act according to that." It is reported that the Prophet approved of his answer (Ramadan 2009, 24).

From this tradition, ijtihad became a secondary source for further developing the Islamic legal system. It is the means by which a jurist can make a ruling on an unprecedented case, allowing for expansion of the law to include new phenomena. However, in the development of shari'ah, this ability was relegated only to jurists who met the qualifications for ijtihad. These qualifications included a mastery of Arabic grammar, an exhaustive knowledge of the source texts, and a high level of competence in utilizing legal principle and precedent. In the Sunni tradition, the founders of the four legal schools were deemed to be mujtahids of the first rank.

As the shari'ah was being codified, Islam simultaneously expanded westward through Africa to Andalusia and eastward through Iran to the boundaries of China. This expansion soon turned into an exchange or coalescence of ideas, beliefs, and customs, ultimately dissolving cultural borders while ushering in an age of intercultural knowledge. Such exposure to diverse communities led to the construction of new systematic thinking, newly positioned identities, and pluralistic realities. Paradoxically, this time of great dynamism and transfusion concomitantly became a time of enhanced efforts to homogenize as well as concretize tradition through law. By the end of the eleventh century many jurists and rulers felt an increasing need for a closed system of legalistic knowledge. This consensual concretization of law ultimately secured the legal structures and schools and brought stability to an already unmanageable political empire.

Starting in the twelfth century, some jurists proposed that the "gates of ijtihad" were closed, that there were no longer any mujtahids left in the community. That is, most legal issues had been solved and there was little to gain by developing new methodologies or revisiting old debates. Muslims would be best served by following one of the four schools of law (*taqlid*) without seeking to develop new legal thought. Jurists in favour of taqlid tended to come from the Hanafi and Maliki schools, while the majority of Hanbalis, as well as some Shafi'is, held that ijtihad was a collective obligation, and hence at least one mujtahid was needed at all times within the Muslim community to apply the law to new circumstances. The debate grew during the following centuries, with some jurists arguing that although there were no longer any mujtahids of the calibre of Abu Hanifa or Shafi'i, there did remain jurists qualified to make ijtihad within one of the four schools of thought. As a result of the debate, jurists developed typologies consisting of different levels of ijtihad.

Many Muslims today believe that ijtihad has been sorely neglected in recent centuries and that Muslims need to revive the practice in order to infuse Islam with new dynamism and to address pressing issues facing the global Muslim community. Some reformers use the term *ijtihad* not in the legal, technical sense, as it has been discussed, but as a general term referring to independent critical thinking amongst Muslims looking to reform Islam in light of the challenges of the modern world.

Jihad: Striving in the Path of God

Jihad is one of the most controversial and misunderstood terms in the Islamic faith. It is a word derived from the Arabic root *jahada*, meaning "to strive with great effort." In the context of Islam, jihad means to make an exhaustive effort for a good cause, whether it be combating one's own destructive inclinations, working to alleviate poverty, or defending one's life and home from assault.

The Qur'an commanded the early Muslim community to make jihad, which in some cases meant to fight against those who opposed the existence of the new Islamic religion. Scholars have noted that the Qur'an did not command Muslims to spread their religion through fighting, but rather to defend themselves from those amongst the Arab tribes who sought to destroy the Islamic faith before it could establish itself. It is the historical circumstances to which the Qur'an responds with calls to fight; fighting is not something that it demands against all.

> God does not forbid you to have friendly, mutually respectful relations with those who have not attacked you because of your religion and have not turned you out of your homes. God simply forbids you to take as your patrons those who attack you because of your religion or turn you out of your homes or conspire with others to turn you out of your homes (60:8).
>
> If they incline towards peace, then you incline thereto, and place your trust in God (8:61).

During the medieval era, Muslim jurists divided the world into two categories, or houses: the house of Islam and the house of war. Recently some commentators have depicted this division as an example of the belligerence of medieval Muslim scholars, of their seeing all non-Islamic lands as places of war. However, this division was again a response to historical realities. Historians note that war between and among peoples was the norm in the pre-modern world. As various religious and ethnic groups fought for dominance and conquest, war, sometimes pre-emptive, was the only means by which to secure a safe space for one's people. Commenting on medieval rulings on jihad, Sherman Jackson notes, "the purpose of jihad, in other words, is to provide for the security and freedom of the Muslims in a world that kept them under constant threat" (2007, 401). Recently Muslim scholars have come together to acknowledge that the establishment of international law, human rights, and the freedom to practise one's religion in most countries means that the division of the world into houses of Islam and war no longer applies as it did in the medieval era.

Veiling in Islam

Before the modern era, most Muslim women practised some form of public veiling, whether by covering their hair and wearing loose clothing or, in some countries, covering their entire body. During the first half of the twentieth century, newly formed secular Muslim states such as Turkey banned veiling altogether, and Muslim women in countries such as Egypt and Tunisia began to dress in ways that reflected modern European norms.

Since the Islamic revival of 1960s and 1970s, many Muslim women now wear the *hijab* (head covering) or

Practices

Some Varieties of Muslim Veiling

Hijab—literally meaning "veil," "partition," "separation," or "screen," referring to clothing that Muslim women wear to fulfil their religious requirements of modest dress, namely long and loose-fitting garments. The term is popularly used to describe a scarf that covers the hair and neck, leaving the face exposed. During the advent of Islam it was connected to higher social status among Arabs, Assyrians, Palestinians, Indians, Greeks, Jews, and Syrians. The original hijab-like scarf in Arabia, called a *khimar*, draped loosely over the hair and back, leaving the breasts exposed. Islam modified this custom because of a Qur'anic revelation that requires women to "draw their veils over their bosoms" (24:31). The hijab was instituted in Islam in the mid-eighth century and became widely adapted in the tenth century. It is worn in a variety of ways across the world and according to individual preference. For instance, decorative pins may be used to hold the scarf in place, or layers of bonnet caps may be worn underneath to add colour. In Turkey women tend to wear brightly coloured polyester scarves folded into a triangle shape and pinned behind the neck, with a bonnet cap underneath; in Iran, scarves made of lightweight material tend to be worn loosely draped over the head, leaving the bangs exposed, and tied in a knot below the chin.

Niqab—a veil that covers not only the hair but also the face, except for the eyes. During the early Islamic period the niqab was worn only by the Prophet Muhammad's wives. The practice entered the mainstream Muslim world in the mid-eighth century when Shafi'i and Hanbali schools of jurisprudence ruled that the entire female body, including the face and hands, be covered in front of men other than close kin. It is usually paired with an *abaya*, a long one-piece, loose-fitting cloak-like garment. The niqab is most popular in the Arabian Peninsula, but it is worn by pockets of Muslim women across the globe.

Burqa—most commonly a garment that conceals the body from head to toe in which vision is obtained only through a latticed fabric panel over the eyes. It is popularly associated with the Taliban in Afghanistan, as Afghani women were forced to wear the burqa under their rule; however, it is also worn among women in north-western Pakistan, along the Afghan border. This garment is not mentioned in the Qur'an, nor is it aligned with the rulings of classical scholars in terms of Muslim women's dress. The term *burqa* is sometimes used synonymously with *niqab*, particularly in Pakistan, India, and Bangladesh.

Dupatta or Chunni—a long, lightweight scarf that is part of South Asian traditional dress styles such as *shalwar khameez* (a long, loose tunic paired with loose trousers). Muslim South Asian women often drape it over the hair to fulfil religious requirements for modesty, but traditionally it may be worn around the neck, leaving the hair exposed. Wearing a dupatta over the hair is common practice among non-Muslim South Asian women as well, for varying reasons.

Source: Muhammad AkramNadwi, *al-Muhaddithat: The Women Scholars in Islam* (Oxford: Interface Publications, 2007)

niqab (face veil) as a personal choice rather than as a cultural norm. However, some Muslim states, such as Saudi Arabia and Iran, enforce public veiling. In Iran women are required to cover everything except for their hands and face, whereas in Saudi Arabia women are required to cover up completely when outside the home.

Because veiling stands as one of the most visible signs of Muslim difference from current Western norms, it has become a flashpoint of controversy and a highly charged political symbol, whether or not Muslim women intend their clothing to function that way. It is important to note that modesty is a value for both women and men in Islam, a value that is expressed in a variety of forms. Muslim women today span the spectrum of clothing practices. Women in Egypt, Malaysia, and Australia may dress according to a finely attuned cosmopolitan fashion sense that differs little from non-Muslim styles. Some choose to cover their hair while otherwise dressing according to current fashions. Others may wear a head covering and more traditional full-body dress.

Schools of Islamic law differ in interpreting the Qur'anic command for women to cover themselves when in public. The following two verses from the Qur'an are most frequently cited as sources for the practice of veiling:

> And tell believing women that they should lower their glances, guard their modesty, and not display their charms beyond what is acceptable to reveal; that they should draw their scarves over their necklines . . . (24:31)

> Prophet, tell your wives, your daughters, and women believers to make their outer garments hang low over them so as to be recognized and not insulted: God is most forgiving, most merciful (33:59)

As evident from these verses, the Qur'an commands believing women to draw a cloak about them when leaving the home and to draw their scarves over their breasts. They are commanded to do so to protect themselves from unwanted attention and to be recognized as believers. Some scholars interpret the word used in the Qur'an for covering, *khimar*, to mean a headscarf. The majority of scholars in the Hanafi and Maliki schools of law hold that women should cover everything but their hands and face when in public, basing this interpretation on the above verses as well as on a hadith indicating that women should cover thus following puberty. Some scholars in the Shafi'i school and most in the Hanbali school hold that women should also cover their hands and face while in public.

Practices

Arguments for Wearing the Hijab

- The hijab is a challenge to the "panoptical power of the male patriarchal gaze" (Nye 2003, 81) that controls women's appearances in terms of their bodies, movements, and dress. It counters the dictates of the fashion world, which, dependent as it is on the corporate power of men, seeks to get women to expose rather than cover their flesh. In this way, the hijab is a direct challenge to Western-style patriarchy.
- For Muslim women living in the West or former colonies of Western powers, wearing the hijab may serve as a rejection of Western cultural images of womanhood and promotion of indigenous ones. It may be used as a symbol of resistance to Western cultural hegemony altogether and, additionally, a symbol of Muslim pride.
- Wearing the hijab in the West allows women to challenge negative media and Orientalist depictions of veiled Muslim women. As more Western women enter public roles in all domains, veiled Muslim women who are seen to enjoy liberties in the same way as other women become tokens of Muslim women's freedom rather than their "oppression."
- Wearing the hijab allows women to express their commitment to Islam and carry sacred space into public realms. The spiritual aspect of covering as a means of constant remembrance of the Divine is empowering for women—and particularly helpful in secular societies—and it provides a deep source of strength when facing everyday challenges.
- Wearing the hijab increases the bonds of sisterhood amongst Muslim women, who traditionally enjoy women-only parties and celebrations. At such events they may not only remove their head coverings but also may wear fashionable hairstyles and less restrictive clothing. This, combined with the act of wearing the hijab in public, allows such women to create bonds through shared experiences that are restricted to women only.

Arguments Against Wearing the Hijab

- Wearing the hijab plays to the expectation that it is women who bear responsibility for upholding decency, Islamic values, and morals in society—an expectation that is gaining more currency in the face of the challenge of Western cultural influence. Wearing "proper" Islamic dress indicates women's compliance with such a double standard, a standard that relieves men of their duties to uphold morality alongside women and unfairly places society's burdens on the shoulders of women.

- If the intent behind veiling is to minimize attention to oneself, in non-Muslim societies it actually serves the opposite function: it draws attention to women. Rather than serving a protective function, it may provoke attack because the woman is visibly "other."
- The idea that Muslim women must wear the hijab in order to not be seen in a sexual manner is problematic because it is impossible to desexualize oneself; Islam confirms that sexuality is a part of being human and a gift from God. The idea also contributes to an aversion toward sexuality among Muslims in general, leaving them unprepared to react to it (Fazili 2005, 77).
- Wearing the hijab in order to be unalluring to men places responsibility on women to avoid arousing them rather than encouraging men to practise self-control and "lower their gaze," as verse 24:31 instructs men to do.
- Because the hijab carries a heavy symbolic load, wearing it restricts a woman's individuality and identity development. She unwittingly becomes a banner of whatever the hijab has come to represent symbolically in her cultural and political context.

Reformist or progressive Muslims have argued that the Qur'an does not specify veiling, but rather only commands a general modesty that can take on various forms depending on cultural context. Progressive Muslims further hold that veiling is a practice that reflects Byzantine and other Middle Eastern cultures that predate Islam.

CULTURAL DIVERSITY

Muslims have adapted their practice of Islam to various cultural settings, leading to distinctive forms of Islam in Africa, China, Southeast Asia, Iran, the Middle East, and now Europe and North America. Although Islam is sometimes wrongly imagined to be a vast, monolithic system, it is a belief and practice that takes on a myriad of forms in different cultural settings. The respect for established cultural practice enshrined in Islamic jurisprudence contributed to the flourishing of different cultural forms within the global Islamic community. As a variety of cultural groups came to adopt Islam, new contributions were made to Islamic thought, art, and practice. Many in Europe and North America associate Islam with Arabs, but although Islam originated in Arabia, Arabs today make up only 13 percent of all Muslims, a cultural minority within Islam.

Turkish, Persian, African, Asian, and European peoples have all played important roles in shaping the Islamic tradition, and Islam remains a multicultural faith. This is readily apparent in the remarkable diversity of mosque architecture. For example, the famed mosque of Djenne in Mali is the largest adobe building in the world. It stands in stark contrast to the great mosque of Xi'an, one of China's oldest mosques, which reflects Chinese architectural principles and resembles traditional Chinese temples.

Recently the well-known Swiss author and activist Tariq Ramadan has advocated for a European or Western Islam. In his many books and lectures around the world, Ramadan encourages Muslims to become active citizens of European and North American nations, respecting local laws, learning the language of the country they reside in, remaining loyal to (though not uncritical of) their country, and making positive use of their liberties. He points out that Islam now is *de facto* a European and North American religion, as there are significant Muslim communities in the West. He calls upon both Muslims and others to acknowledge this fact and for Muslims to feel at home, to put down roots in Western countries. According to Ramadan there should be no problem with being both a committed Muslim and a cultural Westerner (Ramadan 2010, 5).

AUTHORITY

Islam became an incredibly contested term in the twentieth and twenty-first centuries. Unlike the Catholic Church, Islam has no pope or Vatican to determine what all Muslims should believe on a certain matter or what Islam says about something. Although the Ottomans attempted to establish a religious leader loosely analogous to the pope with the position of Shaykh-al-Islam, or Grand Scholar of Islam, this position never crystallized in authority the way that leadership of the Western Church did: the top scholar in the Ottoman realm was believed to be knowledgeable but in no way infallible.

Following colonization of much of the Muslim world in the nineteenth and twentieth centuries, the dissolution of the Ottoman caliphate in 1924, and the establishment of modern nation-states, Islam was displaced from its previously unquestioned role as a formative element in social and cultural life. As something that can no longer be taken for granted in many Muslim societies, Islam has become a phenomenon separable from culture, art, and economics. This has led to what some scholars call the objectification of Islam (Eickelman and Piscatori 1996, 38). No longer embedded in a particular culture and set of social norms, Islam emerges as an object of discussion and debate: What is Islam? What does it say about democracy, about the state, or any current issue? (Roy 2004, 153). New forms of discourse emerge to answer these questions, sometimes defining Islam in modern terms as a system, movement, or ideology. In Chapter 1 of this text, Scott T. Kline points out that the meaning of the term *religion* shifts over time. Likewise, the meaning of terms used to designate particular religions changes over time. Wilfred Cantwell Smith observes that reference to Islam as a system or religion—as opposed to a state of individual submission to God—has increased dramatically in Muslim literature since the nineteenth century. Partly in response to Christian missionaries, Muslims have begun to write and talk about Islam in new ways (Smith 1991, 117).

Traditional religious authorities (ʻulema) have in many cases been displaced by the bureaucracies of the modern state. Administrative functions once fulfilled by religious authorities are now the preserve of modern professionals such as lawyers and economists. What is more, the ʻulema's monopoly over religious knowledge has been dissolved as mass literacy and media technology democratize access to sacred texts. This has led to the emergence of new forms of religious authority. Those defining Islam no longer come exclusively from the class of religious scholars trained in the traditional madrasah system. Many leaders of Islamic movements are modern professionals who may have little formal education in traditional Islamic sciences. Using print and other media, these "new religious intellectuals" can circumvent the ʻulema and gain a popular audience outside traditional academic systems (Eickelman and Piscatori 1996, 38).

The ʻulema still retain significant religious authority, however, and many Muslims choose to follow the rulings of a particularly respected and learned jurist such as Yusuf al-Qaradawi, for example, whose popular television show, *Shariʻah and Life*, is watched by many Muslims throughout the Arab world. Many Shiʻite Muslims follow the opinion of a particularly renowned Shiʻite scholar such as the Grand Ayatollah Ali al-Sistani in Iraq. Though he does not have a state-appointed position, al-Sistani is widely recognized by other Shiʻite leaders in Iraq and Iran, and by Shiʻites throughout the world, as the most knowledgeable of ayatollahs. He continues to have immense influence among Twelver Shiʻites. On his official website (www.sistani.org) al-Sistani addresses questions sent to him by followers from a variety of countries on issues ranging from social justice to whether animal hair on one's clothing affects the validity of prayer. Through his many students, who themselves have established religious schools throughout the world, his thought permeates much contemporary Shiʻite life. In general, within Muslim countries such as Iran, Pakistan, and Saudi Arabia, the ʻulema continue to play important roles in terms of both religious authority and political influence.

IDENTITY

Trends in authority are reflected in trends in identity. With the development of postcolonial modern nation-states in the Muslim world and the decline of traditional religious authority, religion ceases to have a necessary relationship with a particular society or territory. Religion can no longer be simply assumed as the foundation of cultural, political, and social life in a certain geographic region. Furthermore, as Muslims settle in places such as Europe and North America, their religion ceases to be embedded in a particular social context; hence, like other religions, Islam is "deterritorialized" in the modern world (Roy 2004, 38). Religious practice cannot be assumed as a social norm but becomes an individual choice, and is hence frequently grounded more in identity than in society.

Muslims are drawing from a range of sources and values to forge new identities that engage with tradition while opening to contemporary social changes. Especially in Europe and North America, where Islamic norms are neither publicly enforced nor culturally predominant, Muslims negotiate their place in culturally diverse societies and make individual choices about which elements of their Islamic identity to incorporate into their lives (Roy 2004, 148–53). Networks of like-minded friends, Muslim teachers who post lectures on the Internet, weekend intensive courses on Islamic law and spirituality, and annual conferences featuring popular preachers can all play an important role in shaping Muslim identities in places such as Canada and the United States.

ISLAMIC PRACTICE

Compared to Christianity, with its early creedal councils that sought to establish correct belief (orthodoxy), some scholars argue that the Islamic tradition has shown more interest in correct practice (orthopraxy). Correct belief has in fact been an important topic of debate in Islamic history, and as in other faiths, belief and practice are intimately bound to one another in Islam. This relationship is best exemplified by the five pillars of Islam, the first of which lays the foundation of belief, while the following four express this belief in practice. We examine these pillars as examples of what Kline refers to as the performative aspects of a religion. He describes how religious practices mark time and space; note how the following practices relate to these basic categories.

The Five Pillars

Shahadah: Statement of Faith

Islam's first pillar is the statement of faith, or **shahadah**—"There is no god but God and Muhammad is the Messenger of God." *Shahadah* means "to bear witness," and by making the statement of faith a Muslim bears witness that God is the only one worthy of worship, all other gods being illusory; that Muhammad is an authentic prophet of God; and that the revelation he brought—the Qur'an—is an authoritative guide for human life. The first part of the shahadah is the quintessential expression of tawhid—belief in God's oneness—while the second part establishes the reality of God's guidance to humanity as conveyed by prophets and messengers sent by God. This statement hence acts as a basis for all Islamic practice. Someone who wishes to become a Muslim need only state the shahadah, usually in front of an imam or two adult Muslims. The shahadah is not only recited when a person converts to Islam, it is whispered in a newborn baby's ear, is part of the call to prayer, and is recited by Muslims in times of distress or shock or simply when seeking inner peace. As such, the statement of faith, though an expression of belief, is also a practice woven throughout everyday life.

Shahadah: the Islamic statement of faith: "There is no god but God, and Muhammad is the Messenger of God."

Salat: Daily Prayer

Like Jews and Christians, Muslims make spontaneous informal prayers to God, called *du'a*. Muslims also perform a set of formal prayers each day, known as the *salat*. The image of hundreds of Muslims performing salat, standing and bowing together at a mosque or in a city street, is one of the most recognizable depictions of Islam in practice. The salat consists of ritual worship performed five times a day, at daybreak, at noon, during the mid-afternoon, at sunset, and during the evening. The exact times of prayer are based on the cycle of the sun through the day and are codified in Islamic law, based on reports of when the Prophet and his companions prayed.

The Qur'an mentions salat frequently, commanding its performance more than any other action. After the statement of faith, the daily prayer is the most important element of Islamic practice. It is obligatory for all adult Muslims to make the daily prayers. Before prayer, Muslims perform a ritual ablution that involves washing the hands, face, feet, and forearms. After sexual intercourse, Muslims are required to perform a complete ablution, which involves washing the entire body, before they can perform the salat.

Following the ablution, which brings Muslims into a state of ritual purity, the prayer can be performed. Although the salat can be performed alone, at home, at work, or at school, it is deemed praiseworthy for Muslims (especially men) to pray collectively in the mosque. The salat involves a set number of cycles, each of which involves standing while reciting the Qur'an, then bowing, prostrating, and sitting. This cycle of movement is repeated twice during the prayer at daybreak, four times during the noon and mid-afternoon prayers, three times during the sunset prayer, and four times during the evening. Each day Muslims leave what Mircea Eliade called "profane time" and enter into a "sacred time" set aside for prayer and contemplation. Besides the first chapter of the Qur'an, the Fatihah, Muslims usually recite short chapters from the end of the Qur'an during salat. The prayer is performed facing toward the Ka'aba in Mecca.

While it is recommended that Muslims perform the salat collectively when they can, it is obligatory for men to attend communal prayer in the mosque on Fridays. The Friday prayer is held during midday. Besides the prayer itself, an imam delivers a short sermon, usually based on a few verses of the Qur'an and/or hadith. The Friday prayer in local mosques is often well attended, providing an opportunity for Muslims to maintain community ties. Regardless of social status or age, Muslims wash and pray side by side as a community. Local fundraisers such as bake sales or event promotions can sometimes follow the Friday prayer.

Sawm: Fasting During the Month of Ramadan

Like salat, fasting during the month of Ramadan is obligatory for all adult Muslims, or at least those healthy enough to perform the fast. Muslims fast from dawn to sunset, abstaining from food, water, smoking, and sexual activity during the day. Ramadan is the holy month in which the Qur'an is believed to have been first revealed. Besides fasting, throughout Ramadan Muslims are encouraged to refrain from negative speech and actions, to give to charity, to read the Qur'an, and to pray during the evening. Fasting is thought to be not only cleansing for the body but also conducive to increasing devotion and raising awareness of the plight of those without enough food to eat. Ramadan is undoubtedly a time of self-discipline, but it is also a joyous month. Following sunset, people frequently meet with friends and family for festive meals together. Overall, Ramadan is a highly social time, bringing families and communities together in both prayer and celebration.

The Islamic calendar is based on the lunar cycle: a year according to the Islamic calendar is 354 days, whereas a solar year is 365. Because the lunar year is eleven days shorter than the solar year, the months of a lunar calendar occur about eleven days earlier each solar year. This means that the month of Ramadan occurs at varying times of the year, cycling through the entire solar year over a thirty-three-year period. For Canadian Muslims, the time of year in which Ramadan falls can dramatically affect how challenging the month of fasting is. In northern countries the days can be quite short during winter months and exceptionally long during the summer. Thus Canadian Muslims may face a relatively easy month of fasting should Ramadan fall in December, as daylight rarely lasts for more than eight hours during this time of year. In contrast, if Ramadan falls somewhere in June or July, Muslims may need to fast for up to eighteen hours each day. For Muslims in the Far North, where during the height of summer the sun may not set at all, scholars of Islamic law have allowed the fast to be governed by the daylight hours of a more southerly region in order to avoid undue hardship.

Zakat: Almsgiving

General acts of charity are recommended in Islam, based on numerous Qur'anic verses calling upon believers to give of their wealth to the poor, orphans, and widows (that is, those disadvantaged in society). Zakat, however, is a required charitable donation to be given annually. The amount of zakat to be given is calculated as a percentage of the property or profit one has acquired during the year. Depending on the nature of one's wealth and how it was acquired, the amount ranges from 2.5 to 10 percent of one's profit (Murata and Chittick 1994, 16). *Zakat* literally means "purification," and by giving it, Muslims believe that they purify their wealth. Although private ownership is legally binding in Islamic law, private wealth must be purified by public giving. Traditionally, state authorities in Muslim regions collected zakat for use in social welfare projects. Today many Muslims, especially in Western countries such as Canada, voluntarily give zakat to charitable organizations or directly to those in need.

Hajj: Pilgrimage to Mecca

Muslims are required to make the pilgrimage to Mecca at least once during their adult lives if they are able. The pilgrimage is to the Ka'aba, the house of God. Muslims believe that Adam first built the Ka'aba after the fall from the garden. It was rebuilt by Abraham and his son Ishmael, and finally reconsecrated by Muhammad. The

The Ka'aba in Mecca
Source: ayazad/ Shutterstock

Ka'aba for Muslims is hence a symbol of worship of the one true God, beginning with the first human and revived by the prophets throughout history. Although Muslims trace the practice of pilgrimage to Abraham, pre-Islamic Arabs made the pilgrimage to the Ka'aba to worship the various deities it housed. The Prophet Muhammad maintained much of the form of the pre-Islamic pilgrimage but modified it to reflect the story of Abraham and Islamic monotheism.

Before entering the sanctuary surrounding the Ka'aba, the Grand Mosque, pilgrims enter into a state of purity, symbolized by the seamless white garments they wear. Men shave their heads and trim their nails, and women cut off a few locks of hair. After voicing their intention to complete the hajj ritual, pilgrims begin circumambulating the Ka'aba seven times. Following this, they move between the hills of Safah and Marwah outside of Mecca, representing Hagar's search for water for herself and her son Ishmael. After visiting the site of the Prophet's last sermon, Mount Arafat, pilgrims stone the three pillars at Mina, which represent the devil. The completion of the pilgrimage is marked by the sacrifice of a sheep, cow, or lamb, representing Abraham's sacrifice of a sheep in place of his son Ishmael.

The hajj can be an important turning point in a Muslim's life, marking a spiritual rebirth. The pilgrim returns to friends and family purified of sin. Returning pilgrims are often referred to respectfully as *hajji*, one who has completed a pillar of the faith and who strives to maintain the purity gained from the experience.

The Life Cycle

Immediately following a child's birth, Muslim parents recite the *adhan,* or call to prayer, in the baby's ear. Seven days after the child is born, the official birth ceremony is celebrated with friends and family. Usually on this day the child is given a name, its head is shaved, and an animal is sacrificed in thanks to God (Nigosian 2004, 120). The meat is then shared with guests and distributed to the poor. Muslims traditionally give names that reflect their faith, such as the names of prophets—Muhammad being the most popular—or important figures of the early Muslim community, such as Abu Bakr and Ali, or the Prophet's wives, such as Khadijah, Aisha, and Zainab. Other popular names include those that express a person's servanthood to God, such as Abdullah (servant of God), Abdurahman (servant of the All-Merciful), and Abdul Hakim (servant of the Wise). According to the Islamic tradition, God has ninety-nine beautiful names, and Muslims can be named as servants to any of those names. However, it is not mandatory that Muslims be given a religious name, as long as the name does not have a meaning contradictory to the ethos of Islam.

The next important milestone Muslims recognize is puberty. In Islamic law, puberty marks the transition from childhood to the age of responsibility. After reaching puberty, Muslim youth are believed to be accountable to God for their religious obligations: they must begin to perform the salat, fast during the month of Ramadan, and respect the laws governing adult life. Males are required to undergo circumcision. According to some schools of Islamic law, it is recommended that females also undergo a form of circumcision, though not all agree on this. It is important to note that female circumcision ranges from removal of part of the clitoral hood and/or clitoris to the extremes of female genital mutilation (FGM) practiced in certain parts of Africa (not always by Muslims). FGM predates Islam in Africa, and Muslim jurists around the world have made numerous legal rulings prohibiting it. However, the practice persists amongst some East African peoples, despite official religious opposition.

The Prophet reportedly said that "marriage is half of faith." Unlike the Christian, Buddhist, and Hindu traditions, Muslims did not establish celibate religious orders. Following the Prophet's example of marriage and the Qur'an's repudiation of monasticism, the vast majority of Muslims marry. Sexual activity is prohibited for Muslims outside of marriage. Within marriage, however, Muslims believe that God rewards men and women for sharing sexual love. Islamic law permits men to marry up to four wives, with the stipulation that they can do so only if they maintain fair and just treatment of all their wives. Some contemporary Muslim scholars believe this makes polygamy an option that few men would be able to ethically pursue, and most Muslim marriages are monogamous.

Wedding ceremonies are opportunities for families and communities to celebrate the joining of a couple as they enter a new stage in their lives. Wedding customs differ widely amongst Muslims, based on culture and ethnicity. Lebanese Muslims, for example, often perform a popular Arab folk dance known as the dabke at weddings. In Arabic, *dabke* means "stamping the feet," and it is a line dance that indeed involves rhythmic stamping. Muslims from Pakistan, India, and Bangladesh share many wedding customs with Hindus, reflecting the wider Indian cultural milieu. For example, like other Indian brides, Indian Muslim women usually wear a red sari during the marriage ceremony and have elaborate patterns drawn on their hands using a dye, a practice known as mehndi.

Within the Christian tradition, marriage is one of the seven sacraments. According to Islamic law, however, marriage is a legal contract that requires only the consent of both parties, witnesses to the contract, and a dowry or gift from the husband to the bride (Nigosian 2004, 121). An imam performs the marriage ceremony, which is usually quite simple. Although Islam permits divorce, it is regarded as a last resort and something to be avoided if at all possible. According to a hadith, Satan loves nothing more than to split a couple joined in marriage. Another hadith states that "of all the permitted acts, divorce is the most hateful to God." The Qur'an exhorts Muslim men to "live with your wives on a footing of kindness and equity. If you dislike them, it may be that you dislike something in which God has placed great good" (4:19). Although marriage within Islam is a legal contract between two parties, its important spiritual meaning and role in establishing the family is strongly emphasized.

Like marriage, death is something Muslims tend to approach with simplicity and practicality. Following death, a Muslim is immediately prepared for burial, which ideally happens as soon as possible and as close as possible to where the person died. Muslims avoid autopsies or any undue disturbance of the body unless it is necessary. As burial closely follows death, embalming is usually avoided. Family members, close friends, or community members wash the body in a similar manner to the ritual ablution before prayer. The body is then wrapped in a white sheet and transported to the mosque for the funeral prayer. It is seen as meritorious for Muslims to attend the funeral of another Muslim so they can pray for God's mercy upon the soul of the deceased. Following the simple funeral prayer, the body is transported to the cemetery for burial. Usually burials are attended exclusively by male friends and relatives. At the cemetery, the body is buried facing Mecca.

The family of the deceased observe a three-day period of mourning, though widows observe a period of waiting lasting four months and ten days. During this time the widow is not to remarry or to interact with men whom she could legally marry. Following this period, however, the widow is free to pursue another marriage if she chooses.

Festivals

Muharram

On the first day of Muharram, the first month of the Islamic calendar, Muslims celebrate the New Year. For Shiʻite Muslims, this is a particularly important time of year. The New Year marks the beginning of ten days of mourning the martyrdom of Ali and his two sons Hassan and Hussein. During this period devout Shiʻites abstain from shaving or bathing, wear clothes symbolizing their mourning, and maintain a simple diet. The commemoration of the martyrdom of Hussein at Karbala, Iraq, is known as 'Ashura, and it is the emotional pinnacle of the ten-day period. Shiʻites form processions through their neighbourhoods to publicly lament Hussein's martyrdom. During the reenactment of the drama of Hussein's martyrdom at Karbala, some of those involved flog themselves with chains, their blood symbolizing their commitment to stand by the grandsons of the Prophet.

Eid al-Fitr

The feast marking the end of Ramadan is known as Eid al-Fitr. After a month of disciplined fasting during daylight hours, this eid (feast) is a particularly joyous occasion. Celebrants wear their best, give alms to the needy, visit friends and family, and share specially prepared sweets. It is known as the Small Festival in comparison to the Great Festival, Eid al-Adha.

Eid al-Adha

The Eid al-Adha, or Feast of Sacrifice, is also referred to as the Great Festival, Eid al-Kabir. This festival commemorates the story of Abraham's sacrifice of a sheep instead of his son Ishmael. Following the Bible, Jews and Christians believe that Abraham was commanded by God to sacrifice his son Isaac. The story of Abraham as told in the Qur'an, however, holds that Abraham was commanded to sacrifice his son Ishmael. Apart from the difference over which son Abraham was supposed to sacrifice, the narrative structure of the story is almost identical in the Bible and the Qur'an. To commemorate Abraham's sacrifice of a sheep, Muslims sacrifice an animal, usually a goat, but sometimes a cow or camel, depending on what is available and affordable. The animal is placed with its head toward Mecca and then is ritually slaughtered (Nigosian 2004, 126). The meat is divided up into three parts: one part for family, one for friends and neighbours, and one for the poor or needy. The festival is a key element of the hajj pilgrimage to Mecca, where pilgrims celebrate it in the valley of Mina, the site where, according to Islamic tradition, Abraham's original sacrifice took place.

Mawlid al-Nabi

The mawlid, or Mawlid al-Nabi, is the traditional celebration of the Prophet Muhammad's birthday. Mawlid celebrations can include the recitation of poems praising the Prophet, communal prayers, Qur'an recitation, and sometimes a feast, music, dance, and procession (Schussman 1998, 214). The first official mawlid celebrations were held during Shiʻite Fatimid rule in Egypt in the eleventh century, with only the ruling elite participating. Popular manifestations of the mawlid emerged in the twelfth and thirteenth centuries in Syria and Egypt and soon spread through the entirety of the Muslim world, both Shiʻite and Sunni (Schussman 1998, 216). *Mawlid* means "birthday," and Sunnis celebrate not only the Prophet's birthday but also the birthdays of Sufi saints. Shiʻites further celebrate the birthdays of the Prophet's family members, including his daughter Fatima, son-in-law Ali, and grandsons Hassan and Hussein.

Sunni religious authority in particular has had an ambiguous relationship with the Mawlid al-Nabi. Some traditional authorities adamantly opposed mawlid celebrations while others sanctioned them. For example, today in Saudi Arabia the mawlid continues to be forbidden by the official religious establishment.

Mawlid celebrations vary to a great degree depending on social context. In Java, the Garebeg Malud is a state ceremony that connects the Javanese sultanate of Yogyakarta with the Prophet Muhammad (Woodward 1991, 109). In India and Pakistan, mawlid celebrations at Sufi lodges and mosques include *qawwali* (devotional) music performances and a large free meal known as a *langar*. Like the popular ʻurs festivals held in honour of a venerated saint, mawlids in India and Pakistan are truly festive affairs, marked by music, dance, feasting, and coloured lights strewn about the mosques. In Tehran, the capital city of Iran, most mawlid celebrations (in Farsi, *mowludi*) are held by groups of women in private homes. In Egypt, mawlids, especially those celebrating the birthdays of saints, fall into the carnival genre. Permeated by a sense of the ludic, Egyptian mawlid celebrations can involve colourful processions of boats, people, or cars. Inversion is encouraged, and sometimes men dress up as women. Such mawlids include public shouting, spectacles such as horse racing and stick-fighting, and an ethos of public "hilarity" (Hoffman 1995, 109–12). However, Mawlid al-Nabi celebrations held in mosques naturally tend to be more sedate and liturgical in nature.

For many Turkish Muslims in Canada, the mawlid celebration is taken for granted as part of their yearly cycle of celebrations, reflecting both their faith and ethnic heritage. The Turkish religious tradition includes a long history of mawlid celebration, with famed poets such as Yunus Emre praising the mawlid as efficacious for the believer's salvation. Most celebrations of the Prophet's birthday by Turkish Muslims take place in local mosques and include prayer, recitations of poetry, musical performances, and of course food.

THE CANADIAN CONTEXT

Diversity of Muslims in Canadian History

Canada began to receive Muslim immigrants in the late nineteenth century. The first national census, in 1871, reported thirteen Muslims, who were mainly of Middle Eastern origin. By 1901 there were about 300 to 400 Muslim immigrants in Canada, equally divided between Turks and Syrian Arabs. By 1931 the number had risen to 645. Both the onset of the First World War and the Canadian government's attempts to restrict immigration from Asia disrupted the rate of Muslim immigration to Canada. During the war, many Turks were classified as "enemy aliens" and were forced to return to Turkey.

In the early period (late nineteenth to early twentieth centuries), Muslims did not migrate to Canada for religious reasons but rather for economic betterment. The earliest Muslims in Canada—those who arrived at the turn of the century—were mainly males with no capital and little formal education; many of them started out as unskilled labourers or itinerant peddlers. They gravitated toward Canada's urban centres, such as Toronto and Montreal. Through hard work and reciprocal support they managed to broaden their entrepreneurial activities and improve their economic status. The first mosque built in Canada, in 1938, was the Al-Rashid Mosque in Edmonton, Alberta. In 1951, before the unprecedented influx of Muslim immigrants in the 1960s, Canada had 2,000 to 3,000 Muslim residents.

In the second half of the twentieth century, Muslim immigration was characterized by a desire for educational, political, and social freedom. Canada's postwar Muslim community was extremely diverse: it included immigrants from many different parts of the Arab world, such as the Middle East (Jordan, Syria, Lebanon, Palestine, and Egypt), Pakistan, Bangladesh, Turkey, Iran, Eastern Europe, East Africa, and the Caribbean. The number of Muslims in Canada began to increase in the 1950s in particular because of the violence surrounding the partition of India and Pakistan. The South Asian Muslims who arrived in the 1950s, '60s, and '70s were largely educated people with advanced academic degrees. Many of them found work in the professions, at universities, and in the civil service. Political developments in the 1970s brought Muslims of the Ismaili and Ithna Ashariyyah sects to Canada. A large cohort of Shiʻa Imami Ismaili Muslims (generally referred to as Ismailis) came to Canada from Uganda in 1972 after being expelled from the country by its dictator, Idi Amin; they were invited to migrate by Prime Minister Pierre Trudeau. Most of the Ismailis who came to Canada were of South Asian descent.

For most Muslim communities in Canada, their first concern was the building of mosques and Islamic centres in order to stimulate Muslim community life. For example, the Shiʻa Imami Ismaili Muslim community has created a variety of institutes in Ontario such as the Centre for Pluralism in Ottawa and the Ismaili Museum of Art in Toronto. In 1968 the Islamic Circle of North America (ICNA) was established in Montreal. At first the group began with regular meetings to study the Qur'an and hadith, but it has evolved

PEOPLE & PLACES

Demographics

- In 1981 it was reported that 98,165 Muslims were living in Canada. In 1991 Statistics Canada reported that there were 253,265 Muslims living in Canada, and as of 2001, 579,640 Muslims lived in Canada—a 128.9 percent increase.
- In 2001 Muslims comprised about 2 percent of the Canadian population.
- Ontario's Muslim population more than doubled between 1991 and 2001, from 145,600 to 352,500.
- Ontario's Muslim population comprised 3.1 percent of Ontario's total population in 2001.
- Muslims in Ontario accounted for 61 percent of Canadian Muslims in 2001.
- Of the 1.8 million immigrants who came to Canada in the 1990s, Muslims accounted for 15 percent. The median age of these immigrants was 28 years old.
- Montreal's Muslim population doubled between 1991 and 2001, climbing to 100,200 in 2001 and comprising 3 percent of the city's population.
- There are more than eighty mosques in Canada.
- Muslims of South Asian origin are the largest Muslim ethnic group, comprising 35.1 percent of all Muslims living in Canada. Muslims of Arab origin are the next largest group.
- The number of Muslims in Canada who are of European or North American background is less than 2 percent.
- In Canada, the number of Muslims of African background is small, whereas in the United States, African-Americans along with South Asians are the largest ethnic groups.
- The 2001 census reported that there were 33,725 Somalis in Canada. In 1995 there were about 30,000 Somalis living in Toronto, whereas in the early 1980s there was no Somali community there at all.
- There are currently about 75,000 Ismaili Muslims in Canada. They presently hail mainly from Afghanistan, Iran, and Pakistan, with some having arrived in Canada after sojourns in such African countries as Uganda and Tanzania.

since then into an organization that organizes *da'wa* (propagation) field trips, distributes Islamic literature, and is involved in charity. ICNA was established formally in 1971 as a non-sectarian, non-ethnic organization that stresses democratic and peaceful means to promote Islamic values within the North American context. In the early 1970s the Canadian branch of the Islamic Society of North America (ISNA) became active, holding conferences and promoting and building mosques and Islamic schools. ISNA is the first North American Muslim organization to appoint a woman as its executive director: Ingrid Mattson, a Canadian Muslim convert and professor of Islamic studies at the American University of Hartford in Connecticut.

The majority of Muslims are members of the Sunni branch of Islam; however, there are significant numbers of Shi'ite Muslims. According to one estimate, the proportion of Shi'as is as high as 30 percent in North America. One of the largest Shi'ite Islamic centres, the Jaffari Islamic Centre, is based in Toronto, and its congregation is composed mostly of Ithna Ashariyyah, or Twelver, Shi'ites.

It is said that the single most important characteristic of Canada's postwar Muslim community was its diversity, because it would later have implications for the cohesion of the Canadian Muslim community. With such diversity, it is interesting to note that there is no unified voice for Islam in Canada. Unlike many other religions, Islam is not formally hierarchal and has no centralized authority; there is no leader whose word is accepted as law, and imams can only offer their own analyses to their congregations.

Because there is no unified voice in Canada, there are many Muslim advocacy organizations that claim and compete to be the voice for Canadian Muslims. Two of the most frequently profiled Muslim organizations in Canadian newspapers since 2001 are the Canadian Islamic Congress (CIC) and the Muslim Canadian Congress (MCC). The CIC was incorporated in Kitchener, Ontario, in 1997 and is described on its website (under "Objectives and Purpose") as "the independent voice of Canada's Muslims." It aspires to be the non-sectarian voice of Canadian Muslims (Sunni as well as Shi'a) on matters of shared concern such as combating anti-Islamic bias in the media, counteracting discrimination, and advancing Muslim participation in public life. The MCC was formed just a few years after the CIC, in December 2001—three months after the events of September 11. With its office in the multicultural metropolis of Toronto, the founders of the MCC sought to present a different face of Canadian Muslims and, as described in the "Who We Are" page on their website, to give voice to the concerns of those "who are not represented by existing organizations," particularly of those who embrace the vision of a "progressive, liberal, pluralistic, democratic, and secular society." To this day the MCC continues to define its mission in opposition to most existing Muslim organizations, which it pointedly characterizes as "either sectarian or ethnocentric," opposed to modernity, and intolerant of diversity.

The irreducible diversity of Canadian Muslims poses serious challenges for religious leadership. At times this had led to tensions within congregations and between generations. Because the vast majority of imams immigrated here from Muslim-majority countries, their training can be at odds with the reality of the secular and modern culture of Canada. Many younger Muslims who were themselves born in Canada are seeking a newer generation of leaders to whom they can relate.

Sufism in Canada

Canada is home to a variety of Sufi orders, including the Chishti, Halveti-Jerrahi, Qadiri, Nimatullahi, Naqshbandi-Haqqani, and Shadhili, as well as the Sufi Order International. The first Sufi order established in Canada and the United States was Hazrat Inayat Khan's (d. 1927) Sufi Order of the West, now called the Sufi Order International. After arriving in America in 1910, Inayat Khan taught Sufism as a universal spirituality accessible to all. His order attracted mostly Westerners, and today it maintains active branches in cities such as Toronto and New York. Following the reform of immigration laws in the mid-1960s, both Canada and the United States opened their doors to immigrants from around the world, not just from Europe. Sufi teachers were able to settle in North America and, with new communities of Muslim immigrants, they established more traditional Islamic Sufi orders in both countries.

Sufism can be controversial for some Muslims, and anti-Sufi movements remain influential in certain Muslim quarters. As a result, Canadian mosques can be places of contestation over the Islamic authenticity of Sufism, and some Muslims oppose holding Sufi rituals in their mosques. Sufis have established their own mosques where they can perform their devotions without opposition while welcoming any interested Muslims. Further, some Sufi organizations, most notably the Naqshbandi-Haqqani order, have responded to attacks on the legitimacy of Sufism in Islam, arguing that Sufis best represent orthodox Islamic teachings.

Sufis in general have a reputation for tolerance, respect for other religions, and openness to new cultural contexts. Sufi orders have proven attractive to Westerners, and many non-Muslims come to Islam through the spirituality, art, and music of Sufism. As such, some scholars perceive Sufis as potential bridge-builders between Muslims and non-Muslims in the West and around the world.

Some Sufi centres are associated with a particular ethnic community, such as Turkish, South Asian, or Iranian. These centres function not only as places of spiritual practice but also as sites where particular cultural festivals can be celebrated, a community's ethnic language can be shared, and intra-community networking can happen. Many Sufi orders, although they have branches in Canada, are part of transnational worldwide organizations, with branches in the United States, Europe, the Middle East, Africa, and Asia.

Canadian Muslims and the Post 9/11 Context

For most Canadians, the tragic events of 9/11 in Washington, D.C., and New York, 3/11 in Madrid, and 7/7 in London provide a context of relevance for interest in Islam. Many questions have been raised about Islam and Muslims, especially within North

America: Why have a significant minority of Muslims accepted radical teachings? What are these teachings, and how can they be counteracted? Who is the authentic voice for Muslims in Canada?

Among non-Muslims as well as among Muslims in the post 9/11 context, it seems that everyone has become a stakeholder in the future of Islam and that everyone is attempting to frame or reframe the discursive categories within which Islamic interpretation and politics are discussed. Each label for categorizing "desirable" types of Muslims and Islamic interpretations (whether defined by self-identified groups of Muslim interpreters or by non-Muslim observers) seems to have a ready counterpart category for branding adversaries as undesirable others. Conservative Muslims compete with progressive Muslims for air time as traditionalist Muslims denounce self-hating Muslims and Islamophobes. Meanwhile, moderate Muslims challenge militant Muslims, putative Muslim refuseniks denounce Muslim extremists, and would-be reformists repudiate apologists who refuse to embrace the need for change. There are too many binaries—liberal versus conservative, moderate versus militant, orthodox versus heretical. Everyone, it seems, has a party line about who the good Muslims and the bad Muslims are. Sadly, many of these dichotomies distort as much as they reveal, shrouding the complex opinions, beliefs, and sentiments of perceived adversaries with simple labels based on superficial preconceptions and oversimplifications.

From the multiple opposing agendas of Islamic interpreters emerge contradictory messages on a wide range of subjects. At a time of heightened insecurity and acute perceptions of threat, everyone has arrived at the conclusion that their identity and values are under attack—hence the tendency to represent the stakes as total (for example, as a struggle to save the "real" Islam, whether it is defined in staunchly traditional or authoritatively progressive terms) and to aspire to monopolization of public discourse by delegitimizing adversaries.

Because of the ongoing negotiations for construction of a contemporary Canadian Muslim identity, a variety of different debates have emerged in the Canadian post-9/11 context. From the arrests of Muslim youth in Toronto on charges of "home-grown terror" to debates over Muslim faith-based arbitration in Ontario; Quebec's questions about "reasonable accommodation" for minority Muslim communities and the controversial Herouxville "Life Standard's Charter"; the banning of the hijab in soccer and the niqab at the voting polls; and the popularity of CBC's *Little Mosque on the Prairie*—all these have put Canadian Muslims in the media spotlight.

The Toronto 18

Since June 2006, when eighteen Muslim males were arrested on terrorist charges in the Greater Toronto Area, the Canadian media have followed the case and the various responses to it. The arrests and trials created a heightened awareness of security concerns in a post-9/11 context in Canada. It also increased what Juan Cole describes as "Islam anxiety"—a general sense of unease and fear of Islam and Muslims (2009, 115). As a consequence, the construction of contemporary Canadian Muslim identity has become politically charged.

Such extreme cases, though sensational and widely reported, do not reflect wider Muslims' understandings of their place in Canadian society, as illustrated when 120 Canadian imams signed a statement condemning terrorism in July 2005. It is fair to say that opposition to terrorism is one area in which most Canadian Muslims are united. Notably, Imam Syed Sohrawardy, founder of the Islamic Supreme Council of Canada, established Muslims Against Terrorism in Calgary in 1998. In 2008 he also led a Multifaith Walk Against Violence, travelling more than 6,500 kilometres across Canada.

Shari'ah Debate in Ontario

The origins of the Ontario shari'ah controversy lie in the 1991 Ontario Arbitration Act (OAA), which was created to allow private commercial businesses to adjudicate disputes outside provincial courts. The legislation was intended to alleviate the pressure on an already overwhelmed civil court system. This development, reflecting as it did growing interest in alternative dispute resolution in many sectors of society, provided impetus for religious groups (including Jewish, Catholic, Muslim, and Aboriginal communities) to convene their own independent arbitration tribunals for settling civil disputes. Supporters of this initiative argued that the provisions of the OAA were sufficiently accommodating, and that settling civil disputes out of court in accordance with the values and norms of specific communities would benefit individuals while further reducing the load on the provincial court system. The request for religiously based alternative arbitration systems was approved and became the basis for practice by Christian as well as Jewish groups. There was little controversy until 2003, when the Islamic Institute for Civil Justice (ICCJ) announced its own Muslim religious tribunals under the OAA. A number of responses from Muslim organizations to op-ed writers across the country soon added to the debate, with many critics articulating concern that the Province of Ontario was about to grant official legitimacy to Islamic shari'ah law and thereby encourage Islamic movements throughout the world.

Because of public concern about the issue, Ontario Premier Dalton McGuinty commissioned the province's former attorney general, Marion Boyd, to conduct an investigation into whether shari'ah courts should be included in the OAA. In her final report, titled *Dispute Resolution in Family Law: Protecting Choice, Promoting Inclusion* (2004), Boyd recommended that arbitration should continue as an alternative dispute resolution option, and that religious law, including shari'ah, should continue to be allowed for adjudication of civil disputes. Boyd argued that Muslims as well as Jews and other religious groups should be allowed to convene arbitration tribunals so long as a number of recommended safeguards were put in place and observed. She recommended among other things that the OAA be amended to specifically include religious mediators and arbitrators in a list of professionals who were both entitled to act as third parties and obligated to report the needs of all parties being represented. In September 2005, however, McGuinty's government went against the recommendations of the report and banned all religious arbitration.

At the heart of the shari'ah debate was the protection of Muslim women. Supporters and opponents of shari'ah arbitration both characterized Muslim women as especially vulnerable members of the larger community, albeit for opposite reasons. For Muslim supporters of faith-based practices, adding religious arbitration to the mix of options for settling disputes offered more rather than less hope for protecting women from exploitation than reliance on civil law alone. Potential abuses would be minimized because women could still appeal decisions to the formal legal system, and because Canadian-trained lawyers as well as women and elders from the Muslim community would be represented on arbitration panels. Such judgments were not shared by shari'ah detractors. Central to the dissenters' views was a conviction that public endorsement of shari'ah-based arbitration posed a very real threat to the rights of women in the Canadian Muslim community. Opponents argued that women and other vulnerable parties would be coerced into participating in shari'ah arbitration. They demanded that Marion Boyd's review be suspended and the matter be referred to the Ontario Court of Appeal.

Among the more prominent critics of shari'ah-based arbitration were a number of secular Muslim feminists, many of whom were deeply committed to transnational activism for women's rights in Muslim-majority countries such as Pakistan and Iran. Disillusioned by the role of patriarchy in traditional Muslim culture and with the manner in which religious law can be instrumentalized to serve authoritarian ends, these Muslim feminists were concerned that introducing a shari'ah-based option would impede social progress for Muslim women in Canada and perhaps strengthen the hand of fundamentalist movements.

Herouxville Life Standards Charter

On 25 January 2007, the Municipality of Hérouxville in Quebec adopted a list of standards that residents of the town lived by or wished to live by. This "Life Standards" charter states that it is directed at "future residents" of Hérouxville, but it seems equally directed at current residents who maintain traditional values from non-Western cultures. This code was received with a high level of controversy: it was interpreted by both Muslim and non-Muslim Quebecers as specifically targeting the province's Muslim population. The charter aspired to delineate a "code of conduct" for prospective new immigrants to this homogeneous rural community of just over 1,300 persons, singling out as unacceptable such practices as publicly stoning women, burning women alive, throwing acid at the faces of women, female circumcision, covering the face, school prayer, and wearing symbolic weapons to school. It also reaffirmed the rights of every woman in Hérouxville to drive a vehicle, vote, sign cheques, dance, and "decide for herself" (Bruemmer and Dougherty 2007).

On 11 February 2007, a delegation of Muslim women from the Canadian Islamic Congress visited Hérouxville to inform residents about their faith, to dispel myths, and to alleviate concerns. Approximately fifty people attended and the response was largely positive. On 13 February amendments were made to the list of standards, including dropping the reference to stoning women. The offensive nature of the code as well as the wide and varied reaction to it prompted creation of the Bouchard-Taylor Commission.

The Bouchard-Taylor Commission

On 8 February 2007, after a series of highly publicized incidents surrounding the cultural accommodation of ethnic and religious minority groups, Premier Jean Charest of Quebec made an unexpected move. In an apparent attempt to defuse increasingly widespread calls for a reassertion of *pure laine* ("old stock") Quebec culture vis-à-vis the norms of recent immigrants and certain visible minorities, Charest appointed the Consultation Commission on Accommodation Practices Related to Cultural Differences (later known simply as the Bouchard-Taylor Commission). Headed by two prominent academics, philosopher Charles Taylor and sociologist Gérard Bouchard, it was to conduct a public inquiry into the scope and limits of "reasonable accommodation" and draft recommendations for the provincial government (Bouchard and Taylor 2008, 17). As it investigated cultural accommodation practices as well as instances of xenophobia, Islamophobia, and allegedly excessive consideration for minority groups, the commission began a process through which popular attitudes were aired and the concerns of recent immigrant communities heard.

At the time of the commission's formation, the growing public perception that society had "gone too far" in accommodating new immigrants correlated with a dramatic increase in media coverage of accommodation requests and related issues, especially from religious minority groups. The resultant pressure on politicians can be seen in the fact that Charest appointed the commission on the eve of a provincial election that would see his government lose its majority status. This was in no small part on account of Mario Dumont's increasingly popular Action démocratique du Québec party, which promised stricter rules for immigration to its strong rural support base.

sugar-house: A "sugar-house" or "sugar shack" is the English name for the French "cabane à sucre," usually family-owned homes and restaurants where maple syrup and other related maple-products are made and sold.

But what spawned this so-called crisis over reasonable accommodation? Although a number of intertwining factors helped precipitate the political debate, the first and foremost trigger or catalyst was the controversy over Hérouxville's "Life Standards" charter (see above). The charter received immediate and extensive media coverage, coming as it did on the heels of several cases that had similarly sparked public interest. These included a decision to frost the windows of a YMCA located in a Hasidic Jewish community (with the intent of shielding the eyes of men from scantily clad women), the "sugar-house controversy" (in which popular media accounts greatly exaggerated the extent to which a group of Muslim **sugar-house** patrons had imposed their religious values on the management and other patrons), and various incidents in which hijab-wearing Muslim girls were barred from participating in sporting events.

After completing their research, Bouchard and Taylor produced a report that was submitted to the government on 18 May 2008 and made public on 22 May. Some notable conclusions and findings of the report include (1) that the accommodation crisis was largely a "crisis of perception" and immigrants in Québec are generally integrating well; (2) that Quebecers of French-Canadian ancestry are still anxious about their double status as a majority in Québec and a minority in the rest of English North America, but similar identity malaises exist in other Western liberal democracies as well; and (3) that interculturalism and secularism are key themes in this debate and are generally not well understood or yet defined.

Bouchard and Taylor's recommendations fall under the following five themes:

- the definition of policies and programs pertaining to secularism and interculturalism;
- the integration of immigrants, such as measures to recognize diplomas and skills and regionalize immigration;

- "learning diversity," including better training for government employees and initiatives to foster mutual understanding;
- improvement of harmonization policies and management; and
- the fight against inequality and discrimination.

Hijab, Niqab, and Burqa Debates

In the past few years, sentiments against Muslim women's modesty apparel, such as the hijab, niqab and burqa, have been headline news in many Western countries, especially France, Great Britain, and Canada (especially Quebec). Though concerns about co-optation of women's rights discourse for the purposes of warfare are less pronounced in Canada and continental Europe, the status of Muslim women remains a potent symbolic issue. In France and Quebec (as well as in Great Britain), discussions of the hijab and niqab have generated considerable political controversy. They have often reinforced polarization between secular ("assimilated") Muslims and their more culturally conservative counterparts while marginalizing efforts to address more substantive issues such as domestic violence and engagement in the public sphere. Paradoxically, efforts to "help" Muslim women by banning women's head-coverings in schools (France) and sports competitions (Quebec) have increased barriers to their participation in public life.

Although the French hijab debate began in 1989, when school administrators objected to Muslim girls' wearing hair covers to school as a violation of secularism, it was in 2004 that a law was passed barring conspicuous religious apparel (Muslim headscarves, Jewish skullcaps, large Christian crosses) in public schools. In a similar fashion, Muslim girls who wear hijab are being banned from sports activities in Quebec. Asmahan Mansour was expelled from a soccer tournament in Laval, Quebec, for refusing to remove her headscarf; later, Premier Jean Charest condoned the expulsion. In Montreal five Muslim girls were prevented from participating in a tae kwon do competition because of their headscarves. In 2010 the Quebec government brought forward Bill 94, which banned the wearing of the niqab by government employees or by those accessing government services. There have been a variety of responses to such developments, and some fear a growing misunderstanding of Islamic traditions—a slippery slope leading to less rather than greater tolerance and integration.

The Female Imam Controversy

Within several Canadian Muslim circles, particularly in urban centres such as Toronto, there has recently been debate as to whether women can function as imams, that is, whether they can lead prayers for entire congregations. The majority of mosques in Canada allow only men to lead prayers and have erected barriers to separate men and women in the mosque. Yet at least some Ahmadiyyah mosques and all Ismaili mosques, or Jamat Khana, include women in leading prayers.

In April 2005, Pakistani-born Raheel Raza became the first Canadian Muslim female to lead a mixed-gender Sunni congregation in prayers; this took place in a fellow Muslim's backyard. In July 2005, Pamela Taylor, a Euro-Canadian who had accepted Islam in 1986, became the first Muslim female to lead mixed-gender prayer in a Sunni mosque in Canada. This took place at the United Muslim Association in the Etobicoke neighbourhood of Toronto.

The example of women leading mixed-gender prayers is unlikely to be emulated in traditional Muslim contexts, at least for the foreseeable future. Nonetheless, the female imam controversy has added a new degree of intensity to local as well as global discussions about the role of women in Islam. This underscores questions and highlights needs that will be answered in different ways in diverse Muslim contexts as both women and men reengage with one another and their religious texts to address the question "Where do women stand in Islam?"

@

ISLAM AND THE INTERNET

Internet websites are proving to have a significant impact on Muslim understandings of Islam, and hence on the development of Muslim societies and networks (Bunt 2009, 1). Muslims have created Islamic spaces online, with Islamic versions of popular websites such as MuslimSpace, Islamic-Tube, and IslamicTorrents (Bunt 2009, 9). Almost all aspects of Islamic life and practice can be encountered on the Web: Muslims can seek a legal ruling on an issue of concern from a wide variety of religious authorities around the world, can track down a local restaurant serving halal meat, browse fashionable headscarves, or find a local branch of a worldwide Sufi order they are interested in encountering. Muslims can learn their religion online, accessing multimedia presentations instructing them how to perform the daily prayer or properly recite the Qur'an. Some Islamic websites act as umbrella sites that provide literally hundreds of links to more specific pages on Islamic history, theology, law, and spirituality. More scholarly sites provide access to hundreds of ancient and medieval Arabic manuscripts, whether of the Qur'an or early theological texts. For many Muslims, especially youth, the Internet may be the main source from which they learn about their religion, seek out and find a community of like-minded co-religionists, or perhaps even meet their mate on one of the many Muslim matrimonial sites. Some Muslims even mark their religious identity in relation to the Islamic websites they follow.

The Internet provides a forum for new religious authorities to gain a global audience and following, sometimes even eclipsing more traditionally established authorities. Low-status Muslim scholars removed from traditional centres of learning can now attain a global profile through savvy Web offerings, popularizing previously marginal Islamic perspectives (Bunt 2009, 38). Some of these alternative or less prominent perspectives include militant websites that share videos of suicide bombings and military operations carried out by various jihadi groups around the world—in places such as Iraq, Afghanistan, Somalia, Chechnya, and the Philippines—many of whom associate themselves with al-Qaeda. The al-Qaeda organization itself has gone to great lengths to utilize the Internet as a tool for propaganda, recruitment, and networking.

Important theological debates amongst Muslims today frequently take place on the Internet. More conservative Sunni perspectives, sometimes described as Salafi or Wahhabi, have a significant Web presence and seek to present themselves as the only authentic interpretations of the Qur'an and the Sunnah. Some scholars have argued that more conservative or hard-line perspectives dominate the Net, homogenizing Islamic discourse online. However, those who oppose these perspectives, as reformist or progressive Muslims do, have also developed websites promoting their own version of Islamic authenticity. Important debates within Islam can be found taking place at a variety of sites, including the websites of 'ulema and Sufi orders, Muslim blogs, and online forums. Muslims from minority traditions, such as certain Shii'te sects, may find a community and a voice online that is difficult to establish in their daily lives in countries where their particular tradition is marginalized. Muslims can in some sense participate in ritual contexts online that may otherwise be inaccessible. Video recordings of Sufi chanting or the discourses of a Sufi teacher who is no longer living can be accessed by Muslims seeking to receive something of the *barakah*, or blessing, of such events.

CONCLUSION

The Future of Islam in Canada

Recent debates have generated considerable public controversy, but there are also encouraging developments for Muslims in Canada. One such development is the Canadian Broadcasting Corporation's successful TV series *Little Mosque on the Prairie*. It has single-handedly heightened the profile of Muslim Canadians by providing an impetus for dialogue within as well as beyond the boundaries of the country. *Little Mosque* invites viewers to consider Muslims—represented as an internally diverse yet still cohesive community—as "normal" participants in small-town prairie life. It has been interpreted by some as a challenge to the notion that cultural and religious markers such as hijab are impediments to full engagement with North American society. Though designed to inspire laughter with its sitcom style, *Little Mosque* nonetheless explores genuine areas of disagreement among Muslims as well as common misunderstandings between Muslims and their non-Muslim neighbours. The resultant image of Islam in Canada brings to mind the community of Alberta Muslims who built the country's first mosque in 1938, and is arguably much more consistent with day-to-day reality than images derived from newspaper and television coverage of the latest controversy over niqab, hijab, shari'ah, or "reasonable accommodation."

Today Canadian Muslims can be found in all walks of life and in virtually all regions of the country.

They are actively involved in civic life, contributing to the advancement of numerous professions and embracing the same national symbols and aspirations as Canadians from other religious backgrounds, even as they maintain a sense of their own distinctiveness as practitioners of Islam within a Western multicultural nation. Their ethnic and racial diversity is as great as that which can be found in any other Canadian religious community, and their convictions and devotions often differ in ways that outsiders (expecting, perhaps, a degree of uniformity that they do not expect in other contexts) find surprising. Yet for all their diversity, Muslims have been drawn to Canada for the same reasons as Christians and Jews, Hindus and Sikhs: economic opportunity, refuge from persecution, freedom to practise their faith, and hope for a new beginning. The size and internal dynamism of their community give reason to believe that future generations are likely to regard "Muslim" as just another ordinary category of Canadian, and perhaps even a basis for some to hope that the next Gretzky will be an ʻAbdallah.

KEY TERMS

CRITICAL THINKING QUESTIONS

1. Describe some of the ways in which early historical developments in Islam continue to shape Muslim lives today.
2. Discuss the significance of the Qur'an for Muslims and its role in their religious life.
3. Some say Islam is a complete way of life. Considering Muslim beliefs and practices, answer why this is or is not true.
4. How do Islamic websites help shape contemporary Islamic authority and Muslim identities?
5. Describe three issues surrounding Muslim women in Canada in a post-9/11 context.

RECOMMENDED READING

Armstrong, Karen. *Muhammad: A Biography of the Prophet.* San Francisco: Harper SanFrancisco, 1993.

Cole, Juan. *Engaging the Muslim World.* New York: Palgrave Macmillan, 2009.

Fakhry, Majid. *A History of Islamic Philosophy*, 3rd ed. New York: Columbia University Press, 2004.

Halm, Heinz. *Shiʻism*, 2nd ed. New York: Columbia University Press, 2004.

Kamali, Muhammad Hisham. *Principles of Islamic Jurisprudence.* Cambridge: Islamic Texts Society, 2003.

Lapidus, Ira M. *A History of Islamic Societies.* Cambridge: Cambridge University Press, 2002.

Mandaville, Peter. *Global Political Islam.* New York: Routledge, 2007.

Metcalf, Barbara Daly, ed. *Making Muslim Space in North America and Europe.* Berkeley: University of California Press, 1996.

Nasr, Seyyed Hossein. *The Heart of Islam: Enduring Values for Humanity.* New York: HarperCollins, 2002.

Safi, Omid, ed. *Progressive Muslims: On Justice, Gender, and Pluralism.* Oxford: Oneworld Publications, 2003.

Schimmel, Annemarie. *Mystical Dimensions of Islam.* Chapel Hill: University of North Carolina Press, 1975.

Sells, Michael. *Approaching the Qur'an: The Early Revelations.* Ashland, OR: White Cloud Press, 1999.

Zaman, Muhammad Qasim. *The Ulama in Contemporary Islam: Custodians of Change.* Princeton, NJ: Princeton University Press, 2002.

Timeline

- **Time immemorial** Indigenous occupation of North America, by Aboriginal understanding.
- **16,000 or more years ago** Indigenous occupation of North America, by archeological reckoning.
- **1609** First Jesuit mission established in Acadia (eastern North America).
- **1881** Indian Shaker Church created in Washington State, United States.
- **1884** Potlatch banned in Canada in an attempt to control Aboriginal cultural and religious expression.
- **1895** Indian Act amendments in Canada to prohibit Aboriginal cultural and religious practices.
- **1978** American Indian Religious Freedom Act passed in the United States, providing protection for Aboriginal religious and cultural practices.
- **1986** United Church of Canada issues formal apology to First Nations of Canada for efforts to suppress Indigenous cultures.
- **1988** United Church of Canada creates All Native Circle Conference to represent Native congregations and church members.
- **2008** Prime Minister Stephen Harper apologizes in the House of Commons for mistreatment of Aboriginal youth in residential schools.

CHAPTER 5

Indigenous Traditions

Ken Coates

INTRODUCTION

In the late 1990s the United Nations organized a meeting in Whitehorse, Yukon, related to land claims processes and treaties. The meeting was hosted by the Council for Yukon **First Nations** (CYFN), one of the rare occasions when Indigenous groups had taken the leadership of a U.N. event. Difficulties erupted in the minutes before the first plenary session. The council's practices for public gatherings involve asking a local elder to bless the proceedings and to provide spiritual guidance. They had asked a highly respected **elder** from the Teslin Tlingit First Nation to lead the opening prayer. The United Nations, for fairly obvious reasons, avoids mixing religious and political matters and does not authorize prayers for official U.N. events. After several closed-door sessions the organizers decided that the elder could proceed as planned. The logic was simple: a First Nations spiritual blessing was, by definition, not linked to one of the world's major religions and therefore could hardly offend anyone.

The elder spoke from the front of the assembly room. She was a distinguished leader, revered in her community for leading health and education reform. Even more to the point, she was known for being a spiritual leader of considerable authority within her First Nation and beyond. The crowd quieted when she spoke, offering a powerful blessing in Tlingit that conveyed in its tone and passion a message of empowerment. The CYFN host thanked her for the blessing and was turning back toward the room when the elder interrupted. Perhaps, she though, she should translate the blessing so that all would understand what had been said. Nods from around the room, for the delegates gathered from fifteen countries, including many U.N. representatives, were anxious to learn more about these local First Nations who had negotiated such interesting and comprehensive land claim agreements with the Government of Canada. "Okay," she said, beginning, "Our Father, who art in Heaven, hallowed be thy name . . . ." She continued to the considerable dismay of the U.N. officials, who felt there had been a major breach of protocol.

This story illustrates something of the complexity of Native spirituality and religion in the twenty-first century. There is a genuine and growing desire on the part of non-Aboriginal people to know that traditional Indigenous values, worldviews, and practices have survived. There is also considerable despair, even guilt, that expanding European nations did so much to destroy Indigenous cultures and spiritual traditions. There is concern that Indigenous religions have already been irreparably damaged and a growing awareness of the cultural loss to humanity if that is so. Implicit in this reaction is a belief that the major faiths and Indigenous spirituality are incompatible and, indeed, in conflict, and that conversion to non-Indigenous religions really occurred only through force or desperation. It is a

First Nation: a term widely used in Canada to describe Indigenous people of a specific language and cultural group, typically identified with a specific territory.

Elder: a senior member of an Indigenous group who is deemed to have special leadership qualities and is widely believed to be very wise.

confusing and complex situation, made more so by the intense politics around Aboriginal land rights, treaties, and political engagement.

This chapter reviews the nature and evolution of Native religions and Aboriginal spirituality. This subject differs greatly from other sections of this book. Indigenous populations (defined here as populations that developed strong attachments to and were the first inhabitants of their lands) did not and do not have religions that look like many of the organized faith traditions of other countries. Newcomers typically described Indigenous peoples in harsh and derogatory terms: they were called "pagans" and "barbarians," dismissed as "heathens" in need of salvation, and described by the outsiders as lacking in the religious and spiritual foundations of civilized peoples. To this day, commentators struggle to categorize Native religious practices. Are they myths, cultural traditions, superstitions, rituals, or spiritual ceremonies? Native religions have changed and declined in significance over the years, but they have also been exceptionally resilient in the face of extreme pressure to shift or even to disappear (Coates 2004).

The effort to understand Native religions speaks directly to one of the fundamental questions raised by the broader effort to study religions. For generations, commentators rarely described Native spiritual practices as religions. Instead they were viewed as a set of disconnected customs, traditions, and practices, not united by a core theology or a codified or written set of beliefs. Indeed, Native activities that focused on the supernatural were taken as evidence of absence of civilization and backwardness among Indigenous peoples. Efforts to understand Native customs and belief systems within the framework of European religions served only to widen the cultural gap between the original peoples and the newcomers. Later, as the complexity of the human spiritual and religious experience became better known, and as Eurocentric notions of what constitutes a "real" religion gave way to more culturally inclusive and sensitive concepts, the spiritual views and related practices of Indigenous peoples became more widely recognized and appreciated for what they were: sophisticated, multi-generational, and deeply held ways of understanding nature, the human condition, and the relationship between the physical world and the hereafter.

The study of Native religions creates invaluable learning opportunities. Specific objectives for this chapter include understanding the nature and complexity of Indigenous spiritual and religious traditions and appreciating the different traditions among the Indigenous peoples of the world. It is vital as well to recognize the persistence of Indigenous spirituality and religious practices over the centuries, to explore similarities and differences between Indigenous beliefs and practices and those of other faith traditions, and to learn about the relationships between Indigenous spiritual and religious traditions and those of imported faiths, particularly Christianity.

PEOPLE & PLACES

Native Peoples of North America

The Indigenous population of North America, estimated to have comprised as many as ten million people (north of Mexico) before the arrival of Europeans, was and is remarkably diverse. Along the West Coast, substantial and highly artistic cultures flourished that relied on abundant supplies of salmon and the natural wealth of the rainforest. Their totem poles and carved masks are among the most impressive cultural forms on the continent. At the opposite extreme, the **Inuit** inhabited, and still inhabit, one of the harshest areas on the planet, marked by months of extreme cold and darkness and viewed as uninhabitable by most of the newcomers. The vast interior plains were home to many different Native societies, most of which lived off the massive herds of bison that moved across the land. Around the Great Lakes, abundant food supplies and agricultural practices sustained more sedentary societies, which grew corn, hunted, and fished, and which supported the elaborate political systems of the Iroquois and nearby groups. Some of the most impressive architecture on the continent in the pre-European period could be found in the pueblo cultures of the American southwest. Their stone and adobe dwellings reflect the remarkable adaptability and creativity of Indigenous peoples in adjusting to the resources, climate, and natural opportunities of their regions.

Over the generations, the Indigenous peoples came to be viewed in very simple terms: as Indians (the United States) or First Nations (Canada). In fact their cultures varied widely in terms of language, economy, social values, and spirituality. They had complex and generally effective means of managing relations with neighbouring groups—violent military confrontations of the type associated with the newcomers' invasion of North America were very rare—and of sustaining their cultures over many generations.

CENTRAL BELIEFS

The Indigenous religions of the world are remarkably diverse, reflecting the nuances of local cultures, historical influences, relationships with nearby populations, and natural surroundings. Since spirituality and religious expression are so closely connected to the local environment—landforms, plants, animals, seasons, and the like—it follows logically that there are striking differences among the religious activities of the diverse cultures in what is often called the **Fourth World** (McFarlane 1993).

For generations observers described Native religions in disparaging terms. The rituals, customs, ceremonies, and leadership systems of the Indigenous peoples, dismissed as "pagan" and "heathen," were clearly not rooted in the forms of the world's more comprehensive religions. They seemed, in comparison to Christianity, Judaism, Islam, and the like, to be ill-formed, disconnected, and completely localized. That some of their spirituality and religious expression involved ritualistic sacrifice, abuse, body markings or piercings, extreme deprivation, psychological pressure, or other unusual practices convinced outsiders that these Indigenous religious systems were not deserving of respect.

Note that there is often confusion surrounding the words *Indigenous*, *Native*, and *Aboriginal*. Indigenous groups prefer to be described by their specific cultural names and not by such old terms as *Indian* or *Eskimo*. The terms *Indigenous*, *Native* and *Aboriginal* are used interchangeably here, for they all refer to the original inhabitants of **traditional territories** and to groups that have retained their spiritual, ecological, and cultural knowledge over many generations, even though they may have lost control over their lands and resources to newcomers.

Inuit: Indigenous peoples who live in the Arctic, usually above the treeline.

Fourth World: a term used to describe Indigenous peoples around the world.

Traditional territories: the lands occupied and used by a specific Indigenous group in the generations before the arrival of newcomers, most often from Europe.

For many observers who were convinced of the cultural superiority of their society and who held to the belief that their religion was the embodiment of their economic, scientific, and political success, Native spiritual beliefs revealed a lack of understanding of scientific principles and an inherent backwardness. On the primitive–civilized continuum, Europeans viewed themselves as being highly civilized, while the Native cultures were clearly at the opposite end of the scale. The idea that Native people were primitive—unsophisticated and without detailed insight into nature—proved to be remarkably persistent, remaining commonplace to the present. Descriptions of Aboriginal religious practices and spiritual beliefs remained central to the unflattering portrayal of their societies, a perspective that diminished understanding of both the social and intellectual worlds of Indigenous peoples.

In many instances, interestingly, Indigenous peoples viewed the spirituality of the outsiders in a similarly negative manner. The Christian practice of stylized remembrance of Jesus—"the body of Christ, broken for you"—offended some Native observers, who concluded that the newcomers were cannibals. The celibacy of Catholic priests generated endless comment and criticism, especially from cultures that practised polygamy. So too did the formal hierarchy and elaborate ceremonies of the Western religions. The values and practices of other faiths seemed as odd, convoluted, and inexplicable to Native people as Indigenous traditions did to the newcomers.

Native religions, to put it simply, seemed to others to represent a non-spiritual tradition, a value system disconnected from a founding intellect, a charismatic leader, or a clearly defined and written code (Berkhofer 1979). Indigenous spirituality defies easy characterization or summary. Indigenous peoples have inhabited the Aboriginal-dominated areas of the world for thousands of years (a shorter period in the Arctic regions). Over the millennia they established complex social and spiritual systems and developed very sophisticated ways of regulating human behaviour and structuring relations within and between groups. Hundreds of unique cultures emerged across the globe, as different from each other as Spain is from Russia. Some of these groups—for example, the Plains Cree, the Sioux, the Aborigines of Australia, the !Kung people of Botswana—inhabited vast tracts of land. Others, particularly on the resource-rich West Coast of North America and the islands off Malaysia and New Zealand, were much more narrowly based. Cultural forms varied with the nature of the natural resources available to them and with their relationships with surrounding societies. Some groups moved routinely across very large distances; others spent much of their time in much smaller areas. Indigenous spirituality and religious activity therefore existed along a long and complex spectrum and were far from being fixed or singular aspects of Native culture.

Describing the status of Native religion and spirituality in the early twenty-first century is a difficult challenge. In many cases, Aboriginal culture and religion have merged with newcomer traditions, although some Indigenous populations still follow long-standing beliefs and customs. The latter peoples tend to live in remote sections of the Amazon Basin, Papua New Guinea, Suriname, and isolated corners of Africa. Very few Indigenous groups in North America have sufficient separation from the dominant Western society to preserve intact their traditional practices. And even in remote places, the influences of newcomer faiths (typically Christianity) can be readily seen, in some cases transformed by hundreds of years of practice and adaptation. Native peoples are more likely to be recorded in government census data as Christians (Catholics or Protestants) than as following an Indigenous spiritual tradition. In fact, much of the growth of Christian churches over the past century has come from displacement of Indigenous spirituality and religious practice. Understanding Native religions, therefore, requires an appreciation of cultural practices and traditions that are often thousands of years old, of the effects of newcomer faiths and missionary efforts, and of the impressive resilience of core Native beliefs.

SOURCES OF NATIVE RELIGIOUS TRADITION

Indigenous spirituality is from the outset holistic in nature, tying Indigenous peoples to the natural world and revealing that all aspects of an ecosystem hold spiritual authority and insight. Animals, plants, geological formations, rivers, lakes, seasons, clouds, stars, and the elements have spiritual powers that have to be acknowledged. Over hundreds and even thousands of years, Indigenous groups came to an appreciation of their spiritual environment, linking their understanding of creation and the role of human and human/nature relationships to local ecosystems. Among the Indigenous peoples of Taiwan, for example, belief in the power of birds, snakes, and animals provided a unifying element within the society. The Sámi (the Indigenous peoples of northern Scandinavia) had strongly polytheistic religious practices, finding spiritual insight and guidance in many forms: from their ancestors, from animals, and from their physical surroundings.

Aboriginal life is spiritually very rich, with Native people placing themselves amidst—not in dominance over—a complex environmental setting. Nature is all-powerful; human life is transient and subsequently less important and powerful. Traditions and practices vary dramatically but follow a standard pattern of recognizing multiple spiritual authorities and acknowledging that spirituality is a central aspect of all life. Although their belief systems are thin in terms of formality and, to outsiders, largely unrecognizable as formal religion, Aboriginal populations nonetheless have intense spiritual responsibilities and a worldview that focuses on recognizing the connections between the human and natural worlds.

Kwakiutl Ancestor Figure

Native spirituality focuses on strong connections between generations and on the veneration of ancestors. This commitment to spiritual connections between generations is revealed through naming rituals, death feasts and celebrations, a strong pattern of remembrance of key ancestors, and artistic representations from the distant past. Figures such as this West Coast artifact celebrate the long spiritual history of the Native society and remind people of their distant ancestors.

Source: Ancestor Figure, Kwakwaka'wakw, before 1894. Wood, paint, metal. 146 × 83 × 36 cm. UBC Museum of Anthropology, Vancouver, Canada (A1800).

Missionaries: members of a religious organization or church, usually associated with a Christian denomination, who seek to convert members of other faiths to their own.

HISTORY AND DEVELOPMENT

Native religions and spirituality served Indigenous societies extremely well for many centuries. Their values, traditions, customs, and beliefs reflected the natural world and the relationships of the people to their surroundings. Beliefs were regularized within the groups without being written down or otherwise formalized as in other religious traditions, but they were no less powerful, consistent, and influential as a result. Archeologists and anthropologists have studied physical artifacts and worked with Indigenous elders and cultural leaders to understand the complex religious traditions of the distant past. Spirituality and religious expression changed over time, as they did with all world religions, but there is little in the form of written records of transitions that occurred because of local developments, contacts with outsiders, spiritual revelations, or new methods of worship. Many of the practices and beliefs appear to have remained largely unchanged over generations and centuries, although specialists are quick to point out that there is little documentation of shifts and debates within Indigenous groups. Typically—although this is an imprecise and even a false division—Native spirituality and religion are described in their pre-contact and post-contact forms, with the emphasis on transitions in practice and belief that followed direct contact with outsider faiths and spiritual leaders. This divide is artificial because it obscures what were certainly numerous key transitions and even spiritual/religious conflicts within the hundreds of Indigenous cultures that peopled the world before the age of European expansion and exploration.

The Arrival of Missionaries

The continuity with the past changed dramatically with the arrival of Christian missionaries and representatives of other faith traditions as part of the general expansion of Europe and its colonization of the world's peoples. The Christian **missionaries**, committed to sharing

Race for souls: contests between denominations, usually Catholic and Protestant, to claim religious dominion over a specific Indigenous group, usually through conversions and baptism.

the word of God and closely aligned with government objectives of trade, exploration, and expansion, were particularly assertive. These missionaries brought a particularly aggressive form of Christianity with them. They believed it was their God-given mission to convert the "backward" and "uncivilized" Native people to Christianity and thus to save their eternal souls.

The missionaries varied widely in their approach and their impact. Missionaries moved into Sámi territories in the 1400s and expanded their operations the following century. Over time, Christian values competed with, were eventually imposed upon, and came to dominate traditional Sámi views of spirituality and religion. The Society of Jesus (the Jesuits), an assertive Catholic order, pushed very aggressively into Indigenous societies in many areas, eliciting support and animosity in almost equal measure. Other Catholic orders and most of the Protestant denominations took a less forceful role, most of them working slowly to win the adherence of newly encountered peoples. The missionaries promoted education of the young people and in the nineteenth century became active participants in national residential and day-school movements, an engagement with Indigenous peoples that shaped and continues to define the relationship between the churches and Aboriginal societies (Grant 1984).

The Martyrdom of Jean de Brébeuf and Gabriel Lalemant by the Iroquois

Missionaries venturing into Native territory in the early years of contact found themselves in unknown and poorly understood situations. Eager to demonstrate their devotion to God, the Jesuits of the Society of Jesus became internationally known for their willingness to martyr themselves in the service of their faith. Missionaries entered a complex and evolving world, drawn into intertribal rivalries that had been exacerbated by the imperatives of the commercial fur trade, diplomatic alliances involving the French, British, and Dutch, and the devastating impacts of imported diseases. The Jesuit missionaries Brébeuf and Lalemant became ensnared in a rivalry between the Iroquois and the Huron.

Source: The Death of some Jesuit Fathers in Nouvelle-France, from "Historiae Canadensis" by François Ducreux, published in 1664 (engraving) (b/w photo) by Gregoire Huret (1606–70) Bibliotheque Nationale, Paris, France/Giraudon/The Bridgeman Art Library

Missionaries rushed to baptize Aboriginal people, knowing as they did so that the new adherents often had a very sketchy understanding of the nature and meaning of the new faith. The first missionaries into a new area worked to lay claim to the Indigenous population, believing that early baptism would keep out competing denominations. This led to an aggressive "**race for souls**," particularly in newly opened lands, as missionaries sought to establish ongoing relationships with Indigenous groups. The resulting competition was occasionally unseemly, and a cause for considerable amusement among the Aboriginal people. Aboriginal people often became enthusiastic adherents to the new faith, but there were instances of church missionaries attempting to force Indigenous peoples to adopt Christianity, and some of the Christian settlements (both Catholic and Protestant) were run in a very authoritarian manner.

Indigenous Spirituality and Christianity

Scholars examining the evolution of Native religions and spirituality struggle with a very fundamental question: why did so many Aboriginal people surrender their traditional views and become Christians or adopt other faiths? The evidence of the transition is quite dramatic. There are thousands of examples of conversions to Christianity and of communities making the decision to become Catholic or Protestant. Many Aboriginal spiritual leaders, sensing the shifting spiritual winds, became advocates for Christianity, often in a bid to hold on to their authority among their people. Catholics found dedicated adherents by the thousands, as did the Anglicans and other Protestant denominations. People became sincere and committed church members, some as lay leaders and a few as full-time priests. Clearly Aboriginal people had made a shift, sometimes very rapidly, from traditional views to Christian perspectives.

One standard argument, what Canadian historian John Webster Grant describes as the "moon of wintertime" hypothesis, is that Aboriginal people looked to Christianity when Native spiritual traditions failed to protect them in times of great hardship. During the early years of contact, imported European diseases killed 75 percent or more of many Indigenous populations. **Smallpox** was a particular scourge, killing millions of Native people around the world. Societies collapsed in near chaos as leaders died, villages were wiped out, and **traditional medicines** and spiritual prescriptions failed to hold back the devastating diseases. In these times of great turmoil, which were often accompanied by political unrest and reorganization, the argument goes, Indigenous people looked to the obviously greater power of the newly arrived outsiders and their missionary protectors. The newcomers, after all, were not dying from the diseases (indeed, some were accused of bringing the illnesses with them and were punished for their bad medicine). Their medicine or healing power and spiritual authority seemed to be much greater than those of **shamans**, medicine men, and other spiritual leaders (Crosby 2003).

It is a compelling argument, and it fits with the standard view of Indigenous peoples overwhelmed by the arrival of Europeans and struggling to make spiritual sense of a rapidly changing world. It is also consistent with the belief that Aboriginal peoples were forced, by either direct pressure or circumstances, to accept the cultural impositions of Europe. As attractive as that argument may be, however, it is not at all clear that it accounts for the fairly widespread Aboriginal adoption of Christianity. Indeed, many Native people and groups became adherents when disease was not destroying the population, when the harvesting economies were strong and people felt confident about their future. Nor does this explanation adequately account for the long-term adherence of many Indigenous peoples to the new religions.

Indigenous peoples had many reasons for joining the new faith traditions. At times, picking the Catholics, the Protestants, or others could bring commercial advantage. While many missionaries had only casual contact with the local population, some of them were deeply committed to their congregations. Charismatic priests and pastors, many of whom lived for extended periods with the Indigenous peoples, inspired adherents through their words and deeds. It is clear, as well, that many Indigenous people were taken by the message and the vision of Christianity. Indeed, the descriptions of **communitarian** values for society outlined in the Gospels bear a striking resemblance to the redistributive traditions within Native communities. To put it more simply, many Indigenous peoples became Christians or joined some other faith because they came to believe in the message of the newly arrived church.

Becoming Christian did not, however, necessarily mean that the Native people had abandoned their traditional values and beliefs. The missionaries certainly hoped they would, and at times they exerted great pressure to eliminate Aboriginal practices. Many missionaries, however, realized that trying to compel wholesale changes would push the Native people away. They remained flexible in their insistence on adherence to certain practices, discouraging **polygamy**, for example, while tolerating the continuance of Indigenous burial rites and many seasonal rituals. There is considerable evidence that Christian and Aboriginal spiritual perspectives coexisted for many decades. Contrary to standard assumptions about faith and adherence, Aboriginal people appear to have found it possible to follow both Christian and Indigenous beliefs simultaneously.

Smallpox: a deadly virus, perhaps the most serious in history, that spread throughout the world during the age of European expansion and was responsible for the deaths of millions of Indigenous peoples.

Traditional medicines: local products, particularly herbs and other plants, used by Indigenous healers to treat illness.

Shaman: an Indigenous spiritual and religious leader.

Communitarian: describes a belief that the needs of the group are central to society and that the authority of the individual is often subsumed by the requirements of the larger population.

Polygamy: the practice of a man having more than one wife.

Revitalization movements: efforts by Indigenous religious leaders to rebuild their society, often through efforts to rehabilitate traditional beliefs and customs.

Syncretistic movements: intense spiritual revivals that combine elements of Indigenous and other (typically Christian) religions.

Conflict between the two belief systems may well have been minimal. After all, the versions of Christianity practised before the late twentieth century focused primarily on relationships between humans and between humans and God, offering strict and firm guidelines for belief and conduct in both areas. Aboriginal spirituality, in contrast, focused substantially on relationships between humans and animals and humans and the environment. Indigenous views of the spiritual world place the individual within a broader natural system and make it clear that paying attention to the spirits of the animals, elements, plants, mountains, and water are a crucial part of human existence. Christianity had relatively little to say about the natural world, and certainly did not imbue animals and nature in general with spiritual authority in the way that Indigenous belief systems did.

Indigenous Spiritual Responses

Not all Indigenous peoples were comfortable with the role of the missionaries and their assaults on traditional values and beliefs. The Jesuits, who were among the first to establish extensive ties with Indigenous groups, generated considerable hostility and occasionally brutal assaults on individuals. From time to time, charismatic leaders emerged in the Aboriginal population who promised to reintroduce native beliefs or develop new ways of understanding the spiritual world through what became known as **revitalization** or **syncretistic** movements (which are not unique to Indigenous peoples). These movements often combined elements of traditional customs and rituals with aspects of Christianity and focused on prominent prophets and their visions. They ranged from major, wide-ranging efforts—such as the movement started by Handsome Lake among the Iroquois of North America in the early nineteenth

PEOPLE & PLACES

Handsome Lake

Handsome Lake was an important leader of the Iroquois Confederacy in the early 1800s. He sought to rebuild commitment to the Haudenosaunee tradition in the wake of decades of dislocation associated with the arrival of Europeans. The charismatic man was profoundly distressed by the social and economic decay he was witnessing among his people and worried about the prospect of further conflict and war with the newcomers. Traditional spiritual leaders lacked the ability to revive Indigenous pride and culture. As he was recovering from a prolonged period of despair, Handsome Lake reported several striking visions and committed himself to the spiritual renewal of his people. His code, which purported to be a restatement of the core values of the Iroquois Confederacy, offered strong moral direction and called on the people to avoid witchcraft and other evil practices. Handsome Lake's combination of Christianity and traditional values, his evocation of Indigenous identity, and his appeals against immoral activity made him popular throughout the Iroquois territories and beyond, although the emergence of this "new religion" divided the Iroquois people. After his death in 1815, Handsome Lake's Code (*gai'wioo*) became a central part of Iroquois identity and spiritual practice, although not without opposition from some people who claimed it did not fully represent traditional Iroquois beliefs and values. In the decades that followed, the code left by Handsome Lake featured prominently in spiritual and religious activity (Parker, 2008).

century—to tiny and little-known local revivals. In general these movements emerged at times of profound social change, when communities were questioning their spiritual and social direction and worried about the loss of traditional values. These charismatic leaders often drew liberally on both Indigenous and Christian traditions as they promised to provide guidance to the Indigenous communities (Harkin 2004).

The revitalization, or "new religion," movements were typically dismissed by contemporary observers as a power play against the missionaries. They clearly represented an Aboriginal attempt to reassert some measure of spiritual control, for they happened at times when Indigenous groups were losing their lands and resources and facing many pressures from the newcomers. The revitalization movements also represented an effort by Native people to make spiritual sense of the rapidly changing times.

The challenges posed by incoming religious traditions were only part of a new order that included new technology, industrialization, dramatic population growth, military or administrative control by external governments, and many other disturbing influences. Aboriginal people were struggling amidst the uprooting of a social and environmental order that had remained fundamentally the same for centuries. Spirituality played an important role in that struggle as Indigenous prophets, shamans, and leaders sought the means to explain, through visions and Aboriginally inspired insights, the turmoil and chaos around them.

Assimilation and Acculturation Efforts

Missionaries and governments were not content with the fairly easily won dominance of the Christian church among the Native people. A combination of muscular Christianity—the Catholic and Protestant idea that Christianity was the preeminent religion in the world and had to be shared globally—assertive European colonial authority, and the assumed primacy of Western civilization gave missionaries and government officials alike the idea that it was their duty to eradicate traditional Indigenous customs and practices. It was, they argued, clearly in their interests to eradicate Aboriginal spirituality as one of the final elements of a dying social

Practices

The Ghost Dance

One of the most famous examples of Aboriginal revitalization through religion occurred in the late nineteenth century. The Ghost Dance, introduced by the Paiute spiritual leader Wovoka (Jack Wilson), arose out of a combination of traditional practices, particularly the Circle Dance, and represented a strong assertion of Indigenous identity at a time of great dislocation and hardship among Aboriginal populations in the American west. Wovoka based his prophecies on instructions from God, promising adherents that a life of peace and cooperation on earth would lead to greater harmony in the hereafter. The message merged Christian and Indigenous understandings of spiritual worlds and sought to reconcile Aboriginal communities to the massive changes sweeping across the continent at the time.

The prophet and the dance itself, a long and gruelling multi-day activity, attracted interest across much of the western United States. Describing the Ghost Dance as a dance strips the experience of much of its emotional power. Adapted by local spiritual leaders or shamans to suit specific circumstances, it focused on an apocalyptic vision of the future, promised a return to independence for Indigenous peoples, and engulfed whole communities in prolonged periods of religious fervour and enthusiasm. It was an intense and memorable experience that served to remind participants of the power of spirituality (Kehoe 1989).

Residential schools: special boarding schools for Indigenous children, designed to both convert them to Christianity and prepare them for integration into mainstream society.

Potlatch: a gathering or feast, often with spiritual elements, in which the host family redistributes much of its wealth to guests.

and cultural order. They sought to accomplish this in several ways, including aggressive proselytizing, education of Native youth (particularly through **residential schools**, which gave them full control of the children for many years), and imposition of a sedentary, farm-based lifestyle, which was more susceptible to Christian teachings than a mobile harvesting existence. The belief seemed to be that through such demonstrations the Euro-Christian order would prevail and Aboriginal people would move quickly toward a more modern and sustainable lifestyle (Miller 2000).

Indigenous peoples and communities adapted, almost as much as the promoters of the new way hoped they would. Many became farmers or industrial workers. Children attended schools, typically voluntarily, and parents arranged for them to go to the often distant residential schools. Aboriginal people could see that the world was changing and that the future required adaptation. But many key Indigenous practices remained: the **potlatch** (a West Coast system for redistribution of wealth), the Sun Dance on the prairies, burying rituals, appeals to animal and natural spirits, and the like. Other practices, particularly polygamy, disappeared quite rapidly. To the degree that they could control their own lives and make their own choices, Indigenous peoples sustained many of their spiritual practices and beliefs.

Church and government officials wanted to eliminate the last vestiges of the old order. Certain of their moral righteousness and of God's blessing and convinced that harsh measures were necessary to stamp out Native spirituality, national governments and state-sanctioned churches agreed to eliminate "undesirable practices." Major ceremonial activities were banned, and in several cases practitioners were imprisoned for continuing centuries-old customs. Many of the central practices continued underground, away from the prying eyes of the missionary and the government agent. The prohibitions had a considerable impact over time, however; the new regulations attacked the status and profile of key ceremonies and criminalized vital social and spiritual activities. Importantly, very few non-Aboriginal people rallied to the defence of Indigenous spiritual and religious expression at the time, even as they and their governments were making concessions to accommodate dissenting religious groups from other faiths.

There were ironic twists to this suppression of Aboriginal spirituality. In the early twentieth century, several governments, including Canada and the United States, prohibited or restricted Aboriginal political organization and banned meetings designed to challenge government actions or policies. Many groups, however, particularly in British Columbia, had no desire to comply with this limitation on their freedom. Since they were allowed to assemble for religious purposes, they quickly organized political gatherings under the guise of church events. Lookouts would keep watch for missionaries, police officers, or government officials. If any approached, the political discussions would cease and song would break out. "Onward, Christian Soldiers" was a favourite, and the hymn eventually became a subversive demonstration of Aboriginal protest and solidarity (Neylan 2003).

The experience of Native peoples, including their evolving relationships with Christian and other external religious groups, has long been held up as a prime example of the processes of colonization and decolonization. From the time of contact, Native people were seen as culturally and spiritually inferior to the newcomers, who used their technological, commercial, and military advantages to impose their will on the original peoples. Religion played a central role in the domination of Native cultures, with missionaries working closely with government and military officials to impose the will of the imperial powers and to undermine Native values, customs, and religious practices. Over time, Indigenous societies became extensively (but not entirely) colonized, aligned with imperial cultures and socio-economic practices and increasingly separated from traditional life-ways and spiritual practices. Native peoples found some aspects of the newcomers' systems to their liking, and they resisted the dominance inherent in the colonial system. However, the power of the state and, in many areas, the influx of hundreds of thousands of immigrants pushed Native societies to the margins and left them outsiders in their traditional territories.

Native resistance nevertheless proved very strong, and even the systematic efforts of governments and churches to undermine Aboriginal cultures ultimately failed. With many Indigenous people still spending a lot of time on the land and water—and therefore away from non-Aboriginal influences and in close connection with the natural world that defined their spiritual existence—a great deal of informal spiritual and religious activity continued. During the social turmoil of the 1960s, a period marked by the rise of **anticolonial** movements and Aboriginal protests, the mainstream churches substantially recanted. They decided that their aggressive attacks on Indigenous spirituality and culture had been wrong. Most of the residential schools, the majority of which had already been taken over the government, were closed. Missionary efforts largely ceased (to be picked up later by fundamentalist Protestant groups), although the churches remained connected with long-standing Christian faith communities. The churches also became stalwart defenders of Indigenous land and resource rights—which, though most people do not know it, they had often been in the past as well.

The newfound respect for Indigenous values and traditions was reflected in large-scale efforts to celebrate and support Aboriginal culture. Education, long used as a tool to suppress Indigenous customs and practices, was now used to build—or rebuild—Native spiritual and cultural activities. New Age adherents and environmentalists became enamoured of Indigenous values and argued that efforts toward sustainability and coexistence with nature required the rediscovery and general application of Native spiritual beliefs. After being ignored and then vigorously suppressed, Indigenous religion and spirituality became a cause for celebration and recognition. A layer of guilt overlay much of the non-Aboriginal response to Indigenous spiritual activity in the 1960s and 1970s, although this sense of sorrow slowly shifted to admiration and respect over time. Outsider enthusiasm for Indigenous art is due at least in part to interest in Indigenous spirituality. By the end of the twentieth century, the general population was accepting of and even enthusiastic about Indigenous spiritual and religion practices.

Traditional spiritual beliefs experienced a revival of sorts in the years after the Second World War. The gradual decline of state and Christian domination provided an opportunity for Native peoples to re-engage with Indigenous practices. In a few places this led to significant connection with traditional religious beliefs and activities, even though the Indigenous peoples had been separated for many generations from fully Native-controlled spirituality. Among groups such as the Sámi in northern Europe, symbolic practices such as yoiking (chanting) experienced a revival, representing a substantial political statement about the persistence of Indigenous traditions. The same is true of potlatches on the West Coast of North America and ceremonial activities among the Indigenous peoples of Hawaii. More general practices, such as the sweat lodge, were adopted by different Native groups as a way of separating themselves spiritually from the dominant religious cultures.

Anticolonial: against external control or domination, typically by a different ethnic group and often associated with protests against European imperial powers.

SPIRITUAL AND RELIGIOUS PRACTICES

Despite the historical and cultural misunderstandings—the root of a great deal of the conflict, discrimination, and hostility between Native peoples and newcomers—Indigenous spiritual and religious traditions share a great deal in common with other world religions. Despite the remarkable diversity of Native religious expression, Indigenous societies sought spiritual understanding and guidance, established systems for recognizing key transitions in life, and identified the spiritual forces that affected their lives. In other words, Native religions operated through structures, activities, and concepts that differed in the specifics but not in their general contours from other faith traditions. A review of the key elements that occur regularly in Indigenous spiritual traditions illustrates this point.

Creation Stories

Indigenous religions place considerable emphasis on creation stories that explain the origins of the world, the emergence of animal and plant life, and the arrival of human beings. These stories, which vary widely among Indigenous cultures, are often associated with specific geographic or natural phenomena within the traditional territory of the group. Aborigines in Australia believe—in a series of understandings that newcomers later labelled "the Dreamtime"—that the earth has existed for all time and was inhabited by a series of beings associated with various animals. These beings created all life on earth, including human beings, animals, and plants, and left marks on the planet that marked their passing and provided physical evidence of the creation of the world.

The Maori of New Zealand attribute the emergence of the earth and of humans to two key figures, Rangi (heaven) and Papa (earth). The sons of this pair represent the key powers of the natural world. The brothers argue about how best to emerge out of darkness, and they assign Papa to become the earth and Rangi to form the heavens, creating the world and humanity in the process.

In Canada's Maritimes, the Mi'kmaq and Maliseet believe that Glooscap arranged the peopling of the world, shaping the land, creating animals, and destroying the evil forces that dominated the earth. In this tradition, Glooscap comes from the sky world to remake the planet, create human beings, and prepare them to survive in the new land. His twin, Malsm, introduces deceit and evil into the world. In the Huron tradition, Sky Woman (Aataentsic) falls from the sky and her descent is seen by the Great Turtle. The Turtle orders other animals to pile soil on his back, creating the earth, which provides a soft landing for Aataentsic. Made pregnant by the spirit of the Great Turtle, she gives birth to Iouskeha (good) and Tawiscaron (evil); the latter kills his mother at birth. Iouskeha defeats his brother and thereafter provides guidance to the people (Trigger 1976).

Deities

Religion requires a spiritual focus, an understanding that some strong non-human force governs the known world. Deities figure prominently in Indigenous religions but rarely in the form of a dominant single God. Instead, spiritual power is typically distributed amongst and throughout the natural world. Major spirits are deemed responsible for all manner of human and natural events, often with their spiritual authority distributed by function or aspect of life.

African Indigenous peoples express their spirituality in many different ways, with some worshipping a single god and others seeing spiritual authority in several gods. There is great complexity in traditional African understandings of God, although there is considerable similarity in that God (or the gods) is powerful, influential in individual lives, responsible for creation and the emergence of humanity, and a moral guide for society. Concepts of supreme beings in Africa range from single gods such as the Chukwu among the Igbo to Mawu-Lisa, a twin female/androgynous god. Female gods figure prominently in African spirituality, either as deities in their own right or as important spiritual guides. So it was with North American Aboriginal religions and spiritual traditions, which called on a large number of spiritual influences and authorities.

PEOPLE & PLACES

Trickster Characters

Indigenous religions often have mischievous characters called tricksters who figure prominently in storytelling, song, dance, and ritual. The trickster tradition is quite strong in many traditions, including those of Africa and Asia. The character is something of an anti-authority figure—devious, funny, crass, and occasionally bawdy. Tricksters in Indigenous traditions change character, personality, and roles, proving their flexibility and unreliability. Among First Nations in Canada, the most prominent trickster characters include Coyote, Nanabush, and Raven. The trickster is a source of both humour and concern, alternately light-hearted and devious. Tricksters change genders and physical appearance, generate great fun, and celebrate sex. They are at once influential spiritual leaders and silly creatures who highlight the absurd aspects of life. In many traditions, tricksters are given credit for creating stability and a semblance of order in the world and for transforming spiritual reality into a physical presence. They are celebrated, therefore, for being agents of change while retaining the image of cultural hero for their impish behaviour (Erdoes and Ortiz 1984).

Spiritual Leadership

For centuries before Christian missionaries and leaders of other faiths arrived, Native peoples sought and found solace and direction through spiritual guides. In some societies these people were called witch doctors and were believed to possess the power to punish or reward as the spirits dictated. Other cultures called them shamans or medicine men and relied on them to provide direction or to invoke traditional customs and ceremonies to meet local needs. (In many instances, when outside religions arrived on the scene, these leaders sought prominent roles in the new faith so they could retain their position of prominence and authority.) In some Indigenous groups around the world spiritual leadership came from powerful women who understood and interpreted the spiritual world.

Shamans play a vital role in areas where Native religions remain active. They perform a variety of healing and spiritual functions, depending on the local culture, using traditional medicines, spiritual connections, and understandings to provide advice, ensure cultural continuity, interpret dreams, mediate disputes over resource use, and connect people to the spiritual world. They dominate ceremonial life, including naming the newborn, and provide protection for members of their communities by invoking spiritual protection and by using their medicines, spiritual connections, and understanding of the spiritual world to guide human behaviour (Vitebsky 2001).

Shamans and Religious Ceremonies

These men, dressed in the dramatic ceremonial clothing of the Pacific Northwest coast, demonstrate the important role that spirituality played in Indigenous communities. Before the arrival of the Europeans in North America, the shaman was responsible for healing the sick, interpreting the spiritual world, and providing guidance in ritual and spiritual practices. When the Europeans arrived, the shamans were shown to be incapable of stopping their dreaded diseases, against which Native people had little immunity. The Christian missionaries provided alternative spiritual guidance, often sparking intense rivalries and conflict with the local shaman. Some adapted by moving closer to Christianity (often while continuing traditional practices); others who adhered publicly to traditional approaches found themselves shunted aside by their communities.

Source: Image # 42314, American Museum of Natural History Library

Practices

The Iroquois False Face Society

Indigenous societies called on the spiritual world to keep them well, to keep them fed, and to bring health to the people. The False Face Society played this pivotal role among the Iroquois, with particular responsible for healing. Led by women but with numerous male members, the Society invoked spiritual powers through singing, chanting, and dancing, while the leaders used their hands or special salves on those affected by the illness. The members wore masks that were highly symbolic and dramatic in shape and colouring, representing key figures that stood for prominent elements in Iroquois spirituality. Individuals entered the False Face Society after being visited by a spirit, which was then represented by the mask they wore. False Face events served primarily to heal, drawing on spiritual powers to ward off illness and disease. They played important roles in community rituals designed to celebrate the passage of the seasons and to chase off evil spirits that might target the people (Blau 1966).

Adulthood

Aboriginal cultures placed a great deal of emphasis on rites of passage into adulthood. The rituals and practices associated with puberty and the assumption of adult responsibilities often had strong spiritual elements, such as the spirit quests of the people of the North American plains. In these quests, young Aboriginal men would leave the community, often for extended periods, and subject themselves to lengthy periods without food. The expectation was that they would have an intense spiritual experience, typically in the form of a dream or vision, during the period of deprivation. This **vision quest** would provide the participant with guidance into adulthood and usually a new name that captured the essence of the spiritual experience.

Vision quest: an intense spiritual experience, typically involving prolonged deprivation, during which participants make contact with their guardian spirit.

Practices

Sweetgrass

The use of sweetgrass (smudging) was among the most common Aboriginal spiritual rituals in Canada, and it remains in regular use. After the sweetgrass is harvested it is typically braided or tied into a sheaf. It is then lit and used for smudging. In a sweetgrass ceremony, the smoke from the grass (also called the smudge) is waved toward the face and over the head, allowing its gentle smell to surround the individual. The sweetgrass is passed from person to person, drawing peace into the gathering. This ceremony is designed to be a celebration of the spiritual world—the Creator, in many traditions—and is intended to be a reminder of the place of humans within creation. The sweetgrass purifies and cleanses the soul, making it more receptive and encouraging the individual to follow spiritual guidance. Sweetgrass ceremonies have become commonplace across North America and are one of the primary pan-Indian rituals. The practice has become an important part of psychological and personal healing processes, particularly in prisons, where Aboriginal rights advocates had to fight for permission to engage in the ceremony.

Female puberty rituals remain important (more so than those of males) among Indigenous peoples. Young women are expected to provide moral strength for the people, so they are given special preparation for the responsibilities of adulthood. Often sequestered for a period of training and preparation, the young women are blessed by the dominant spirits of the society, from which are requested protection and fertility in motherhood. The rituals involve elaborate dances and presentation of the young men, who use the ceremonies to identify the one they wish to marry (Dugan 1985).

Late Nineteenth-Century Cree Sun Dance Ceremony

Indigenous spirituality underwent profound changes following the arrival of Europeans and the spread of Christianity and government authority. Newcomers, while often impressed by the spectacle of Native ceremonial and religious practices, recoiled at the intensity and power of many Indigenous spiritual activities, including the lengthy and highly potent Sun Dance. Governments in Canada and the United States actively suppressed these cultural practices in the late nineteenth and early twentieth centuries.

Source: © Bettmann/CORBIS

Practices

The Sun Dance

The Sun Dance was one of the most important spiritual rituals of Native people of the northern plains, and it spread widely among the various tribal societies. The ritual appears to be connected with the social and cultural turmoil in the region during the nineteenth century, picking up on and expanding Indigenous practices in response to the rapid changes associated with development of the west. They were typically held to follow up on a vision received by a community member or when the people needed to draw on spiritual authority. These long events, which lasted for more than a week, required extensive organization and preparation, often undertaken by the women of the community. Cleansing and preparatory rituals began the process, which culminated in the raising of a sacred pole and construction of a sacred lodge.

These powerful events drew people together, gave prestige to the dancers and organizers, celebrated spiritual connections, and encouraged cultural renewal. In some societies, including among the Crows, Dakota, and Blackfeet, cutting rituals figured prominently in the Sun Dance, while other groups did not include cutting. The Government of Canada banned Sun Dances in the late nineteenth century, believing that such "pagan" practices undermined efforts to assimilate them into European and Christian traditions. The effort to restrict the dances failed—government agents could not watch over Native people all the time—and the tradition continued underground. The Sun Dance resurfaced when the government lifted the ban and has re-emerged as a central element of the cultural and religious traditions of the Plains peoples (Twofeathers 1997).

Harvesting

Indigenous peoples lived closely with their environment and believed that spirits guided their pursuit of food and, therefore, their survival. Animals, many held, gave themselves up voluntarily to be killed for human sustenance. Thus the spirit of the animal had to be recognized and addressed, for the animal was sure to be reborn to make itself available for food in the future. The Inuit of the Arctic relied heavily on spiritual tools—songs, carved amulets, and the like—to draw bowhead whales toward their spears. Killing a whale was an act of reverence, not bloodthirstiness. After a successful kill the whale would be honoured and, in thanks, given water from a bucket specially made for that purpose.

The Nuu-chah-nulth on the West Coast of Canada also connected spirituality and harvesting. The lead whaler would prepare himself carefully for pursuit of the whales, undergoing a long period of fasting and spiritual reflection. The whaler would bathe and scrub himself in order to ensure cleanliness for the hunt. His wife was then expected to remain in her bed without moving while her husband pursued the whale. Hunters also invoked the spirits of deceased members of their community, believing that they would direct them to the whales. When a whale was killed, the hunters and the community would thank the animal for surrendering itself and would seek to mollify its spirit.

Marriage

The union of a man and a woman, one of the core elements in societal organization, likewise requires formal recognition from the community. While specific ceremonies vary widely, the idea of recognizing marriage (and, in some cultures, multiple marriages or divorce) and celebrating the formation of a new family unit figures prominently in Native tradition. Spirituality figured prominently in Kwakiutl marriage ceremonies, even when these were dominated by substantial exchanges of material wealth. The parents would arrive at an acceptable price for the woman's hand and arrange the ceremony. According to a description of a turn-of-the-twentieth-century marriage, the woman would be collected by men from the groom's family and escorted to the ceremonial site. There, amidst much singing and dancing, and with participants often donning impressive spirit masks, the marriage ritual would continue. The elaborate masks represented key spiritual figures, including monsters who would eat anyone who dared compete for the woman's hand. Chiefs and spiritual leaders would speak at the ceremony, invoking protection for the couple, while the families completed the exchange of material goods agreed upon earlier. While observers describe the marriage ritual as a symbolic representation of war, and though material exchange featured prominently in the ceremony, the events included significant representations of spiritual beliefs and calls for spiritual guidance.

Women in Native Religions

Women play very important roles in Native societies and have had a significant presence in religious values and practices. Among the Aztecs, for example, Coatlicue was described as "the mother of gods" and was the deity responsible for the emergence of the moon and stars. Takanaluk, or Sea Woman, is one of the most prominent figures in Inuit spirituality and is seen as responsible for controlling the fish and sea mammals that inhabit Arctic waters. Female figures feature prominently in Native creation stories and descriptions of the spiritual world, reflecting the prominent place of women within the broader society.

Indigenous societies typically had strong rituals and conventions governing women's activities during menstruation. Menstruating women were often separated from their families and the community, housed in separate facilities, and given an opportunity to pray and reflect on spiritual and social matters. These ceremonial activities reinforced the key roles that women played in the society, particularly those of mother and caregiver, and emphasized their special spiritual responsibilities. The retreat from family and community, which the Anishinabe refer to as "moontime," celebrated the reproductive role of women and illustrated how close they are to the rhythms and power of the natural world.

Illness

Sickness tests a person's faith and challenges spiritual leaders. So it was in Indigenous religions. Spiritual leaders often handled illnesses, relying on traditional medicines or healing mechanisms, evoking powerful spirits, or blaming malevolent forces or spells for the illness. Successful healing could strengthen connections; failed healing could test resolve.

Practices

Sweat Lodges

Purification rituals are very important in many Native religious traditions. They are designed to purge the body of evil and malicious influences and to open both body and mind to the spirits and to religious teachings. In most Canadian Aboriginal communities, small lodges, for either individual or group use, are built specifically for a sweat. Heated stones are placed on a hearth in the middle of the lodge and water is poured over the rocks, producing a steady flow of steam. Temperatures rise dramatically inside the lodge, and the resulting perspiration rids both body and soul of unwanted elements.

The sweat lodge is more than an Aboriginal sauna. Traditional practices determine the orientation of the lodge and a spiritual leader leads the sweat. The sharing of a pipe is commonplace, as are prayers and singing. Elders call on the spirits for assistance and guidance and instruct participants to open themselves to the wisdom of the spirits. Sweats can go on for lengthy periods, the heat and steam combining with the prayers and rituals to create an intense emotional experience for the participants.

PEOPLE & PLACES

Midewiwin

Organized medicine societies were common among Native groups in Canada, bringing together individuals with special medical or spiritual powers. Midewiwin, or Grand Medicine Society, emerged during the early years of European contact in the areas north and west of the Great Lakes. (Like many aspects of Aboriginal spirituality, this tradition has connections to pre-contact practices but appears to have been a specifically post-contact development.) These highly organized groups of men had special ways of selecting and initiating individuals into the order, and they operated according to highly ritualized practices that included shooting rituals and sacred shells. Individuals worked their way through several stages of membership, each level indicating a greater depth of understanding and cultural awareness. Other members of society, who alternately feared and treasured their spiritual powers, held the leaders in high esteem.

Members were taught the core concepts and ideas of the group, introduced to the songs that played a crucial role in healing processes, learned Indigenous healing systems, and were given medicine bundles to support their communion with the spiritual world. The Midewiwin passed on their traditions through songs, ceremonies, and visual representations of their practices, and they served as a central element in the social and spiritual lives of their people. Indigenous spirituality continued to evolve over time, either through greater incorporation of Christian practices or, as in the case of the Chippewa, transformation of the Midewiwin tradition into the Drum Dance (Harrison 1982).

The !Kung of southern Africa emphasized a healing ritual called the trance dance. Illness, in this tradition, came from the spirits. A healing dance had the power, they believed, to stop the spirits from affecting the individual or the group. The ritual involved lengthy, active dances by men or women that left participants in a trance, providing a powerful counterbalance to the spirits. Those in a trance had the ability, they believed, to heal all the people at the ceremony. Like many Indigenous spiritual rituals, the trance dance had an important social function as well, the singing and joy of the event adding to both the enjoyment of participants and the spiritual power of those seeking to provide healing.

Death

Rituals of death and dying provide the best illustration of belief in and respect for spiritual faith. Concepts held about the life hereafter outline fundamental understandings about spiritual power and the existence of otherworldly realities. Native religions have elaborate end-of-life rituals that incorporate deeply embedded beliefs about the spiritual world. The preparation of bodies, funeral pyres, inclusion of personal effects with the body (to arm the individual for life in the world of the spirits), and other ceremonial elements demonstrate the depth and sincerity of Indigenous beliefs about deities and spirits.

The Aborigines of Australia attach great importance to the funeral experience, celebrating the life of the departed spirit, which is supposed to return to its point of birth for later reincarnation. Sombre and colourful dances and rituals are followed, in much of the country, by preparation and presentation of the body for the hereafter. The body is typically first placed on an elevated platform, where it is allowed to decompose. Later the bones are handled with great care, being carried by a relative for some time, placed in a cave, or deposited in a fallen tree. This reverence for the dead is an expression of confidence in the spirit world and the inevitable return to life of the deceased. The Plains peoples of North America likewise placed the body off the ground, usually with key personal possessions to serve the individual in the afterlife. Women mourned extensively and would often hurt themselves—cutting off a fingertip, for example, if they had lost their child or husband.

PEOPLE & PLACES

Medicine Wheels

Aboriginal religions in Canada left few monuments or dramatic physical manifestations of their spirituality or religious practices, save for the majestic totem poles of the West Coast. Considerable interest, therefore, has been given to the large and dramatic medicine wheels (this description is one used by newcomers and archeologists, not Indigenous people) found on the northern plains. The medicine wheels typically involve a configuration of rocks or cairns set up in a circle with spoke-like ribs. These symmetrical forms were clearly created for a particular (but not clearly understood) purpose using locally available materials, and they often show signs of being temporary structures. One of the more prominent—the Ellis Medicine Wheel in Alberta—includes a central circle about 5 metres in diameter and a series of spokes radiating from it for up to 20 metres.

The purpose of the wheels, some of which were clearly used many times while others were apparently designed for a single ceremony, is not completely clear, although some appear to serve as death memorials for prominent leaders. Some analysts say they were connected to Sun Dances and other large ceremonial activities. The concepts of the medicine wheel, particularly the emphasis on circles and a holistic approach to life and wellness, have become familiar parts of contemporary spirituality, healing practices, and definitions of Indigenous worldviews. Ironically, these concepts have more consistent application and resonance in the present than they appear to have had in the past. (Wilson 1994).

AUTHORITIES

Given the nature of Indigenous societies and the absence of literacy, it is hardly surprising that Native traditions did not include written texts or elaborate social and religious codes. There are no Indigenous counterparts to the Bible or the Qur'an, and human or charismatic leadership plays a relatively small role in Native spirituality. Importantly, even the advent of writing and literacy among Indigenous groups did not produce an effort to codify existing beliefs in written form. **Orality**—reliance on the spoken word passed on from generation to generation—remained and remains a cornerstone of Indigenous spirituality. Learning to write, ironically, typically focused on learning to read the Bible, and only very rarely was writing used to record and pass on Native spiritual concepts and traditions.

Aboriginal groups had multiple deities (some accorded special powers to one or a small number of gods) and believed that spiritual authority existed all around the individual and the group. This approach ensured that Aboriginal people were highly vigilant with regard to spiritual behaviour and well aware that spiritual authorities were abundant in their lives. Many Indigenous traditions had powerful figures—the Trickster was commonplace among North American Native peoples—who played influential roles in community life. For example, Wisakedjak (Plains Cree) and Naapi (Blackfoot) were complex characters that alternated between offering strong guidance and at other times seeming vengeful and even silly. Their unconventional behaviour replicated the unreliability of the human and natural worlds.

Most world religions have clear authorities, in the form of a deity, a prophet, a foundational text, or religious structures. The hundreds of Native religions around the world typically have none of these, but this does not mean that their spirituality lacks focus, meaning, or real power. Authority rests in the land, the animals, and the elements, and it is expressed through human recognition of the power, mystery, and spiritual intensity of the natural world. It was this absence of formality that led newcomers to describe Indigenous peoples as being without religion and without spiritual guidance, living in superstition and guided by self-important shamans or medicine men. This also meant that the incoming people missed the depth and persistence of Indigenous spirituality, which continued long after many of the public rituals and ceremonies had been eliminated, modified, or transformed into the practices of imported faith traditions.

Orality: the deep and powerful influences of oral traditions, such as storytelling, elders' lessons, dances, and singing, on cultures that do not communicate extensively through writing.

Practices

Medicine Bags or Bundles

The Indigenous peoples of the northern plains organized much of their spiritual and religious practice around special medicine bags or bundles. These bags carried items of spiritual importance to the individual or the community, typically containing animal parts, artifacts, and important plants. They did not contain medicine—and therefore were not the Aboriginal counterpart to the Western doctor's bag—but rather held items of spiritual and cultural significance. The bag represented or added to the shaman's healing powers. There was no fixed size, format, or design for medicine bags; they reflected the personal history, beliefs, and spiritual understandings of the owner. They were passed on through the generations and were guarded with reverence and great care. Often items in the bags were associated with powerful and culturally important songs that themselves were owned by the possessor of the bag (Frisbie 1987). When the bag wore out, the contents would be carefully moved to another bag.

RELIGIOUS IDENTITY

Indigenous societies, while varying dramatically in size, cultural characteristics, lifestyles, and worldviews, nonetheless have several spiritual and religious elements in common. They do not have formal churches or extensively managed religious organizations, and spirituality is highly individualistic and religious leadership is quite fluid. Organized religion of the type common in Europe and much of Asia at the time of contact had no counterpart among the small, mobile Indigenous populations of the world. Identity came through family, language, and, most powerfully, relationship to traditional territories. Religion was not a cultural badge or a means of marking identity, as it was with many other approaches to faith and spirituality.

That being said, Native groups did have spiritual leaders who were at some times quite powerful and influential, but they did not share a common training or a systematic means of being prepared for leadership. Native people had many fixed traditions, customs, and practices associated with their spiritual beliefs, and these were sustained over hundreds of years. They ranged from cycle-of-life rituals (birth, adulthood, marriage, death) to requirements that animals killed for food be honoured and thanked by those who killed them. These traditions allowed for a great diversity of spiritual reflection, belief, and ceremony. While certain practices were maintained within the group, individual spirituality rested on family and group experiences and, typically, a very personal relationship with the natural environment. The use of the term *two-spirited* by some Indigenous groups to describe individuals with a homosexual orientation is but one indication of this openness to the diversity of human spiritualities.

In past generations, well-developed rituals tied to key stages in the cycle of life played a central role in identity formation and personal growth. Since the arrival of newcomers and dominant external governments, values, and traditions in Native territories, many of these traditions have receded in importance. Where they are still practised—in rural Australia and remote regions of Asia, North America, Africa, and Latin America—Indigenous societies count on their rituals to mark important events that indicate the place of an individual or family within the society and in relationship to the spiritual world. Oftentimes these traditions come into conflict with changing values. In remote parts of Australia, young men have been taken against their will to participate in initiation ceremonies. On rare occasions the young men fought back after their return, charging community members with abduction and assault for forcing them to participate in the ceremonies.

Spirituality plays a role in the contemporary self-image of Indigenous peoples, but not in a deep and well-organized manner. As the oppression of Indigenous peoples and cultures declined and as institutions and the public at large came to accept the diversity and complexity of Aboriginal values and beliefs, Native spirituality and religious practices experienced a significant resurgence. There was no substantial nation-wide or international movement coalesced around a single idea, leader, or organization. Revitalization movements of the type experienced in the nineteenth century have been extremely rare and short-lived. Instead, under the leadership of elders and local leaders, community-specific practices, customs, and traditions have been reintroduced. Political meetings and school classrooms have become the most important venues for the positive celebration and use of Indigenous spiritual approaches. However, many Aboriginal people remain distant from these religious practices, and indeed, Christian churches and traditions remain much stronger and higher-profile in most Native communities. Much of the renaissance, if such a word is appropriate, has been ceremonial in nature. Sweetgrass ceremonies or local variants open many public meetings. Elders are regularly brought in to bless events and to offer prayers and words of wisdom, albeit in languages that are often as little understood as Latin is at a Canadian Catholic mass.

There is value, for both Aboriginal and non-Aboriginal people, in public displays of Aboriginal ceremony and tradition. For the Indigenous participants and onlookers, the use of Native practices demonstrates that their cultures are alive and relevant in the twenty-first century. They provide, further, an opportunity to educate non-Aboriginal people about Indigenous values and traditions, and so to place the Aboriginal participants in a position of some prestige and relevance. Non-Aboriginal people, for their part, are often enthusiastic supporters of Indigenous spiritual and religious activities, for they provide a unique glimpse into a different world, an affirmation of open-mindedness, and a means of showing respect for Indigenous cultures.

The practices themselves might be inconsequential and brief, but they are generally well regarded by all the participants and seek to forge connections of equality and appreciation.

One of the strongest and most consistent uses of Indigenous spirituality is found in the prison and rehabilitation systems. Aboriginal rates of incarceration, self-destructive behaviour, and internally directed violence are well above those in the general newcomer populations. Officials in the prisons, halfway houses, and other parts of the correction system have long searched for the best means of reaching Aboriginal offenders and placing them on the right path. Elders, Aboriginal spiritual leaders, Indigenous activists, family members, and others have discovered that a substantial number of these men and women respond to Indigenous spiritual teachings and experiences. Sweat lodges have become quite commonplace in Canadian prisons, as have Aboriginal religious and spiritual practitioners. The use of Indigenous spirituality to reach hitherto lost and directionless people is tied strongly to their problems with self-esteem and Aboriginal self-identity: spiritual customs and actions provide a positive connection and outlet.

Health-care providers have also come to understand the importance of Aboriginal religion and spiritual practices, even if they cannot explain their scientific relevance. Some hospitals, particularly in the northern parts of the prairie provinces, have included Native healers in their practice, seeking to provide Indigenous clients with services and support that are culturally relevant and acceptable. More than a decade ago, a prominent and outspoken Native political leader appeared close to death. He was wasting away and could not fight against what seemed to be the imminent collapse of his bodily functions. Medical doctors struggled in vain to identity cause and treatment. While visiting his community, a healer approached and asked the man if he was sick. Then the medicine man provided a solution: he told the politician that he was too angry and that all the anger was hurting him. He counselled him to find peace and to make peace. The advice was followed and the politician recovered, becoming a very different kind of leader and with newfound respect for his community's spiritual traditions and teachings.

Pan-Indigeneity: the convergence of Indigenous traditions around a set of common practices that collectively highlight the commonality of Indigenous cultures and worldviews.

Peace pipe: originally smoked to mark the end of conflict and the creation of alliances and trading relationships; now one of the most widely recognized Indigenous traditions evoking spiritual powers to support human endeavours.

Pan-Indigenous Practices

Pan-Indigeneity is one of the most important religious and spiritual phenomena observable among Indigenous populations today in the more economically developed parts of the world. Before the arrival of the Europeans, Indigenous cultures remained within relatively narrow confines; there was little sharing across cultural and geographic boundaries. The arrival of the Europeans offered Christianity, although in various denominational formats, as a unifying religious force, although doctrinal disputes between Catholics and Protestants prevented large-scale connections from developing. The combination of sharing space in residential schools and the post-Second World War movement of Indigenous peoples from reserves to towns and cities, and from one part of the country to another, mingled Aboriginal populations as never before. Indigenous peoples from many cultures came together in the major cities and, through cultural centres, Aboriginal-run schools, and other outlets, began to make connections across Aboriginal divides (Blaser et al. 2010).

One outcome of this mingling of peoples was the development of shared Indigenous customs and practices. Certain traditions of North America—the **peace pipe**, the sweat lodge, sweetgrass ceremonies—became commonplace as they were adopted and adapted by Aboriginal groups of many types. These standard activities became symbols of Aboriginality and could soon be seen at many different Indigenous gatherings and settings. Pan-Indigenity became particularly prevalent in prisons, where the large Aboriginal populations are drawn from all parts of the country. The ceremonies drew prisoners together and provided confidence-building and culturally enriching experiences, particularly as many of the prisoners had long been separated from their local spiritual traditions.

Pan-Indigenous practices, purists point out, are not "authentic" and therefore, they assert, they are not truly Aboriginal in character. The emergence of shared spiritual traditions is, however, a fairly logical outgrowth of social and demographic change. The practices provide a symbolic and practical identifier for Indigenous people and a recognizable means of asserting Aboriginality to non-Indigenous peoples. Over the past few decades, these practices have become entrenched in Aboriginal communities and have provided a cultural bridge that has drawn disparate Indigenous cultures together, if only weakly. The practices do not at this point have the strength, substance, and continuity to become a full-scale religious movement, and there is no substantial organizational strength behind the pan-Indigenous spirituality. They are however, a sign of continued Indigenous interest in culture, religion, and spirituality and an indication that Aboriginal people continue to seek appropriate means of exploring and expressing their spirituality.

RELIGIOUS DIVERSITY

In a statistical sense, Native religions have all but disappeared in many countries. Religious diversity in Indigenous communities typically refers not to different Aboriginal approaches to spiritual expression but rather to the degree of dominance by imported religious traditions. In Zambia, where hundreds of thousands of people live in remote villages, Indigenous religions account for only 1 percent of the professed faiths of residents. Much the same is true in New Zealand, where the Catholic and Anglican churches are very active, and in Indigenous regions of Japan, where Shinto traditions have replaced the most public expressions of Aboriginal traditions.

Close to 90 percent of Aboriginal Canadians indicate a religious affiliation (roughly the same as for the population as a whole); of this number, only 2 percent indicate that they follow a religion other than Catholic or Protestant. As a percentage of the total Canadian population, the number of individuals indicating attachment to a Native religion is exceptionally small. Indeed, Native religions are lumped together in the "other" statistical category—along with atheists, free thinkers, humanists, New Age, Scientology, and New Thought—which represents just 0.4 percent of the Canadian population. The "no religion" category, at more than 16 percent, dwarfs the category that includes Aboriginal religions. Statistically, then, Native religions are so small as to be irrelevant. Those professing the Jewish faith, while less than 1 percent of all Canadians, are much greater in number than those claiming adherence to a Native religion. Interestingly, statistical reporting on the prevalence of Indigenous religions in Africa, where many Native rituals, beliefs, and practices remain commonplace, shows a similar dominance of Christian faiths and very few people claiming a Native religion. If one uses statistics as a guide to beliefs and customs, then, it would seem that Native spirituality and religions have all but vanished from the face of the earth.

These data, however, misstate and misrepresent the current state of Aboriginal religion and Native spirituality. First, Indigenous people are very uncomfortable with national census data collection and tend to shy away from reporting their activities. Boycotts of censuses are common, particularly in Canada. Second, Native religions lack the organizational structure and formality that governments and census-takers associate with religions. Aboriginal people who follow their Native spiritual traditions very rarely have official membership in a church or a church-like institution. Religious groups that gather according to cultural traditions generally do not make donations or otherwise financially support entities duly constituted under national charitable regulations.

Most important, however, is the simple fact that Native religions do not fit the standard Western definitions of religion. Many Aboriginal people who self-identify as Catholic, Protestant, or some other imported faith do indeed follow traditional spiritual and religious practices. Aboriginal spiritual activities remain fairly widespread and commonplace, particularly in remote and northern regions. These traditions are deeply imbedded in both life on the land and in the seasonal and cultural movements of Indigenous peoples. A family might well hold a formal funeral in a Christian church for a recently deceased relative—and then hold a potlatch or other ceremony of remembrance in traditional Aboriginal fashion. Does this mean that the family is Christian?

Or does it indicate that they follow an Aboriginal religion or Native spiritual tradition? The answer, of course, is that they are both, a situation that is confusing to census-takers and external observers alike.

The simple point is this: very few Indigenous people describe themselves as practitioners of Aboriginal religions. This is an accurate reflection of reality, as *religion*, as commonly understood, does not equate well with the practices and traditions of most Indigenous communities. Many more Aboriginal people have strong Indigenous spiritual beliefs and seek ways—more often private than public—of expressing their spirituality. In this complex cultural and social system where the system used for recording religious affiliations is based on a non-Indigenous conception of spirituality and religion, the impression remains that Aboriginal religion has largely disappeared and that Indigenous spirituality is but a thin vestige of the past. Neither is true, for there is much more resilience and continuity in the spiritual and religious life of Aboriginal peoples than is generally believed.

Native religions and spirituality face significant challenges in the twenty-first century, as daunting as the forces for change and cultural transformation that occurred in the previous three centuries. The threats and influences come primarily from non-religious sources, although a few major issues have been created by the interaction of Aboriginal people and mainstream religions. An overview of the various challenges illustrates some of the ways in which the contemporary world is transforming Native religious practices, traditions, and worldviews that have persisted for many centuries.

Young Aboriginal people are increasingly disengaged from their communities and from the teaching and wisdom of their elders. In general, they are spending much less time on the land, have limited experience with fishing, hunting, trapping, and gathering, and are losing the intimate connection with traditional territories that has long been integral to Indigenous spirituality. The generation gap has been widened by the migration of Native families and individuals from reserves to towns and cities, which has reshaped the social and cultural dynamics of many Indigenous communities. Major urban centres—Toronto in Canada, Auckland in New Zealand, Sydney in Australia, Los Angeles in the United States—have some of the largest concentrations of Aboriginal people in their respective countries. The separation of families and between young people and elders has strained community relations and made the transmittal of cultural values and spiritual traditions increasingly difficult. While the actual cultural impact of this demographic shift has likely been overstated, the reality is that distance and separation have subverted relationships that rely heavily on regular interaction.

The informality and inclusiveness of Aboriginal religious and spiritual engagement work against these forms of faith expression in the twenty-first century. The old order relied heavily on frequent and relevant storytelling, one-on-one conversations, time on the land with elders, and community gatherings. With the latter taken over largely by political and management processes, and with less time than ever for the personal connections that sustained spiritual connections across generations, Aboriginal communities lack the larger and more inclusive events and processes that can build spiritual understanding and reinforce traditional practices. Not surprisingly, more organized religions, particularly Christian denominations, are moving with various degrees of aggressiveness to expand their place in Aboriginal societies. The mainstream churches—Anglican, Catholic, and other faiths—are quite inclusive in their approaches, aware that their legacy of cultural attack on Indigenous peoples precedes them in the communities. The Baha'i faith, for example, provides ample room for spiritual differentiation and exploration and has actually highlighted the religious contributions of Indigenous peoples. Pentecostal churches, some of which impose strict rules on adherents, have found many followers and at the same time have driven a wedge between church members and others in their communities.

Popular culture is, as for many other religions, having a marked effect on Aboriginal communities. Television, radio, video games, movies, and the like have given once isolated Indigenous peoples a much more comprehensive view of the world, albeit one obscured by advertisers and mythmakers. Young people raised on a steady diet of *Grand Theft Auto*, music videos, and action movies have little room left for spiritual reflection and participation in religious traditions. This cultural breakdown has led to serious challenges. The social pathology of many Aboriginal communities, marked by high rates of suicide, drug and alcohol abuse, teen pregnancy, violence, and incarceration, both reflects a spiritual void and accelerates separation from traditional cultural practices. Communities and individuals at risk may need spiritual comfort and direction, but at times of crisis, negative forces tend to overwhelm. Community leaders working hard to rebuild or expand cultural traditions find the various social challenges extremely difficult to overcome.

The forces undermining Native religion and spirituality are impressive, but the situation is not all negative. There are countervailing influences supporting Native religious beliefs and practices that hold considerable potential for the future. Only time will tell if factors supporting cultural and spiritual continuity will ensure the ongoing presence and importance of Native religious views. For example, elders are determined to keep Aboriginal values and traditions alive and relevant. There are literally hundreds of community leaders in all corners of the world working very hard to introduce young children to Indigenous customs and spiritual perspectives. This effort is carried out by volunteers, extremely sincere and backed by community-wide support. With the elders leading the way, Aboriginal communities in general have become more assertive about protecting and demonstrating their culture and their values. The demoralization of the past century and more is slowly being replaced by cultural and spiritual confidence. The expansion of Native spiritual practices and improvements in Native community engagement efforts beyond political radicalism have enhanced Native spiritual engagement and reinvigorated Indigenous cultural practices.

Native spiritual leaders have identified strong connections between spirituality and cultural strength and between an Indigenous worldview and personal rehabilitation. Indigenous communities speak openly and frankly about the social, economic, and cultural problems affecting their people. They work collectively to identify solutions for individuals and for groups. The coordination of efforts to improve circumstances for individuals at risk and communities that are struggling has given the Native religious movement a clear purpose and strong support. Because of the mingling of Indigenous peoples in cities, prisons, hospitals, and other settings, a pan-Aboriginal spirituality has emerged that is changing the nature of Native religious activity. Historically, Indigenous communities explored and celebrated their understanding of the spiritual world through culture-specific activities and traditions. In more recent times, In more recent times, a small set of cultural practices, like sweat lodges, smudging and death ceremonies, are the public markets of Indigenous spiritual practice. This transition is providing a more substantial base for Aboriginal spirituality and religion.

Relations with outsiders have also improved. Christian denominations have often been quite flexible in their relations with Aboriginal spiritual beliefs. That they bulldozed Indigenous practices and insisted on strict adherence to Christian structures was occasionally true but is no longer commonplace. The more inclusive value systems of the mainstream Christian churches (but not, in the main, more fundamentalist and evangelical branches) have allowed congregations to incorporate Native concepts and teachings. At the same time, the growing non-Aboriginal interest in Aboriginal spirituality has raised the profile of Indigenous worldviews and added to Indigenous confidence about their belief systems. And the same is true in reverse. When Christian missionaries, government agents, and the general non-Aboriginal public maligned Indigenous religious and spiritual practices, Native communities and individuals took the criticism to heart. Some moved away from traditional values precisely because the Europeans had described them so harshly and tried to eliminate their practices. Now, with non-Indigenous peoples seeking out elders and spiritual leaders for guidance and insight, non-Aboriginal interest is making Aboriginal spirituality more acceptable within the Indigenous population.

New technologies and Indigenous adaptation to the dominant societies have created additional opportunities. New media outlets, including Aboriginal television stations, regional radio broadcasts, and Aboriginal-controlled magazines and newspapers, have broadened the reach of Aboriginal cultural leaders. Among the most promising developments in this regard have been community and regionally based educational materials. The inclusion of cultural and spiritual content—particularly in the three northern Canadian territories—allows cultural leaders to place their ideas and concepts in the hands of teachers and children. Collectively, Aboriginal peoples have gained a greater ability to speak within and across cultures and to share stories, practices, traditions, and ideas about religion and spirituality in a way that could not be imagined only a few decades ago.

THE CANADIAN CONTEXT

The discussion above both includes and reflects spirituality and tradition among Aboriginal groups in the West. There are literally dozens of Aboriginal cultures within North and South America, and considerable diversity in practice within linguistic and cultural groups. Not surprisingly, therefore, Indigenous spirituality differs widely. More sedentary groups developed more elaborate ceremonies and greater formality than very mobile Indigenous peoples. However, spiritual expression through dance, singing, stage-of-life rituals, relationships with animals and the rest of the natural world, and concepts of deities and spiritual authority followed general Indigenous patterns.

Spiritual and religious practices among the Indigenous peoples of Canada replicated the diversity of other Native traditions in the West. The Indigenous populations themselves varied widely, from the mobile and remarkably adaptive Inuit of the Far North to the more sedentary and agricultural peoples of the Great Lakes region, among them the Huron and Iroquoian cultures. West Coast traditions reflected the unique conditions along the Pacific watershed, including one of the densest populations of any non-agricultural area in the preindustrial world, and the spiritual and economic importance of the salmon fishery. In much of the country, from the Maritimes across the subarctic and through the northern Great Plains, Indigenous populations moved with the seasons and the availability of food, developing cultures and ways of living that reflected the potential of their particular region. Each group, from the Mi'kmaq to the Coast Salish, from the Plains Cree to the Han of the Upper Yukon River Basin, had its own spiritual understandings and religious practices, although they adhered in general to the broader pattern of Indigenous peoples across the Americas. The religious diversity of Indigenous peoples, which includes the rich Christian traditions that emerged after contact with Europeans and the practices of the **Métis**—people of mixed Aboriginal and European ancestry—remains evident to the present day and plays a strong and re-emerging role in Aboriginal culture and public life (McMillan and Yellowhorn, 2004).

The subarctic peoples, who lived in harsh environments and travelled extensively, had fewer religious traditions and activities. But, as with the Inuit, they inhabited a world filled with spirits and explained by elaborate accounts, typically called *myths*. In contrast, the people of the northwest coast, the plains and parklands of the northern Prairies, and around and north of the Great Lakes, had much more complex spiritual traditions and practices. The religions of these diverse peoples all include creation stories that describe the emergence of the earth and humans. In varying forms, the creation stories describe how a dominant spirit reached to the bottom of the sea, collected dirt or mud, and from it created the Earth. Most traditions have a prominent spiritual figure possessed of great powers that shaped creation into its contemporary form, usually through an act of great bravery or wisdom.

Understandings of the origins of the earth and the spiritual beings that created order subsequently informed spiritual and religious practices as the Indigenous peoples sought the most appropriate means of celebrating, recognizing, and appeasing the powerful spirits that filled and defined their worlds. These means include, as for other Indigenous peoples, a complex web of celebrations and feasts, fertility rituals, purification rites, and invocations of the spirits. Many of the Indigenous religions in Canada contain notions of a **Great Spirit** or a dominant spiritual authority and speak of a life hereafter. Described as the world or land of the dead, the place where the spirits of the deceased gather, this afterworld is revered in Indigenous traditions. And, like Aboriginal spiritual traditions and religions the world over, the Indigenous practices recognize the crucial role that the spirits play in the availability of animals, fish, and birds and the nature of the seasons.

Native peoples of Canada counted on shamans to guide them on their spiritual journey and to protect them from evil spirits, which were often blamed for illness or hardship. The shaman interpreted the spiritual world, organized community celebrations, and managed the various spiritual and social groups

Métis: people of mixed Indigenous and European ancestry, typically French-speaking and associated with the Catholic Church.

Great Spirit: one of many names given to the dominant or most prominent spirit within Indigenous knowledge and faith systems.

PEOPLE & PLACES

Native Peoples of Canada

Iroquois

The peoples of the Iroquois Confederacy, whose lands spanned the border between what is now Canada and the United States, are among the best-known Indigenous peoples in the Americas. They earned a reputation as fierce warriors, strong allies, and people determined to maintain control of their destiny after the arrival of the outsiders. They had complex and effective governance systems, and their Confederacy made them a formidable presence in the early contact period. They lived in a bountiful area where they were able to mix agriculture, hunting, and fishing in a manner that allowed for more stability and less moving around than for many other Indigenous peoples in the West.

Their spiritual world centred on the Great Spirit, who was responsible for directing their affairs and who influenced the world through other gods and spiritual guides. The Great Spirit fought the forces of evil that tested the resolve and loyalty of the people. The Iroquois belief system emphasized the afterlife and challenged people to attend to the wishes of the Great Spirit if they hoped to make a peaceful transition after death. Given the strength of the Great Spirit and the other spiritual forces in their lives, it is not surprising that the Iroquois, led by "keepers of the faith," maintained a rich ceremonial tradition, which focused largely on changes in the seasons. Their traditions were complex, stable, and vital, governing personal relationships, celebrating the availability of food, and fortifying the people during times of conflict. These spiritual beliefs influenced both personal and group behaviour and served as the backbone of the society. Their belief and ceremonial system had much more structure than those of many Indigenous groups in the Americas but did not have the rigidity and formality of the imported Christian faith (Trigger 1976; Snow 1996).

Haida

The Indigenous peoples of the Pacific Northwest coast are known for their dramatic longhouses, impressive totem poles, and rich spiritual traditions. Their dances, masks and costumes, and refined ceremonial activities are all evidence of a complex and spiritually intense society, as were the activities of the shaman, who was responsible for monitoring the spiritual well-being of the society and invoking the spirits against enemies. The totem poles and other artistic expressions relied heavily on stylistic representations of the natural world, highlighting the Haida's strong reliance on animal and bird symbolism. The animal kingdom featured prominently in Haida spiritual understandings, for to them mammals, birds, fish, and other natural phenomena were as significant as human beings and imbued with considerable spiritual authority. A strong belief in reincarnation—and the movement of spirits between human and animal forms and worlds—influenced religious practice.

The Haida celebrated frequently and were known for the size and duration of their potlatches. These major celebrations often involved the presentation of gifts to spiritual guides and authorities, and included naming rituals for children, dances, singing, and storytelling. The highly stylized dances, which also drew on the animation of spirits from the animal world, featured handsomely carved masks and costumes that became the hallmark of West Coast Indigenous cultures. Haida celebrations of death included separation of the bodies by class or status (slaves were disposed of without ceremony), the use of a grave house to hold the body, often for an extended period, and for those of high status, placement of the deceased's remains on a **mortuary pole** and a funeral potlatch (a major cultural event of the Pacific Northwest, typically involving distribution to community members of material goods). The Haida believed that human beings would be reborn after death after they had waited in the spirit world for an opportunity to re-enter human experience.

Mortuary poles: in West Coast Indigenous cultures, large carved totem poles that recognized the lives of individuals and ancestral ties.

Inuit

The Inuit have long attracted attention as being among the Americas' most remarkable peoples, living as they do in an area that seems to outsiders devoid of food and other resources, hostile, and even dangerous. They moved widely over their Arctic territories, using both the land and the ice-covered sea during the long winter season. Theirs was a flexible society that involved making the most of the limited resources of the region; for example, women married young but often changed partners or lived in polygamous relationships. The extended family unit was the central social organization, with larger groups coming together as the seasons and food supplies permitted. Their world was awash with spirits, from the powerful imagery of the northern lights to the great authority of the whales and walruses. Inuit spiritual views had ample room for ghosts and mythical creatures: the long winter nights and fierce environment lent themselves to an assumption of powerful forces at play in their world and provided ample time for sharing stories and culture. They knew of their vulnerability in the Arctic environment and knew that attending to the wishes of the spirits was central to their survival.

The Inuit world had many gods, including the powerful undersea woman called Sedna, who exerted great influence over their lives. The northern lights were alternatively forces of great danger, the spirits of ancestors, or spirit guides. Religious practice was not codified or formal, although shamans (called *angakkuit*) provided interpretations of the spiritual world and guided their people through the complex interplay of animal spirits, people, and the natural world. The shaman called on spirits at times of hunting, illness, or conflict and offered explanations for that which could not readily be explained. The Inuit did not claim control over the spiritual world but sought, through the shaman and daily rituals (such as thanking animals that sacrificed themselves to provide food), to maintain a balanced relationship with the many spirits and forces around them (Damas 1981).

Métis

The Métis represent a distinctive Indigenous culture born from the intermarriage of Indigenous peoples and newcomers, principally French-speaking Catholics associated with the fur trade. The children of the fur trade developed a strong and stable culture based around the North West and Hudson's Bay companies and, in the nineteenth century, the prairie buffalo hunt. The Métis drew heavily on both their Indigenous and European ancestry, becoming different from but connected to both cultural lines. Economically they relied strongly on traditional Indigenous skills, serving as *voyageurs* for the fur traders and suppliers for the fur-trading posts.

The Catholic Church worked very hard to keep the Métis within its faith community while recognizing their distinctive life-ways and habits. The Anglican Church, in contrast, encouraged English-speaking people of mixed ancestry to assimilate into the broader Canadian society. Not all did, of course, and a sizeable number of Métis people with Anglican affiliations nonetheless retained a more traditional Métis lifestyle. Catholic priests lived and even travelled with the Métis on their major journeys, particularly during the massive buffalo hunts, and Catholicism became strongly identified with them from the early days. Métis families often maintained social and cultural ties with their First Nations relatives and participated in their social and religious activities. In general, however, the Métis remained devout Catholics (Brown 1985).

that operated within a population. A shaman's ability to heal or to help an individual overcome a severe difficulty determined his or her authority within the group—having "strong medicine" was a sign of a particularly effective connection to the spiritual world.

Seasonal rituals reflected the harvesting activities of the area. West Coast peoples celebrated the return of the salmon (the first salmon caught in a year was often singled out for particular respect and thanked for surrendering itself to the people); the rituals of the plains peoples focused on the return and harvesting of the buffalo. Indigenous peoples in what became Canada had rich spiritual traditions in which their seasonal rounds and personal activities were influenced by their understanding of the spiritual world and their efforts to evoke the spirits for their benefit. They feared evil spirits and worried that the mistreatment of the natural environment could result in harm to humans. Celebrations related to the cycles of life were commonplace, as were events tied to the seasons and to harvesting. While practices varied dramatically and were not codified in the same manner as Western religions, Indigenous spiritual and religious traditions nonetheless lasted for many centuries and played a prominent and continuing role in Aboriginal communities.

Canadian Indigenous peoples, starting in the Maritimes and around the Great Lakes, had extensive contact with missionaries from the early seventeenth century. The last groups to have regular contact with external church representatives—the Inuit—came in contact with the outsiders in the early twentieth century, more than three hundred years later. The Christian churches (other faiths had very little contact with Indigenous peoples up to the present) were aggressive in their outreach to the "heathens" of northern North America and worked very hard to bring them to the Christian way. Christianity for both Catholics and Protestants was about lifestyle and work patterns as much as Bible study and sermons. Indigenous peoples were encouraged to leave the land, become educated in Western ways, and assume a position in the changing wage and industrial economy. The churches had the ear of the Government of Canada and secured its substantial financial, legal, and administrative support. The federal government banned many Indigenous practices, including the central potlatch tradition of the West Coast, and sent Native children to church-run residential schools, where they were separated from their parents and culture and taught to disparage traditional values and beliefs.

While the Christian churches were often dogmatic, they also demonstrated considerable flexibility—what religious scholars describe as *latitudinarianism*, or creating space within an organized religion for conflicting practices. Missionaries tolerated traditional burial practices and a wide variety of cultural and spiritual issues and accepted the fact that many who had been baptized as Christians had a

PEOPLE & PLACES

Lac Ste. Anne

Lac Ste. Anne in Alberta is one of the most important spiritual sites for the Métis people of Canada. The lake, revered by the Sioux and Cree for its powerful monsters, has long held an important place in Indigenous religion. The Catholics, let initially by Father Thibault, established a Catholic mission at the site that ministered to the growing Métis population in the area. In the late 1850s the Grey Nuns arrived at the mission, drawing an ever larger number of Métis to the settlement. The lake had been known as a place of healing, and the shrine established at the mission came to be seen by the Métis as a site of miracles. An annual migration attracts as many as 40,000 people per year, and many stories circulate of miraculous cures and instant healing. In more recent times, Lac St. Anne has been a focal point for dealing with alcohol and drug addictions as well as cures for illness and disease, and it has emerged as a key centre for Métis cultural expression.

John Slocum and Louis Yowaluck, Leaders of the Indian Shaker Church

Native religions and spiritual practices have not been static over the generations but have responded to changing conditions in the natural, Indigenous, and broader world. While many Native practices continued, even in the face of efforts by churches and government to suppress them, numerous communities and peoples responded creatively to the arrival of Christianity. Some adapted readily to the newly arrived religion and became avid adherents of various Christian denominations. Others, as in the Indian Shaker Church led by Slocum and Yowaluck, melded Christianity and traditional spiritual views.

Source: BAE GN 03021 06487500, National Anthropological Archives, Smithsonian Institution

PERSPECTIVES

The Shaker Religion

The Shaker religion is a good example of the interconnections between Indigenous spiritual traditions and Christianity. The Shaker tradition, described less favourably as a messianic cult, emerged in the nineteenth century near Olympia, Washington, during a time of great upheaval and distress among Aboriginal people in western North America. John Slocum and his wife, building upon some of the guardian spirit concepts common in Indigenous spiritual traditions, introduced the new faith. Slocum, who was near death from illness, experienced direct contact with God and returned to life to preach about the inevitable return of Christ. Mary, his wife, healed him when he became seriously ill a second time. Her shaking during the healing rituals—reflecting a pattern of spirit possession that has been noted in both Indigenous and Christian faiths—gave the name to the new religion. It was a unique amalgam of faith traditions, drawing from Indigenous spiritual practices and the Catholic and Protestant branches of the Christian church.

Shaker churches included regular services, dramatic healing activities, and declarations of direct connection to God. In its initial formulation, the Shaker religion challenged both Indigenous and Christian traditions and sought to replace them both. The healing practices in particular threatened both the power of the local shaman and the claims of the Western world to scientific and medical understanding. Over time, however, many Indigenous groups and Christian congregations reconciled with the Shakers, finding ways to incorporate Native spirituality within their services and to accept elements of Shaker tradition into Christian ceremony. This blending of Indigenous spiritual practices with other religious activities in both the Christian and new faith traditions has been important in the perpetuation of Indigenous religious traditions. Importantly, the Shaker religion (like other new Indigenous religions) played a significant role in alcohol-abuse intervention as a means of helping Indigenous peoples cope with cultural change and turmoil (Ruby 1996).

very thin understanding of the values and substance of the faith and were continuing many traditional spiritual activities. With the collapse of Christian confidence in the 1960s, the Canadian churches became even more accommodating, establishing separate Aboriginal church organizations (including the All Native Circle Conference of the United Church of Canada), celebrating Indigenous traditions during church services, and reaching out to learn more about Indigenous beliefs and practices.

The churches' decision to offer an apology for their roles in the residential schools (and for their lack of oversight of evil behaviour by some of their staff members) and to participate in providing financial compensation for their actions provided an opportunity for a new relationship between the mainstream churches and Indigenous peoples. The financial and demographic weaknesses of the Catholic and Protestant churches, however, have undercut the their ability to expand their relationships substantially. Pentecostal churches have become increasingly active in Aboriginal communities, and the general Pentecostal emphasis on socializing only within the faith tradition has caused considerable rifts between believers and non-believers in Native communities. In one memorable instance in British Columbia, an evangelical group, aided by non-Aboriginal outsiders, erected a small church in a village only to incur the wrath of non–church members. The village council ordered the church closed and insisted that it be dismantled entirely. Non-Christian faiths, save for the Baha'i, have had relatively little contact with Indigenous groups. Immigrant populations have not been particularly supportive of Indigenous land and resource rights and have in general not found common ground on spiritual or cultural matters. There have been some promising connections, however, starting with business contacts and slowly expanding to the cultural and social realms, that suggest greater cultural and potentially spiritual interaction may be forthcoming.

Native spirituality is making a small public comeback, with increasing and respectful inclusion of elders and Indigenous spiritual traditions at public events and, particularly, at Native social and political gatherings. The diversity of Indigenous spirituality, however, which means that there are no common structure, traditions, practices, or formalized belief systems across the country, has worked against a comprehensive revitalization movement. Nevertheless, the Christian churches, at one time bitter opponents of Indigenous worldviews and social practices, have become among their greatest supporters. External observers often mix up Indigenous cultural practices with spirituality and religion. They can be connected but are not necessarily so: community gatherings, wealth exchanges, and rituals associated with life passages have often had much of their spiritual content removed, or replaced by newcomer traditions and concepts.

@

NATIVE RELIGION AND THE INTERNET

While new communication technologies and the Internet have enlivened and even revitalized many religions, the opposite appears to be true in the case of Native spirituality and practice. Many Indigenous populations are not well connected to the Internet and lack computing infrastructure and technological training within their communities. Furthermore, Indigenous spiritual expression lacks the organizational structure and administrative capacity that is needed to capitalize on communications advances.

There is a great deal of Indigenous spiritual material available online, but it is disorganized, unsystematic, and not designed to recruit or organize disparate community members. Much of the Internet content focuses on pre-contact traditions and practices, with the unintended consequence of reinforcing the idea that Native religions are dying, if not already dead. There has been, as well, a considerable amount of pre-emption of Native religion by other spiritual explorers and New Age thinkers, resulting in a blurring of the lines around Indigenous authenticity and cultural control. This is a long-standing issue for Indigenous peoples, who have long opposed the removal of cultural and spiritual artifacts from their communities and the control of Indigenous knowledge by outsiders. While the Internet has the potential to give Indigenous communities control over their spiritual story and representation, the poor infrastructure in many Native settlements and limited local ability to capitalize on new technologies are resulting in a digital profile that reinforces old images of Indigenous spirituality and allows outsiders to define the image and understanding of Native religions.

Perhaps more significantly, the Internet has permitted a proliferation of misinformation about and inaccurate representations of Aboriginal spirituality and religion. Numerous commentators and writers have appropriated Indigenous concepts. Critics of Aboriginal cultures have provided inaccurate and culturally dismissive commentaries on Native religions. With very few substantial authorities providing guidance or central control over the presentation of Aboriginal spirituality and religions, the Internet produces serious misrepresentations of Indigenous religions and adds to the fairly general sense that these spiritual formulations are no longer of much significance in the world. Some Indigenous communities, particularly those in the wealthier nations, have been using digital media to record, share, and sustain their spiritual and religious teachings, but this activity is comparatively slight and has yet to have much impact.

PEOPLE & PLACES

Native Sacred Sites and the Law

Aboriginal religious practices are no longer interfered with by the state, and there is growing respect for Indigenous spirituality in society at large. In one area, though—the protection of Aboriginal sacred sites—conflict remains. Native peoples have many places that hold special religious significance. These may be prominent landmarks such as lakes, mountains, waterfalls, unique stands of timber, islands, or the like, or less prominent features or areas that are nonetheless considered spiritually important.

Australia has seen many legal clashes over Aboriginal control of sacred sites and has enacted special legislation—for example, the Northern Territory Aboriginal Sacred Sites Act—that protects Indigenous interests in this area. This legislation has been used to stop the development of mines, to block roads, and to otherwise preserve these special locations. The transfer of Uluru (Ayers Rock) from the government to the local Pitjantjatjara and Yankunytjatjara Aborigine populations is the best-known example. The United States has provided some assurances—including the much-amended National Historic Sites Preservation Act, which includes numerous provisions to underscore the special interests of Native Americans, and President Clinton's executive order of 1996, which provided for Native use of federal lands for spiritual purposes—while also providing Native groups with the right to claim ancestral remains and artifacts that were taken without their consent.

Aboriginal identification of sacred sites can be extremely controversial. Sacred sites are often secret or semi-secret, and identifying them through any kind of open process can attract attention to locations that are supposed to be kept for very special purposes. It causes great anxiety among Indigenous peoples to have to identify and defend sacred locations. In addition, non-Aboriginal people repeatedly challenge Indigenous claims that a site is truly sacred, touching off extensive debate and creating divisions between groups. In rural areas, where plans to open a mine, build a road, harvest timber, or otherwise develop the land can come into conflict with burial and spiritual sites, bitter disputes can erupt.

The proposed Hindmarsh Island Bridge in Australia sparked great controversy. Some local Aborigines declared that the site was sacred but refused to disclose the reasons. After much legal and public wrangling, it appeared that the claim had been made up, and the bridge was built. The controversy did not die, however, as further debate suggested that the claim was indeed substantive. For Aboriginal people, any proposal to destroy or desecrate a spiritual site is taken most seriously, often sparking legal action, blockades, and civil disobedience, such as the Gustafsen Lake standoff over proposed development of a gravesite in the interior of British Columbia in 1995.

CONCLUSION

While any accounting of the spiritual and religious challenges facing Native peoples provides a daunting list of threats and influences pulling Indigenous peoples toward other religious traditions, a crucial point must be kept in mind. Outsider commentators have been killing off Native spirituality for hundreds of years. Christian missionaries as early as the fifteenth century declared that "primitive" and "savage" worldviews would soon be overwhelmed by European values and traditions. Governments supported the Christians' efforts through residential schools and restrictions on cultural practices. Sharply negative attitudes toward Native spiritual traditions built up over time, further marginalizing Indigenous spiritual practices.

But Native spirituality persisted. Religious practices and expression changed, as they have done in all religions in Canada and globally. No religion or spiritual view of the world stands apart from the society in which it operates. But despite formidable forces seeking to undermine and even destroy Indigenous spirituality, many Native people continue to hold to practices, beliefs, values, and traditions that are connected to centuries-old Aboriginal religions. That Aboriginal people go to Christian churches, spend less time on the land than they did historically, and seem integrated into the Canadian mainstream does not mean that Native spirituality has disappeared, or that it will disappear anytime soon.

What is clear is that Native religious practices do not follow the public, formal structures of other, more mainstream religions but rather represent more personal and community values and traditions. Native religion, therefore, is less obvious and more difficult to identify than the traditional Western religions. This does not mean, however, that they have died or are about to disappear. The lack of high-profile Native religious facilities, formal religious structures, easily identifiable and charismatic religious leaders does not mean that Aboriginal spirituality has withered away or that no Indigenous spiritual practices remain. The temptation within the dominant societies, evident for hundreds of years now, is to assume that Indigenous spirituality and religion will simply fade away, becoming a cultural remnant of a dying group of societies. In spite of these predictions, however, Native spirituality remains, as before, deeply connected to land and community, and is still an integral part of Indigenous understanding of humanity and nature.

As outlined at the outset of this chapter, Indigenous spirituality and religion warrant careful study. While Indigenous spirituality and religious practices share core elements, there is considerable diversity among the various Indigenous peoples of the world. In-digenous traditions are rich, complex, and of very long standing; they have persisted in the face of many powerful forces of change and destruction. Indigenous belief systems have adapted to the arrival of new religions, particularly Christianity, but they clearly have not disappeared. The centrepiece to understanding Indigenous religion is to recognize that spirituality and religious practices are deeply imbedded within Native cultures, and resilience, not disappearance, is one of the core characteristics of Indigenous faith.

The effort to explain Native religion and spirituality raises important questions about what Scott Klein described in Chapter 1 as the "insider/outsider problem."

***The Spirit of Haida Gwaii*, by Bill Reid**

While there is a strong tendency to see Aboriginal spirituality as a historical and cultural artifact, a dying if not dead remnant of distant values and practices, the reality is that Native religion remains vibrant and diverse. Native art such as this famous sculpture by Haida artist Bill Reid remains a prominent means of sharing religious stories and spiritual values. *The Spirit of Haida Gwaii*, which represents the spiritual forces of British Columbia's northwest coast Haida people, is one of Canada's best-known pieces of modern art. One version highlights the Canadian Embassy in Washington, D.C., and the other is prominently displayed at Vancouver International Airport.

Source: *The Spirit of Haida Gwaii: The Jade Canoe* by Haida artist Bill Reid, 1993. The second and final bronze casting. In the collection of the Vancouver International Airport Authority.

Outsiders, particularly anthropologists, ethnographers, and historians, have prepared almost all of the extended definitions of Aboriginal spiritual understanding and practice. The small number of Indigenous people who have written about their religious beliefs have done so primarily to make personal statements about their spirituality and to emphasize the persistence of traditional practices and worldviews. The intellectualizing of Native religion has allowed for greater comparisons and deeper analysis, but it has also highlighted the gap between practitioners and analysts. Given the evolution of Indigenous practice and belief, particularly through its connections to Christianity, contemporary Aboriginal activities do not match easily with descriptions of pre-contact spirituality. One is left, in the absence of codified religious texts and formalized practice (to say nothing of the integration of Indigenous and Christian beliefs), with externally constructed definitions of Aboriginal religion and numerous efforts to rationalize Aboriginal practice in light of the demands of subsistence lifestyles, rather than as a rich intellectual and spiritual tradition. The effort to truly understand Aboriginal spirituality and religious practice remains, therefore, clouded by cross-cultural contact and Western intellectual traditions and standards. The usual approaches to the study of religions do not transfer well to the Indigenous situation. This often leads to the impression that Aboriginal cultures were historically only partially formed and that the damage caused by colonization and missionization left deep spiritual scars on Indigenous peoples that may never be healed.

In the final analysis, Native religious and spiritual practice represents—as do all the world's religions—the evolution of human experience and thought over time. Aboriginal spirituality has evolved dramatically, and contact with other cultures has introduced major and significant change. Many Native people remain active spiritually and have found ways to bridge the perceived gap between Indigenous and Western worldviews. There is clearly no singular Aboriginal religion or spiritual formation and none of the formal texts or codes that help students of religion delve deep into the intellectual and cultural nuances of a belief system. What there is, however, is abundant evidence of deeply spiritual peoples who developed complex and sophisticated beliefs and practices over many generations. Native people, after all, share the profoundly human propensity to seek an ultimate meaning for the place of humanity within natural and supra-human realities. Like other peoples, Aboriginal societies founded the institutions, customs, traditions, rituals, and belief systems necessary to situate themselves within the physical–spiritual continuum and continue to seek the best means possible of understanding the mysteries of the human condition.

KEY TERMS

Anticolonial, p. 213
Communitarian, p. 209
Elder, p. 203
First Nation, p. 203
Fourth World, p. 205
Great Spirit, p. 227
Inuit, p. 205
Métis, p. 227
Missionaries, p. 207
Mortuary poles, p. 229
Orality, p. 221
Pan-Indigeneity, p. 223
Peace pipe, p. 223
Polygamy, p. 209
Potlatch, p. 212
Race for souls, p. 208
Residential schools, p. 212
Revitalization movements, p. 210
Shaman, p. 209
Smallpox, p. 209
Syncretistic movements, p. 210
Traditional medicines, p. 209
Traditional territories, p. 205
Vision quest, p. 216

CRITICAL THINKING QUESTIONS

1. Do you think that Christianity or other introduced faiths can coexist with Indigenous spirituality and religion?
2. Is it appropriate to describe Indigenous spirituality and spiritual practices as a religion?
3. Why did Indigenous spirituality and spiritual customs focus so strongly on relationships between humans and animals and between humans and nature?
4. Are Indigenous spiritual and religious beliefs and traditions relevant and helpful in the twenty-first century?

RECOMMENDED READING

Deloria, Vine. *God Is Red: A Native View of Religion.* New York: Dell, 1975.

Dickason, Olive, and David McNab. *Canada's First Nations: A History of Founding Peoples from Earliest Times.* Toronto: Oxford, 2009.

Goldman, I. *The Mouth of Heaven: An Introduction to Kwakiutl Religious Thought.* New York: John Wiley, 1975.

Hultkrantz, A. *Belief and Worship in Native North America.* Syracuse: Syracuse University Press, 1981.

———. *Native Religions of North America.* Toronto: Harper & Row, 1987.

———. *Prairie and Plains Indians.* Leiden: Brill, 1973.

———. *The Religions of the American Indians.* Berkeley: University of California Press, 1982.

McMillan, A., and E. Yellowhorn. *First Peoples in Canada.* Vancouver: Douglas and McIntyre, 2004.

Morrison, R. B., and C. R. Wilson. *Native Peoples: The Canadian Experience.* Toronto: Oxford University Press, 2004.

Schaeffer, C. E., *Blackfoot Shaking Tent.* Calgary: Glenbow Institute, 1969.

Stewart, Omer C. *Peyote Religion: A History.* Norman: University of Oklahoma Press, 1987.

Thompson, S. *Tales of the North American Indians.* Bloomington: Indiana University Press,1966.

Underhill, R. *Red Man's Religion: Beliefs and Practices of the Indians North of Mexico.* Chicago: University of Chicago Press, 1965.

Waugh, E. H., and K. Dad Prithipaul. *Native Religious Traditions.* Waterloo, ON: Wilfrid Laurier University Press, 1979.

RECOMMENDED VIEWING

A Man Called Horse. Dir. Elliot Silverstein. Perf. Richard Harris, Judith Anderson, Jean Gascon. Cinema Center Films, 1970. Film.

The Mission. Dir. Roland Joffé. Perf. Robert De Niro, Jeremy Irons. Enigma Productions/Kingsmere Productions/Warner Bros., 1986. Film.

Black Robe. Dir. Bruce Beresford. Perf. Lothaire Bluteau, Aden Young, Sandrine Holt. Alliance Communications/ Samson Productions, 1991. Film.

First Nations: The Circle Unbroken. National Film Board of Canada, 1998. Video series.

USEFUL WEBSITES

Ancient Wisdom: Native Religions of North America
A link site to valuable primary and secondary materials on Indigenous spirituality and religion.

Canada's First Nations
A useful overview site with considerable background on Indigenous cultures. *Canada's First Nations* is a joint project of the University of Calgary and Red Deer College.

First Peoples' Cultural Foundation
A very interesting site designed to preserve Indigenous languages and cultures.

Four Directions Teachings
Introduction to the core values and traditions of four North American Indigenous groups.

Internet Sacred Text Archives: Native American Religions
Primary (original) texts relating to Indigenous spirituality and religious practice.

Legends Project (CBC Radio)
Traditional stories and legends from Indigenous groups across Canada.

Multicultural Canada
Brief introductions to cultures in Canada, including Indigenous groups.

Native American Spirituality and Religion Directory of Online Resources
Link site to important online materials.

Native Religions of Newfoundland and Labrador
Overview of Indigenous religious traditions on the East Coast.

Native Spirituality Guide
A handbook prepared for police officers to help them understand Indigenous spiritual and religious practices.

Native Web
Link site to valuable Internet collections relating to Indigenous peoples.

Truth and Reconciliation Commission of Canada
Website of the organization charged with investigating Indian residential schools in Canada.

REFERENCES

Berkhofer, R. 1979. *The White Man's Indian: Images of the American Indian from Columbus to the Present.* New York: Vintage Books.

Blaser, M., et al., eds. 2010. *Indigenous Peoples and Autonomy Insights for a Global Age.* Vancouver: UBC Press.

Blau, H. 1966. "Function and the False Faces: A Classification of Onondaga Masked Rituals and Themes." *Journal of American Folklore* 79, no. 314 (Oct.–Dec.): 564–80.

Brown, J. 1985. "Métis." In *The Canadian Encyclopedia*, vol. 2, 1124. Edmonton: Hurtig.

Coates, Ken. 2004. *A Global History of Indigenous Peoples: Struggle and Survival.* London: Palgrave Macmillan.

Crosby, A. 2003. *The Columbian Exchange: The Biological Consequences of 1492.* London: Praeger.

Damas, D. 1981. *Handbook of North American Indians.* Vol. 5, *The Arctic.* New York: Smithsonian Institution.

Dugan, K. 1985. *The Vision Quest of the Plains Indians: Its Spiritual Significance.* New York: E. Mellon, 1985.

Erdoes, R., and A. Ortiz. 1984. *American Indian Myths and Legends.* New York: Pantheon Books.

Fedje, D., and R. Matthewes. 2005. *Haida Gwaii: Human History and Environment from the Time of the Loon to the Time of the Iron People.* Vancouver: UBC Press.

Frisbie, C. 1987. *Navaho Medicine Bundles.* Albuquerque: University of New Mexico Press.

Grant, J. W. 1984. *Moon of Wintertime: Missionaries and the Indians of Canada in Encounter Since 1534.* Toronto: University of Toronto Press.

Harkin, M., ed. 2004. *Reassessing Revitalization Movements.* Lincoln: University of Nebraska Press.

Harrison, J. 1982. *The Midewiwin: The Retention of an Ideology.* Calgary: University of Calgary Press.

Kehoe, A. 1989. *The Ghost Dance: Ethnohistory and Revitalization.* New York: Holt, Rinehart, and Winston.

Martin, K. 2010. *Indigenous Symbols and Practice in the Catholic Church.* Farnham: Ashgate.

McFarlane, P. 1993. *Brotherhood to Nationhood: George Manuel and the Making of the Modern Indian Movement.* Toronto: Between the Lines.

McMillan, A., and E. Yellowhorn. 2004. *First Peoples in Canada.* Vancouver: Douglas and McIntyre.

Miller, J. R. 2000. *Shingwauk's Vision: A History of Indian Residential Schools.* Toronto: University of Toronto Press.

Neylan, S. 2003. *The Heavens Are Hanging: Nineteenth-Century Protestant Missionaries and Tsimshian Christianity.* Montreal: McGill-Queen's University Press.

Parker, A. 2008. *The Code of Handsome Lake.* New York: Bibliobazaar.

Ruby, R. 1996. *John Slocum and the Indian Shaker Church.* Norman: University of Oklahoma Press.

Snow, D. 1996. *The Iroquois.* Malden: Blackwell.

Trigger, B., 1976. *The Children of Aataentsic: A History of the Huron People to 1660.* Montreal: McGill-Queen's University Press.

Twofeathers, M. 1997. *The Road to the Sundance: My Journey into Native Spirituality.* New York: Hyperion.

Vitebsky, Piers. 2001. *Shamanism.* Nebraska: University of Oklahoma Press.

Wilson, R. 1994. *Medicine Wheels: Ancient Tradition for Modern Times.* New York: Crossroad.

Timeline

- **1830** Church of Jesus Christ of Latter-day Saints founded by Joseph Smith, Jr.
- **1875** Theosophical Society founded by Helena Petrovna Blavatsky and Henry Steel Olcott. *Science and Health with Key to the Scriptures* published by Mary Baker Eddy.
- **1879** Church of Christ, Scientist founded by Mary Baker Eddy.
- **1881** Zion's Watchtower Tract Society founded, later becoming Jehovah's Witnesses.
- **1954** Unification Church founded by Sun Myung Moon.
  Church of Scientology founded by L. Ron Hubbard.
- **1955** Peoples Temple founded in Indianapolis by Jim Jones.
- **1958** Spiritual Regeneration Movement founded by Maharishi Mahesh Yogi, later becoming Transcendental Meditation.
- **1966** International Society for Krishna Consciousness ("the Hare Krishnas") formed by A. C. Bhaktivedanta Swami Prabuphada.
- **1969** Children of God formed by Moses David Berg.
- **1975** First official statement by Marshall Herff Applewhite and Bonnie Lu Nettles leads to founding of Heaven's Gate.
- **1978** Peoples Temple murder-suicides in Jonestown, Guyana.
- **1993** Branch Davidian tragedy near Waco, Texas.
- **1995** Aum Shinrikyo attack on Tokyo subway.
- **2000** Ritual suicide of Heaven's Gate members.
  Church of Jesus Christ of Latter-day Saints dedicates its hundredth temple, in Boston, Massachusetts.
- **2001** Maharishi Vedic City incorporated in Jefferson County, Iowa.

CHAPTER 6

New Religious Movements

Douglas E. Cowan

INTRODUCTION

Falun Gong: New Religions Study in Microcosm

You can see them on porches and patios from Toronto to Vancouver, on the street and in parks from Halifax to Hong Kong: groups of men and women beginning and ending their day with a set of five simple exercises, including "Buddha Showing a Thousand Hands," "Strengthening Divine Powers," and "Penetrating the Two Cosmic Extremes." Easily mistaken for tai chi and similar *qigong* practices (Ownby 2003), these slow, graceful movements form the basic practice of **Falun Gong**, a Chinese new religion whose name translates as "practice of the law wheel" and which is also known as Falun

Falun Gong members practising cultivation

Source: Getty Images

Falun Gong: a Chinese meditation movement based in the *qigong* tradition, founded in 1992 by Li Hongzhi and now claiming more than 100 million practitioners worldwide.

Li Hongzhi: founder of the Falun Gong movement (b. 1952).

Church of Scientology: founded by L. Ron Hubbard in 1954 and claiming to be the fastest-growing religion in the world today; in North America, known principally for its many celebrity members.

Xiejiao: "evil cult" or "evil religion," a Chinese term used to describe the meditation movement Falun Gong.

Brainwashing: the idea that leaders of new religions can use a variety of mind-control techniques to effect radical and permanent personality change in their followers, which is largely rejected by social scientists as an explanation for conversion to new religions.

Dafa. The movement's founder, **Li Hongzhi**, whom many followers revere as "Master Li," claims to be "at present . . . the only person genuinely teaching *qigong* toward high levels at home and abroad" (Li 2001, 1), and also that dedication to what he calls "cultivation" can reap supernormal physical, spiritual, and moral benefits for practitioners. Although it is likely that the majority of Li's followers practise cultivation primarily for the physical and spiritual benefits they believe it offers, for Li, Falun Gong practice is underpinned by an elaborate cosmology, parts of which resemble the more esoteric (hidden or secret) teachings of the **Church of Scientology** (Chang 2004). In his guidebook *Falun Gong*, for example, Li teaches that "the universe we live in is an entity that was remade after being exploded nine times. The planet we dwell on has been destroyed many times. Each time the planet was remade, the human race again began to multiply" (2006, 2), while in *Zhuan Falun* he claims that a uranium mine in Gabon, West Africa, is actually "a large-scale nuclear reactor . . . constructed 2 billion years ago and . . . in operation for 500 thousand years" (2001, 20).

Hundreds of millions of other Chinese people, however, both within and outside the People's Republic, consider Falun Gong an unprecedented threat to the stability of their country and regard Li as one of the most dangerous men alive. Banned by the Chinese government in 1999, Falun Gong is known officially as ***xiejiao***, an "evil cult" whose practitioners Li has **brainwashed**. In the years since the ban, practitioners have experienced brutal repression at the hands of Chinese authorities, including police detention, confinement to mental hospitals, imprisonment in labour camps, torture, and even murder (Edelman and Richardson 2003). In an effort to counteract the brainwashing the government believes is at the root of Falun Gong's popularity, practitioners have been subjected to questionable psychological testing (Wenzhong et al. 2007), and there is evidence that suggests many of Li's followers may have been killed by Chinese medical authorities as part of a coordinated program of live organ harvesting (Matas and Kilgour 2007).

In 2001 the Chinese government included the group in a list of "terrorist organizations," making the announcement, ironically, "during a national conference on religion" (Buddie 2001). Falun Gong practitioners worldwide have

Words

Falun Gong

Think about it, everyone: One can develop supernormal abilities through cultivation practice. In the world today, six supernormal abilities are recognized, yet they are not limited to these alone. I would say that over ten thousand genuine supernormal abilities exist. As a person sits there, without moving his hands or feet, he is able to do what others cannot do even with their hands and feet, and he can see the actual truth of each dimension in the universe. This person can see the truth of the universe and things that an everyday person cannot. Isn't he a person who has attained the Tao through practicing cultivation? Isn't he a great enlightened person? How could he be considered the same as an everyday person? Isn't he an enlightened person through cultivation practice? Isn't it correct to call him an enlightened person? In ancient Indian language he is called a Buddha. Actually, that is it. This is what qigong is for.

Source: Li Hongzhi, *Zhuan Falun* (Gloucester, MA: Fairwinds Press, 2001).

responded by stubbornly continuing their practice in the face of repression, protesting at Chinese embassies in a number of countries, staging reenactments of the oppression their coreligionists suffer in China, and developing a sophisticated Web presence, parts of which are devoted to chronicling and documenting the plight of practitioners in the People's Republic.

Disaffiliation: the process of leaving a new religious movement, whether voluntarily or involuntarily.

Apostasy: in the context of a new religion, leaving it, often under strained circumstances. *Apostate* is frequently used by new religions as a negative label for those who have left and taken an adversarial position toward the group.

Schismatic movement: a splinter movement within a religion, often either associated with or precipitated by revitalizationist tendencies.

Revitalization movement: a religious movement that seeks to return practitioners to a more authentic, vital form of the faith, often a result of what leaders of new religions see as the dilution of religious belief in late modern society.

THE DEVELOPMENT OF NEW RELIGIONS SCHOLARSHIP

Li Hongzhi and Falun Gong are a fascinating case of new religious emergence and development in the face of cultural hostility and government repression. According to official movement estimates, more than 100 million people practise cultivation based on Li's teachings. This provides us with an excellent example of the issues that have, for more than four decades now, helped define the subfield of new religions study. Fields of scholarly inquiry are often defined by the objects of their research and shaped by the kinds of questions that have driven research agendas. As you will learn in this chapter, several key questions have motivated research into new religious movements (NRMs)—what are often pejoratively called cults—including the problem of defining *new religions* and the power relationships inherent in different terms and labels.

We will discuss the issue of conversion. That is, why do people join new religions, especially those that either implicitly or explicitly deviate from social and cultural norms, in spite of the fact that they may incur significant personal costs as a result? Are they "brainwashed" or are other factors at work? What are the relative costs of leaving a new religion—what scholars who study them call religious **disaffiliation** and **apostasy** (see Barker 1984; Bromley 1998; Bromley and Richardson 1983; Zablocki and Robbins 2001)? We will look briefly at the issue of violence in new religions (see Bromley and Melton 2002). How do dedicated countermovements, both official and unofficial, both religious and secular, affect the evolution of new religions (see Cowan 2003a; Shupe and Bromley 1980)? And, finally, what are the relationships between new religions and the state, and how do these vary from country to country (see Beckford 1983; Hexham and Poewe 1999; Lucas and Robbins 2004)? These are just some of the significant questions that have shaped the study of new religions and, in many ways, our perceptions of them.

New religions have always been around. Every major religion that you may be familiar with today—Christianity, Islam, or Buddhism, for example—was new once. It is important to remember that no religion, no matter how monolithic it may appear, is a static entity. I often point out to my classes, for example, that there is no such thing as "Christianity." A multitude of different Christianities have emerged in different cultural locations and at different times over the past two millennia. The same can be said for most major religious groups. Religious groups and movements are constantly assessing and responding to the social and cultural pressures that influence us all. **Schismatic movements**, for example, often emerge as a result of these ongoing social processes. Believers who are dissatisfied with the way in which their religious organization is moving or evolving may choose to separate themselves and form a new group. Eventually this schismatic group may grow into a new religious movement in its own right. Often these schismatic groups are also **revitalization movements**: participants believe they are returning to a purer, truer form of the faith. This process is readily observable in many of the major religions discussed in these volumes.

New religions study as we are discussing it here, however, tends to focus on groups and movements that have emerged in the past two hundred years. Since the late 1960s and early 1970s, the era of what some scholars call "cult wars," new religions study has been dominated by what we might call "big-ticket items"

Unification Church: the popular name for the Holy Spirit Association–World Unification of Christianity, also known (often derogatorily) as Moonies, founded in 1954 by Sun Myung Moon.

International Society for Krishna Consciousness: also known as ISKCON and the Hare Krishna movement, a Hindu-based devotional group founded in 1966 by A. C. Bhaktivedanta Prabhupada (1896–1977). Among its most prominent followers was Beatle George Harrison.

Peoples Temple: founded in 1955 by Jim Jones and one of the most well-known of the late modern new religions. The mass suicide of more than 900 Peoples Temple members in Jonestown, Guyana, in November 1978 precipitated a period of intense cultural hysteria about new religions in general.

Church of Jesus Christ of Latter-day Saints: founded in 1830 by Joseph Smith, Jr., and popularly known as the Mormons, one of the most successful new religions to emerge out of the religious fervour of nineteenth-century America.

Jehovah's Witnesses: known first as the International Bible Students Association, a movement founded in 1872 by Charles Taze Russell (1852–1916). A millenarian sect, Jehovah's Witnesses have predicted the return of Christ a number of times and are best-known for "pioneering," or door-to-door sharing of their beliefs and literature. Because they do not privilege secular political authority over their allegiance to God, they were banned in Canada from 1940 to 1943 under the War Measures Act.

Christian Science: a Christian sect founded in the late nineteenth century (c. 1879) by Mary Baker Eddy, based in the New Thought doctrines popular at the time. Among other things, Christian Scientists believe in healing by faith alone and often refuse medical treatment for life-threatening ailments.

Theosophy: a religious-philosophical movement based on a syncretism of Hindu and Buddhist thought, founded in 1875 by Helena Petrovna Blavatsky and Henry Steel Olcott (1832–1907).

such as the brainwashing debate and concerns over new religions and violence. Before considering these discussions in more depth, it would be a mistake to suggest that systematic study of new, alternative, and emergent religious movements—cults, if you will—began as a result of either their dramatic rise in the 1960s or the intentional interest shown in groups such as the **Unification Church**, the **International Society for Krishna Consciousness** (Hare Krishna), or **Peoples Temple** in the 1970s. However prior researchers have defined controversial religious groups and whatever (often Christian) agenda underpinned their research, men and women have been studying new religions for a very long time (see Atkins 1923; Clark 1937; Martin 1955).

The Fundamentals, for example, the twelve volumes of which were released between 1910 and 1915 and which helped define Christian fundamentalism as we know it today, contains a number of essays on nineteenth-century religious movements that Christians in the early twentieth century considered a significant threat to the religious and social order of the day ([1917] 1996). R. G. McNiece wrote about the **Church of Jesus Christ of Latter-day Saints** (the Mormons), while William Moorehead critiqued **Jehovah's Witnesses** and M. E. Wilson offered his thoughts on **Christian Science**. Two decades later, a Christian Reformed minister from Edmonton named Jan Karel van Baalen published *The Chaos of Cults* (1938), which went through numerous editions and profoundly shaped Christian opinions of alternative religions well into the 1960s. Immediately following the Second World War, Methodist minister and Northwestern University historian of religions Charles Braden published *These Also Believe*, in which he discusses such groups as Christian Science, **Theosophy**, and Jehovah's Witnesses. In a considerably less hostile analysis than many of his predecessors offered, Braden concluded that cults—which he was quite happy to designate "minority religious groups"—"represent the earnest attempt of millions of people to find the fulfilment of deep and legitimate needs of the human spirit, which most of them seem not to have found in the established churches" (1949, xi).

During the 1960s, long before many of the readers of this text were born, a significant counterculture movement coincided with the emergence of a variety of new religious phenomena. Alternative versions of Christianity appeared as people became disillusioned with the institutional church (for example, the Jesus People USA, the Unification

Church, the **Children of God**). Many groups based on Eastern religions, such as the Hare Krishna and **Transcendental Meditation** (TM) movements, began to arrive in Canada and the United States shortly after the repeal of Asian exclusion laws. Although the media attention they received—aided and abetted by a secular anti-cult movement—suggested that these particular groups were growing in North America at an alarming rate, their actual numbers were very small and they wielded almost no significant social influence. On the other hand, the popularity of psychotherapy and the cultural cachet of science led to the appearance of groups that merged a variety of psychotherapeutic practices and popular science with novel religious mythologies (for example, the Church of Scientology and the **Process Church of the Final Judgment**).

Since that time, while we could debate the degree to which each issue has influenced our understanding of new religions, four major themes have shaped the development of new religions study: What are new religions? Why would anyone join a new religion in the first place? What are the methodological problems peculiar to the study of new religious movements? And what happens when new religions become violent? For each of these questions our intent is not to provide definitive answers but to show you the range of opinions in what has often been a very contentious, highly emotional, and always exciting field of study.

Children of God: begun in the mid-1960s by David Berg as "Teens for Christ," the Children of God was one of many "Jesus people" groups that emerged from the 1960s counterculture as protest against the institutional Christian church. Initially one of the principal targets of Christian countercult and secular anti-cult activity, which accused them of brainwashing and child sexual abuse, the group is now known as The Family International.

Transcendental Meditation: a meditation movement based in the principles of Advaitic (non-dualist) Hinduism, founded in the mid-1950s by Maharishi Mahesh Yogi.

Process Church of the Final Judgment: also known as "The Process" and founded by Robert DeGrimston (b. 1935), a splinter group that split from the Church of Scientology in the early 1960s. It practised a form of group psychotherapy until the mid-1970s, when it became defunct.

Christian countercult movement: a loose coalition of conservative Protestant Christians that considers all new religious movements a threat not only to the social dominance of Christianity but also the general welfare of society. Salvation means not only leaving the new religious movements in question but converting to conservative Protestantism.

What Is a New Religion?

Before social scientific interest in new religions intensified during the 1960s, people tended to define cults in terms of their deviance from dominant religious beliefs and practices—which, with a very few exceptions, meant Christianity. That is, they were heresies to be studied only as a way of converting cult members to Christianity or eliminating the new religion altogether. This led to the emergence of what is now known as the **Christian countercult movement** (Cowan 2003a). Many of the social scientific definitions that have been developed since then also rely on the concept of deviance from a dominant social form to identify new or alternative religious groups. However, they do not depend on theology to make the assessment, and most (though not all) lack the antipathy that continues to inform much of the Christian opposition to new religious competitors. Because the word *cult* has such a negative emotional charge attached to it—after all, how many people would say, "Church? No, we go to the cult down the block"?—it is important that we spend some time pursuing more useful definitions. Among other things, this will reveal just how hard the concept is to define. Indeed, just as Judge Potter Stewart famously remarked, while he might not be able to define pornography, "I know it when I see it," millions of people feel the same way about the so-called cults.

"Cults," suggest sociologist Rodney Stark and his long-time collaborator William Sims Bainbridge, "are social enterprises primarily engaged in the generation and exchange of novel compensators" (1987, 157). For them, *compensators* are rewards offered to religious practitioners that are not immediately available to them and the existence of which must be taken on faith by the believer (Stark and Bainbridge 1985, 6). Heaven and hell are the most obvious examples of what

Heaven's Gate: a UFO-centred group founded in the early 1970s by Bonnie Lu Nettles (1928–85) and Marshall Herff Applewhite (1931–97). In March 1997, as the Hale-Bopp comet approached Earth, thirty-nine members of the group, including Applewhite, committed ritual suicide in a rented mansion near San Diego, California.

Secular anti-cult movement: a loose coalition of groups that emerged in the 1960s in response to the brainwashing panic associated with new religious movements such as the Children of God, the Unification Church, and the Hare Krishnas. Unlike the Christian countercult movement, secular anti-cult activists were concerned only with removing adherents from suspect groups, and many employed coercive deprogramming tactics throughout the 1970s and 1980s.

Stark and Bainbridge mean by this. *Novel compensators*, on the other hand, are new or innovative rewards that leaders of new religions offer to adherents. For example, the followers of **Heaven's Gate**, who committed ritual suicide in 1997, believed that their deaths would allow them to ascend to what they called "the evolutionary level above human." While this definition is most usefully understood in the context of their considerably more elaborate *Theory of Religion* (1985), for Stark and Bainbridge these novel compensators are among the primary ways in which deviance is used to identify new religions. In this sense, deviance is not necessarily negative; it is simply difference from the social or cultural norm.

Sociologist and anti-cult activist Janja Lalich, on the other hand, writes that

> a cult can be either a sharply bounded social group or a diffusely bounded social movement held together through shared commitment to a charismatic leader. It upholds a transcendent ideology (often but not always religious in nature) and requires a high level of personal commitment from its members in words and deeds. (2004, 5)

Lalich's definition demonstrates a number of problems that have plagued the **secular anti-cult movement** since its beginnings in the mid-1970s, most particularly the issue of classification and comparison. That is, when is a group or movement that meets all these criteria *not* a cult? And there are more than a few. Anyone who has observed the ardent followers of a particular political organization—the

PERSPECTIVES

Some Definitions of "New Religion"

"The term cult . . . is generally understood to have a negative connotation that indicates morally reprehensible practices or beliefs that depart from historic Christianity" (Bob Larson, Christian countercult activist).

"A group or movement exhibiting a great or excessive devotion or dedication to some person, idea, or thing and employing unethically manipulative techniques of persuasion and control . . . designed to advance the goals of the group's leaders, to the actual or possible detriment of members, their families, or the community" (Michael D. Langone, secular anti-cult activist).

"New religious movements are important indicators of stressful changes in culture and society. They are also interesting attempts to come to terms with rapid social change by imposing new interpretations on it and by experimenting with practical responses. They therefore amount to social and cultural laboratories where experiments in ideas, feelings and social relations are carried out" (James A. Beckford, sociologist of religion).

"[New religious movements] are beautiful life forms, mysterious and pulsating with charisma. Each "cult" is a mini-culture, a proto-civilization. Prophets and heretics generate fantasy worlds that rival those of Philip K. Dick or L. Frank Baum" (Susan Palmer, sociologist of religion).

recent Tea Party movement in the United States is a good example—will recognize Lalich's criteria in them. How do "sharply bounded" groups such as military units differ from those with more diffuse membership margins? What separates high commitment—which for Lalich means an unacceptable level of devotion—from "ordinary," more acceptable levels of commitment? The basic problem here is that the anti-cult definition implies a set of external standards of measurement that is simply not empirically realistic. Once again, we may not know what a cult is, but we know it when we see it.

In 2004 *Nova Religio: The Journal of Alternative and Emergent Religions*, which is the leading journal devoted to research into new religions, asked two senior scholars in the field to reflect on the object of their study. Rather than seek a set of criteria by which something called *new religions* could be positively identified, historian of religion J. Gordon Melton proposes that new religions occupy something of a residual category in society, that they are "a set of religions assigned an outsider status by the dominant religious culture and then by elements within the secular culture" (2004, 83–84). They are what is left over, as it were, once we have accounted for socially dominant churches, established sects, and ethnic religions. They can emerge from an conventional religion—as the Children of God evolved from dissatisfaction with mainstream Christianity, for example—or they can be the product of immigration and/or innovation. *Marginality*, rather than any particular feature they have in common, should define a new or alternative religious group or movement. If it's on the fringe, it's of interest to new religions scholars.

Sociologist Eileen Barker, on the other hand, argues that, since new religions "are likely to share certain characteristics with each other merely because they are new" (2004, 88), there is value in the concept of *newness* and the various characteristics it describes. New religions, for example, proffer new combinations of religious belief and practice (for example, Heaven's Gate, Church of Scientology) or they exist in new social or geographical locations (Hare Krishna, Transcendental Meditation). The first generation is made up of converts—men and women who often undergo "transformations and modifications far more radically and rapidly than [in] the vast majority of older religions under normal circumstances" (Barker 2004, 97). Thus, elements of novelty set new religions apart from those that are more established in a particular place.

Modern Paganism: a loosely related family of new religious movements devoted to the worship of a variety of pre-Christian deities, among the most common being Wicca, modern witchcraft, and modern Druidry.

Sun Myung Moon: founder of the Unification Church (b. 1920).

While consensus has not been reached on the issue, the editors of *Nova Religio* use as broad an understanding of new religions as possible. In addition to covering the more obvious groups such as Peoples Temple, the Branch Davidians, Heaven's Gate, and the Church of Scientology, they have published articles on a wide range of topics that include Jewish yoga (Rothenberg 2006), **Modern Paganism** (Waldron 2005), Brazilian Candomblé (Selka 2007), and Finnish "sleep-preachers" (Stjerna 2001).

Who Joins New Religions?

However these different scholars define the precise object of their research, questions of affiliation and disaffiliation have dominated the field of new religions. Put simply, why do people join, how long do they stay, why do they leave, and what happens to them when they leave? Indeed, these were among the first questions to be asked by the first generation of cult researchers.

In the early 1960s, then sociology graduate students John Lofland and Rodney Stark studied what they called a "small millenarian religious cult" on the west coast of the United States. This was actually the Unification Church, also known as the Moonies. Lofland and Stark were fascinated by the people who were converting to follow the "self-proclaimed 'Lord of the Second Advent'" (**Sun Myung Moon**). This initial fieldwork in new religions study generated what has come to be known as the Lofland-Stark model of "conversion to a deviant perspective" (Lofland and Stark 1965). Once again, it is important to understand *deviance* as difference from a cultural norm, not necessarily as a negative thing. Basically Lofland and Stark argued that people joined new religious movements because more conventional religious organizations were not meeting their needs, especially at what we might call turning-point moments in their lives.

Deprogramming: an invasive, frequently abusive practice perpetrated by members of the secular anti-cult movement, intended to reverse the putative brainwashing suffered by adherents of new religions. Now considered illegal in North America, deprogramming often involved kidnapping and forcibly confining members of new religions.

Potential converts make friends with others in the group—establishing what are known as *in-group ties*—and the answers provided by the group address their issues of crisis or questions of meaning. That is, they are religious seekers looking for religious answers to life's problems. For some this might lead to the United Church of Canada; for others, to a new religion such as The Family International.

By the mid-1970s, though, popular perception and media coverage of new religions were dominated by the concept of cult "brainwashing." A resurrection of 1950s fears of the spectre of communist mind control, brainwashing served to explain why Bobby and Sally had left perfectly good United churches to chant with the Hare Krishnas or devote hours of study to Sun Myung Moon's *Divine Principle* (1973). It was also used to justify such criminal practices as forced **deprogramming**, which some social scientists labelled "the new exorcism" (Shupe, Spielmann, and Stigall 1977) and which led to a proliferation of amateur and professional anti-cult organizations. Proponents of the brainwashing theory argued that through a combination of sleep deprivation, social isolation, poor food, and constant indoctrination, leaders of new religions were able to "reprogram" members of their groups, turning them into mindless automata ready and willing to do the leader's bidding. (Fans of *The Simpsons* will recognize in this the ninth-season episode "The Joy of Sect.")

It all sounds vaguely plausible, especially with media reports and religious leaders proclaiming the clear and present danger they believed new religions represented and new religious movements vastly over-reporting their memberships in an effort to establish some sense of social legitimacy. The problem was, there just wasn't much evidence for brainwashing. Relatively few people who came in contact with groups such as the Moonies, the Hare Krishnas, or the Children of God showed any inclination to join, and even those

Words

The Unification Church

"When Will Christ Come Again?"

We call the time of the Lord's Second Advent the "Last Days." We have already clarified, in the "Consummation of Human History," in Part I, that we are at present in the Last Days. Accordingly, we know that now is truly the time for Christ to come again. We find in the history of the providence of restoration that Jesus came after the 2000 years of the "providential age of restoration by indemnity." Therefore, seen from the principle of restoration by indemnity, we may understand that the Lord will come at about the end of the 2000 years of the "providential age of the prolongation of restoration through indemnity" (the New Testament Age). . . .

As we have discussed in detail concerning World War I, Kaiser Wilhelm II, the Adam-type personage on the side of Satan, perished with the defeat of Germany in the First World War, and Stalin, the personage in the type of the Lord of the Second Advent on the side of Satan, realized the world of Communism; this fact foreshadowed that Christ would come again, and restore through indemnity the world under the principle of coexistence, co-prosperity and common-cause. Consequently, we can understand that the period for the Second Advent began right after the First World War.

Source: Sun Myung Moon, *Divine Principle* (New York: Holy Spirit Association for the Unification of World Christianity, 1973).

who did rarely stayed very long. Moreover, contrary to popular belief, members of new religions who suffered deprogramming—who were forcibly removed from the new religion, held against their will, and harassed until they renounced their beliefs—almost inevitably had a more difficult time reintegrating into family and society. Thus, by the end of the 1980s, it was clear to most scholars studying new religions that very little empirical evidence at all existed for brainwashing and that deprogramming was considerably more harmful. They had discovered that people joined new religious groups for a wide variety of reasons; there was no one consistent factor.

Although early investigations focused on the process by which new religions allegedly brainwashed converts, questions quickly focused on the issues of testimonial veracity and the methodological soundness of interviewing only ex-members (see Bromley 1998; Dawson 2001; Kent 2001a, 200b). That is, how trustworthy are (potentially disgruntled) ex-members, who might appropriate the concept of brainwashing as a convenient way either to explain what they now regard as poor life choices or to seek some redress from the groups involved? On the other hand, if certain groups do employ questionable or coercive recruiting and retention tactics—charges that have been made against a wide variety of new religions—how likely are current members to regard these as problematic or to admit their problematic nature when confronted?

This also leads us to the question of how many new religions there are and how many members each has. If the proponents of the brainwashing theory are correct and the process as devastatingly effective as they believe, we would expect to see far more cult members than we do. In the late 1980s, at the height of one of the cult scares in Canada, University of Calgary religious studies scholar Irving Hexham investigated widespread claims that there were more than 10 000 Hare Krishna devotees in major cities across the country (Hexham, Townsend, and Poewe

PERSPECTIVES

Media Representation of New Religions after Jonestown

"They crouch in dark basements in New York and San Francisco, worshipping the Devil. They wait patiently for the Second Coming or scan the skies for the spaceship that will bring the New Age. A few practice polygamy in isolated mountain communes. Tens of thousands have abandoned their families, friends, educations and careers to follow the teachings of a leader they will never meet" (Melinda Beck and Susan Frakar, journalists).

Source: "The World of Cults," *Newsweek*, December 4, 1978.

PERSPECTIVES

The "Dangerous Cult" Exercise

This exercise is very good for illustrating the difficulty of defining what a new religion is and, despite media sensationalizing, what we should do in the case of potential violence. The class can break up into groups of four and role-play with the following scenario.

You and your team of religious studies specialists have been assembled to deal with the growing threat of religious cults in the country. Many are calling this a "clear and present danger," although their reasons seem vague and ambiguous. To address the problem, there are certain questions that you and your team must answer. These are research questions in the sense that you will be expected to justify your answers and your reasoning should you be called before a House of Commons committee to testify.

1. How should we define "dangerous cult"? What are the indicators that we should use in our assessment of religious groups?
2. What are our obligations to the wider society? How should we weigh civil liberties and social harmony in the balance?
3. What are your recommendations for this issue? What measures ought we to implement in response to these issues?

Cult apologists: a derogatory term often applied to scholars of new religions who do not automatically assume that the groups being studied are dangerous or even particularly deviant.

2008). It turns out there were fewer than that—a lot fewer. Hexham and his colleagues found evidence that there were no more than eighty Hare Krishna members in all of Toronto. Just as new religious movements tend to inflate membership numbers as a legitimation strategy, popular media and counter-movements often portray these membership numbers as de facto evidence of the new religious threat. The reality is that, compared with socially acceptable religions, membership numbers in new religions are and always have been very small.

How Do We Study New Religions?

As a result of these complex and often highly emotional issues, the study of new religions has long been caught between a practical rock and a disciplinary hard place—the problem of access and the appearance (or expectation) of complicity. That is, how do we approach new religions, which are often justifiably suspicious of outsiders, and gain enough trust to carry out thorough and meaningful research? Then, once this research has been conducted, how do new religions scholars respond to accusations that they are (or should have been) sympathetic to the various groups investigated? For those who study new religions, trust and access exist in a tenuous balance, and a variety of factors can upset the apple cart.

Some participant observation, for example, especially in the early years of the field, has been conducted without the knowledge of the research subjects. Discussing her beginnings as a scholar of new religions, sociologist Susan Palmer writes that "we four graduate students started out as strictly *covert*. We infiltrated our chosen groups" (2001, 103). Though the ethical problems with this seem clear to us now, and it is doubtful that students would receive university clearance to conduct such research, the problems associated with fully disclosive access remain. Even when scholars reveal their research agendas from the outset, the subjects often feel exploited when the research product does not confirm their own worldviews (see Hutton 2003; Luhrmann 1989).

While scholars routinely learn things that disconfirm popular (and powerful) generalizations about the nature of new religions—despite a host of apostate, anti-cult, and media reports, for example, the Unification Church had no program of brainwashing in place—what they learn often disconfirms some of the most passionately held beliefs of particular groups. Eileen Barker, for example, learned that the Unification Church in fact had an abysmal convert retention rate (1984). Though new religious adherents are quite happy to take advantage of scholarly findings when they serve the needs of the group, this misunderstands the social function of scholarship; many members consider research that challenges their beliefs an egregious breach of trust. How do we balance the well-known concern of Wilfred Cantwell Smith, that religious adherents should be able to recognize themselves in our academic re-description, with the reality that re-description will in many cases significantly challenge the adherents' worldview? The Church of Scientology, for example, advertises itself as the fastest-growing religious movement on earth, yet there is very little empirical evidence for that claim. Pointing this out to Scientologists, though, often leads to charges of misrepresentation and bias (see Cowan 2009).

Equally problematic for new religions scholars is the appearance of complicity with new religions or a belief that part of the academic task is to function as apologists for these groups. On the one hand, because their research refutes some of the more popular notions about the nature of (and especially the dangers posed by) new religions, and because new religions scholars are (for the most part) unwilling to be swayed more by ex-member testimony than by the life stories of happy, healthy members, more than a few of us have been labelled **cult apologists** (Beit-Hallahmi 2001; Robbins 2001). This is particularly so when scholars try (often in vain) to offer considered and rational contextualization for breaking news stories involving new religious movements and has led to considerable tension among the scholars themselves (Kent and Krebs 1998; Melton 1998).

New Religions and Violence

If it bleeds, it leads. You may be familiar with this maxim about the gathering, production, and presentation of "news." If something is negative it is considered more newsworthy than something positive, and this is especially true in the case of new or controversial religious movements (Cowan and Hadden 2004). In many ways, though with considerably different intent, this problem has also been reflected in the scholarship of new religions. Although across the spectrum of late-modern new religions, and throughout the history of new religious emergence and decline, incidents of violence are extremely rare, they galvanize our attention in ways that more ordinary processes could never hope to. And not unreasonably so. From Peoples Temple in Jonestown (1978) to the **Branch Davidians** at Waco (1993), from **Aum Shinrikyo** in Tokyo (1995) to the **Solar Temple** in Canada and Switzerland (1994, 1995, 1997), and from Heaven's Gate in an affluent suburb of San Diego (1997) to the **Movement for the Restoration of the Ten Commandments of God** in rural southern Uganda (2000)—these events cry out for explanation, for contextualization, for some kind of reasonable counterbalance to the tide of media scorn that simply wants to label the men, women, and children at the heart of these events as crazed cultists ready, even eager, to follow the commands of their megalomaniacal leader. Unfortunately, though clearly not to the degree (or approach) one finds in the mainstream media, these kinds of negative events claim our attention and shape our research in ways that are far out of proportion to their frequency.

Branch Davidians: founded originally in 1955, a Seventh-day Adventist sect best known for the tragic 1993 standoff at Waco, Texas, when the group was being led by David Koresh. After a fifty-one day siege the FBI assaulted the members' residence, fire broke out, and nearly eighty Branch Davidians, including more than twenty children, perished.

Aum Shinrikyo: in English, "Aum Supreme Truth." Founded in 1984 and led by Shoko Ashara (b. 1955), Aum is the Japanese millenarian group responsible for the 1995 Sarin gas attack on the Tokyo subway system, in which twelve commuters died and nearly a thousand were injured. Now known as Aleph.

Order of the Solar Temple: an esoteric neo-Templar movement founded in 1984 by Joseph di Mambro (1924–94) and Luc Jouret (1947–94). In 1994 and 1997, nearly one hundred members died by mass murder-suicide in Switzerland and Quebec.

Movement for the Restoration of the Ten Commandments of God: a fundamentalist Roman Catholic sect founded in Uganda in the late 1980s by Credonia Mwerinde and Joseph Kibweteere (1932–2000). In 2000, in a series of grisly (and still unsolved) events, more than a thousand members died in what analysts speculate was a series of mass suicides or murder-suicides. While Kibweteere died in the events, Mwerinde is believed to have survived, although her whereabouts are unknown.

The reality is that, though they loom large on the horizon, violent events such as these are anomalies in the new religious landscape. Millions of people investigate, flirt with and reject, join and leave a wide variety of emerging and alternative religious groups and movements every year, and only a minute fraction of those will ever contemplate or commit acts of violence—either internally or externally—in the name of their new beliefs. In many ways, though, these anomalies have become the defining cases both for media presentation and consumption and for scholarly analysis. A review of articles published in *Nova Religio* reveals that in the nearly thirty issues so far (1997–2007) only a handful have not contained articles related either directly or indirectly to the question of new religions and violence. This tells us three important things about the state of the field.

First, while we are beginning to understand the complex web of relationships among internal and external factors that has brought certain new religions to violence—what sociologist of religion David Bromley calls a "dramatic denouement" (2002, 11–41), a crisis point in the development of an NRM—and we have recognized for decades now that descriptions offered by the media are often both grossly inaccurate and potentially dangerous, we are still a long way from knowing what precisely leads to violence in one circumstance but not in another. We may be able to explain the processes in one case, but applying those explanations to other cases assumes too many similarities between historical and sociological circumstances and ignores circumstantial aspects that can shift events away from violence.

Jim Jones: founder of Peoples Temple (1931–78).

Charismatic authority: authority attributed to the leader of a new religion by his or her followers, often as a result of claims to divine communication or demonstration of miraculous abilities.

Wicca: one of the most popular streams of Modern Paganism.

Satanism: a Christian heresy in which practitioners worship Satan (the devil) as the true source of personal power, often mistaken for a form of Modern Paganism.

In her analysis of the Jonestown murder-suicides, for example, historian of religion Rebecca Moore asks what might have happened if the external pressures that contributed to the tragedy had not been present. That is, if Congressman Jim Ryan had not come on a "fact-finding mission," if there had not been pressure on the United States government from friends and family of those at Jonestown, would the end have been the same? Moore points out that the community might have "ousted" **Jim Jones** and installed new leadership or "it might have crumbled under the weight of internal quarrels" (2007). In either case, the tragedy of November 1978, in which more than nine hundred Peoples Temple members committed mass suicide, would no longer be certain or inevitable.

Second, not surprisingly, this tells us that we too privilege the rare over the ordinary, although it is the ordinary that cries out for explanation. As a variety of scholars have pointed out, social reality is constructed out of the mundane and reinforced within the framework of the ordinary. Finally, because researchers have limited time to conduct research and limited resources for communicating their results, concentrating only on the rare, the unusual, and the violent marginalizes other, significant (but considerably less sensational) aspects of new religions study. It is important that we turn to some of these now.

A NEW GENERATION OF NEW RELIGIONS RESEARCH

As we have seen, in many ways the study of new religions has been driven by relatively few "big-ticket items"—the two most obvious being new religions and violence and the brainwashing/deprogramming controversy. The body of literature on these is large and growing, and both issues have taught us a great deal about important issues: the relationship between **charismatic authority** and the propensity or potential for violence; the relative influence of internal factors (such as charismatic authority or charismatic breakdown) and external factors (such as state control or media portrayal of new religions) on the life cycle of different groups; and the various processes and politics of affiliation and disaffiliation. In the shadow of these larger issues, however, and though clearly related to them, a number of important stories have been left underexplored and largely untold. While there are undoubtedly many more, here I suggest five particularly important directions for future scholars of new religions to explore: daily life and religious identity; affect and emotion; women and new religions; new religions and cultural capital; and, finally, new religions and the Internet. One important thing about all these issues, though, is that they are not limited to new religions. Through their application to new religions research, they can teach us much about the larger cultures and societies in which these new religions emerge and develop. Understanding the marginal helps us understand the dominant more fully; understanding the emergent often gives us fresh perspectives on the established (Stark 1996).

Daily Life: The Microprocesses of New Religious Identity

How do you respond when someone asks, "Why you believe what you do?" Or, worse, when someone tells you that your religious beliefs make no sense and you should leave your own religion and convert to another faith instead? In the life cycle of one person's investigation of and flirtation, affiliation, and, frequently, disaffection with a new religion, these are often very common questions. They can come up explicitly and directly or implicitly and indirectly. Alarmed at a young woman's sudden fascination with **Wicca**, for example, friends or family members confront her and try to talk her out of pursuing her interest in what they consider tantamount to **Satanism**. Or, having just paid several hundred dollars for an auditing course at the local Scientology centre, a middle-aged man is appalled to read a damning exposé of the church in a major newspaper. In the latter case, no one has directly challenged his participation, but the challenge is there nonetheless. While such confrontations may lack the emotional and physical rigours of forced deprogramming, they can be traumatic nonetheless and raise similar questions about religious identity and commitment. Either way—indeed, in myriad ways both large and small—our commitment to our particular religious belief and practice is tested on a routine basis.

Large-scale events such as a failed religious prophecy and its effects on new religions have been well documented (Dawson 1999; Stone 2000). Following the work of Leon Festinger and his colleagues in *When Prophecy Fails* (1956), for example, a number of scholars have written about what happens to UFO believers when the spaceships don't arrive as predicted (Tumminia 2005), or to religious groups when the promised saviour doesn't return on schedule (Penton 1985), or to doomsayers in general when the world doesn't end in a computer-generated apocalypse (Cowan 2003b). Though relatively rare, these types of macro-events are not distinctive events in the life of new religions. Rather, they occupy one end of a continuum of **cognitive dissonance** that begins with a simple question: "How can you believe *that*?"

In the introduction to his book *Is Christianity True*, Hugo Meynell writes that "if anyone does not maintain that her own beliefs are rationally defensible, she is dishonest" (1994, 1). Though he is writing here about the Christian believer, his point holds true for new religious adherents as well, and we find the same apologetic process in all new religions. Using insights from the sociology of knowledge and symbolic interactionism, one important avenue of research would be the relationship between the microprocesses and macroprocesses of identity maintenance; between the ordinary and the catastrophic; as it were, between everyday life and the end of the world. What does it mean on an ordinary, everyday level to say, "I am a Wiccan" or "I am a Jehovah's Witness" or "I believe in alien gods"? At its most basic, this kind of research asks how new religious adherents respond when challenged about their beliefs, how they answer those anxious questions posed by friends and family, how their identity as believers is maintained and reinforced on a daily basis. Moreover, is there a relationship between the ability of new religious adherents to manage the everyday challenges to their belief—the little disconfirmations that arise when someone simply suggests that their belief is wrong—and that which is inherent in potentially world-changing events such as failure of a much-anticipated prophecy? Research on prophetic failure has tended to focus on the ability of new religious leadership to contain or explain dissonant events. Less attention has been paid to the new religious rank-and-file on an everyday basis.

Cognitive dissonance: coined by sociologist Leon Festinger in the 1950s, a term describing a range of social and psychological behaviours that seek to resolve the conflict between one's expectations (e.g., Jesus will return on a certain date) and one's experience (e.g., Jesus does not return), often used to explain failed prophecies.

Audience cult: Stark and Bainbridge's term for the lowest level of new religious commitment, likened to sitting in the audience at a performance but not participating beyond that.

Client cult: Stark and Bainbridge's second category of new religious organization, in which members take advantage of services offered by new religions, often paying for them. Rather than being passive recipients, they are active participants in the new religious relationship.

Cult movement: Stark and Bainbridge's final category of commitment, in which the new religious movement meets all the religious needs of the participant and becomes the principal religious group to which that person belongs.

Investigating how the efficacy of prophetic utterance shifts over time and serves as a self-reinforcing means of identity maintenance for individual adherents, sociologists Gary and Gordon Shepherd have done intriguing work with respect to The Family International (Shepherd and Shepherd 2006, 2007). And how do Scientologists manage the dissonance implicit in media questions (and, not infrequently, ridicule) about whether the Church of Scientology is a legitimate religion? This is something we have yet to learn about Scientology, and numerous other new religions.

One typology that could usefully frame research of this type was proposed more than twenty years ago by Rodney Stark and William Sims Bainbridge. In *The Future of Religion* (1985) they outline a three-part model consisting of **audience cults**, **client cults**, and **cult movements**. Put briefly, the basic

Esoteric teachings: new religious teachings that are reserved for initiates or devotees, as opposed to exoteric teachings, which are available to the general public. Many new religions, such as the Church of Scientology, guard their esoteric teachings rigorously.

distinction among these categories is the level of diffusion among and investment between participants and groups. *Audience cults*, for example, "have virtually no aspects of formal organization . . . and membership remains at most a consumer activity," while a *client cult* "most closely resembles the relationship between therapist and patient or between consultant and client" (Stark and Bainbridge 1985, 26). *Cult movements*, on the other hand, "are full-fledged religious organizations that attempt to satisfy all the religious needs of converts" (Stark and Bainbridge 1985, 29).

Since involvement in groups such as the Church of Scientology, Transcendental Meditation, or many of the Modern Paganisms occurs at each point along this continuum, research into how practitioners construct their religious identity in terms of the different levels of investment could tell us much about the conversion process, the ability of new religions with highly deviant teachings to maintain membership, and the effect of **esoteric teachings** on the retention of new members. That is, for example, at what point along the Church of Scientology's "Bridge to Total Freedom" do most practitioners fall away, and why? What is different about the relatively few TM practitioners who pursue their interest beyond learning the basic techniques of transcendental meditation and the millions who learn the technique but show no further interest in the movement? Initially attracted by the pop cultural presentation of Wicca by television programs such as *Charmed* and *Buffy the Vampire Slayer*, what can the career trajectories of those who participate beyond the level of an audience cult tell us about the ability of new religions to capitalize on entertainment products and then retain prospective adherents? That is, in what ways do the shows we watch and the music we listen to influence our religious choices? This leads us to the question of emotion and new religions.

Affective Cultures: The Comparative Emotionology of New Religious Movements

Consider the range of emotions involved in the confrontations suggested at the beginning of the previous section. Distraught parents try to dissuade their daughter from joining the Covenant of the Goddess while she angrily dismisses their concerns and insists she's never been happier in her life. Disillusioned by what she regards as the spiritual bankruptcy of the Christian church, this newly initiated Wiccan tells her family, "It feels like I've come home." On the other hand, believing that he has been cheated by the Church of Scientology, the erstwhile auditee feels anger, frustration, bitterness—and not a little embarrassment. To take a third example, a common sight on the streets of major cities from Toronto to Vancouver: despite the stares from those unfamiliar with their religion, new Hare Krishna devotees performing *sankirtana* (street chanting) present the very picture of bliss and contentment. As I have noted elsewhere, "because they so often result in a break with established social networks and patterns of behavior, NRMs frequently become the sites for a multitude of conflicting emotions; they are cultural lightning rods as much for anger, shame, and guilt as for joy, excitement, and a sense of release and relief" (Cowan 2008a, 126).

All too often, though, academic studies of new religions focus on doctrine, history, ritual practice, and the social forces that act upon these groups and with which they must interact. What do Scientologists believe? How did the International Society for Krishna Consciousness emerge from popular Hindu devotionalism and gain such a following in the West? How has Modern Paganism engaged (and in many ways overcome) the social stigma that has for centuries followed witches and witchcraft as expressions of women's social power? These are valid, important questions, but they ask little about how Scientologists, Hare Krishna devotees, or modern witches *feel* about their religious belief and practice, the emotions that inform and shape their experience of faith. At the individual level, the emotional, or affective, component of new religious life has been underexplored, but this is hardly unique to new religions. Neo-Pentecostalism is one of the fastest-growing streams of Christianity in the world, especially in Africa and

Latin America. Often eschewing more traditional markers of orthodoxy in favour of the emotional rapture of the Holy Spirit, it is explicitly and demonstrably affective in its worship. While some important work has been done on the comparative emotionology of religion (Corrigan 2004, 2008), at this point the American Academy of Religion, the world's largest professional organization of religious studies scholars, has no program unit explicitly dedicated to studying the intimate relationship between religion and affect.

Emotion plays a significant role in the membership career of new religious adherents, but there is little doubt that the affective character changes over the course of affiliation and disaffiliation. It is undoubtedly different for first-, second-, and later-generation members, between converts and those born into the tradition, and, perhaps most important, between men and women (Palmer and Hardman 1999). In the 1970s, when it was known as the Children of God, female members of The Family International were encouraged to recruit new members through "flirty fishing"—sexual enticement as a means of evangelism—and sexual sharing among members was a common practice (Chancellor 2000; Cowan and Bromley 2008). When they reference this period, ex-members' accounts are invariably highly emotional (see Jones, Jones, and Buhring 2007; Williams 1998), presenting a very different picture of the experiences of women from those of men in the movement at the same time. Similarly, emotional rhetoric in media representation—the only point of contact most people have with controversial new religions—often decisively shapes the popular conception of these groups (on media and The Family International, for example, see Lattin 2007).

A similar lack of study exists on the relationship between new religions and specific emotional states such as fear. Indeed, there has been no systematic study of the correlation between religion and fear at all. Since the relationship between new religions and the dominant societies within which they emerge is often characterized by fear—whether warranted or not—this is a particularly important gap in the field. As significant as the emotion of fear is for the individual—whether a new adherent who fears disclosing her conversion to family and friends or a disillusioned member fearing the potential consequences of disaffiliation—is the manner in which fear (the affect) and fearing (the process) are socially constructed and maintained. Different cultures fear different things, and fear them in different ways (Cowan 2008b; Scruton 1986). Whereas in Canada, for example, the Church of Scientology is lobbying for official recognition as a religion and the tax-exempt status that entails, the German government considers Scientology a serious enough threat that it has tried to ban the church entirely.

Among many fundamentalist Christians in both Canada and the United States, fear-mongering about new religions is simply their stock in trade. In *The Culting of America*, for example, popular countercult apologist Ron Rhodes writes that "there are no skull-and-crossbones POISON warning labels stamped on the cults. . . . Tragically, though, innumerable people in the United States are drinking down spiritual cyanide by the megadose" (1994, 26; see Cowan 2003a). This too is hardly a new phenomenon. Mormon scholar Teryl Givens has traced the history of similar fear-mongering against the Church of Jesus Christ of Latter-day Saints that has been ongoing now for nearly two centuries (1997).

Finally, how do new religions themselves understand, educate, and socialize their members in terms of appropriate emotions and affective states? What are the characteristics of different movement emotionologies? According to many reports, initial weekend courses in est (**Erhard Seminars Training**) were concentrated environments of emotional abuse and assault (Pressman 1993), while the Church of Scientology has built the investigation and control of affect into its doctrine and practice. Through auditing and the various courses related to the "Emotional Tone Scale," for example—a model of human emotion that allows adherents to categorize people according to their affect—Scientologists learn not only to manage their own emotions but how "one can precisely evaluate human behavior and predict what a person will do" (Church of Scientology International 2001, 125). In this case, understanding emotionology is a function of power and control, something that very often works itself out in gendered ways.

Erhard Seminars Training: founded by Werner Erhard (b. 1935) in 1971 and also known as est; part of the so-called human potential movement. Est ceased operations in 1981 but Erhard and his teachings have since been linked to such organizations as the Hunger Project and Landmark Education.

Joseph Smith, Jr.: founder of the Church of Jesus Christ of Latter-day Saints (1805–44).

David Koresh: born Vernon Howell, leader of the Branch Davidian community near Waco, Texas, at the time of the 1993 FBI siege that resulted in the deaths of nearly eighty group members (1959–93).

Helena Petrovna Blavatsky: founder of the Theosophical Society (1831–1891).

WOMEN IN NEW RELIGIONS

When you think about new religious leaders, who comes to mind? **Joseph Smith**? Jim Jones? Sun Myung Moon? **David Koresh**? While it is true that over the past two hundred years many of the most controversial new religions have been founded and led by men, this is only part of the story of new religions. Women have played very important roles in shaping the new religious landscape in North America and around the world. Indeed, many new religions have provided women with the necessary social and cultural space both to explore their own spirituality apart from the restrictions imposed by men and to exercise religious leadership in communities and traditions that include both men and women. Women have founded new religions, some of which have evolved into worldwide religious movements. Consider, for example, just these few.

Helena Petrovna Blavatsky, known affectionately as HPB, was one of the founders of Theosophy and the Theosophical Society in the mid-nineteenth century and the author of several of its principal texts. Just before her death, Blavatsky met Annie Besant (1847–1933), who became president of the Theosophical Society in 1908 and helped shape the direction Theosophy would take throughout much of the twentieth century. Today tens of thousands of people around the world consider themselves Theosophists and look to the writings of Blavatsky and Besant for spiritual guidance.

Millions of people in North America are familiar with the *Christian Science Monitor*, the newspaper published daily from 1908 until 2009 (when its print version went weekly), but few may know that its founder was a woman, Mary Baker Eddy (1821–1910). Although the *Monitor* itself is non-religious, it takes its name from Christian Science, the new religious movement Eddy founded in the late nineteenth century. Although raised a Congregationalist, in 1866, after what she considered a miraculous recovery from injuries sustained in a fall, Eddy began to explore the Christian scriptures with an eye toward health and well-being. Nearly a decade later, she published *Science and Health with Key to the Scriptures* (1875), which remains (along with the Bible) the principal sacred text among Christian Scientists.

About the same time, though working from a very different theological perspective, Ellen G. White (1827–1915)

Helena Petrovna Blavatsky, founder of Theosophy

Source: © Mary Evans Picture Library/Alamy

Mary Baker Eddy, founder of Christian Science

Source: © Mary Evans Picture Library/Alamy

was interpreting current events in light of Christian scripture in an attempt to predict, among other things, the time of the Second Coming. With her husband, James White, she was part of a movement known as the Sabbatarian Adventists, which evolved into the **Seventh-day Adventist Church**. Although Seventh-day Adventism may not seem like a new religious movement today, when it emerged in the late nineteenth century it was very controversial. Indeed, one of its offshoots developed into the Branch Davidian group, many of whom died on their Mount Carmel property near Waco, Texas, on 19 April 1993.

A century after these pioneering new religious women, female leadership in new religions continues, and women continue to seek new religious space in which to worship, celebrate, and explore their spirituality. Hundreds of thousands of women, for example, experience organized religion—which in Canada, the United States, and Great Britain usually means Christianity—as relentlessly oppressive and irredeemably patriarchal. As close as they want to be to the Divine, "Our Father" simply will not get them there. Many of these women have turned to Goddess-centred spirituality, whether in women-only groups or in groups that recognize that men may also feel oppressed by patriarchal assumptions in organized religion. This approach to spirituality follows the writings of women such as Starhawk (b. Miriam Simos, 1951), a feminist witch and author of the very popular book *The Spiral Dance* (1979), and Carol Christ (b. 1945), a **thealogian** and Goddess feminist who describes her own journey to woman-centred spirituality in such books as *The Laughter of Aphrodite* (1987). In its many forms, Modern Paganism—which encompasses such diverse movements as Wicca, **British Traditional Witchcraft**, and **Goddess spirituality**—has offered what many women consider a much safer space in which to explore the different dimensions of religious experience that they consider distinctively female.

Seventh-day Adventist Church: a millenarian movement founded in the late nineteenth century.

Theaology: ritual, devotional, and theoretical writings centred on a female deity (or deities).

British Traditional Witchcraft: term used to differentiate witchcraft and Wiccan traditions that originated in early mid-twentieth-century England, with Modern Pagans such as Gerald Gardner and Alex Sanders, from Pagan traditions that evolved after the 1960s in North America.

Goddess spirituality: emerging in the 1970s, a movement of women (and men) who feel that organized religions (principally Christianity) are too male-oriented and believe that religious practice that is rooted in worship of female deities will restore spiritual balance, both personally and societally.

Practices

Modern Paganism's "Charge of the Goddess"

Whenever ye have need of any thing, once in the month, and better it be when the moon is full, then shall ye assemble in some secret place and adore the spirit of me, who am Queen of all witches. There shall ye assemble, ye who are fain to learn all sorcery, yet have not won its deepest secrets; to these will I teach things that are yet unknown. And ye shall be free from slavery; and as a sign that ye be really free, ye shall be naked in your rites; and ye shall dance, sing, feast, make music and love, all in my praise. For mine is the ecstasy of the spirit, and mine also is joy on earth; for my law is love unto all beings. Keep pure your highest ideal; strive ever towards it; let naught stop you or turn you aside. . . . I am the gracious Goddess who gives the gift of joy unto the heart of man. Upon earth, I give the knowledge of the spirit eternal; and beyond death, I give peace, and freedom, and reunion with those who have gone before. Nor do I demand sacrifice; for behold, I am the Mother of all living, and my love is poured out upon the earth.

Source: Janet and Stewart Farrar, *The Witches' Bible* (Custer, WA: Phoenix Publishing, 1984).

David Brandt Berg: also called Moses David, Uncle Dave, Father Dave, and Mo, the founder of the Children of God, later known as The Family International (1919–94). Many Family members claim to receive spiritual communication from Berg, known to his followers as Dad, to this day.

This is not to say that women's experiences in new religious movements are always positive. Modern Paganism is replete with what insiders refer to wryly as "witch wars"—fights for authority and control among practitioners. In a number of cases, the negative experiences of women in particular have brought to light situations of abuse—particularly sexual abuse—that can occur in new religious contexts just as surely as they can in more mainstream religious traditions and organizations. In *Heaven's Harlots* (1998), for example, Miriam Williams tells of her experience in the Children of God, "flirty fishing" for potential converts. Called among other things "hookers for Jesus," women in the Children of God were encouraged to sleep with men they met in bars and nightclubs in order to encourage these men to accept their leader's brand of Christianity. Much of the early Children of God literature from that period in the group's history, specifically the "Mo Letters" from founder **David Berg**, included sexually explicit (many would argue pornographic) illustrations to accompany his instructions on flirty fishing. One of the most disturbing of these images shows a naked woman spread-eagled on a bed, a spike driven into her vagina. Superimposed to her left is a classic illustration of Jesus's crucifixion, and the text at the top reads: "You *are* the love of God!" Not surprisingly, allegations of sexual abuse—including sexual contact with minors—has been at the heart of controversy surrounding the Children of God for many years. Although the practice of flirty fishing was discontinued by the early 1990s and sexual contact with children firmly repudiated by the group a few years later, the stigma attached to such behaviour has made it impossible for The Family International (as Children of God is called now) to achieve the kind of social acceptance other new religions have found.

Cover art from one of Children of God founder David Berg's Mo Letters

Source: © Jeff Morgan 04/Alamy

GAINING CULTURAL SUPPORT: NEW RELIGIONS AND DOMINANT SOCIETY

While new religions still tend to be regarded with suspicion in North America, some groups or movements have managed to secure a measure of support, whether explicitly or implicitly, from different sectors of the dominant society. This support can occur in a number of ways, including appeals to popular culture, economic investments, legal reparation, political affiliation, and exploiting the relationships among these.

Over the past several years, when new religions scholars have been contacted with regard to the Church of Scientology, one of the questions that invariably comes up is about the attraction of Scientology for cultural celebrities. While in many countries around the world the Church of Scientology continues to battle for official recognition as a religion, the celebrity status of many North American members—Tom Cruise, John Travolta, Isaac Hayes, Jenna Elfman, and Kirstie Alley, to name just a few—has accrued to Scientology a measure of cultural capital unavailable to groups who count no prominent figures among their ranks. The relationship between new religions and cultural celebrities, however, is hardly new; Tom Cruise and the Church of Scientology, Madonna and Kabbalah, and Richard Gere and Tibetan Buddhism are simply the latest.

During the countercultural emergence of new religions in the 1960s, it was the Beatles and their visit to the **Maharishi Mahesh Yogi**'s ashram that did more to promote Transcendental Meditation than many of TM's other recruiting methods put together (Lapham 2005). Would Tibetan Buddhism be as popular in the West as it is if not for the cultural capital it accrues through such celebrities as Richard Gere? Though many people in North America still have a deeply rooted cultural fear of witches and witchcraft (Barner-Barry 2005), Modern Paganism has seen significant growth in the past fifteen years. As I have suggested, how much of that is due to the cultural capital accruing from such mass entertainment products as *Buffy the Vampire Slayer*, *Charmed*, *Sabrina the Teenage Witch*, *The Craft*, *Practical Magic*, and the worldwide phenomenon that is Harry Potter? Although many Modern Pagan scholars are offended by what they see as crass commercialization of their religious beliefs (Ezzy 2001; Foltz 2005), they fail to consider that the very commodification they condemn is at least partly responsibly for the Modern Pagan growth they often rapturously celebrate. How popular culture shapes popular understanding of new religions—and how new religions participate in that process—is another relationship that has been left seriously understudied.

Maharishi Mahesh Yogi: founder of the Transcendental Meditation (TM) movement (1917–2008).

The Beatles with the Maharishi Mahesh Yogi
Source: © Trinity Mirror/Mirrorpix/Alamy

Cultural capital accrues in other ways as well. During the 1970s and much of the 1980s, the Unification Church was regarded as the epitome of the dangerous, brainwashing cult (Barker 1984). However, by aligning itself with some of the more virulent proponents of American anti-communism, by diversifying its business interests so that the group itself was no longer dependent on money raised by members, and by opening itself up to mainstream scholars of new religions, it has shed some of the social stigma that marked it just a few decades ago. Of course, its highly publicized mass wedding ceremonies still raise a cultural eyebrow or two, but that appears to be offset by the visibility of such enterprises as the church-owned *Washington Times* newspaper and Sun Myung Moon's array of powerful political and religious friends. At the invitations of Richard Nixon and Mikhail Gorbachev, for example, Moon visited both the White House and the Kremlin. He has twice addressed the United States Congress, and his wife, Hak Ja Han Moon (b. 1943), once delivered a speech to the United Nations. When Moon celebrated his eightieth birthday, his guests included former vice-president Dan Quayle and former British prime minister Edward Heath.

Though some research has been conducted on the finances of new religions (Bromley and Shupe 1980; Richardson 1982), this too is an area in which much more remains to be done. How, for example, does the Church of Scientology pay for the magnificent buildings it erects or renovates, or fund the lavish events that seem to mark every important moment in the life of the group? Do the celebrities who attend pay on an exorbitant per plate basis or are the costs borne in some other way? Is the sale of Scientology products—a complete course of which can run into several hundreds of thousands of dollars—enough to finance the organization, or are there other investments that are keeping the Church afloat? At the other end of the economic scale, The Family International spent most of its movement life at a subsistence level, procuring goods and services where and as they could according to the needs of the moment, and occasionally living off the proceeds of flirty fishing. Between these two are a host of new religions that have experimented with, and taken advantage of, a wide variety of fundraising efforts. As sociologist James T. Richardson pointed out twenty-five years ago, however important it is to learn what people believe or why they choose to join one group over another, such questions "cannot be answered properly without also understanding the economic policies and practices of the groups, and the interaction of important elements of group life with fund-raising and internal allocation schemes" (1982, 255).

NEW RELIGIONS AND THE INTERNET

Shortly after the release of the Wachowski brothers' special effects blockbuster *The Matrix* in 1999, messages began appearing on the Internet inviting people to join a new online religion called "Matrixism." For the price of a single mouse-click, men and women around the world could choose to follow the "path of the One." Psychedelics are a sacrament, pornography is equated with prostitution, and all the teachings seem to come not so much from the future as from the early teachings of the Baha'i. Although I still receive the occasional email about them, the last time I checked, the Matrixism site hadn't been updated in more than five years.

Early in the twenty-first century, few if any new religions have no online presence, either officially or as part of a countermovement website. Loath as I am to admit it, even Wikipedia is occasionally a source of useful information. But Matrixism illustrates three particular issues that face new religions on the Internet just as surely as they do more established traditions: the paradox of "ephemeral resilience," the problem of innovation and promotion, and the relationship between the online and offline worlds.

First there is the paradox of *ephemeral resilience*—the reality that online material is both fragile (it can disappear or change quickly) and durable (it is difficult to erase one's electronic footprint entirely). Although the Matrixism website has not been updated in several years and its graphics and interface are considerably out-of-date, you can still find it on the Net. For some new religions, such as the Church of Scientology, this has caused tremendous problems. In the mid-1990s, for example, a number of esoteric Scientology documents were uploaded to the Internet as a result of a court case in which the Church was involved. Although Scientology tried to limit their exposure on the Web, the documents—which contain a number of teachings reserved for upper-level devotees—were posted and reposted to sites all over the Internet. When they disappeared from one site, they reappeared elsewhere, and the Church tried in vain to remove them entirely.

Second, there is the problem of innovation and promotion. The reality is that simply because you invent a new religion and offer it in the late-modern spiritual marketplace, there is no guarantee that anyone will take your particular red pill and follow you down the rabbit hole. Most new religions emerge, flourish for a time (or not), and disappear before we learn anything significant about them. Some collapse because they could not socialize a second generation; others fade away as adherents simply lose interest. Some are absorbed by larger organizational institutions, while still others modify their beliefs and practices to accommodate social and cultural norms. There are many thousands of new religions at any one time, most of which we never hear about and most of which will not survive their formative stages and first generation. As *The Matrix* recedes from our cultural horizon—replaced, for example, as I write this by James Cameron's *Avatar*—the concept of Matrixism will steadily lose relevance and the power to compel even nominal membership. For all those learning to speak Na'vi today, perhaps in the hopes of making Avatarism a new religion, the same will be true in the future.

Third, there is the Holy Grail of Internet faith: a new religion innovated, established, and operated entirely online. Although there are some new religions that claim to exist entirely online, I have yet to find one for which this is the case. Much of their communication may take place in chat rooms, through instant messaging, or via email, but the people still exist offline. As I point out in *Cyberhenge* (2005), they still live in their physical bodies, and only very rarely does what happens online not relate directly to offline beliefs and behaviour. Commercial hyperbole and enthusiast rhetoric notwithstanding, we do not live our lives online but rather use the online world as way to supplement our activities, our interests, and our identities offline.

CONCLUSION

Though at this point many scholars of new religions feel the field is in something of a lull, there is little danger of new religions disappearing any time soon. If we have learned nothing else, it is that humans are endlessly inventive when it comes to their different visions of the unseen order, and endlessly creative in the ways they seek to manage and negotiate their relationships with that order. The first generation of new religions scholarship taught us that new religions must be considered in the context of the larger social and cultural movements within and out of which they emerge, that they cannot be reduced to a simplistic set of criteria bounded by a charismatic leader at one end and a group of dullard followers at the other. Those who join new religions exercise a wide range of agency, and while relatively few of those who investigate a particular new religion will ultimately commit to it, there is little evidence that the new religious experience is detrimental in and of itself.

We have also learned that new religions cannot be stereotyped according to the "big-ticket items" that have occupied so much popular and scholarly attention throughout the years. Though "dramatic denouements" such as these will, undoubtedly, occur from time to time, they are the exceptions rather than the rule of new religious behaviour. They should not shape either the agenda of new religions scholarship or the popular cultural understanding of new religions. What we must always bear in mind is that these are real people engaged in what is for them a very real search for meaning.

KEY TERMS

CRITICAL THINKING QUESTIONS

1. When you hear the phrase "dangerous cult" on the news, what do you think? How would you identify a dangerous cult if asked? If possible, role-play the "Dangerous Cult" exercise in class. How did you feel while wrestling with the questions? Did it make the issue of new religions simpler for you or more complex?
2. Do you know anyone who is a member of one of the groups described in this chapter? Do you think of them as part of a cult?
3. Most, if not all, of the issues related to new religious movements are also part of established religious groups. What groups can you identify that share

some of these issues, and how do you explain the difference between the way these groups are treated and new religious movements?

4. Most people learn what little they know about new religions through the mainstream media. How do you think these media portray new religions and why? Is there another side to the NRM story, and, if so, how should it be told?

5. Some countries have passed laws that significantly restrict the rights and freedoms of new religions. In some cases, new religions are criminalized and repressed. What do you think about this? Should the rights of individuals to believe as they choose be curtailed if others think that it is in their own best interest?

6. This chapter has only scratched the surface of new religions. What are some other new religions that you know of? Have you ever heard of other groups being called cults? Why do you think that is?

RECOMMENDED READING

Barker, Eileen. *The Making of a Moonie: Choice or Brainwashing?* London: Basil Blackwell, 1984.

Bromley, David G., and J. Gordon Melton, eds. *Cults, Religion, and Violence.* Cambridge: Cambridge University Press, 2002.

Bromley, David G., and James T. Richardson, eds. *The Brainwashing/Deprogramming Controversy: Sociological, Psychological, Historical, and Legal Perspectives.* New York: Edwin Mellen Press, 1983.

Cowan, Douglas E. *Bearing False Witness? An Introduction to the Christian Countercult.* Westport, CT: Praeger, 2003.

Cowan, Douglas E., and David G. Bromley. *Cults and New Religions: A Brief History.* Oxford: Blackwell, 2008.

Dawson, Lorne L. *Comprehending Cults: The Sociology of New Religious Movements*, rev. ed. New York: Oxford University Press, 2006.

Lucas, Phillip C., and Thomas Robbins, eds. *New Religious Movements in the 21st Century: Legal, Political, and Social Challenges.* New York: Routledge, 2004.

Palmer, Susan J., and Charlotte E. Hardman, eds. *Children in New Religions.* New Brunswick, NJ: Rutgers University Press, 1999.

Stone, Jon R., ed. *Expecting Armageddon: Essential Readings in Failed Prophecy.* New York: Routledge, 2000.

Zablocki, Benjamin, and Thomas Robbins, eds. *Misunderstanding Cults: Searching for Objectivity in a Controversial Field.* Toronto: University of Toronto Press, 2001.

RECOMMENDED VIEWING

Although numerous films and television programs include new religious movements as part of their plotlines (see Cowan 2008b, 2010), relatively few feature films are about new religious movements per se—and almost all present new religions in a negative light.

The Believers. Dir. John Schlesinger. Perf. Martin Sheen, Helen Shaver, Harley Cross. Orion Pictures, 1987. Ostensibly about Santería, this film builds on popular fears of ritual sacrifice and supposed death cults.

The Craft. Dir. Andrew Fleming. Perf. Robin Tunney, Fairuza Balk, Neve Campbell. Columbia Pictures, 1996. Considered by many a recruitment film for Wicca and witchcraft, this film appeared at the height of popular interest in Modern Paganism.

The God Makers. Documentary by J. Edward Decker, T. A. McMahon, and Dave Hunt. Jeremiah Films, 1982. Regarded by many as "religious pornography," this is a notorious example of evangelical Christian countercult propaganda against the Church of Jesus Christ of Latter-day Saints.

Holy Smoke. Dir. Jane Campion. Perf. Kate Winslet, Harvey Keitel, Julie Hamilton. India Take One/Miramax, 1999. An excellent if occasionally disturbing film about the abduction and forced deprogramming of a young Australian woman who joined a new religious movement while travelling in India.

September Dawn. Dir. Christopher Cain. Perf. Jon Voight, Trent Ford, Tamara Hope. September Dawn/Voice Pictures, 2007. Feature film about the Mountain Meadows massacre, one of the truly dark moments in Latter-day Saints history.

Waco: The Rules of Engagement. Documentary by William Gazecki, Dan Gifford, and Michael McNulty. Fifth Estate/SomFord Entertainment, 1997. Considered by new religions scholars to be one of the best documentaries on the 1993 Branch Davidian tragedy.

USEFUL WEBSITES

Apologetics Index

Extensive countercult website maintained by a Dutch fundamentalist Christian.

Church of Scientology

The official website of the Church of Scientology. Lots of publicly available information, but relatively little about the inner workings of the organization.

Ex-Family
One of many ex–Family International or ex–Children of God websites. Contains scans of hundreds of internal Family/COG documents, including "Mo letters."

Falun Gong
The official website of Falun Gong. Many of their primary materials are available here for free download.

The Family International
Official website of The Family International (formerly the Children of God).

International Cultic Studies Association
Official website of the last remaining large anti-cult organization in North America (formerly the American Family Foundation).

Modern Paganism
The largest general information portal for Modern Paganism, including Wicca, witchcraft, Druidry, heathenism, and Asatru. This is *the* place to start.

Operation Clambake
One of the most prominent anti-Scientology websites, run by a Dutch anti-Scientology activist. Contains scans of hundreds of internal Scientology documents.

Transcendental Meditation
Official website of the Transcendental Meditation movement.

REFERENCES

Atkins, Gaius Glenn. 1923. *Modern Religious Cults and Movements.* New York: Fleming H. Revell.

Barker, Eileen. 1984. *The Making of a Moonie: Choice or Brainwashing?* London: Basil Blackwell.

Barner-Barry, Carol. 2005. *Contemporary Paganism: Minority Faith in a Majoritarian America.* New York: Palgrave.

Beckford, James A. 1983. "The 'Cult' Problem in Five Countries: The Social Construction of Religious Controversy." In *Of Gods and Men: New Religious Movements in the West*, ed. Eileen Barker, 195–214. Macon, GA: Mercer University Press.

Beit-Hallahmi, Benjamin. "'O Truant Muse': Collaborationism and Research Integrity." In *Misunderstanding Cults*, ed. Benjamin Zablocki and Thomas Robbins, 35–70. Toronto: University of Toronto Press.

Braden, Charles S. 1949. *These Also Believe: A Study of Modern American Cults and Minority Religious Movements.* New York: Macmillan.

Bromley, David G., ed. 1998. *The Politics of Religious Apostasy: The Role of Apostates in the Transformation of New Religious Movements.* Westport, CT: Praeger.

———. 2002. "Dramatic Denouements." In *Cults, Religion, and Violence*, ed. David G. Bromley J. Gordon Melton, 11–41. Cambridge: Cambridge University Press.

———. 2004. "Wither New Religions Studies?" *Nova Religio* 8, no. 2: 83–97.

Bromley, David G., and J. Gordon Melton, eds. 2002. *Cults, Religion, and Violence.* Cambridge: Cambridge University Press.

Bromley, David G., and James T. Richardson, eds. 1983. *The Brainwashing/Deprogramming Controversy: Sociological, Psychological, Historical, and Legal Perspectives.* New York: Edwin Mellen Press.

Bromley, David G., and Anson D. Shupe, Jr. 1980. "Financing the New Religions: A Resource Mobilization Approach." *Journal for the Scientific Study of Religion* 19, no. 3: 227–39.

Buddie, C. 2001. "Feeling Insecure over Security Laws." *South China Morning Post*, 21 December.

Chancellor, James D. 2000. *Life in The Family: An Oral History of the Children of God.* Syracuse, NY: Syracuse University Press.

Chang, Maria Hsia. 2004. *Falun Gong: The End of Days.* New Haven, CT: Yale University Press.

Church of Scientology International. 2001. *The Scientology Handbook.* Los Angeles: Bridge Publications.

Clark, Elmer T. 1937. *The Small Sects in America.* Nashville, TN: Cokesbury Press.

Corrigan, John, ed. 2004. *Religion and Emotion: Approaches and Interpretations.* Oxford: Oxford University Press.

———. 2008. *The Oxford Handbook of Religion and Emotion.* Oxford: Oxford University Press.

Cowan, Douglas E. 2003a. *Bearing False Witness? An Introduction to the Christian Countercult.* Westport, CT: Praeger.

———. 2003b. "Confronting the Failed Failure: Y2K and Evangelical Eschatology in Light of the Passed Millennium." *Nova Religio* 7, no. 2: 71–85.

———. 2005. *Cyberhenge: Modern Pagans on the Internet.* New York: Routledge.

———. 2008a. "New Religious Movements." In *The Oxford Handbook of Religion and Emotion*, ed. John Corrigan, 125–40. Oxford: Oxford University Press.

———. 2008b. *Sacred Terror: Religion and Horror on the Silver Screen.* Waco, TX: Baylor University Press.

———. 2009. "Research Scientology: Perceptions, Premises, Promises, and Problematics." In *Scientology*, ed. James R. Lewis, 53–79. Oxford: Oxford University Press.

———. 2010. *Sacred Space: The Quest for Transcendence in Science Fiction Film and Television*. Waco, TX: Baylor University Press.

Cowan, Douglas E., and David G. Bromley. 2008. *Cults and New Religions: A Brief History*. London: Blackwell Publishing.

Cowan, Douglas E., and Jeffrey K. Hadden. 2004. "God, Guns, and Grist for the Media's Mill: Constructing the Narratives of New Religious Movements and Violence." *Nova Religio* 8, no. 2: 64–82.

Dawson, Lorne L. 1999. "When Prophecy Fails and Faith Persists: A Theoretical Overview." *Nova Religio* 3, no. 1: 60–82.

———. 2001. "Raising Lazarus: A Methodological Critique of Stephen Kent's *Revival of the Brainwashing Model*." In *Misunderstanding Cults*, ed. Benjamin Zablocki and Thomas Robbins, 379–400. Toronto: University of Toronto Press.

Edelman, Bryan, and James T. Richardson. 2003. "Falun Gong and the Law: Development of Legal Social Control in China." *Nova Religio* 6, no. 2: 312–31.

Ezzy, Douglas. 2001. "The Commodification of Witchcraft." *Australian Religious Studies Review* 14, no. 1: 31–44.

Festinger, Leon, Henry W. Riecken, and Stanley Schacter. 1956. *When Prophecy Fails: A Social and Psychological Study of a Group That Predicted the Destruction of the World*. New York: Harper & Row.

Foltz, Tanice. 2005. "The Commodification of Witchcraft." In *Witchcraft and Magic: Contemporary North America*, ed. Helen A. Berger, 137–68. Philadelphia: University of Pennsylvania Press.

Givens, Teryl L. 1997. *The Viper on the Hearth: Mormons, Myths, and the Construction of Heresy*. Oxford: Oxford University Press.

Hexham, Irving, and Karla Poewe. 1999. "'*Verfassungsfeindlich*': Church, State, and New Religions in Germany." *Nova Religio* 2, no. 2: 208–27.

Hexham, Irving, Joan Townsend, and Karla Poewe. 2008. "New Religious Movements." In *The Canadian Encyclopedia*. http://www.thecanadianencyclopedia.com.

Hutton, Ronald. 2003. *Witches, Druids, and King Arthur*. London: Hambledon and London.

Jones, Kristina, Celeste Jones, and Juliana Buhring. 2007. *Not Without My Sister: The True Story of Three Girls Violated and Betrayed*. London: HarperCollins.

Kent, Stephen A. 2001a. "Brainwashing Programs in The Family/Children of God and Scientology." In *Misunderstanding Cults*, ed. Benjamin Zablocki and Thomas Robbins, 349–78. Toronto: University of Toronto Press.

———. 2001b. "Compelling Evidence: A Rejoinder to Lorne Dawson's Chapter." In *Misunderstanding Cults*, ed. Benjamin Zablocki and Thomas Robbins, 401–11. Toronto: University of Toronto Press.

Kent, Stephen A., and Theresa Krebs. 1998. "When Scholars Know Sin: Alternative Religions and Their Academic Supporters." *Skeptic Magazine* 6, no. 3: 36–44.

Lalich, Janja. 2004. *Bounded Choice: True Believers and Charismatic Cults*. Berkeley: University of California Press.

Lapham, Lewis. 2005. *With the Beatles*. Hoboken, NJ: Melville House.

Lattin, Don. 2007. *Jesus Freaks: A True Story of Murder and Madness on the Evangelical Edge*. New York: HarperOne.

Li Hongzhi. 2001. *Zhuan Falun: The Complete Teachings of Falun Gong*. Gloucester, MA: Fairwinds Press.

———. 2006. *Falun Gong* (English version), 5th ed. http://www.falundafa.org/ book/eng/pdf/flg_2006.pdf.

Lofland, John, and Rodney Stark. 1965. "Becoming a World-Saver: A Theory of Conversion to a Deviant Perspective." *American Sociological Review* 30: 862–75.

Lucas, Phillip C., and Thomas Robbins, eds. 2004. *New Religious Movements in the 21st Century: Legal, Political, and Social Challenges*. New York: Routledge.

Luhrmann, Tanya M. 1989. *Persuasions of the Witch's Craft: Ritual Magic in Contemporary England*. Cambridge, MA: Harvard University Press.

Martin, Walter M. 1955. *The Rise of the Cults: An Introductory Guide to the Non-Christian Cults*. Grand Rapids, MI: Zondervan.

Matas, David, and David Kilgour. 2007. *Bloody Harvest: Revised Report into Allegations of Organ Harvesting of Falun Gong Practitioners in China*. Washington, DC: Coalition to Investigate the Persecution of the Falun Gong in China. http://organharvestinvestigation.net/report0701/report20070131-eng.pdf.

McNiece, R. G. (1917) 1996. "Mormonism: Its Origin, Characteristics, and Doctrines." In *The Fundamentals: A Testimony to the Truth*, ed. R. A Torrey et al. Vol. 3, 288–300. Grand Rapids, MI: Baker Books.

Melton, J. Gordon. 1998. "Mea Culpa! Mea Culpa!" http://www.cesnur.org/testi/ melton98.htm.

———. 2004. "Toward a Definition of 'New Religion.'" *Nova Religio* 8, no. 1: 73–87.

Meynell, Hugo A. 1994. *Is Christianity True?* Washington, DC: Catholic University of America Press.

Moon, Sun Myung. 1973. *Divine Principle*. Washington, DC: Holy Spirit Association for the Unification of World Christianity.

Moore, Rebecca. 2007. "The Power of Cultural Opponents: The Case of Peoples Temple." Paper presented at the International Symposium of Cultic Studies, Chinese Academy of Social Sciences, Shenzhen, China, 6–8 December.

Moorehead, William G. (1917) 1996. "Millennial Dawn: A Counterfeit of Christianity." In *The Fundamentals: A Testimony to the Truth*, ed. R. A Torrey et al. Vol. 4, 109–30. Grand Rapids, MI: Baker Books.

Ownby, David. 2003. "A History of Falun Gong: Popular Religion and the Chinese State Since the Ming Dynasty." *Nova Religio* 6, no. 2: 223–43.

Palmer, Susan J. 2001. "Caught Up in the Cult Wars: Confessions of a Canadian Researcher." In *Misunderstanding Cults*, ed. Benjamin Zablocki and Thomas Robbins, 99–122. Toronto: University of Toronto Press.

Palmer, Susan J., and Charlotte E. Hardman, eds. 1999. *Children in New Religions*. New Brunswick, NJ: Rutgers University Press.

Penton, M. James. 1985. *Apocalypse Delayed: The Story of Jehovah's Witnesses*. Toronto: University of Toronto Press.

Pressman, Steven. 1993. *Outrageous Betrayal: The Dark Journey of Werner Erhard from est to Exile*. New York: St. Martin's Press.

Rhodes, Ron. 1994. *The Culting of America*. Eugene, OR: Harvest House.

Richardson, James T. 1982. "Financing the New Religions: Comparative and Theoretical Considerations." *Journal for the Scientific Study of Religion* 21, no. 3: 255–68.

Robbins, Thomas. 2001. "Balance and Fairness in the Study of Alternative Religions." In *Misunderstanding Cults*, ed. Benjamin Zablocki and Thomas Robbins, 71–98. Toronto: University of Toronto Press.

Rothenberg, Celia. 2006. "Jewish Yoga: Experiencing Flexible, Sacred, and Jewish Bodies." *Nova Religio* 10, no. 2: 57–74.

Scruton, David L., ed. 1986. *Sociophobics: The Anthropology of Fear*. Boulder, CO: Westview Press.

Selka, Stephen. 2007. "Mediated Authenticity: Tradition, Modernity, and Postmodernity in Brazilian Candomblé." *Nova Religio* 11, no. 1: 5–30.

Shepherd, Gary, and Gordon Shepherd. 2006. "The Social Construction of Prophecy in The Family International." *Nova Religio* 10, no. 2: 29–56.

———. 2007. "Grassroots Prophecy in The Family International." *Nova Religio* 10, no. 4: 38–71.

Shupe, Anson D., Jr., and David G. Bromley. 1980. *The New Vigilantes: Deprogrammers, Anti-Cultists, and the New Religions*. Beverly Hills, CA: Sage.

Shupe, Anson D., Jr., R. Spielmann, and S. Stigall. 1977. "Deprogramming: The New Exorcism." *American Behavioral Scientist* 20, no. 6: 941–56.

Stark, Rodney. 1996. *The Rise of Christianity: How the Obscure, Marginal Jesus Movement Became the Dominant Religious Force in the Western World in a Few Centuries*. Princeton, NJ: Princeton University Press.

Stark, Rodney, and William Sims Bainbridge. 1985. *The Future of Religion: Secularization, Revival, and Cult Formation*. Berkeley: University of California Press.

———. 1987. *A Theory of Religion*. New Brunswick, NJ: Rutgers University Press.

Stjerna, Kirsi. 2001. "Finnish Sleep-Preachers: An Example of Women's Spiritual Power." *Nova Religio* 5, no. 1: 102–20.

Stone, Jon R., ed. 2000. *Expecting Armageddon: Essential Readings in Failed Prophecy*. New York: Routledge.

Tumminia, Diana. 2005. *When Prophecy Never Fails: Myth and Reality in a Flying-Saucer Group*. Oxford: Oxford University Press.

van Baalen, Jan Karel. 1938. *The Chaos of Cults: A Study in Present-Day Isms*. Grand Rapids, MI: Wm. B. Eerdmans.

Waldron, David. 2005. "Witchcraft for Sale! Commodity vs. Community in the Neopagan Movement." *Nova Religio*, 9, no. 1: 32–48.

Wang Wenzhong et al. 2007. "Research on Causes of Practicing the Evil Cult 'Falun Gong,' Its Influences upon Its Practitioners, and Psychological Help to Them." Paper presented at the International Symposium of Cultic Studies, Chinese Academy of Social Sciences, Shenzhen, China, 6–8 December.

Williams, Miriam. 1998. *Heaven's Harlots: My Fifteen Years as a Sacred Prostitute in the Children of God Cult*. New York: William Morrow.

Wilson, M. E. (1917) 1996. "Eddyism, Commonly Called 'Christian Science.'" In *The Fundamentals: A Testimony to the Truth*, ed. R. A Torrey et al. Vol. 4, 149–65. Grand Rapids, MI: Baker Books.

Zablocki, Benjamin, and Thomas Robbins, eds. 2001. *Misunderstanding Cults: Searching for Objectivity in a Controversial Field*. Toronto: University of Toronto Press.